WHO KILLED KURT COBAIN?

OTERO

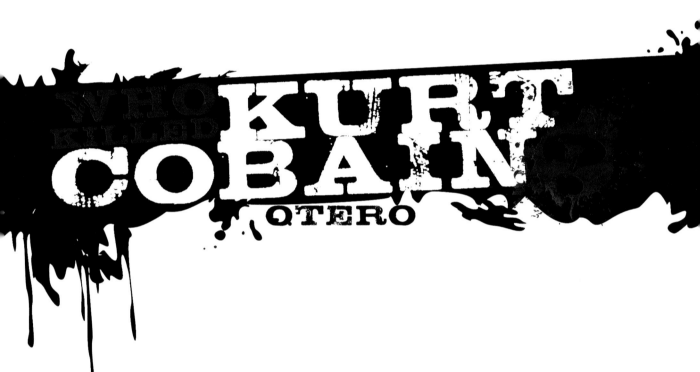

Become our fan on Facebook **facebook.com/idwpublishing**
Follow us on Twitter **@idwpublishing**
Subscribe to us on YouTube **youtube.com/idwpublishing**
See what's new on Tumblr **tumblr.idwpublishing.com**
Check us out on Instagram **instagram.com/idwpublishing**

COVER ART BY
VÉRANE OTERO

PRODUCTION & DESIGN BY
ROBBIE ROBBINS

PUBLISHED BY
TED ADAMS

ISBN: 978-1-63140-726-0
19 18 17 16   1 2 3 4

Originally published by Glénat as
"Le Roman de Boddah."

Ted Adams, CEO & Publisher
Greg Goldstein, President & COO
Robbie Robbins, EVP/Sr. Graphic Artist
Chris Ryall, Chief Creative Officer/Editor-in-Chief
Laurie Windrow, Senior Vice President of Sales & Marketing
Matthew Ruzicka, CPA, Chief Financial Officer
Dirk Wood, VP of Marketing
Lorelei Bunjes, VP of Digital Services
Jeff Webber, VP of Digital Publishing & Business Development
Jerry Bennington, VP of New Product Development

For international rights, please contact
licensing@idwpublishing.com

WRITTEN & ILLUSTRATED BY
NICOLAS OTERO

LETTERED BY
TROY LITTLE

TRANSLATED BY
IVANKA HAHNENBERGER

EDITED BY
JUSTIN EISINGER

EDITORIAL ASSISTANCE BY
SARAH DUFFY
AND
ALONZO SIMON

... THE STORY OF BODDAH ...

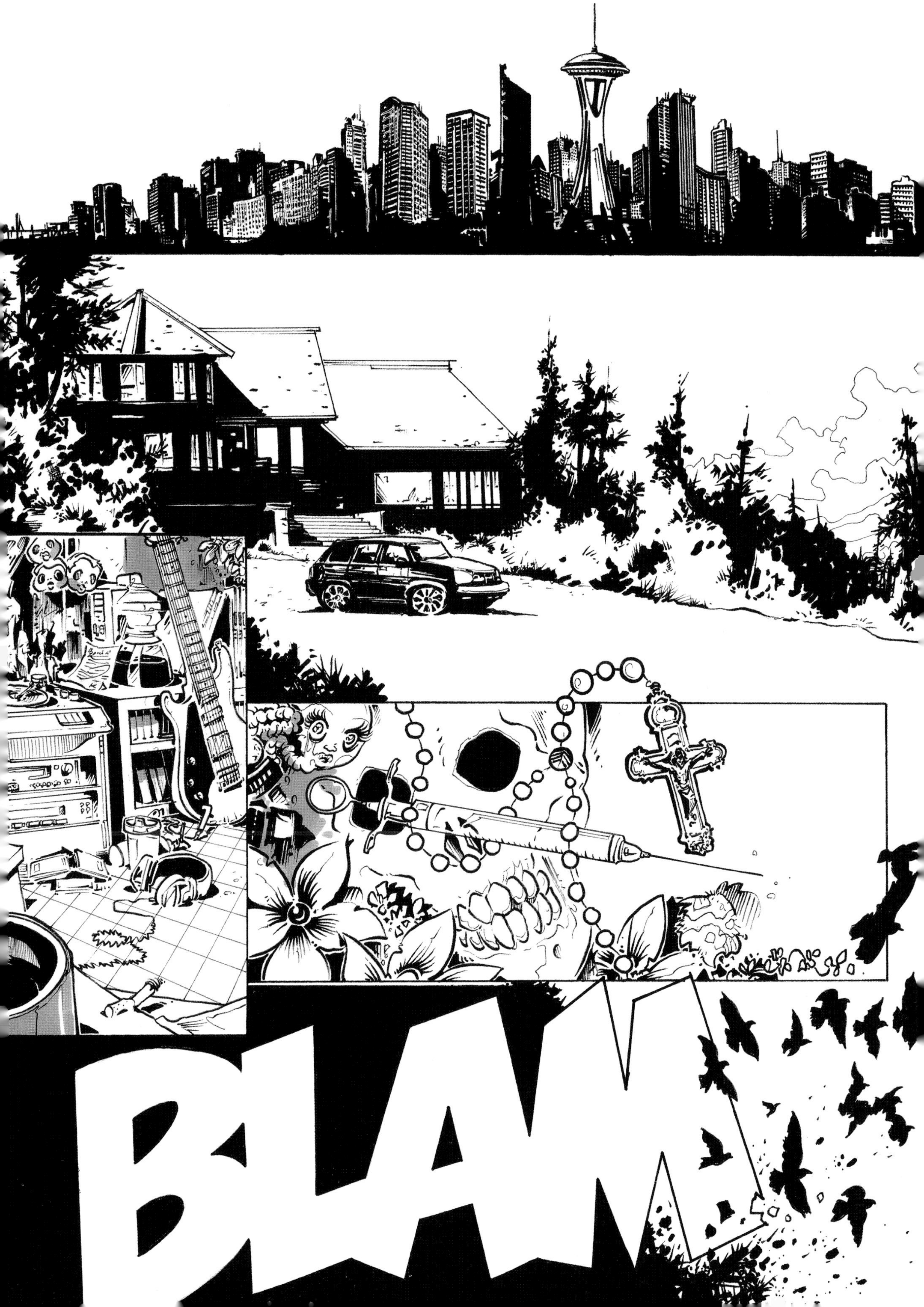
BLAM!

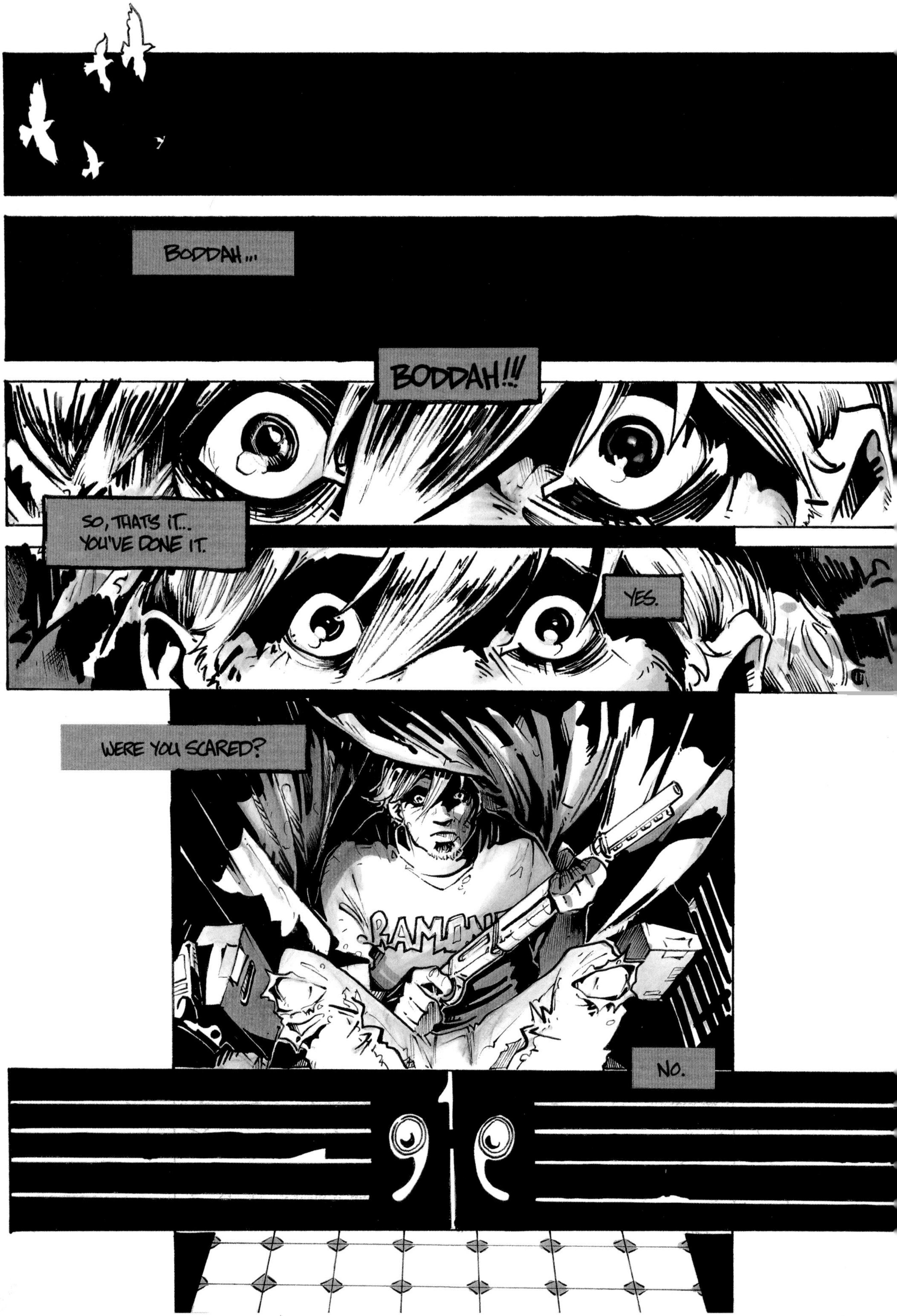
BODDAH...
BODDAH!!!
SO, THAT'S IT... YOU'VE DONE IT.
YES.
WERE YOU SCARED?
RAMONE
NO.

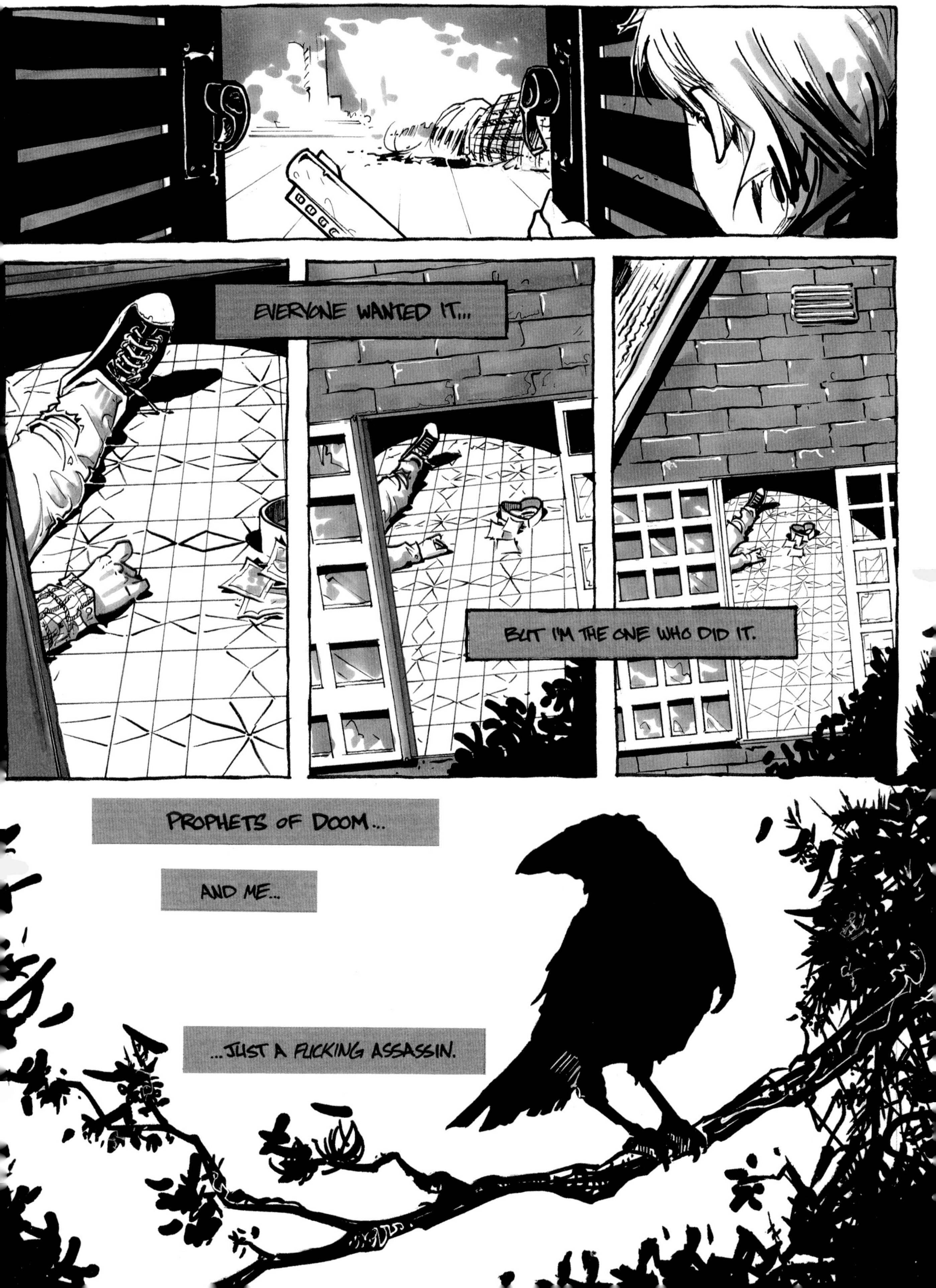
EVERYONE WANTED IT...
BUT I'M THE ONE WHO DID IT.
PROPHETS OF DOOM...
AND ME...
...JUST A FUCKING ASSASSIN.

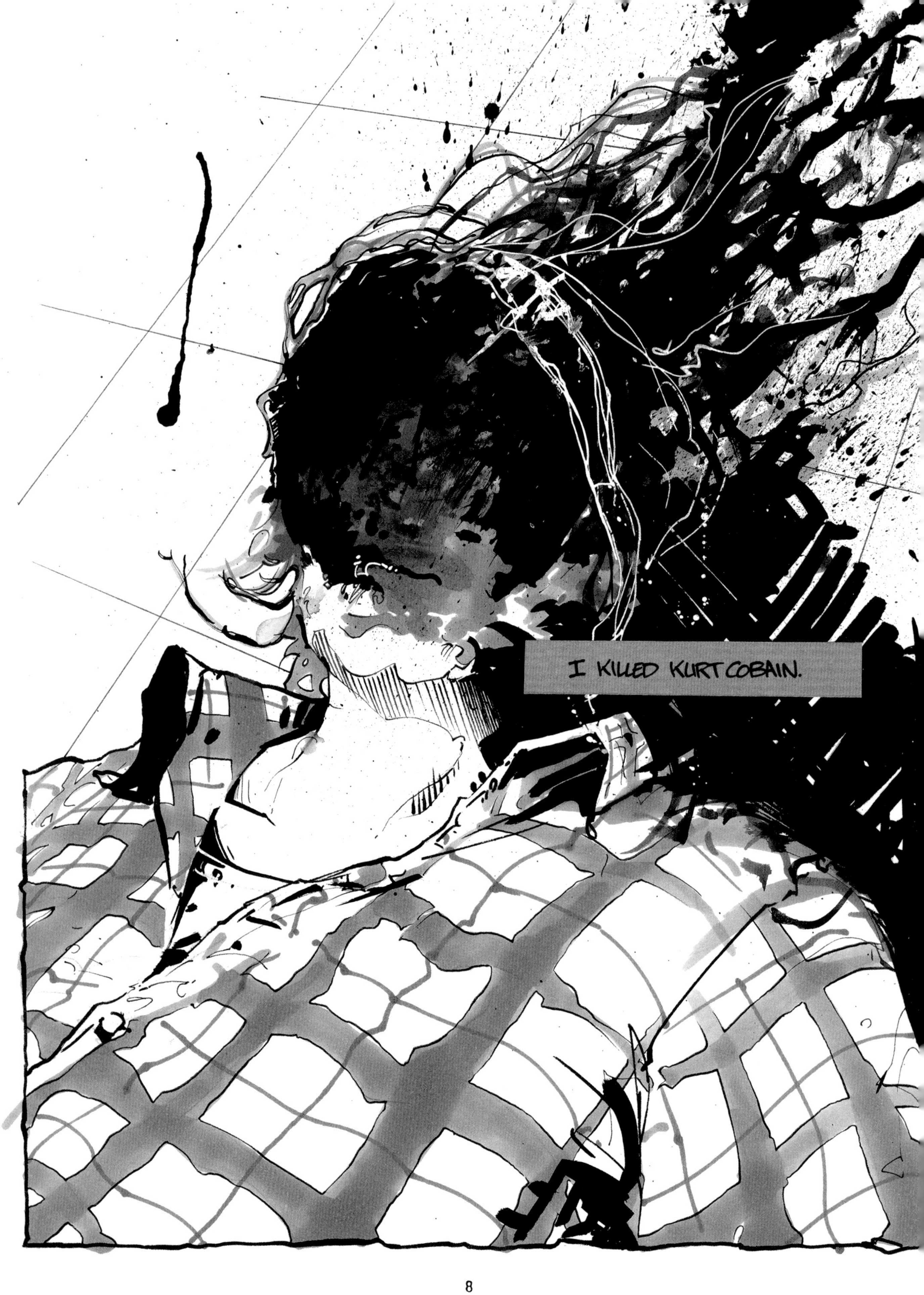
I KILLED KURT COBAIN.

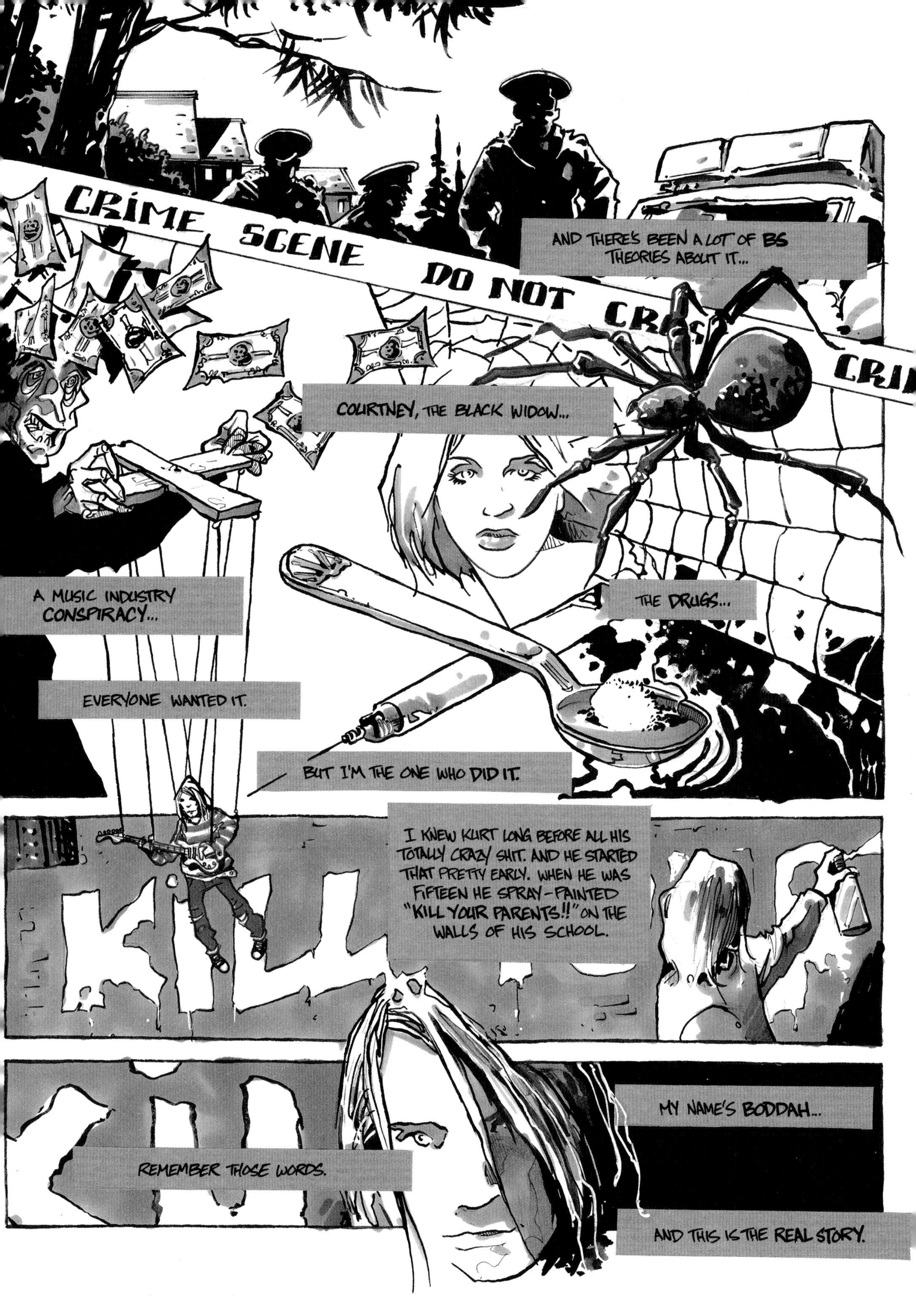
CRIME SCENE DO NOT CROSS
AND THERE'S BEEN A LOT OF BS THEORIES ABOUT IT...
COURTNEY, THE BLACK WIDOW...
A MUSIC INDUSTRY CONSPIRACY...
THE DRUGS...
EVERYONE WANTED IT.
BUT I'M THE ONE WHO DID IT.
I KNEW KURT LONG BEFORE ALL HIS TOTALLY CRAZY SHIT. AND HE STARTED THAT PRETTY EARLY. WHEN HE WAS FIFTEEN HE SPRAY-PAINTED "KILL YOUR PARENTS!!" ON THE WALLS OF HIS SCHOOL.
MY NAME'S BODDAH...
REMEMBER THOSE WORDS.
AND THIS IS THE REAL STORY.

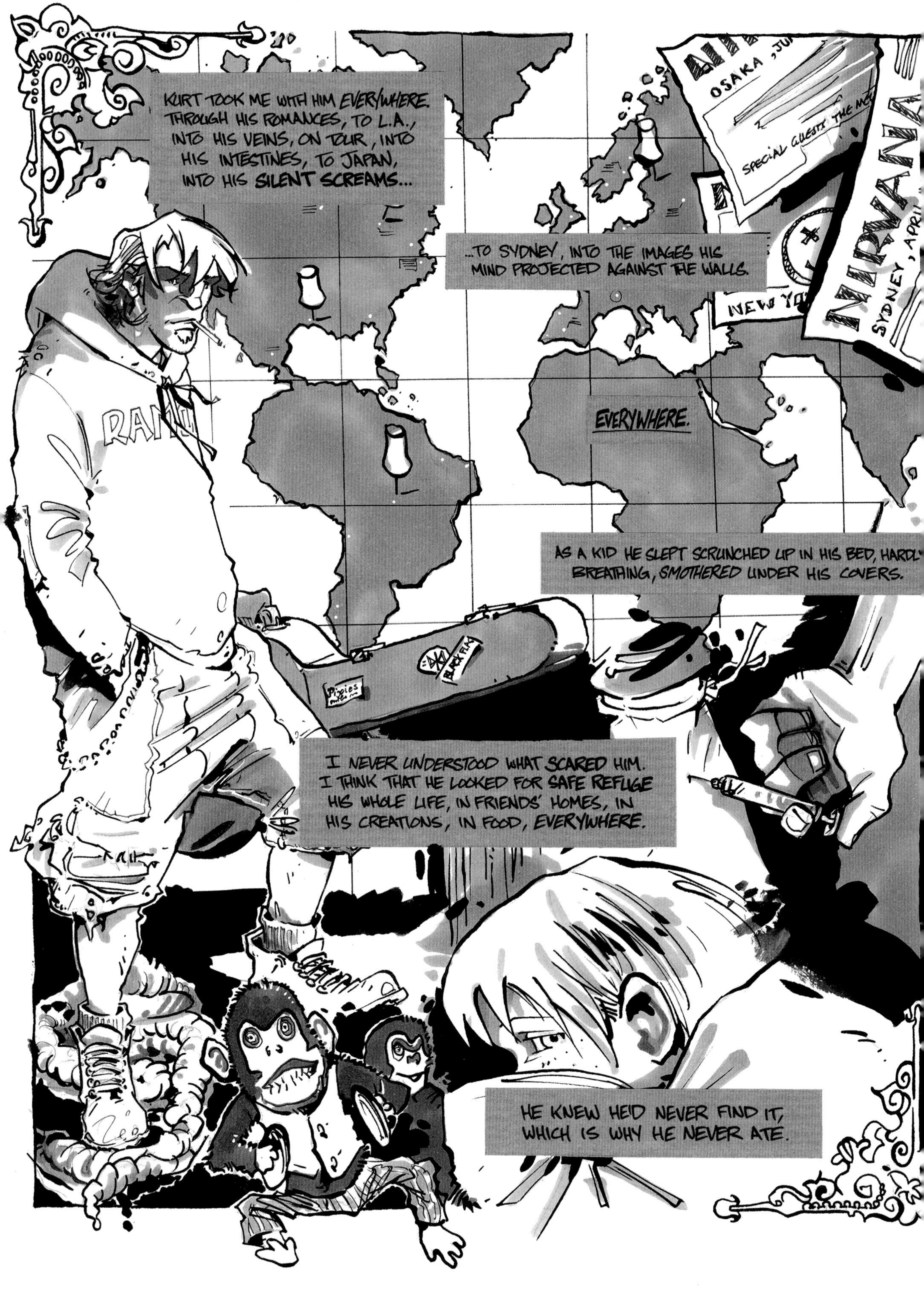
KURT TOOK ME WITH HIM EVERYWHERE. THROUGH HIS ROMANCES, TO L.A., INTO HIS VEINS, ON TOUR, INTO HIS INTESTINES, TO JAPAN, INTO HIS SILENT SCREAMS...
...TO SYDNEY, INTO THE IMAGES HIS MIND PROJECTED AGAINST THE WALLS.
EVERYWHERE.
AS A KID HE SLEPT SCRUNCHED UP IN HIS BED, HARDLY BREATHING, SMOTHERED UNDER HIS COVERS.
I NEVER UNDERSTOOD WHAT SCARED HIM. I THINK THAT HE LOOKED FOR SAFE REFUGE HIS WHOLE LIFE, IN FRIENDS' HOMES, IN HIS CREATIONS, IN FOOD, EVERYWHERE.
HE KNEW HE'D NEVER FIND IT, WHICH IS WHY HE NEVER ATE.

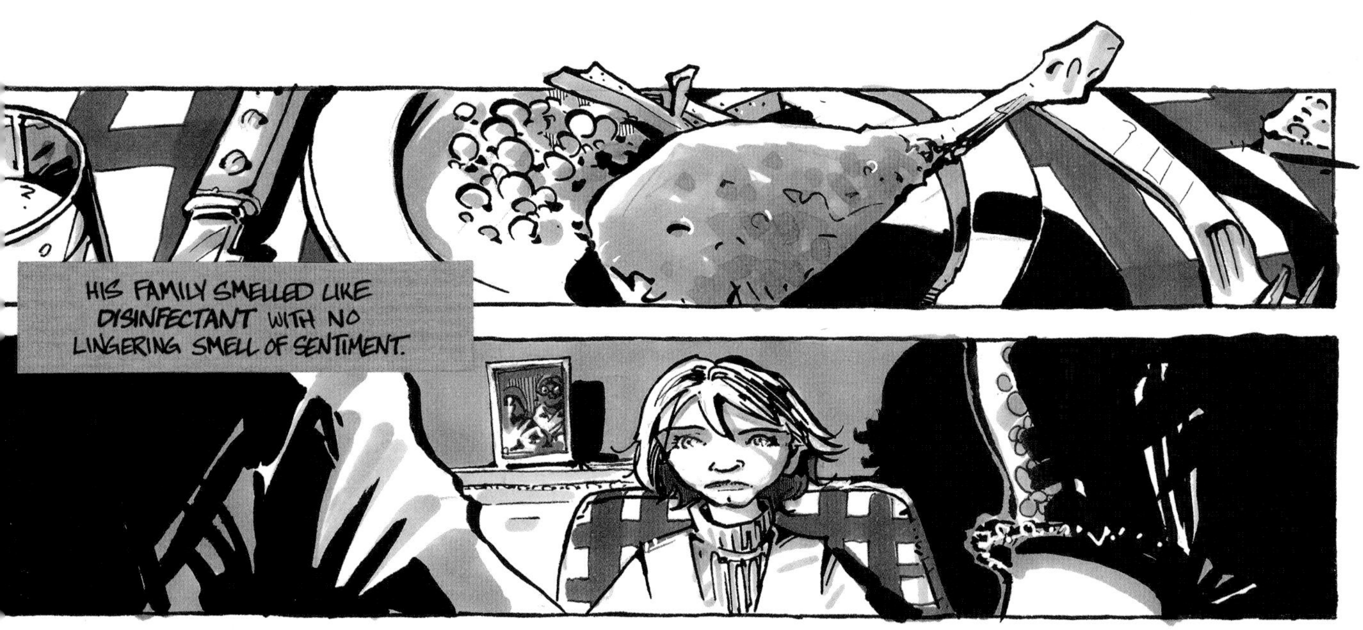
HIS FAMILY SMELLED LIKE DISINFECTANT WITH NO LINGERING SMELL OF SENTIMENT.

CHAPTER ONE ONE, TWO, NIRVANA

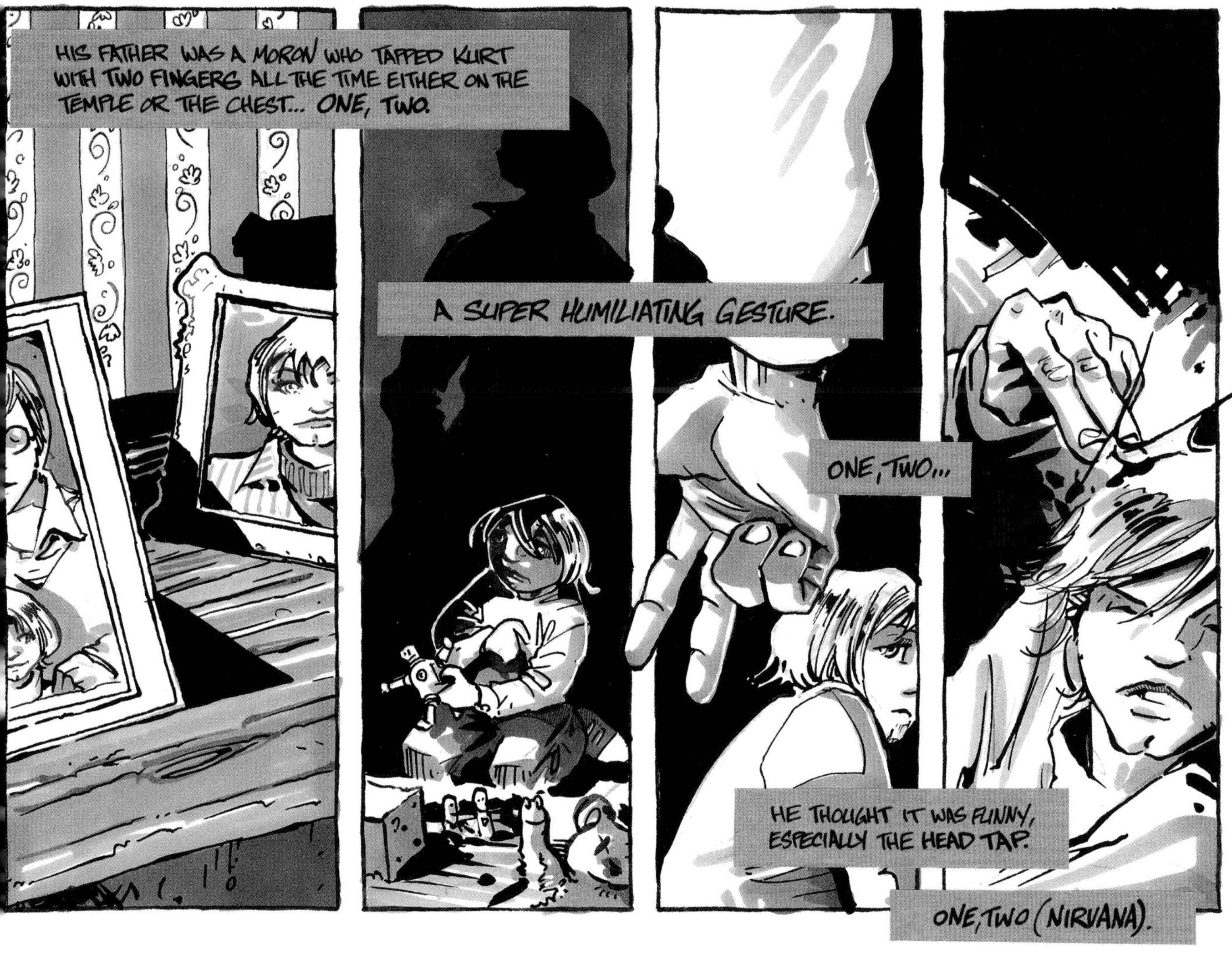
HIS FATHER WAS A MORON WHO TAPPED KURT WITH TWO FINGERS ALL THE TIME EITHER ON THE TEMPLE OR THE CHEST... ONE, TWO.
A SUPER HUMILIATING GESTURE.
ONE, TWO...
HE THOUGHT IT WAS FUNNY, ESPECIALLY THE HEAD TAP.
ONE, TWO (NIRVANA).

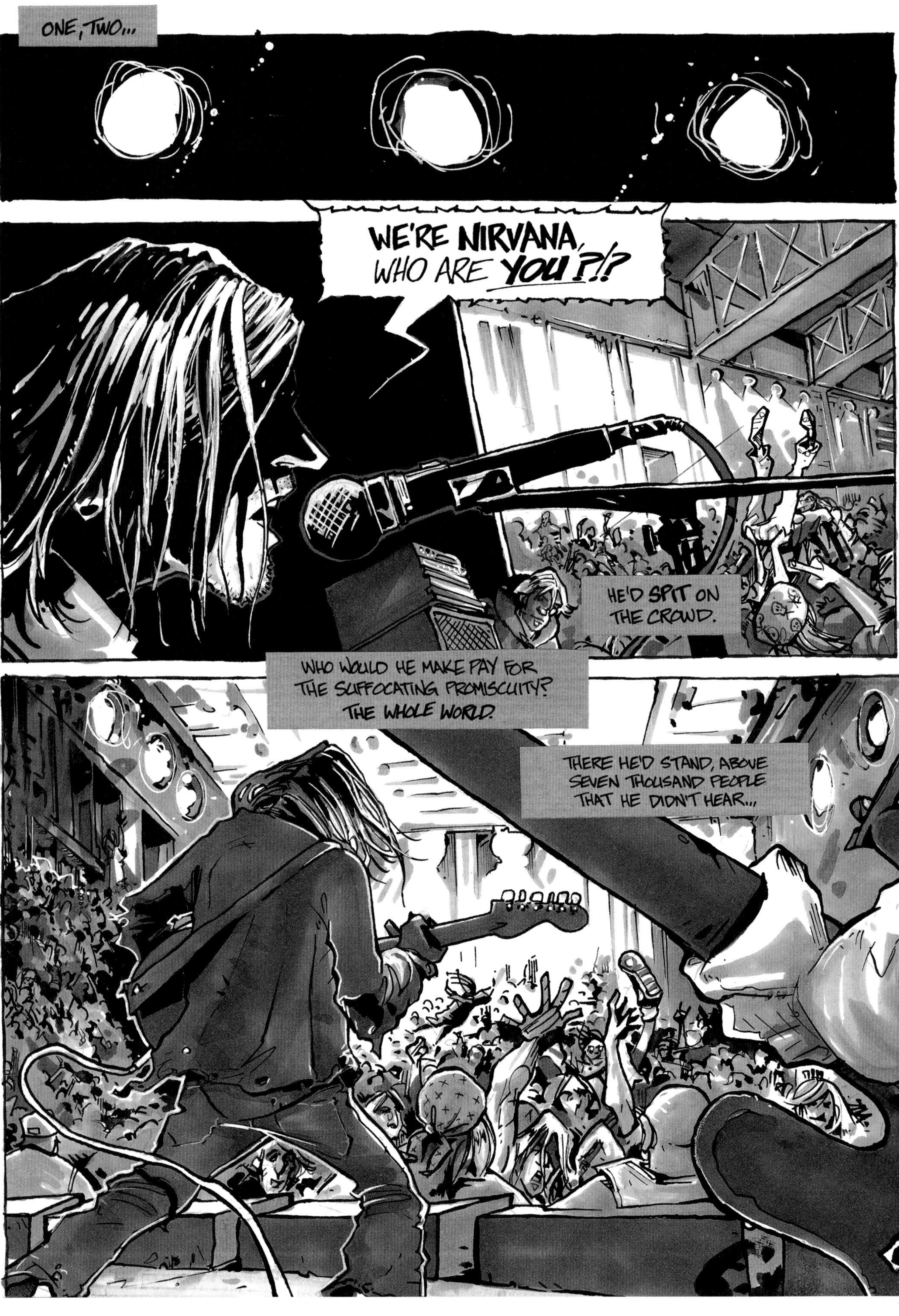
ONE, TWO...
WE'RE NIRVANA, WHO ARE YOU?!?
HE'D SPIT ON THE CROWD.
WHO WOULD HE MAKE PAY FOR THE SUFFOCATING PROMISCUITY? THE WHOLE WORLD.
THERE HE'D STAND, ABOVE SEVEN THOUSAND PEOPLE THAT HE DIDN'T HEAR...

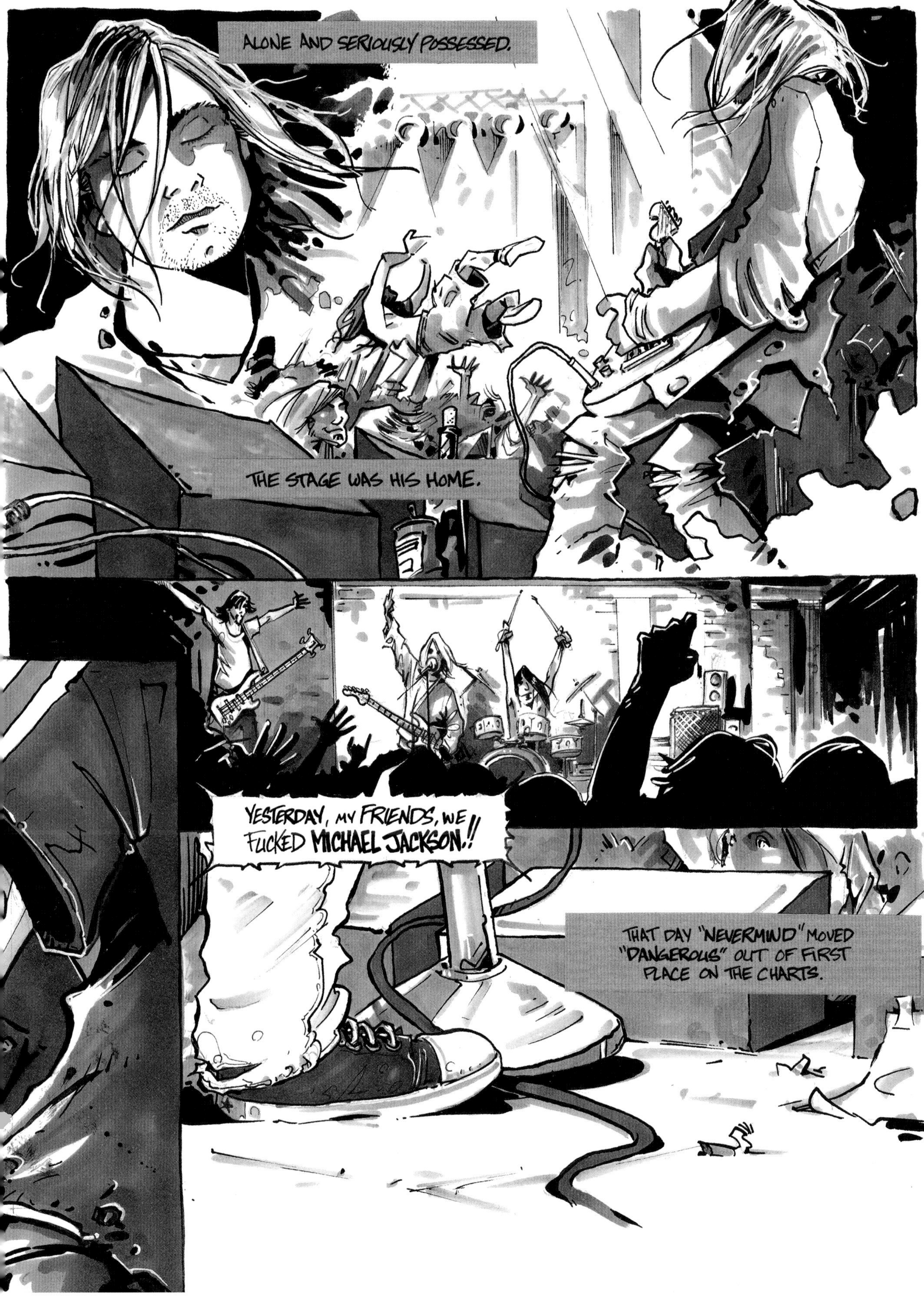
ALONE AND SERIOUSLY POSSESSED.
THE STAGE WAS HIS HOME.
YESTERDAY, MY FRIENDS, WE FUCKED MICHAEL JACKSON!!
THAT DAY "NEVERMIND" MOVED "DANGEROUS" OUT OF FIRST PLACE ON THE CHARTS.

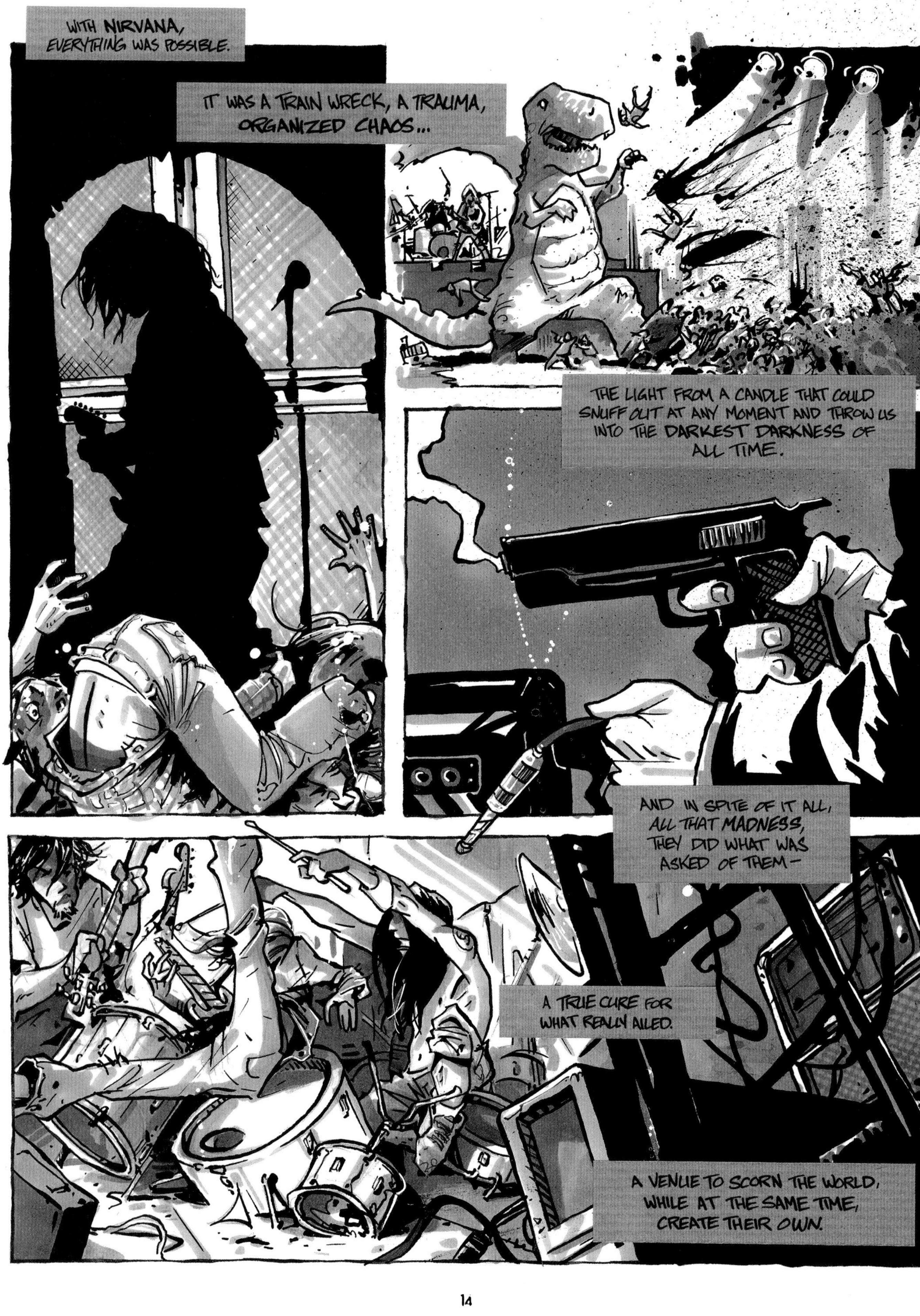
WITH NIRVANA, EVERYTHING WAS POSSIBLE.
IT WAS A TRAIN WRECK, A TRAUMA, ORGANIZED CHAOS...
THE LIGHT FROM A CANDLE THAT COULD SNUFF OUT AT ANY MOMENT AND THROW US INTO THE DARKEST DARKNESS OF ALL TIME.
AND IN SPITE OF IT ALL, ALL THAT MADNESS, THEY DID WHAT WAS ASKED OF THEM–
A TRUE CURE FOR WHAT REALLY AILED.
A VENUE TO SCORN THE WORLD, WHILE AT THE SAME TIME, CREATE THEIR OWN.

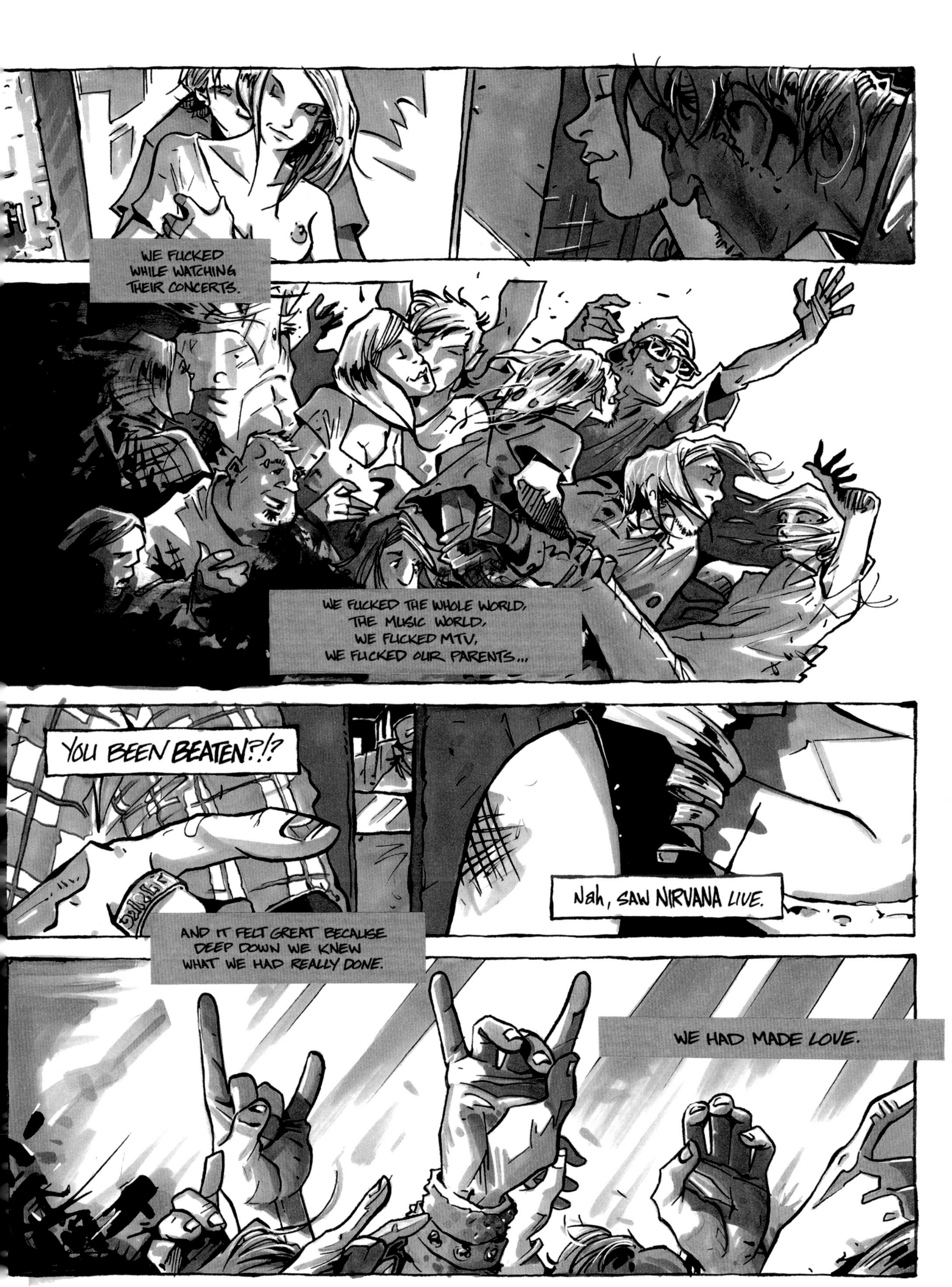
WE FUCKED
WHILE WATCHING
THEIR CONCERTS.
WE FUCKED THE WHOLE WORLD,
THE MUSIC WORLD,
WE FUCKED MTV,
WE FUCKED OUR PARENTS...
YOU BEEN BEATEN?!?
Nah, SAW NIRVANA LIVE.
AND IT FELT GREAT BECAUSE
DEEP DOWN WE KNEW
WHAT WE HAD REALLY DONE.
WE HAD MADE LOVE.

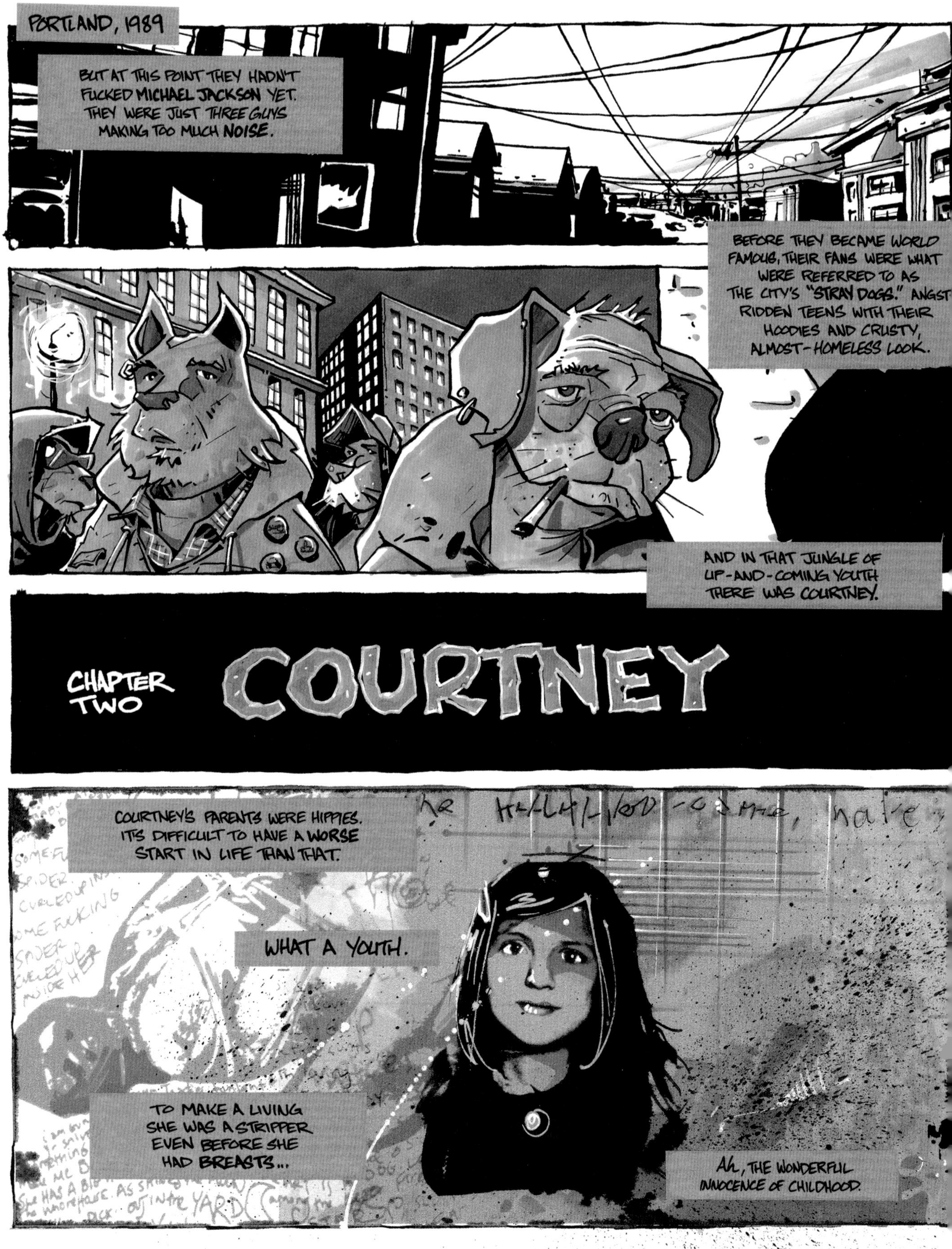
PORTLAND, 1989
BUT AT THIS POINT THEY HADN'T FUCKED MICHAEL JACKSON YET. THEY WERE JUST THREE GUYS MAKING TOO MUCH NOISE.
BEFORE THEY BECAME WORLD FAMOUS, THEIR FANS WERE WHAT WERE REFERRED TO AS THE CITY'S "STRAY DOGS." ANGST RIDDEN TEENS WITH THEIR HOODIES AND CRUSTY, ALMOST-HOMELESS LOOK.
AND IN THAT JUNGLE OF UP-AND-COMING YOUTH THERE WAS COURTNEY.
CHAPTER TWO
COURTNEY
COURTNEY'S PARENTS WERE HIPPIES. IT'S DIFFICULT TO HAVE A WORSE START IN LIFE THAN THAT.
WHAT A YOUTH.
TO MAKE A LIVING SHE WAS A STRIPPER EVEN BEFORE SHE HAD BREASTS...
Ah, THE WONDERFUL INNOCENCE OF CHILDHOOD.

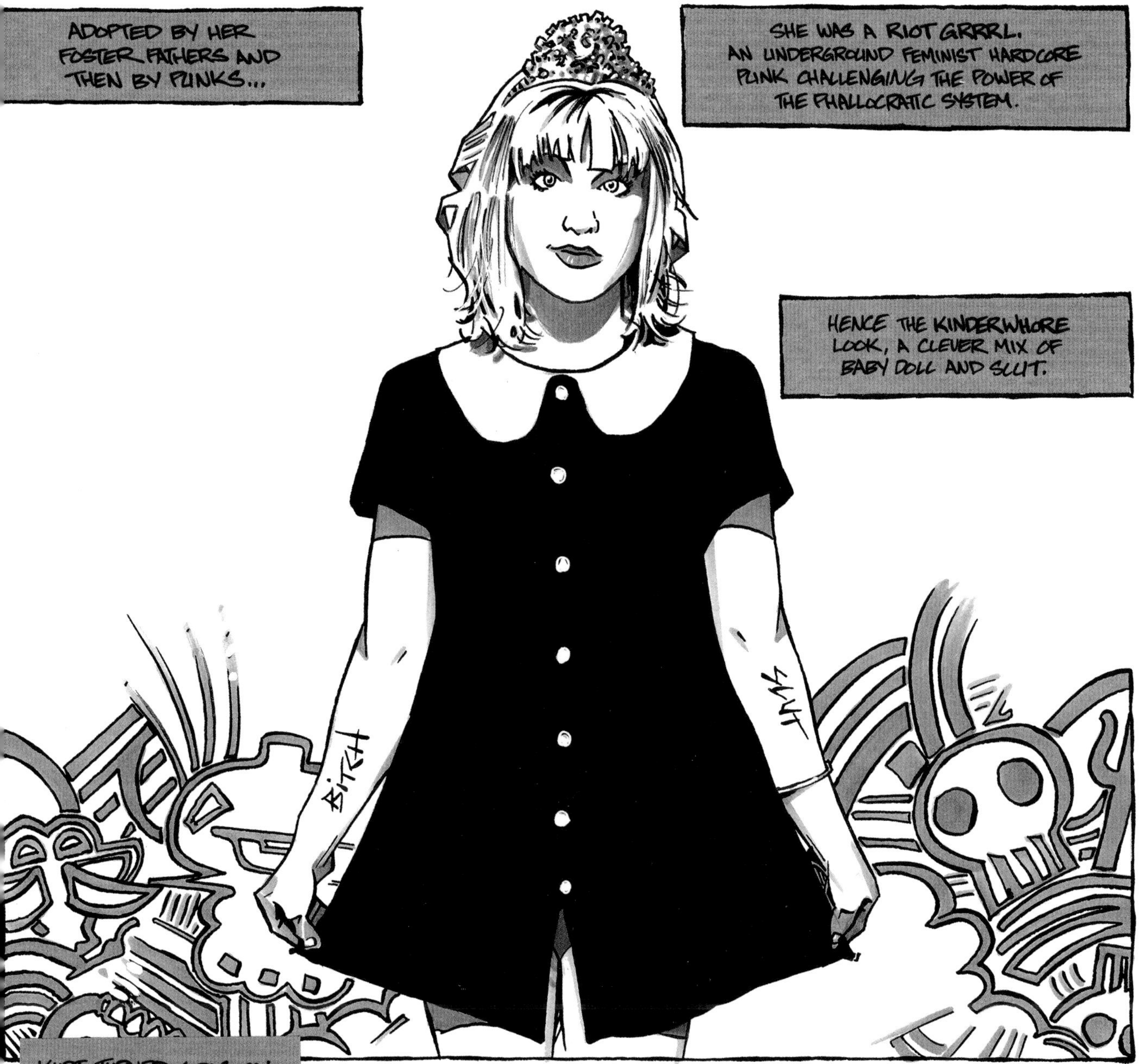
ADOPTED BY HER FOSTER FATHERS AND THEN BY PUNKS...
SHE WAS A RIOT GRRRL. AN UNDERGROUND FEMINIST HARDCORE PUNK CHALLENGING THE POWER OF THE PHALLOCRATIC SYSTEM.
HENCE THE KINDERWHORE LOOK, A CLEVER MIX OF BABY DOLL AND SLUT.
BITCH
SLUT

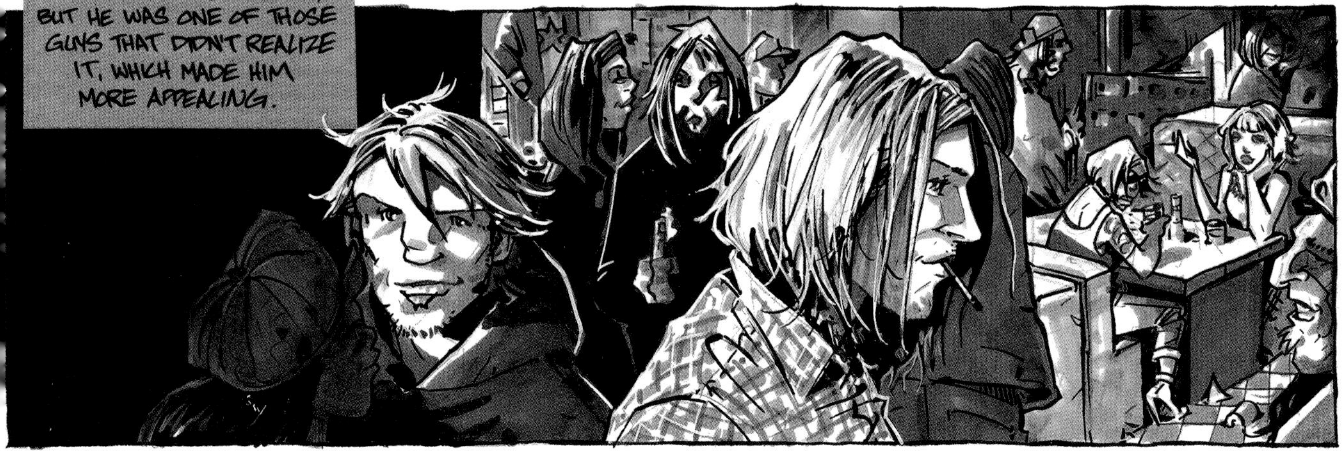
KURT TURNED GIRLS ON, BUT HE WAS ONE OF THOSE GUYS THAT DIDN'T REALIZE IT, WHICH MADE HIM MORE APPEALING.

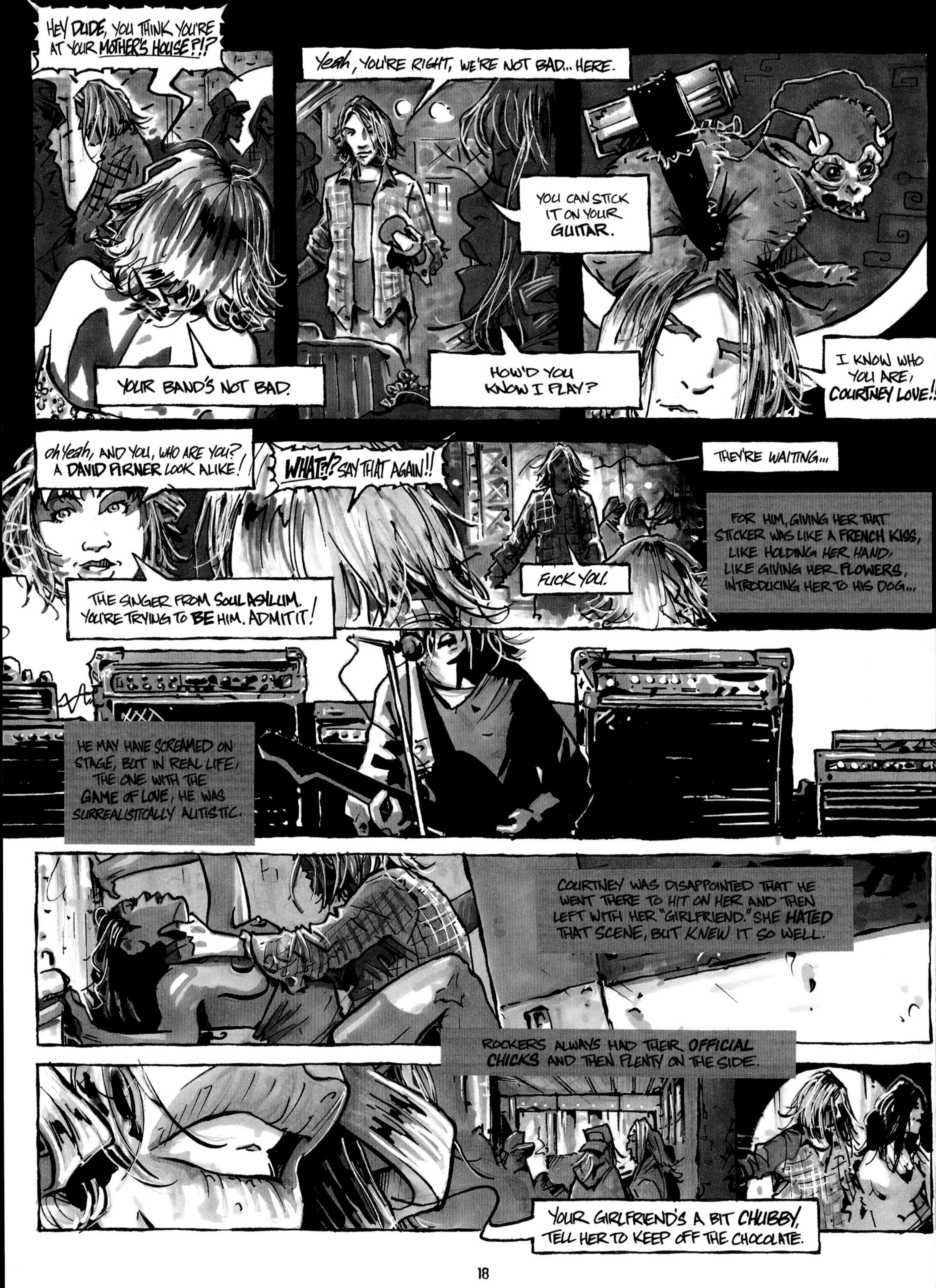
HEY DUDE, YOU THINK YOU'RE AT YOUR MOTHER'S HOUSE?!?
YOUR BAND'S NOT BAD.
Yeah, YOU'RE RIGHT, WE'RE NOT BAD... HERE.
YOU CAN STICK IT ON YOUR GUITAR.
HOW'D YOU KNOW I PLAY?
I KNOW WHO YOU ARE, COURTNEY LOVE!!
oh Yeah, AND YOU, WHO ARE YOU? A DAVID PIRNER LOOK ALIKE!
THE SINGER FROM SOUL ASYLUM. YOU'RE TRYING TO BE HIM. ADMIT IT!
WHAT?!? SAY THAT AGAIN!!
FUCK YOU.
THEY'RE WAITING...
FOR HIM, GIVING HER THAT STICKER WAS LIKE A FRENCH KISS, LIKE HOLDING HER HAND, LIKE GIVING HER FLOWERS, INTRODUCING HER TO HIS DOG...
HE MAY HAVE SCREAMED ON STAGE, BUT IN REAL LIFE, THE ONE WITH THE GAME OF LOVE, HE WAS SURREALISTICALLY AUTISTIC.
COURTNEY WAS DISAPPOINTED THAT HE WENT THERE TO HIT ON HER AND THEN LEFT WITH HER "GIRLFRIEND." SHE HATED THAT SCENE, BUT KNEW IT SO WELL.
ROCKERS ALWAYS HAD THEIR OFFICIAL CHICKS AND THEN PLENTY ON THE SIDE.
YOUR GIRLFRIEND'S A BIT CHUBBY, TELL HER TO KEEP OFF THE CHOCOLATE.

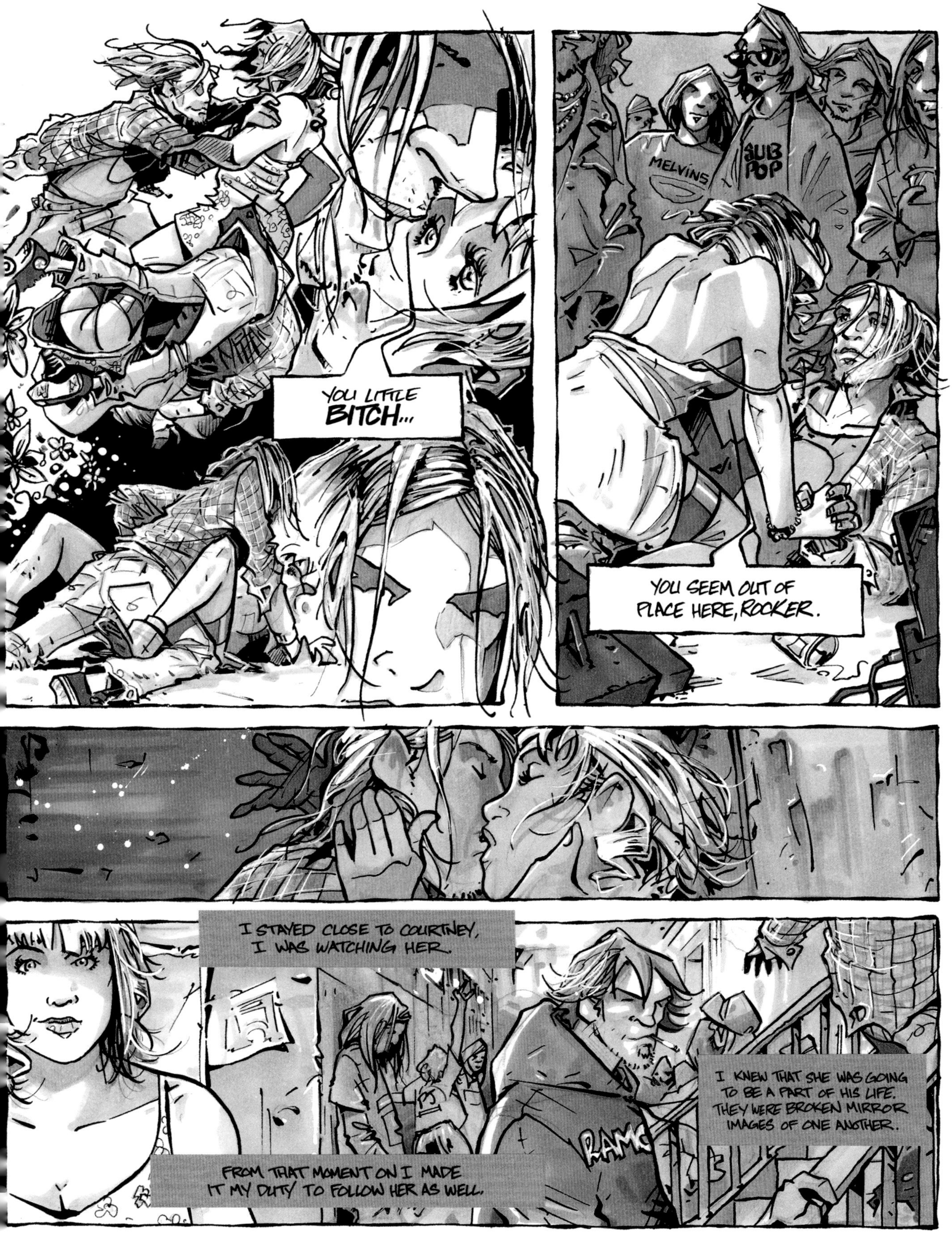
YOU LITTLE BITCH...
YOU SEEM OUT OF PLACE HERE, ROCKER.
MELVINS
SUB POP
I STAYED CLOSE TO COURTNEY, I WAS WATCHING HER.
I KNEW THAT SHE WAS GOING TO BE A PART OF HIS LIFE. THEY WERE BROKEN MIRROR IMAGES OF ONE ANOTHER.
FROM THAT MOMENT ON I MADE IT MY DUTY TO FOLLOW HER AS WELL.

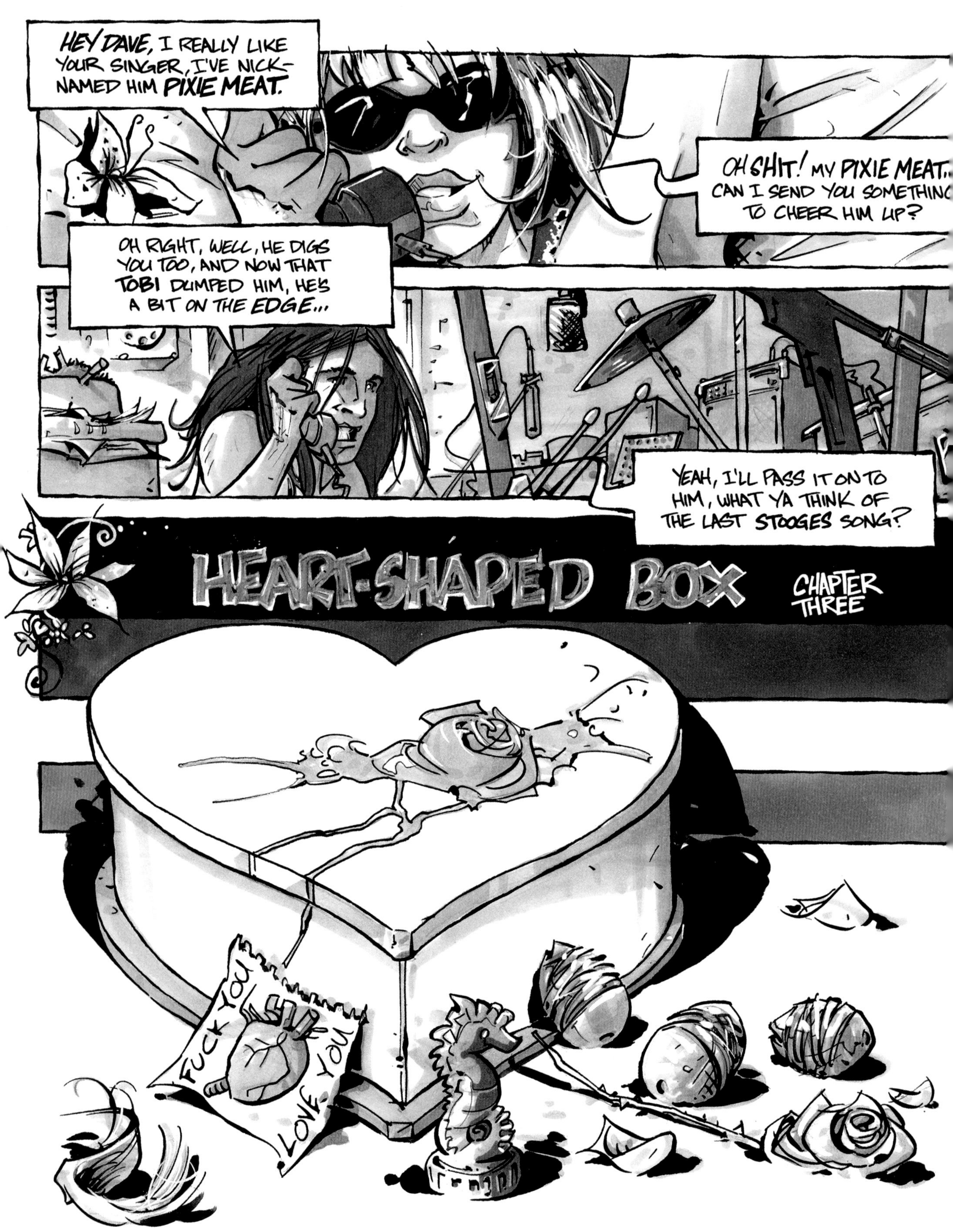
HEY DAVE, I REALLY LIKE YOUR SINGER, I'VE NICK-NAMED HIM PIXIE MEAT.
OH RIGHT, WELL, HE DIGS YOU TOO, AND NOW THAT TOBI DUMPED HIM, HE'S A BIT ON THE EDGE...
OH SHIT! MY PIXIE MEAT... CAN I SEND YOU SOMETHING TO CHEER HIM UP?
YEAH, I'LL PASS IT ON TO HIM, WHAT YA THINK OF THE LAST STOOGES SONG?
HEART-SHAPED BOX
CHAPTER THREE
FUCK YOU
LOVE YOU

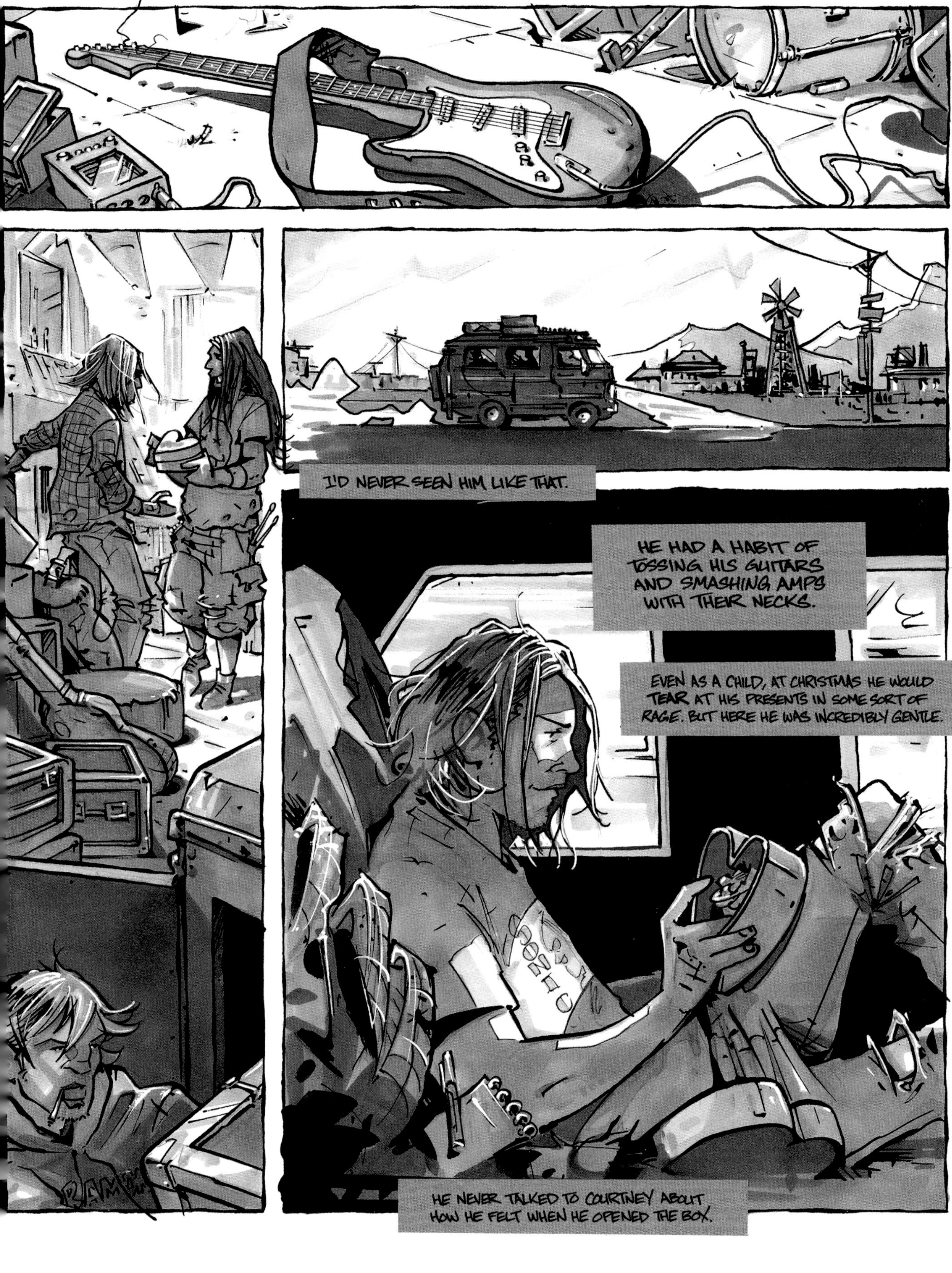
I'D NEVER SEEN HIM LIKE THAT.
HE HAD A HABIT OF TOSSING HIS GUITARS AND SMASHING AMPS WITH THEIR NECKS.
EVEN AS A CHILD, AT CHRISTMAS HE WOULD TEAR AT HIS PRESENTS IN SOME SORT OF RAGE. BUT HERE HE WAS INCREDIBLY GENTLE.
HE NEVER TALKED TO COURTNEY ABOUT HOW HE FELT WHEN HE OPENED THE BOX.

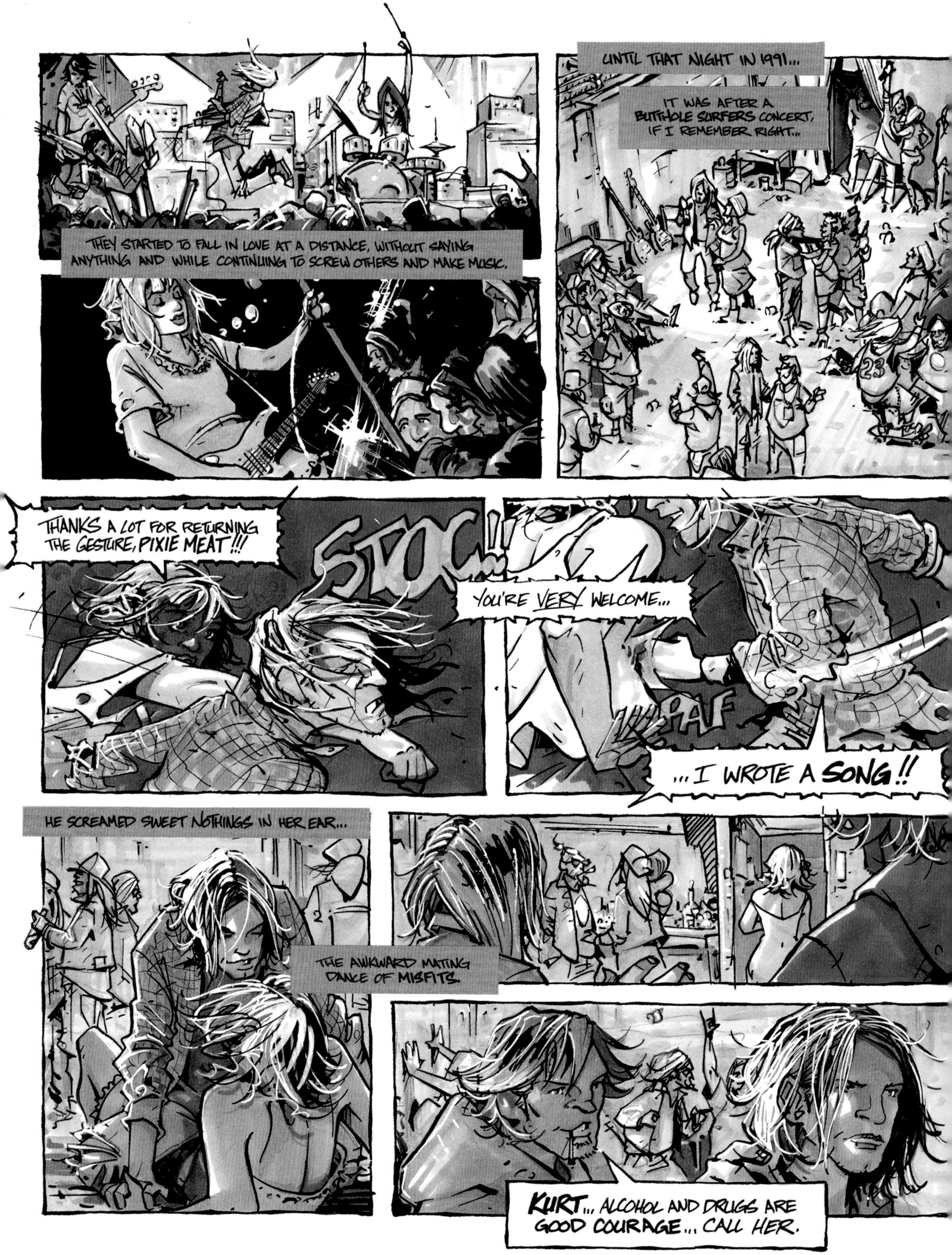

THEY STARTED TO FALL IN LOVE AT A DISTANCE, WITHOUT SAYING ANYTHING AND WHILE CONTINUING TO SCREW OTHERS AND MAKE MUSIC.
UNTIL THAT NIGHT IN 1991...
IT WAS AFTER A BUTTHOLE SURFERS CONCERT, IF I REMEMBER RIGHT...
THANKS A LOT FOR RETURNING THE GESTURE, PIXIE MEAT!!!
STOC!!
YOU'RE VERY WELCOME...
PAF
...I WROTE A SONG!!
HE SCREAMED SWEET NOTHINGS IN HER EAR...
THE AWKWARD MATING DANCE OF MISFITS.
KURT... ALCOHOL AND DRUGS ARE GOOD COURAGE... CALL HER.

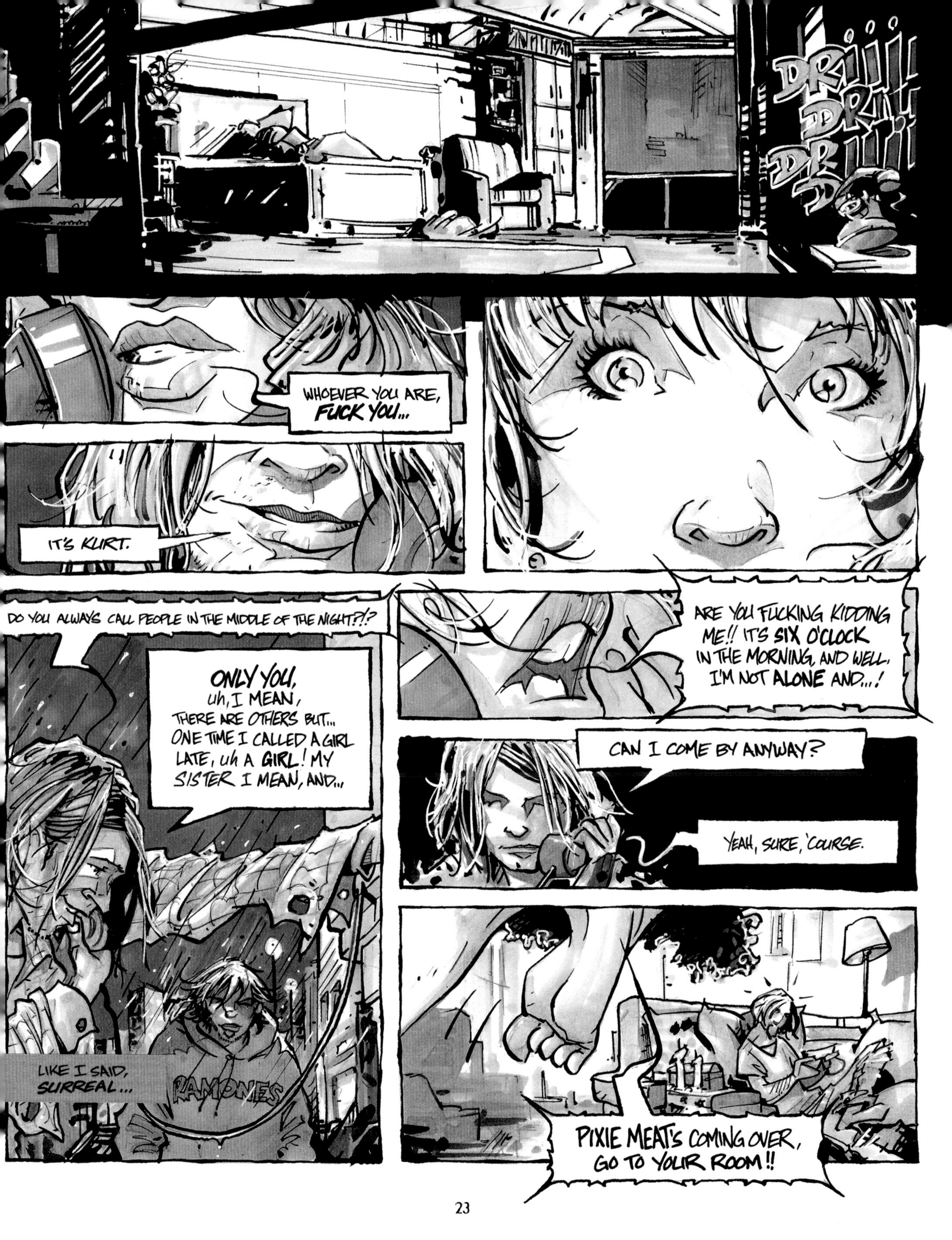
DRIIII DRIII DRIII DRIII
WHOEVER YOU ARE, FUCK YOU...
IT'S KURT.
DO YOU ALWAYS CALL PEOPLE IN THE MIDDLE OF THE NIGHT?!?
ONLY YOU, uh, I MEAN, THERE ARE OTHERS BUT... ONE TIME I CALLED A GIRL LATE, uh A GIRL! MY SISTER I MEAN, AND...
LIKE I SAID, SURREAL...
RAMONES
ARE YOU FUCKING KIDDING ME!! IT'S SIX O'CLOCK IN THE MORNING, AND WELL, I'M NOT ALONE AND...!
CAN I COME BY ANYWAY?
YEAH, SURE, 'COURSE.
PIXIE MEAT'S COMING OVER, GO TO YOUR ROOM!!

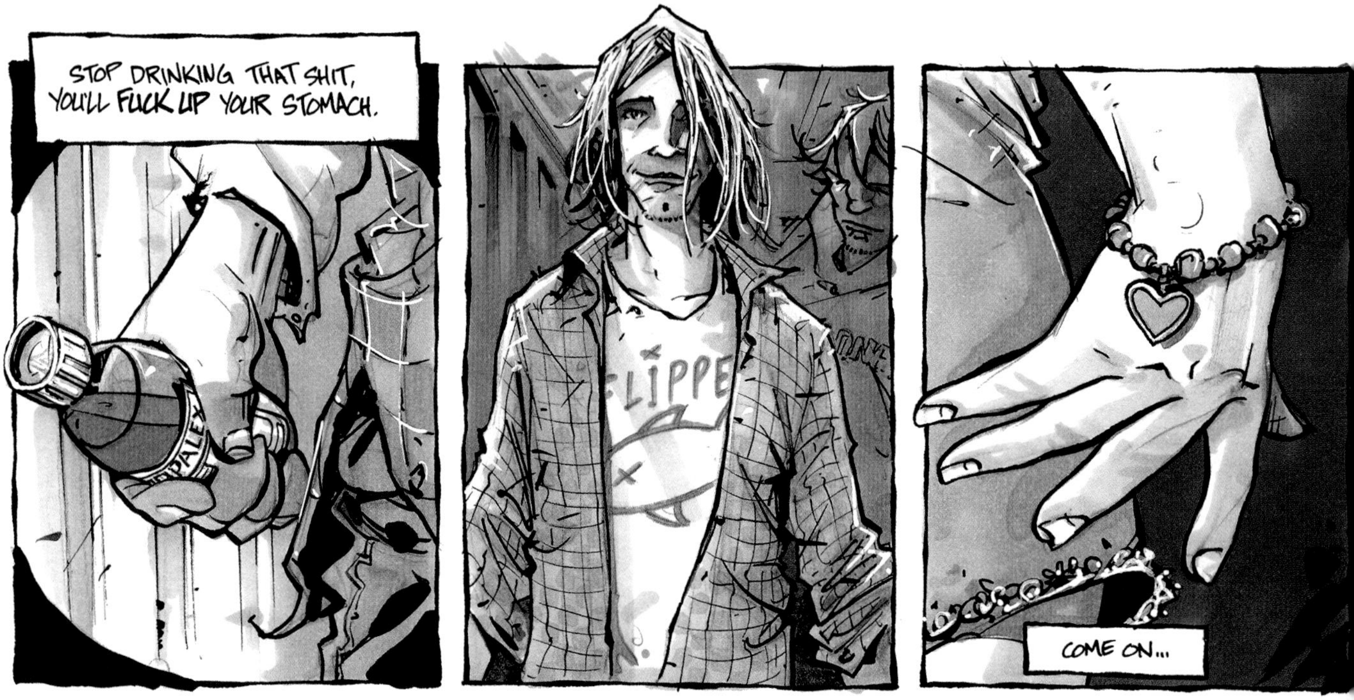
STOP DRINKING THAT SHIT, YOU'LL FUCK UP YOUR STOMACH.
COME ON...

CHAPTER FOUR VICODIN

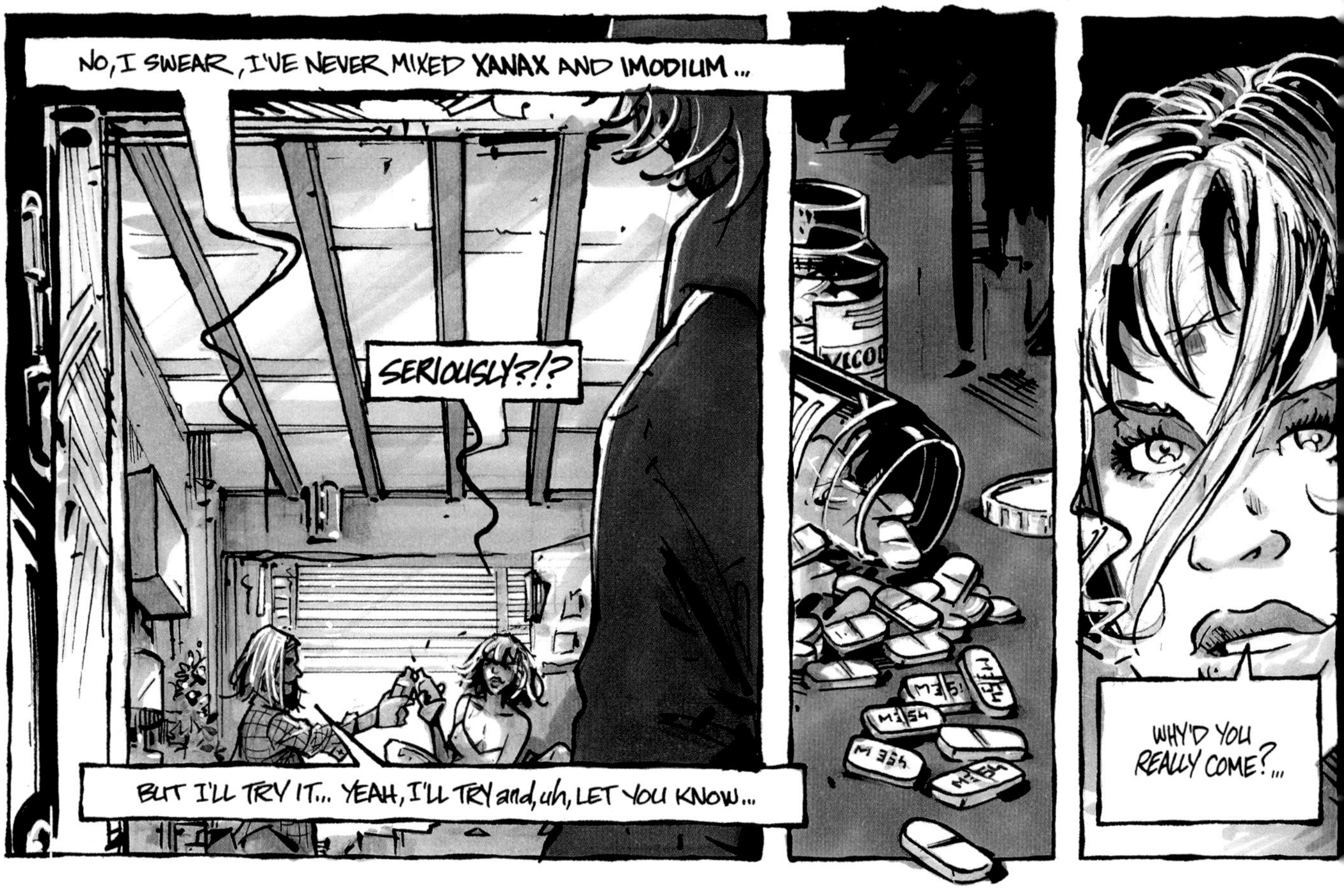
NO, I SWEAR, I'VE NEVER MIXED XANAX AND IMODIUM...
SERIOUSLY?!?
BUT I'LL TRY IT... YEAH, I'LL TRY and, uh, LET YOU KNOW...
WHY'D YOU REALLY COME?...

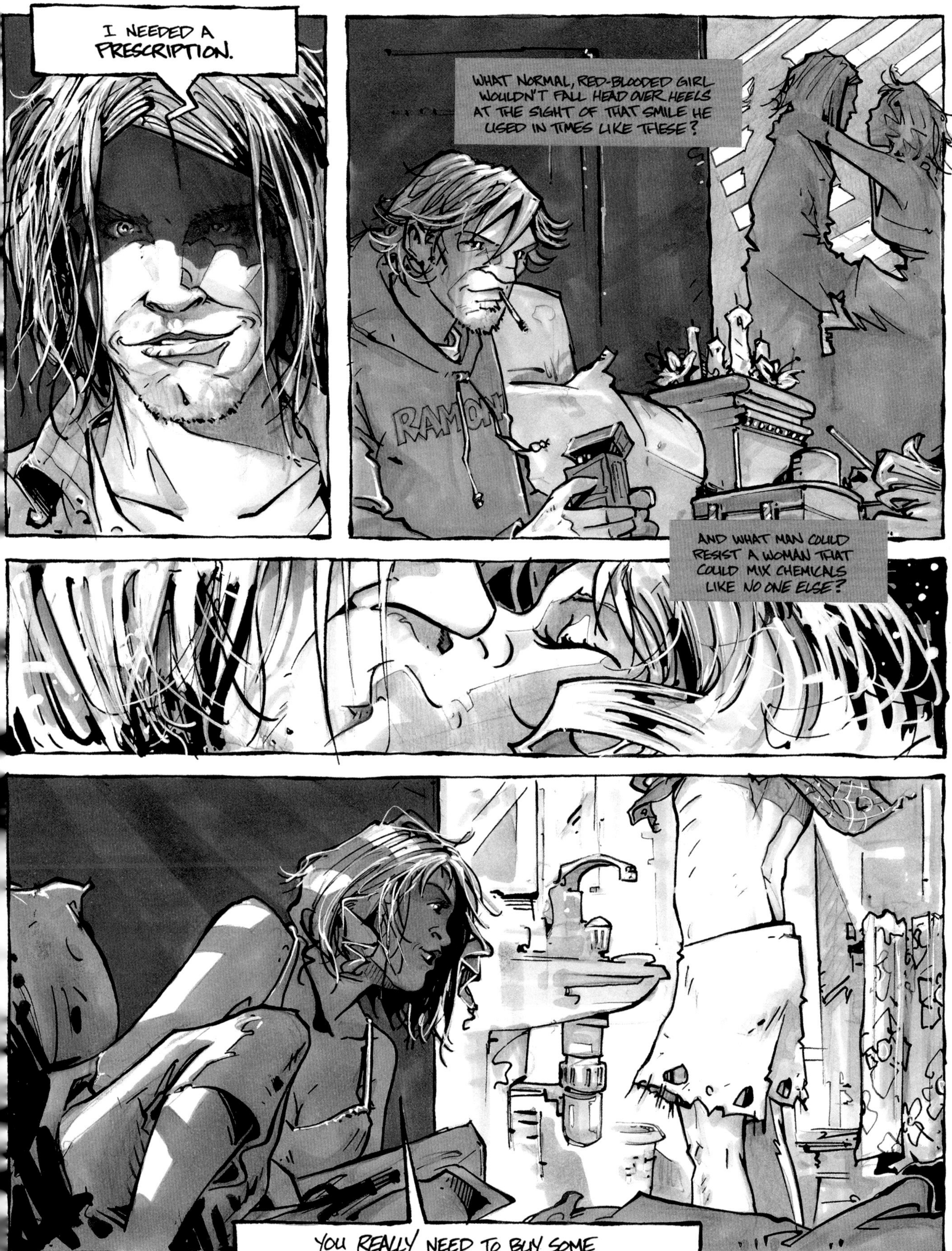

I NEEDED A PRESCRIPTION.
WHAT NORMAL, RED-BLOODED GIRL WOULDN'T FALL HEAD OVER HEELS AT THE SIGHT OF THAT SMILE HE USED IN TIMES LIKE THESE?
RAMONES
AND WHAT MAN COULD RESIST A WOMAN THAT COULD MIX CHEMICALS LIKE NO ONE ELSE?
YOU REALLY NEED TO BUY SOME UNDERWEAR, THOSE ARE RIDICULOUS.

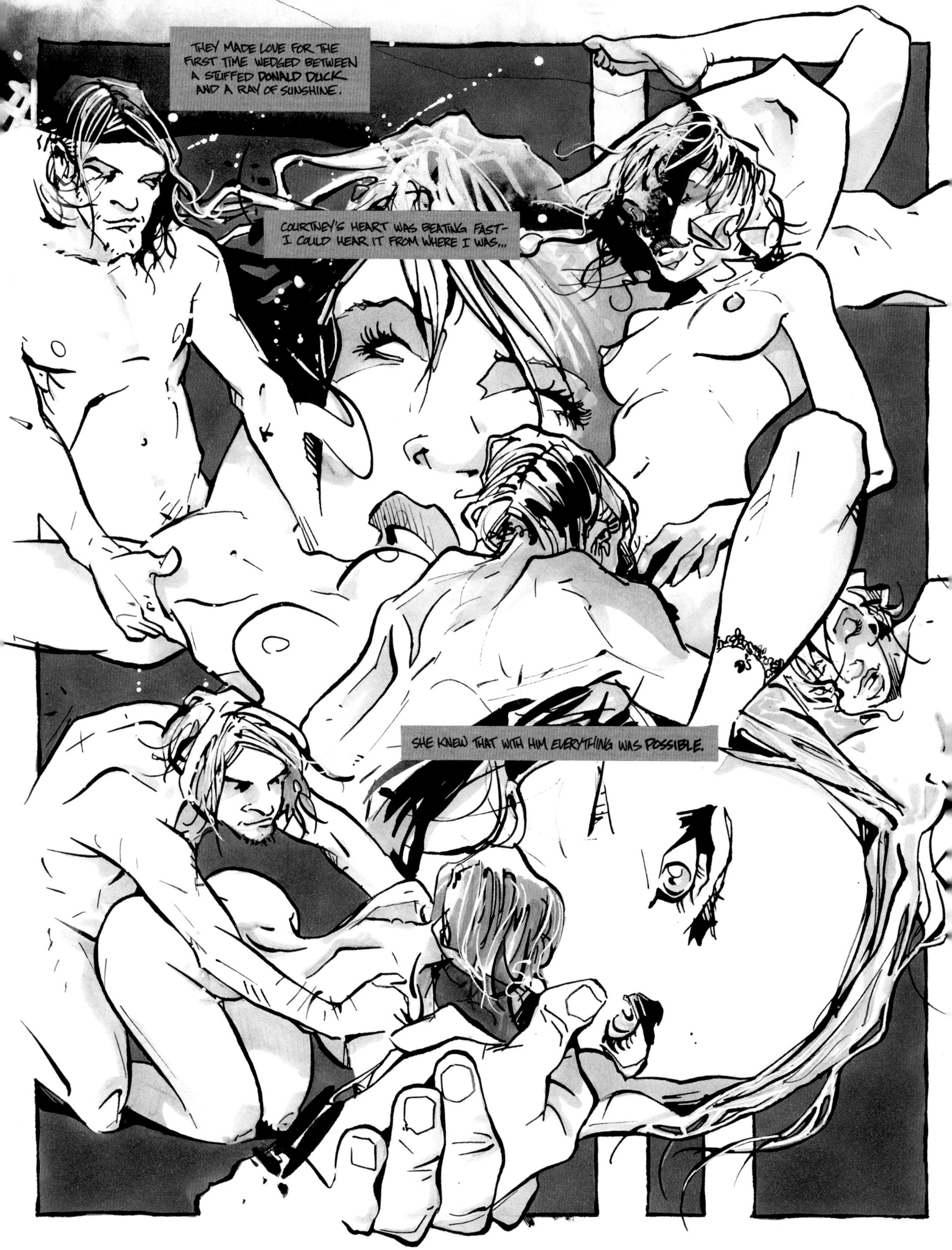
THEY MADE LOVE FOR THE FIRST TIME WEDGED BETWEEN A STUFFED DONALD DUCK AND A RAY OF SUNSHINE.
COURTNEY'S HEART WAS BEATING FAST- I COULD HEAR IT FROM WHERE I WAS...
SHE KNEW THAT WITH HIM EVERYTHING WAS POSSIBLE.

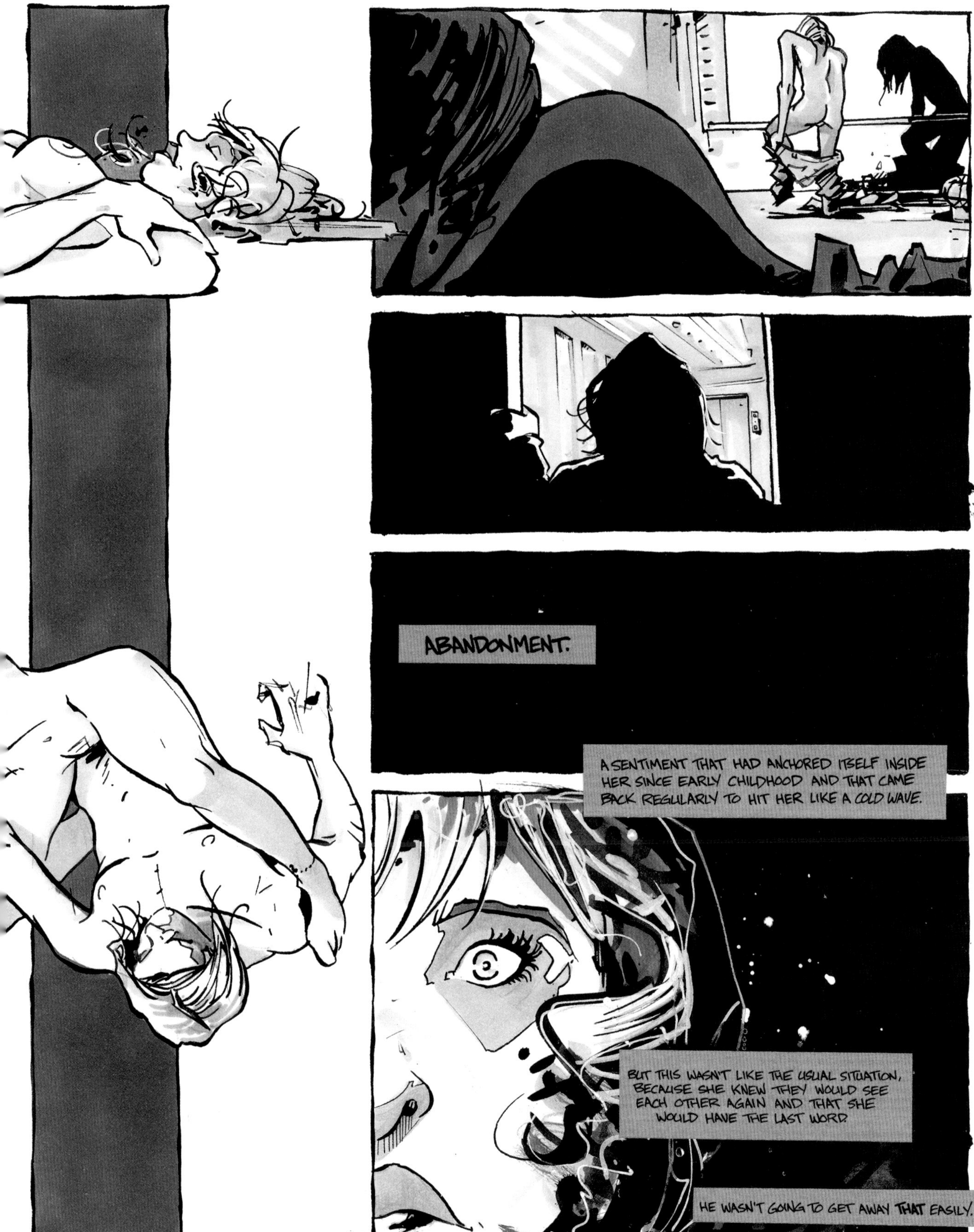
ABANDONMENT.
A SENTIMENT THAT HAD ANCHORED ITSELF INSIDE HER SINCE EARLY CHILDHOOD AND THAT CAME BACK REGULARLY TO HIT HER LIKE A COLD WAVE.
BUT THIS WASN'T LIKE THE USUAL SITUATION, BECAUSE SHE KNEW THEY WOULD SEE EACH OTHER AGAIN AND THAT SHE WOULD HAVE THE LAST WORD.
HE WASN'T GOING TO GET AWAY THAT EASILY.

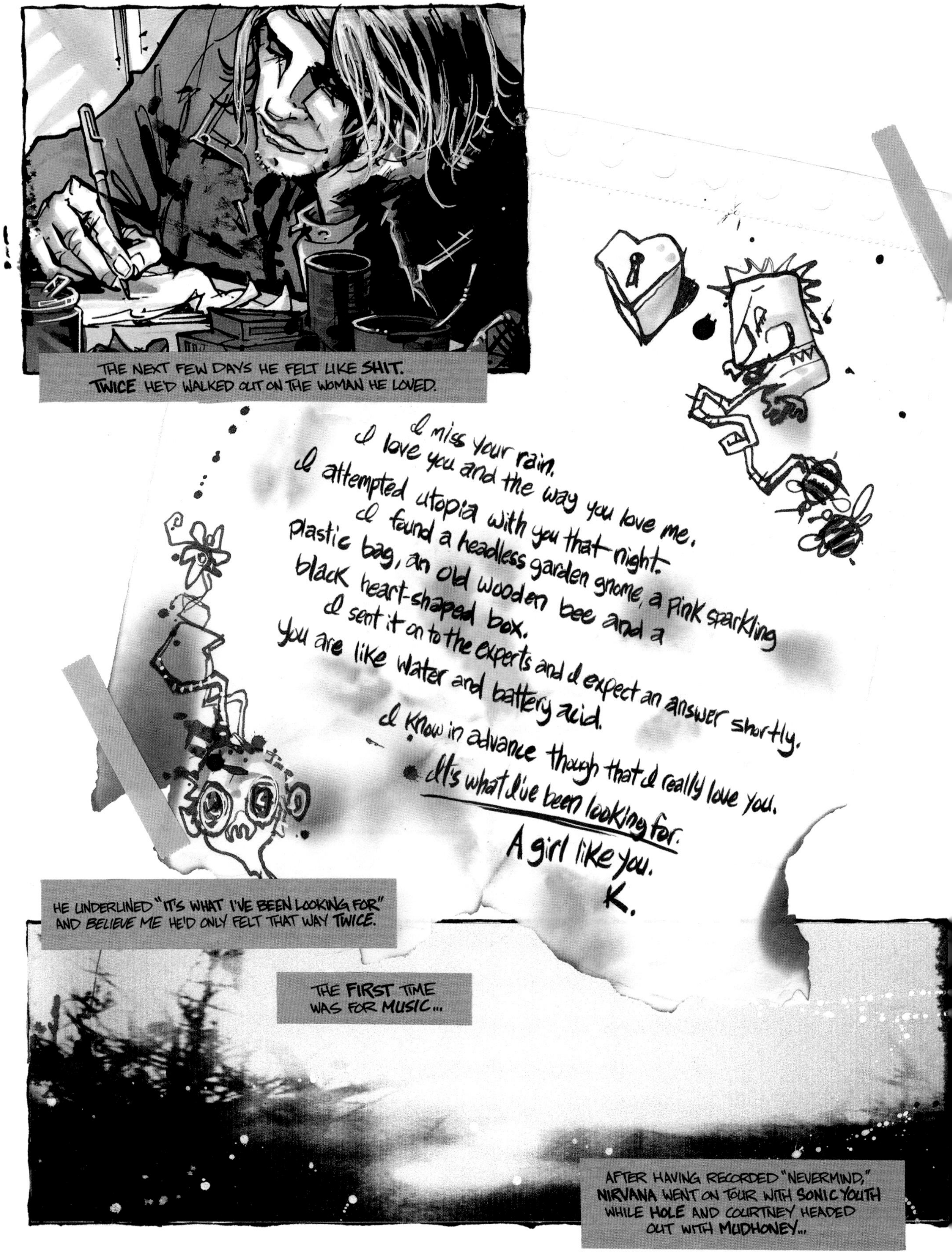
THE NEXT FEW DAYS HE FELT LIKE SHIT. TWICE HE'D WALKED OUT ON THE WOMAN HE LOVED.
I miss your rain.
I love you and the way you love me.
I attempted utopia with you that night.
I found a headless garden gnome, a pink sparkling plastic bag, an old wooden bee and a black heart-shaped box.
I sent it on to the experts and I expect an answer shortly.
You are like water and battery acid.
I know in advance though that I really love you.
It's what I've been looking for.
A girl like you.
K.
HE UNDERLINED "IT'S WHAT I'VE BEEN LOOKING FOR" AND BELIEVE ME HE'D ONLY FELT THAT WAY TWICE.
THE FIRST TIME WAS FOR MUSIC...
AFTER HAVING RECORDED "NEVERMIND," NIRVANA WENT ON TOUR WITH SONIC YOUTH WHILE HOLE AND COURTNEY HEADED OUT WITH MUDHONEY...

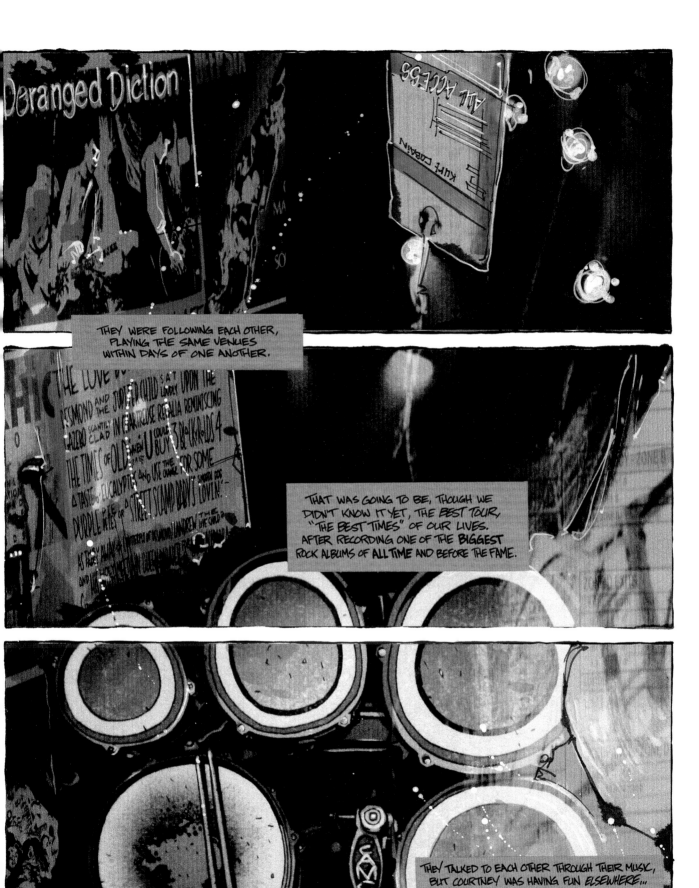

Deranged Diction

ALL ACCESS

Kurt Cobain

THEY WERE FOLLOWING EACH OTHER, PLAYING THE SAME VENUES WITHIN DAYS OF ONE ANOTHER.

THAT WAS GOING TO BE, THOUGH WE DIDN'T KNOW IT YET, THE *BEST* TOUR, "THE BEST TIMES" OF OUR LIVES. AFTER RECORDING ONE OF THE *BIGGEST* ROCK ALBUMS OF *ALL TIME* AND BEFORE THE FAME.

THEY TALKED TO EACH OTHER THROUGH THEIR MUSIC, BUT COURTNEY WAS HAVING FUN *ELSEWHERE...*

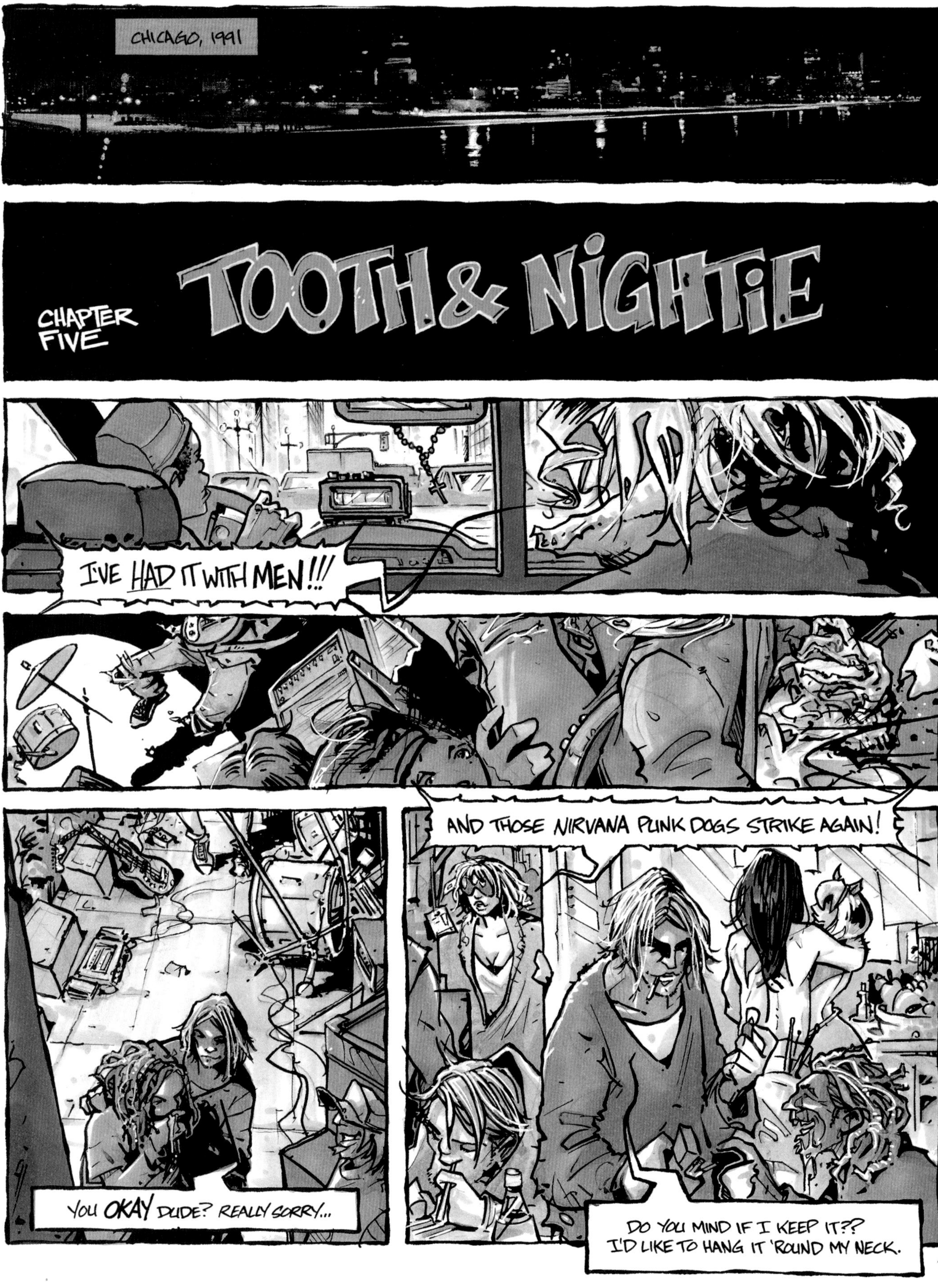
CHICAGO, 1991
CHAPTER FIVE
TOOTH & NIGHTIE
I'VE HAD IT WITH MEN!!!
AND THOSE NIRVANA PUNK DOGS STRIKE AGAIN!
YOU OKAY DUDE? REALLY SORRY...
DO YOU MIND IF I KEEP IT??
I'D LIKE TO HANG IT 'ROUND MY NECK.

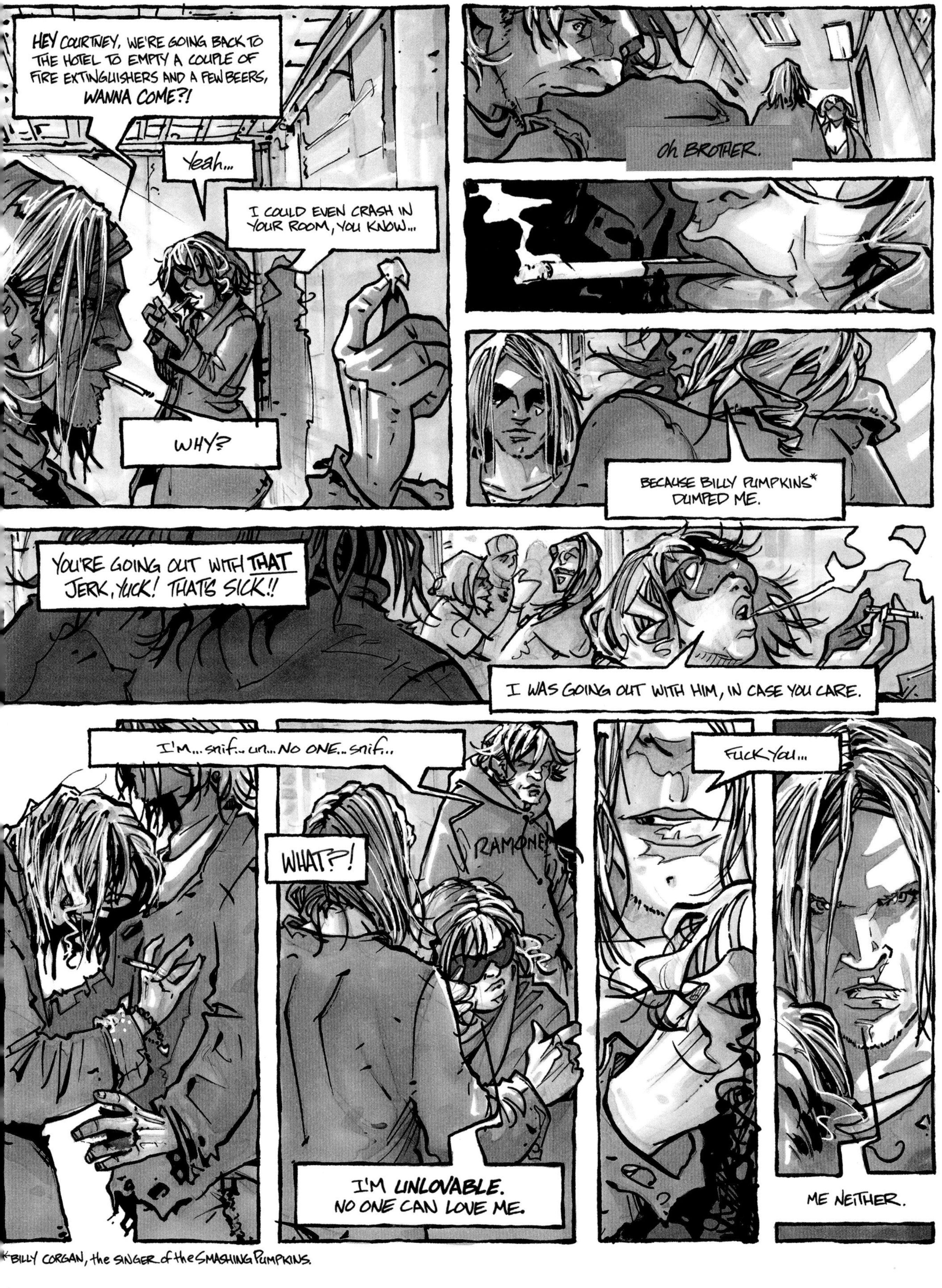
HEY COURTNEY, WE'RE GOING BACK TO THE HOTEL TO EMPTY A COUPLE OF FIRE EXTINGUISHERS AND A FEW BEERS, WANNA COME?!
Yeah...
I COULD EVEN CRASH IN YOUR ROOM, YOU KNOW...
WHY?
Oh BROTHER.
BECAUSE BILLY PUMPKINS* DUMPED ME.
YOU'RE GOING OUT WITH THAT JERK, YUCK! THAT'S SICK!!
I WAS GOING OUT WITH HIM, IN CASE YOU CARE.
I'M... snif... un... NO ONE... snif...
WHAT?!
RAMONES
I'M UNLOVABLE. NO ONE CAN LOVE ME.
FUCK YOU...
ME NEITHER.

*BILLY CORGAN, the SINGER of the SMASHING PUMPKINS.

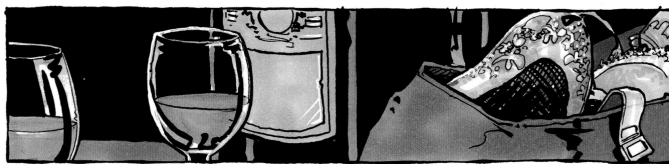

PUTTING ON HER LINGERIE WAS
LIKE REACHING INTO HER SOUL.

HE WAS INCAPABLE OF UNDRESSING A WOMAN,
BUT HAD NO PROBLEM PUTTING ON HER GEAR.

THE MOMENT HE POSED IN FRONT OF THE MIRROR
HE BECAME HIS OWN GROUPIE, ONE HE WOULD VOLUNTARILY
FUCK ON THE SLIPPERY SLOPE OF HIS BROKEN CHILDHOOD.

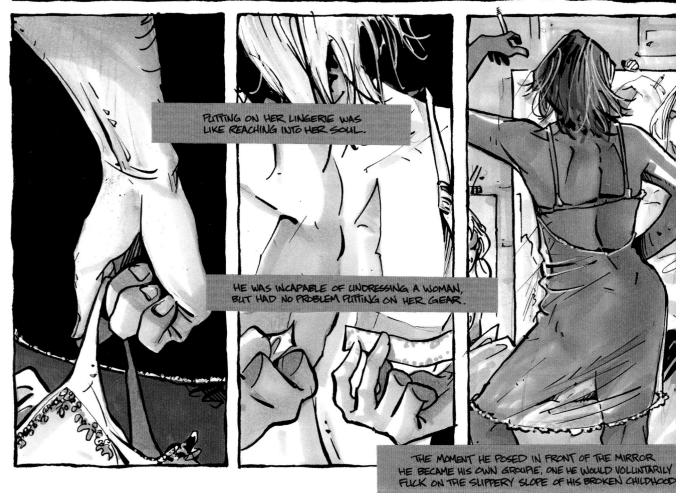

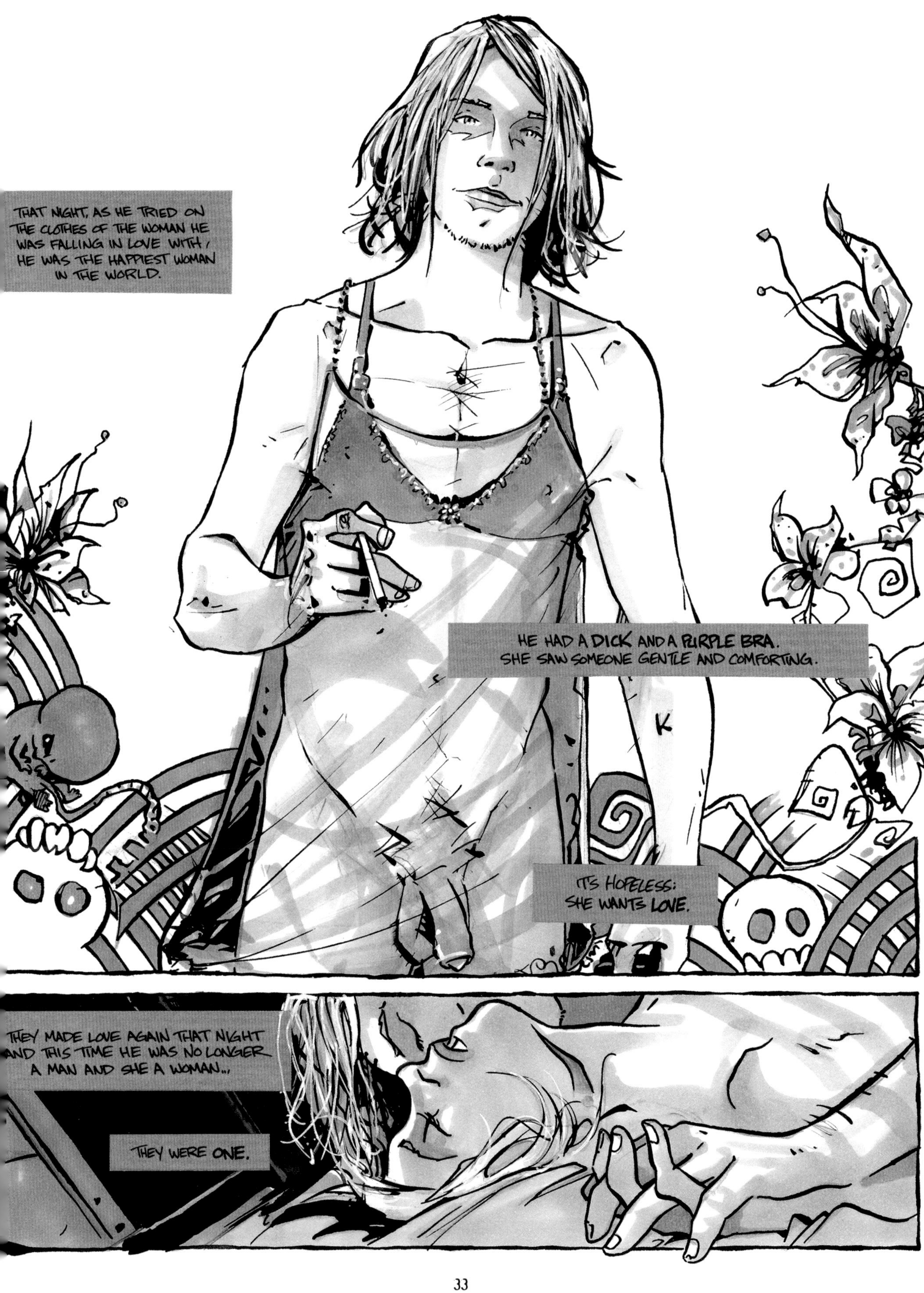
THAT NIGHT, AS HE TRIED ON THE CLOTHES OF THE WOMAN HE WAS FALLING IN LOVE WITH, HE WAS THE HAPPIEST WOMAN IN THE WORLD.
HE HAD A DICK AND A PURPLE BRA. SHE SAW SOMEONE GENTLE AND COMFORTING.
IT'S HOPELESS: SHE WANTS LOVE.
THEY MADE LOVE AGAIN THAT NIGHT AND THIS TIME HE WAS NO LONGER A MAN AND SHE A WOMAN...
THEY WERE ONE.

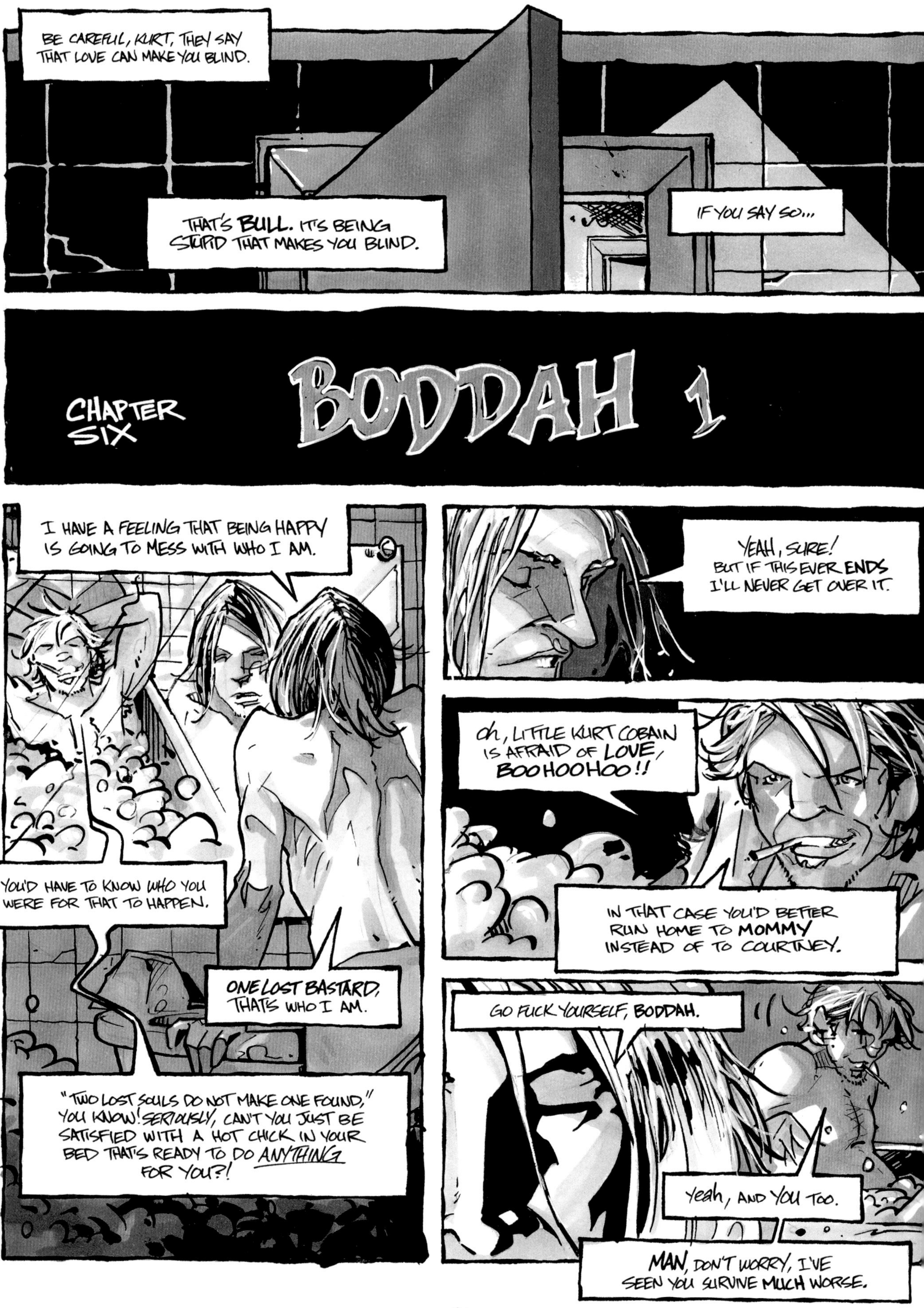
BE CAREFUL, KURT, THEY SAY THAT LOVE CAN MAKE YOU BLIND.
THAT'S BULL. IT'S BEING STUPID THAT MAKES YOU BLIND.
IF YOU SAY SO...
CHAPTER SIX
BODDAH 1
I HAVE A FEELING THAT BEING HAPPY IS GOING TO MESS WITH WHO I AM.
YOU'D HAVE TO KNOW WHO YOU WERE FOR THAT TO HAPPEN.
ONE LOST BASTARD, THAT'S WHO I AM.
"TWO LOST SOULS DO NOT MAKE ONE FOUND," YOU KNOW! SERIOUSLY, CAN'T YOU JUST BE SATISFIED WITH A HOT CHICK IN YOUR BED THAT'S READY TO DO ANYTHING FOR YOU?!
YEAH, SURE! BUT IF THIS EVER ENDS I'LL NEVER GET OVER IT.
Oh, LITTLE KURT COBAIN IS AFRAID OF LOVE, BOOHOOHOO!!
IN THAT CASE YOU'D BETTER RUN HOME TO MOMMY INSTEAD OF TO COURTNEY.
GO FUCK YOURSELF, BODDAH.
Yeah, AND YOU TOO.
MAN, DON'T WORRY, I'VE SEEN YOU SURVIVE MUCH WORSE.

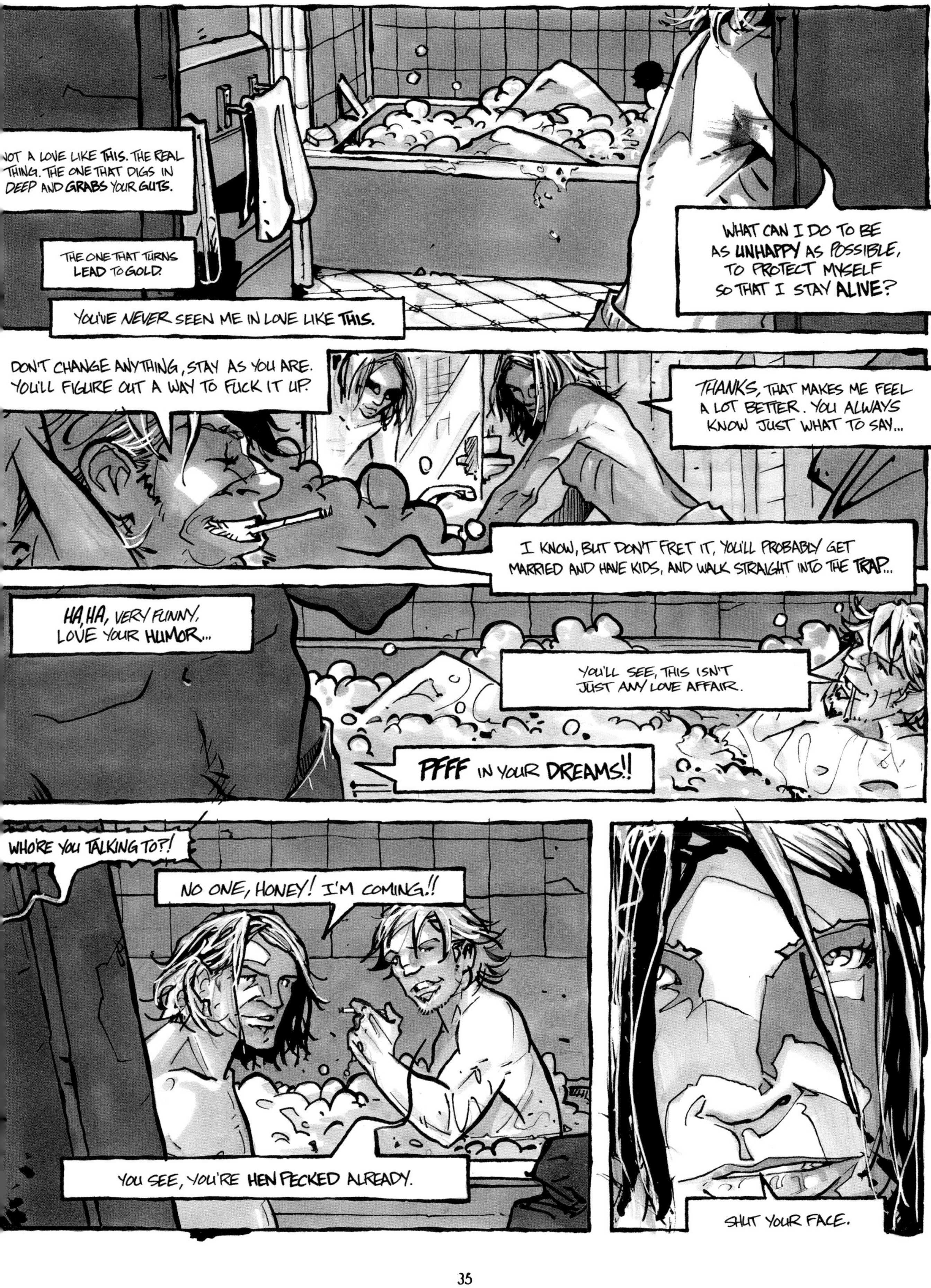

NOT A LOVE LIKE THIS. THE REAL THING. THE ONE THAT DIGS IN DEEP AND GRABS YOUR GUTS.
THE ONE THAT TURNS LEAD TO GOLD.
YOU'VE NEVER SEEN ME IN LOVE LIKE THIS.
WHAT CAN I DO TO BE AS UNHAPPY AS POSSIBLE, TO PROTECT MYSELF SO THAT I STAY ALIVE?
DON'T CHANGE ANYTHING, STAY AS YOU ARE. YOU'LL FIGURE OUT A WAY TO FUCK IT UP.
THANKS, THAT MAKES ME FEEL A LOT BETTER. YOU ALWAYS KNOW JUST WHAT TO SAY...
I KNOW, BUT DON'T FRET IT, YOU'LL PROBABLY GET MARRIED AND HAVE KIDS, AND WALK STRAIGHT INTO THE TRAP...
HA, HA, VERY FUNNY, LOVE YOUR HUMOR...
YOU'LL SEE, THIS ISN'T JUST ANY LOVE AFFAIR.
PFFF IN YOUR DREAMS!!
WHO'RE YOU TALKING TO?!
NO ONE, HONEY! I'M COMING!!
YOU SEE, YOU'RE HEN PECKED ALREADY.
SHUT YOUR FACE.

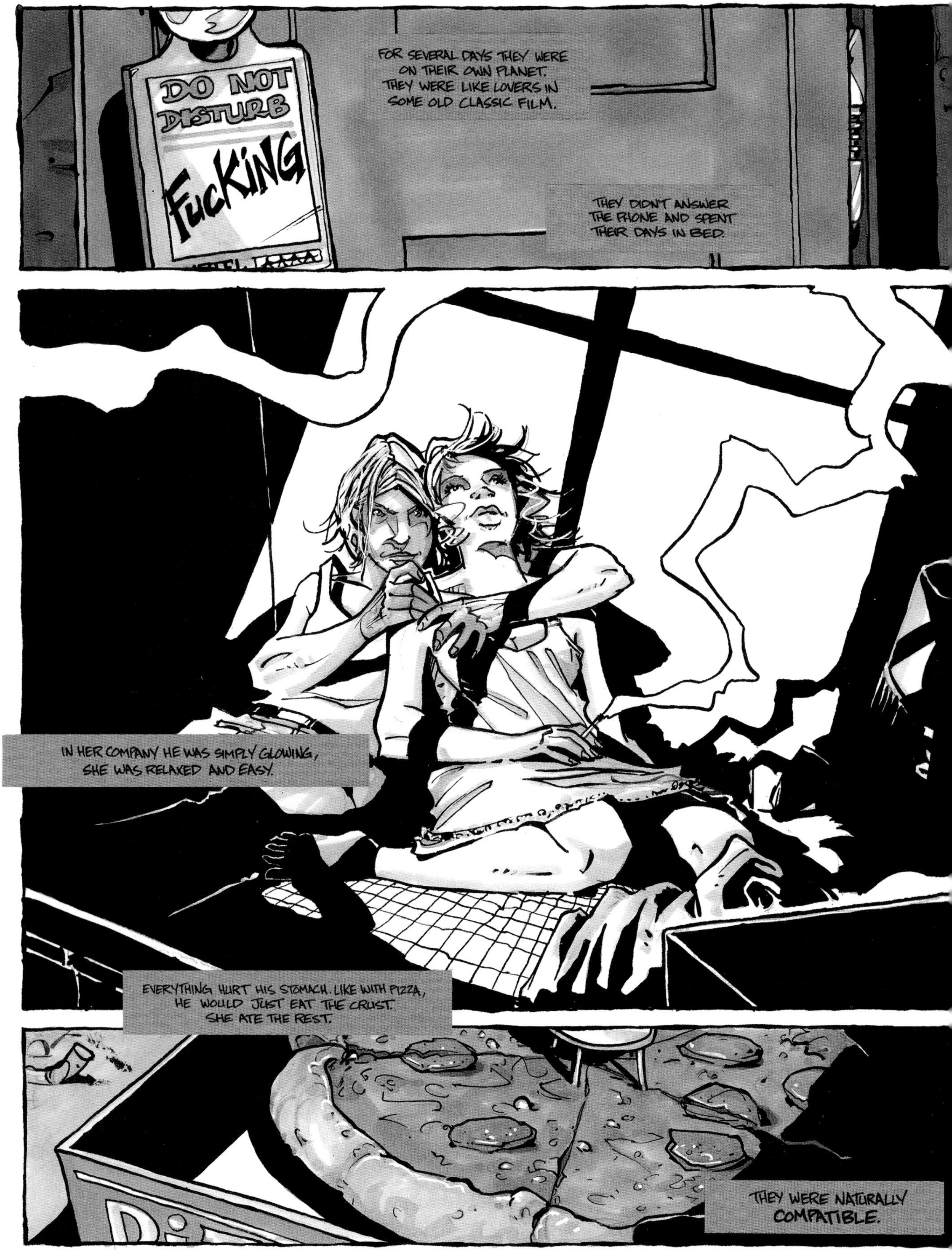
DO NOT DISTURB
FUCKING
FOR SEVERAL DAYS THEY WERE ON THEIR OWN PLANET. THEY WERE LIKE LOVERS IN SOME OLD CLASSIC FILM.
THEY DIDN'T ANSWER THE PHONE AND SPENT THEIR DAYS IN BED.
IN HER COMPANY HE WAS SIMPLY GLOWING, SHE WAS RELAXED AND EASY.
EVERYTHING HURT HIS STOMACH. LIKE WITH PIZZA, HE WOULD JUST EAT THE CRUST. SHE ATE THE REST.
THEY WERE NATURALLY COMPATIBLE.

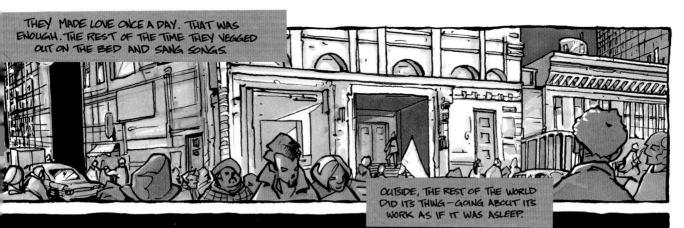

THEY MADE LOVE ONCE A DAY. THAT WAS ENOUGH. THE REST OF THE TIME THEY VEGGED OUT ON THE BED AND SANG SONGS

OUTSIDE, THE REST OF THE WORLD DID ITS THING — GOING ABOUT ITS WORK AS IF IT WAS ASLEEP.

MÉNAGE À TROIS

CHAPTER SEVEN

YOU MAKE A MUCH BETTER J.R. THAN SUE ELLEN, YOU KNOW...

NO ONE HAS EVER SAID THAT TO ME BEFORE, I APPRECIATE YOUR HONESTY. MAN, I LOVE YOU.

HEY...

I WAS WONDERING IF A THIRD PERSON WOULD FIT IN...?

WHAT?!?

I'M GOING TO GET US SOME H...

UH, IF YOU WANT...

OOOFF, A THREESOME, NOT EVEN IN YOUR DREAMS, BUT H, NO PROBLEM.

OKAY.

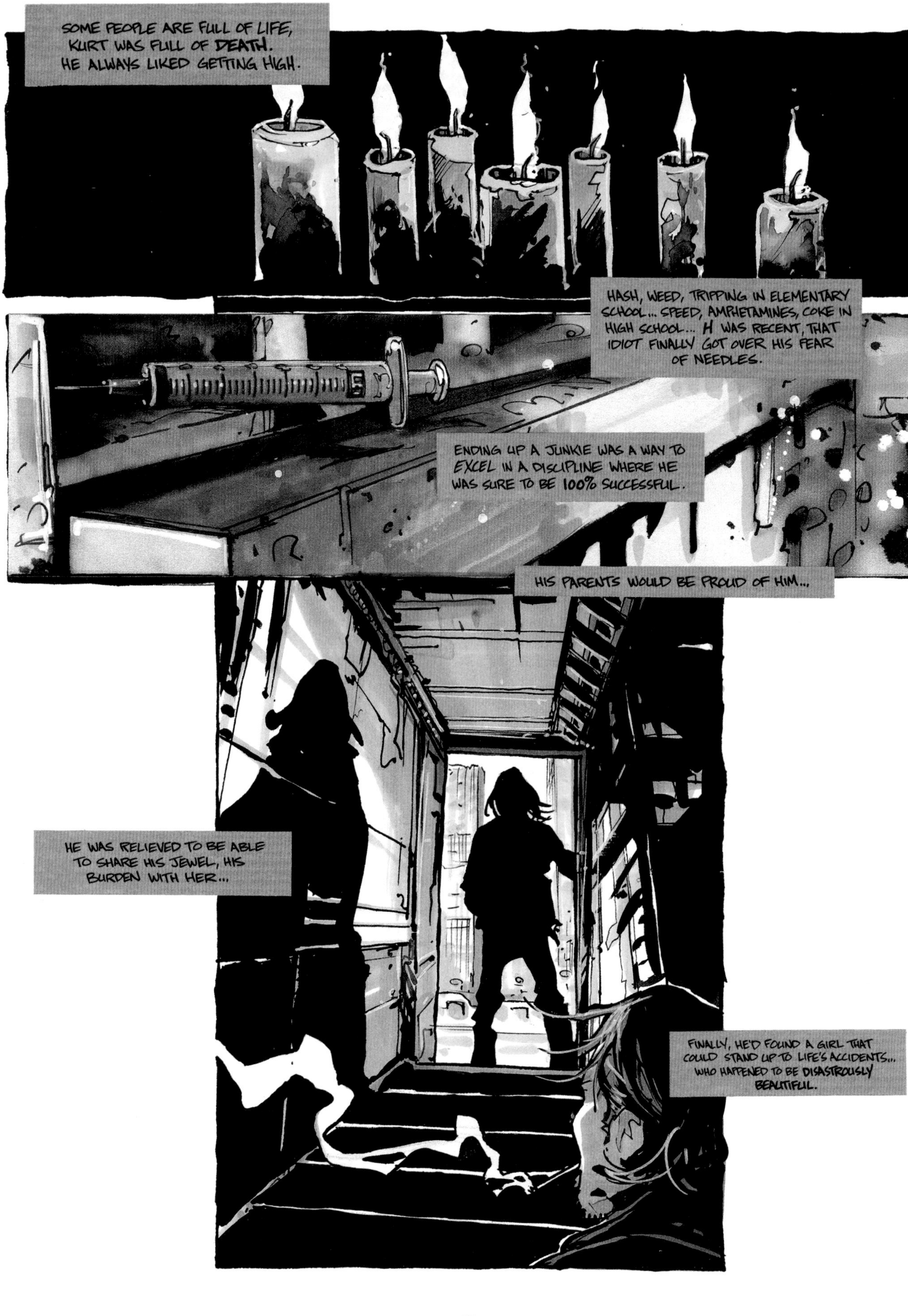
SOME PEOPLE ARE FULL OF LIFE, KURT WAS FULL OF DEATH. HE ALWAYS LIKED GETTING HIGH.
HASH, WEED, TRIPPING IN ELEMENTARY SCHOOL... SPEED, AMPHETAMINES, COKE IN HIGH SCHOOL... H WAS RECENT, THAT IDIOT FINALLY GOT OVER HIS FEAR OF NEEDLES.
ENDING UP A JUNKIE WAS A WAY TO EXCEL IN A DISCIPLINE WHERE HE WAS SURE TO BE 100% SUCCESSFUL.
HIS PARENTS WOULD BE PROUD OF HIM...
HE WAS RELIEVED TO BE ABLE TO SHARE HIS JEWEL, HIS BURDEN WITH HER...
FINALLY, HE'D FOUND A GIRL THAT COULD STAND UP TO LIFE'S ACCIDENTS... WHO HAPPENED TO BE DISASTROUSLY BEAUTIFUL.

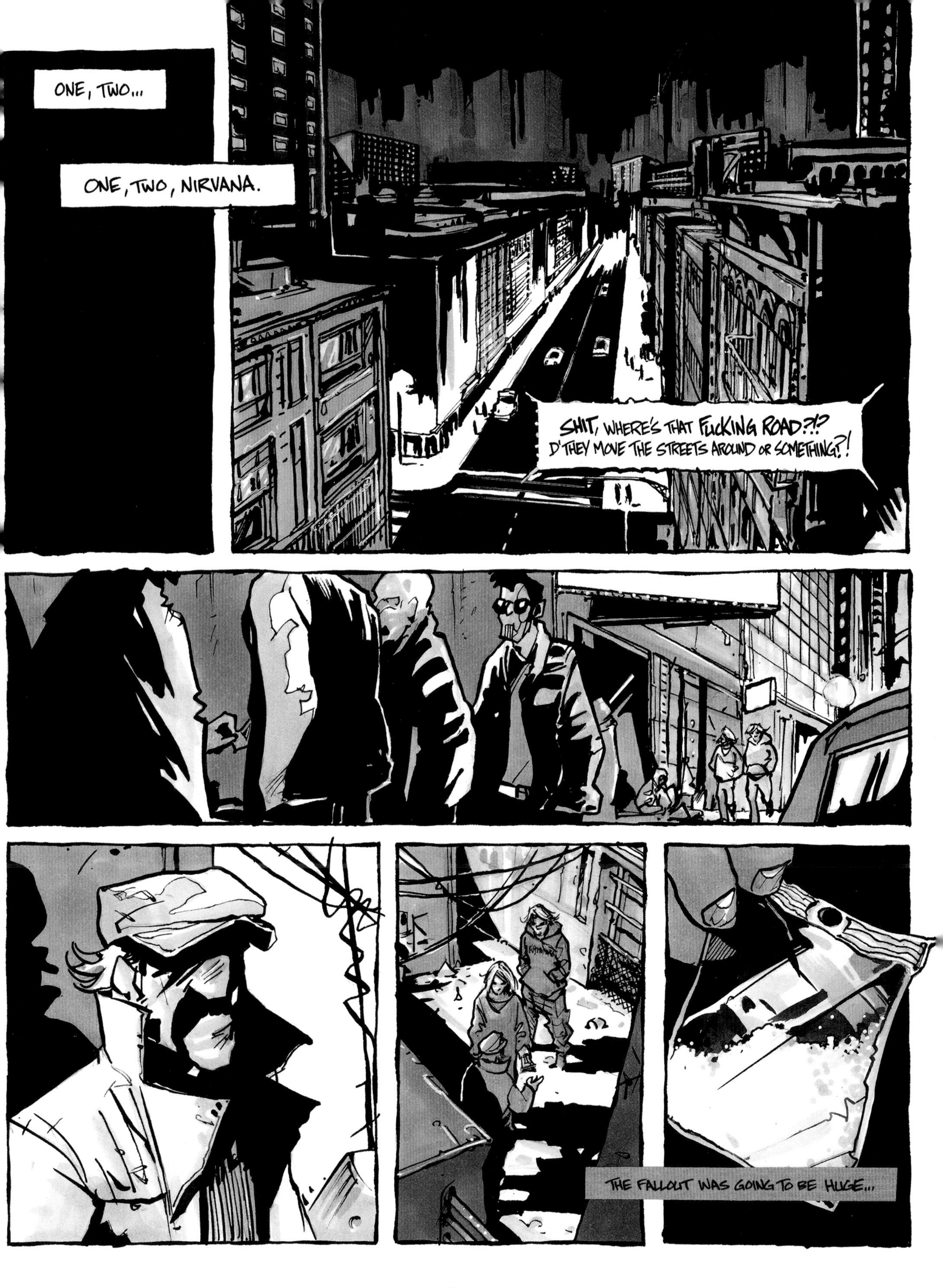
ONE, TWO...
ONE, TWO, NIRVANA.
SHIT, WHERE'S THAT FUCKING ROAD?!? D'THEY MOVE THE STREETS AROUND OR SOMETHING?!
THE FALLOUT WAS GOING TO BE HUGE...

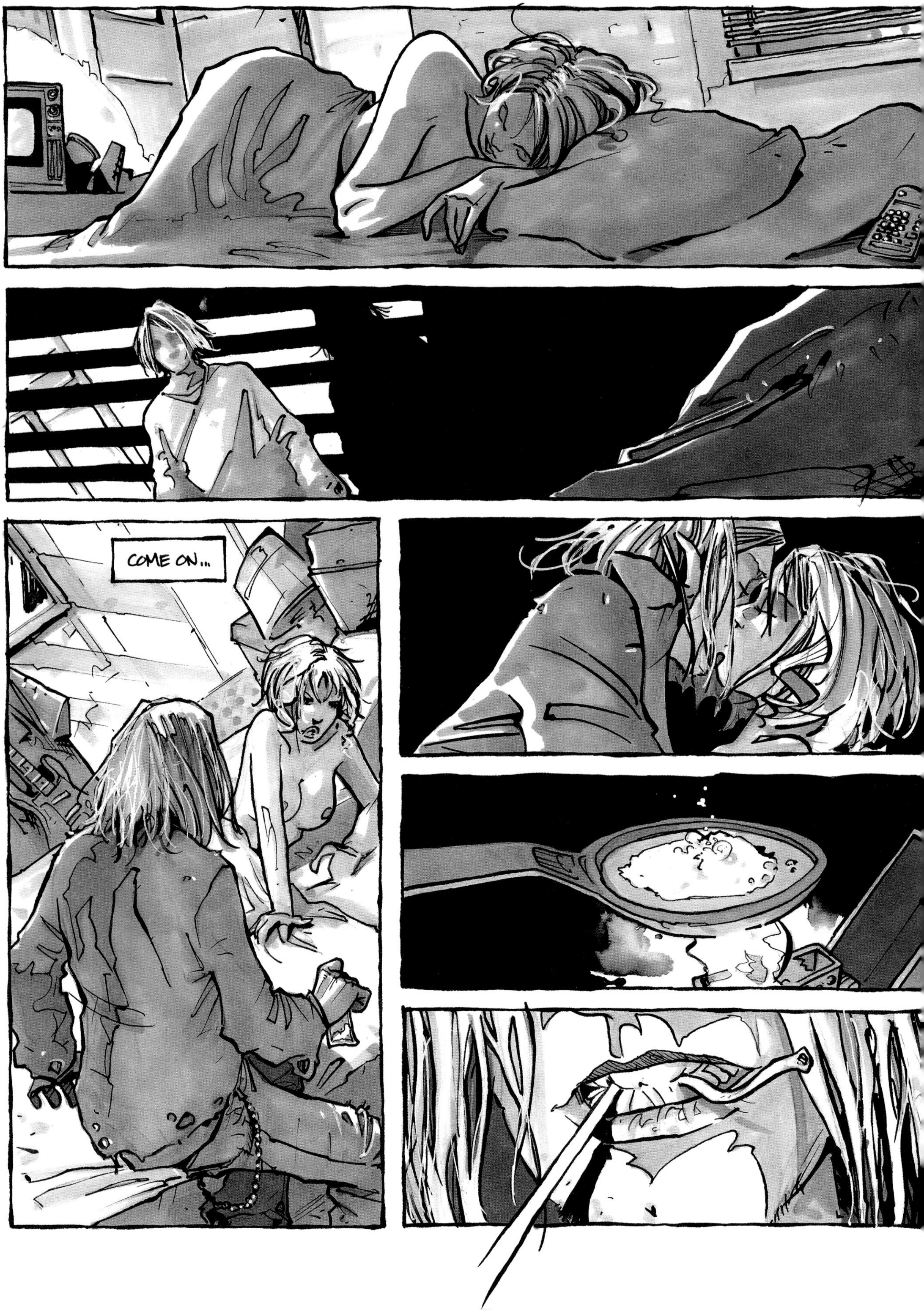
COME ON...

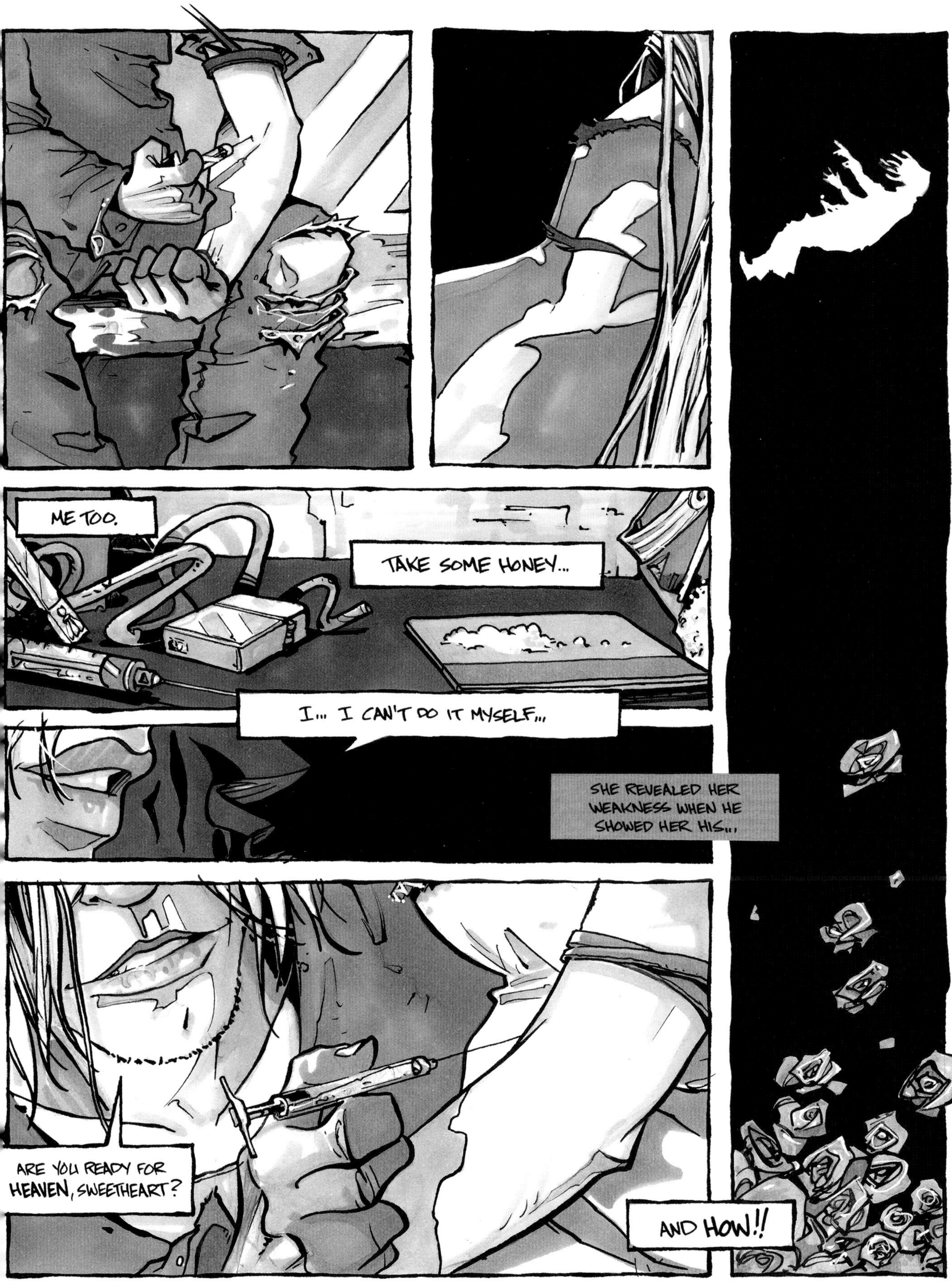
ME TOO.
TAKE SOME HONEY...
I... I CAN'T DO IT MYSELF...
SHE REVEALED HER WEAKNESS WHEN HE SHOWED HER HIS...
ARE YOU READY FOR HEAVEN, SWEETHEART?
AND HOW!!

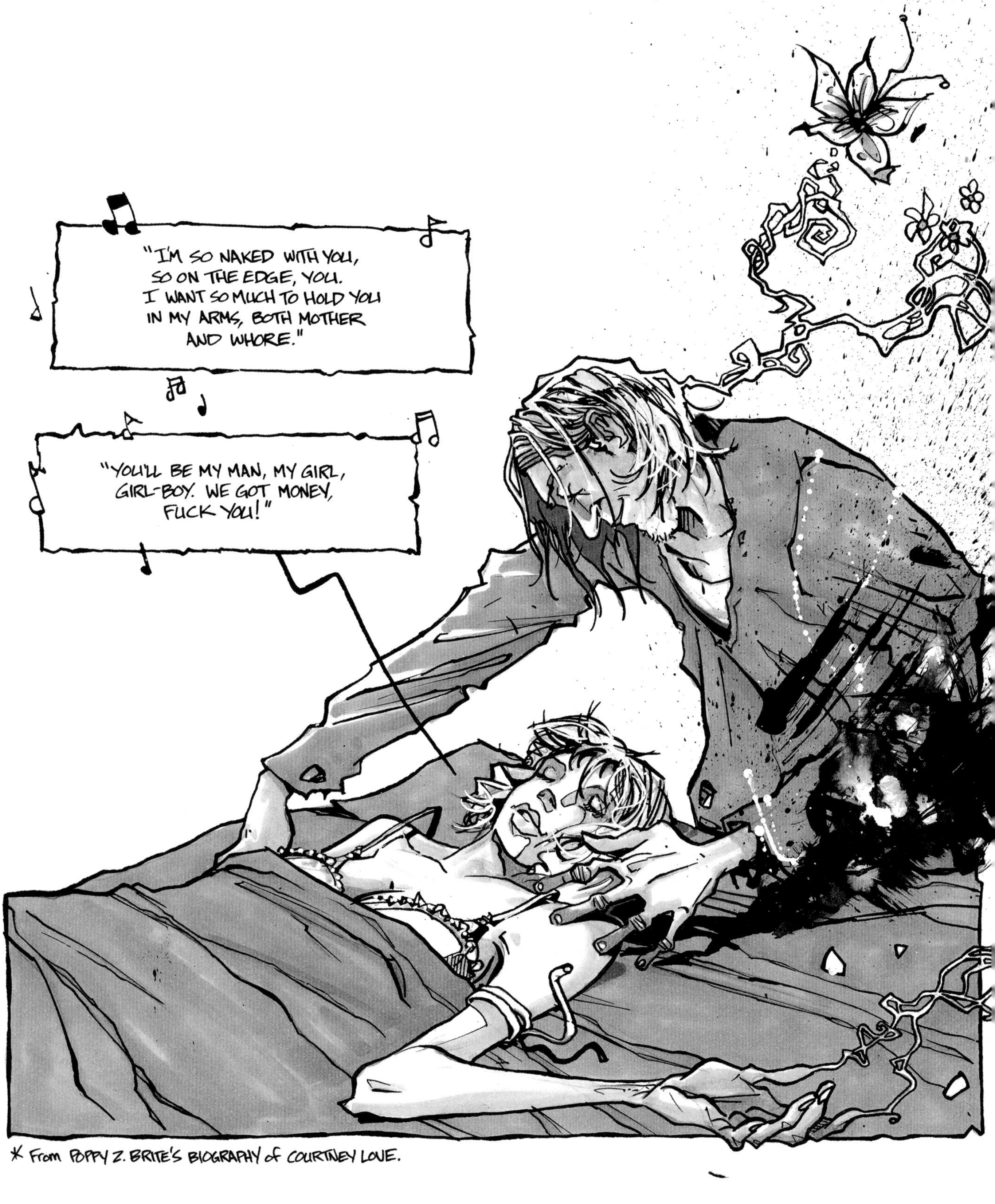
"I'M SO NAKED WITH YOU, SO ON THE EDGE, YOU. I WANT SO MUCH TO HOLD YOU IN MY ARMS, BOTH MOTHER AND WHORE."
"YOU'LL BE MY MAN, MY GIRL, GIRL-BOY. WE GOT MONEY, FUCK YOU!"

* From POPPY Z. BRITE'S BIOGRAPHY of COURTNEY LOVE.

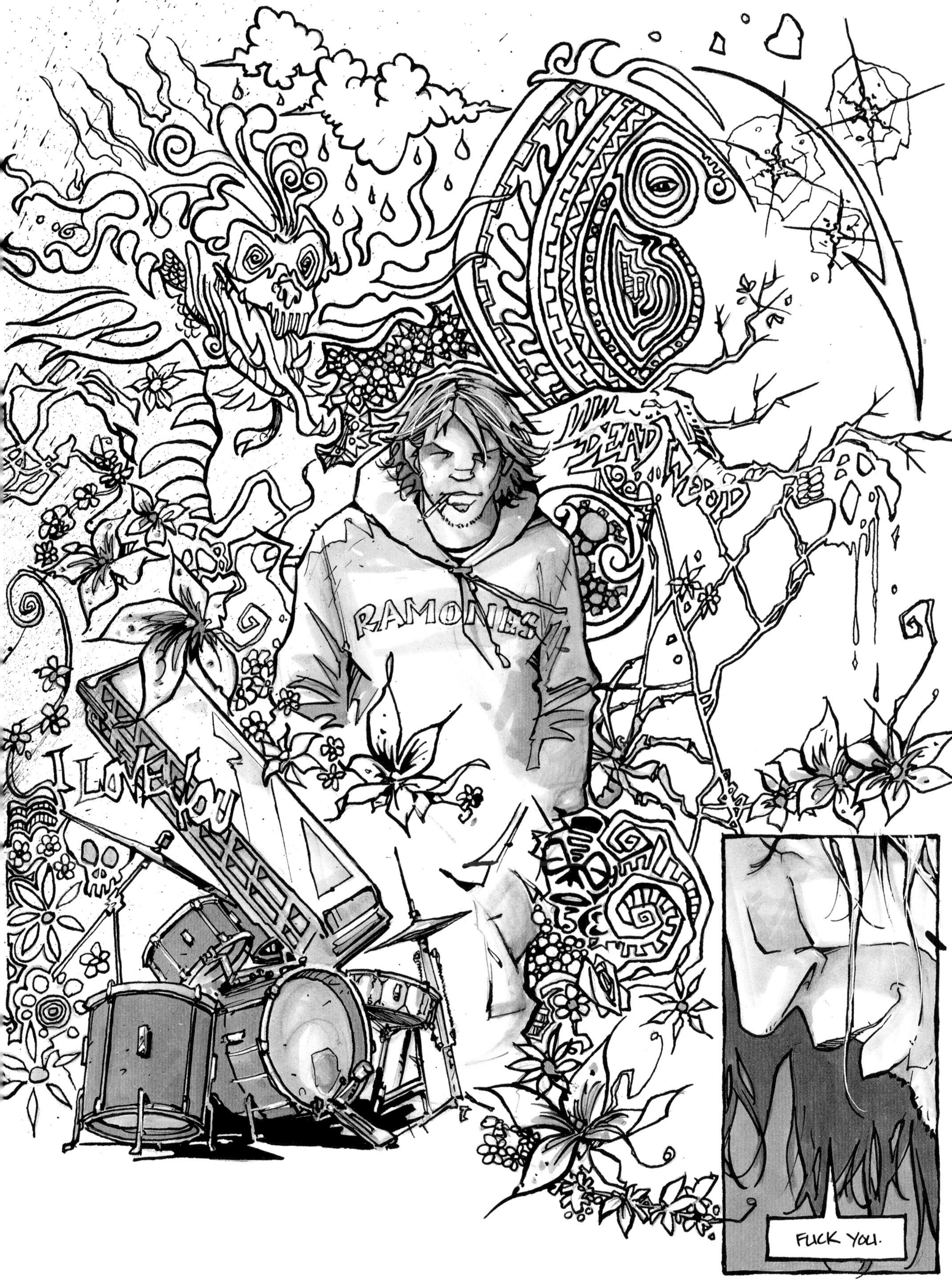
RAMONES
I LOVE YOU
FUCK YOU.

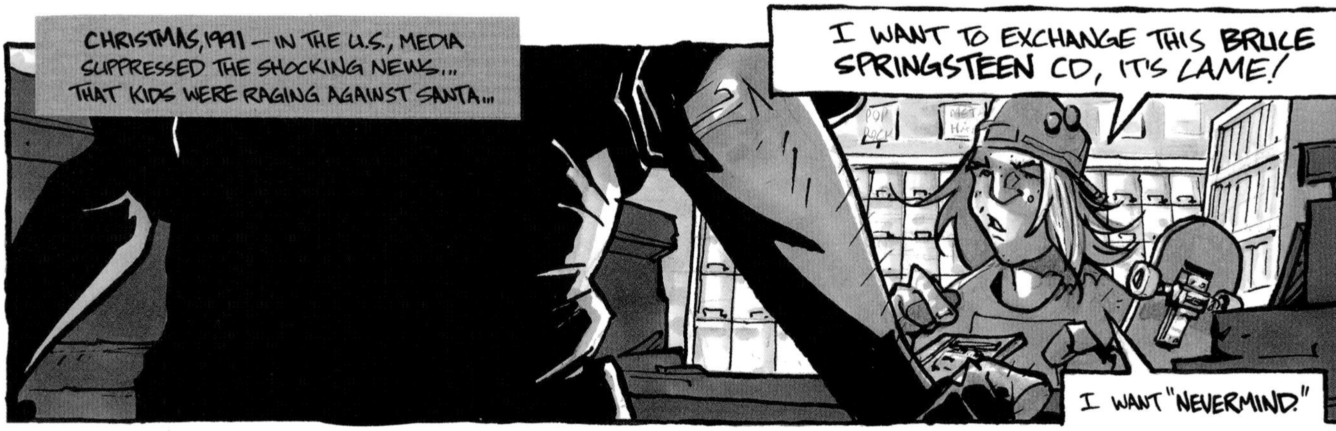
CHRISTMAS, 1991 — IN THE U.S., MEDIA SUPPRESSED THE SHOCKING NEWS... THAT KIDS WERE RAGING AGAINST SANTA...
I WANT TO EXCHANGE THIS BRUCE SPRINGSTEEN CD, IT'S LAME!
I WANT "NEVERMIND."

CHAPTER EIGHT
WONDER KRAVITZ

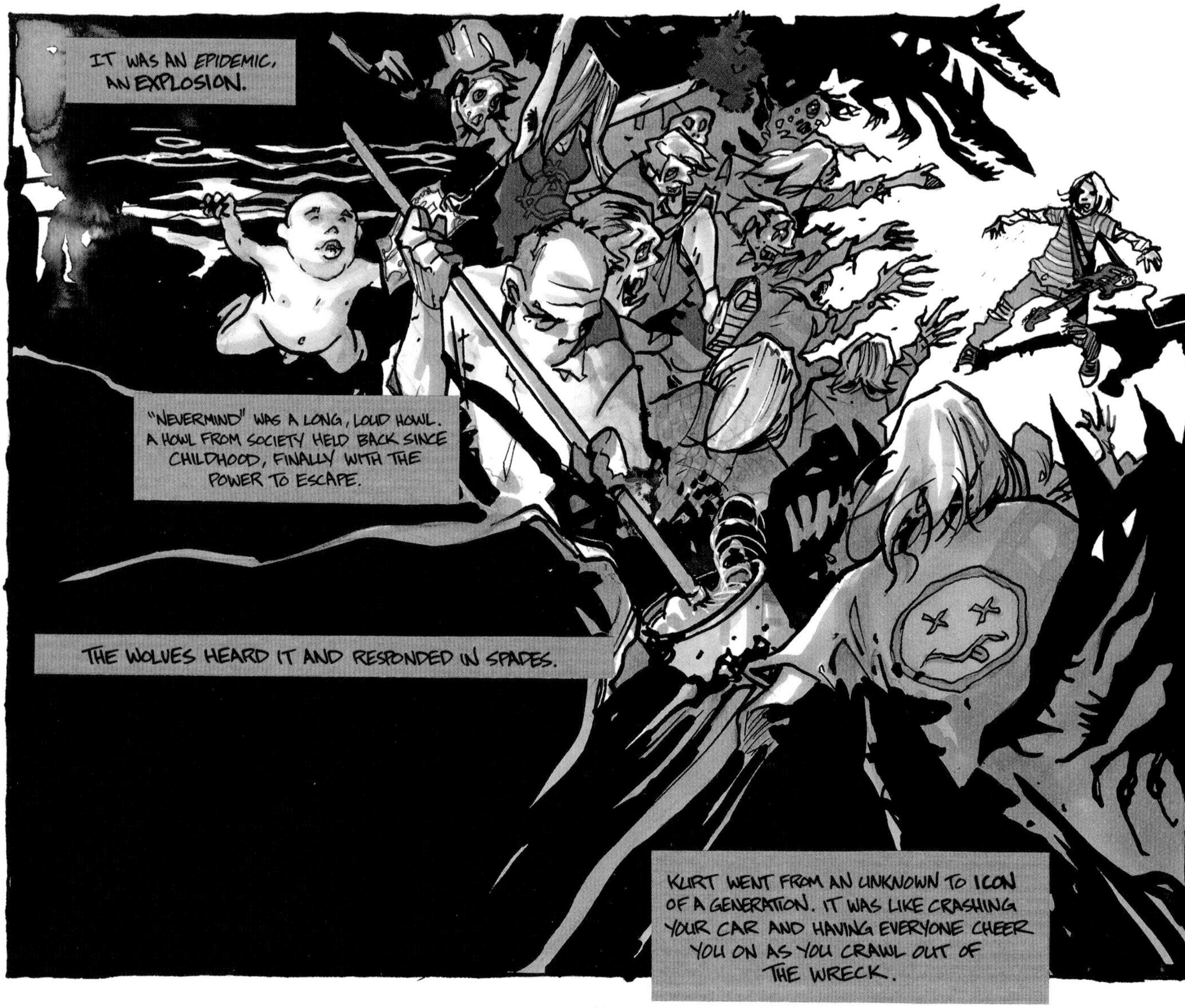
IT WAS AN EPIDEMIC, AN EXPLOSION.
"NEVERMIND" WAS A LONG, LOUD HOWL. A HOWL FROM SOCIETY HELD BACK SINCE CHILDHOOD, FINALLY WITH THE POWER TO ESCAPE.
THE WOLVES HEARD IT AND RESPONDED IN SPADES.
KURT WENT FROM AN UNKNOWN TO ICON OF A GENERATION. IT WAS LIKE CRASHING YOUR CAR AND HAVING EVERYONE CHEER YOU ON AS YOU CRAWL OUT OF THE WRECK.

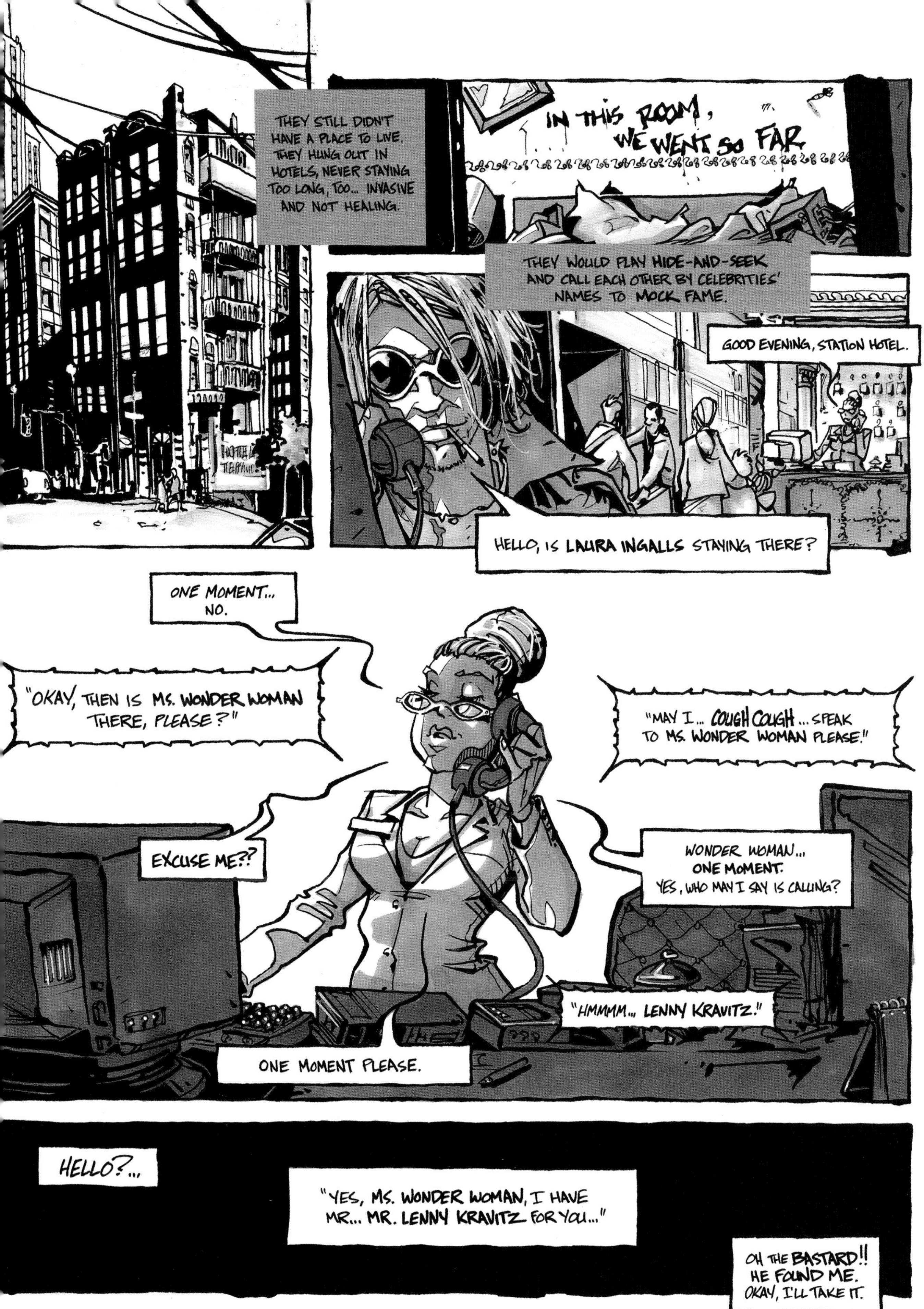

THEY STILL DIDN'T HAVE A PLACE TO LIVE. THEY HUNG OUT IN HOTELS, NEVER STAYING TOO LONG, TOO... INVASIVE AND NOT HEALING.
IN THIS ROOM, WE WENT SO FAR
THEY WOULD PLAY HIDE-AND-SEEK AND CALL EACH OTHER BY CELEBRITIES' NAMES TO MOCK FAME.
GOOD EVENING, STATION HOTEL.
HELLO, IS LAURA INGALLS STAYING THERE?
ONE MOMENT... NO.
"OKAY, THEN IS MS. WONDER WOMAN THERE, PLEASE?"
"MAY I... COUGH COUGH ...SPEAK TO MS. WONDER WOMAN PLEASE."
EXCUSE ME??
WONDER WOMAN... ONE MOMENT. YES, WHO MAY I SAY IS CALLING?
"HMMMM... LENNY KRAVITZ."
ONE MOMENT PLEASE.
HELLO?...
"YES, MS. WONDER WOMAN, I HAVE MR... MR. LENNY KRAVITZ FOR YOU..."
OH THE BASTARD!! HE FOUND ME. OKAY, I'LL TAKE IT.

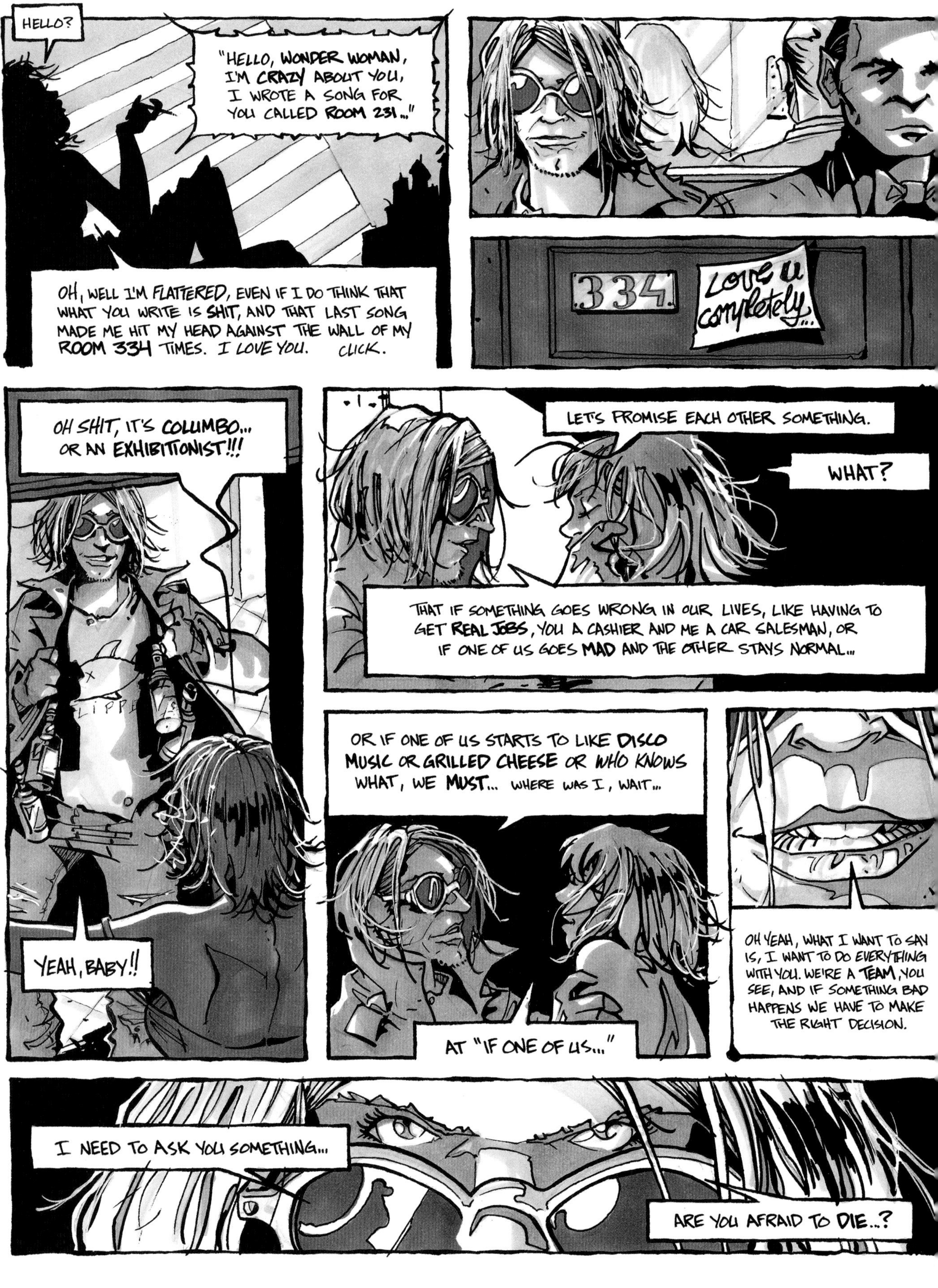
HELLO?
"HELLO, WONDER WOMAN, I'M CRAZY ABOUT YOU, I WROTE A SONG FOR YOU CALLED ROOM 231..."
OH, WELL I'M FLATTERED, EVEN IF I DO THINK THAT WHAT YOU WRITE IS SHIT, AND THAT LAST SONG MADE ME HIT MY HEAD AGAINST THE WALL OF MY ROOM 334 TIMES. I LOVE YOU. CLICK.
334
Love u completely...
OH SHIT, IT'S COLUMBO... OR AN EXHIBITIONIST!!!
YEAH, BABY!!
LET'S PROMISE EACH OTHER SOMETHING.
WHAT?
THAT IF SOMETHING GOES WRONG IN OUR LIVES, LIKE HAVING TO GET REAL JOBS, YOU A CASHIER AND ME A CAR SALESMAN, OR IF ONE OF US GOES MAD AND THE OTHER STAYS NORMAL...
OR IF ONE OF US STARTS TO LIKE DISCO MUSIC OR GRILLED CHEESE OR WHO KNOWS WHAT, WE MUST... WHERE WAS I, WAIT...
AT "IF ONE OF US..."
OH YEAH, WHAT I WANT TO SAY IS, I WANT TO DO EVERYTHING WITH YOU. WE'RE A TEAM, YOU SEE, AND IF SOMETHING BAD HAPPENS WE HAVE TO MAKE THE RIGHT DECISION.
I NEED TO ASK YOU SOMETHING...
ARE YOU AFRAID TO DIE...?

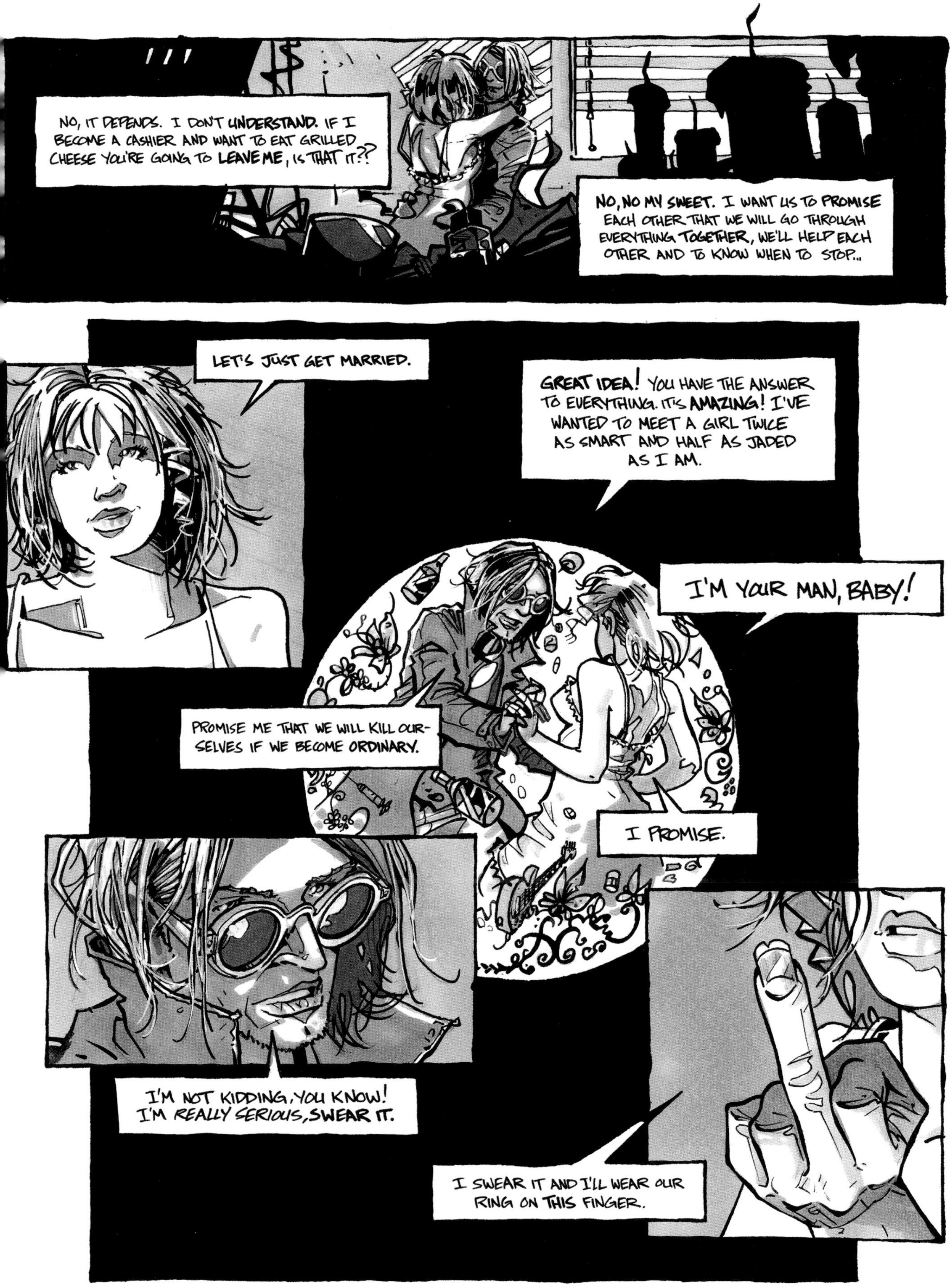
NO, IT DEPENDS. I DON'T UNDERSTAND. IF I BECOME A CASHIER AND WANT TO EAT GRILLED CHEESE YOU'RE GOING TO LEAVE ME, IS THAT IT??
NO, NO MY SWEET. I WANT US TO PROMISE EACH OTHER THAT WE WILL GO THROUGH EVERYTHING TOGETHER, WE'LL HELP EACH OTHER AND TO KNOW WHEN TO STOP..
LET'S JUST GET MARRIED.
GREAT IDEA! YOU HAVE THE ANSWER TO EVERYTHING. IT'S AMAZING! I'VE WANTED TO MEET A GIRL TWICE AS SMART AND HALF AS JADED AS I AM.
I'M YOUR MAN, BABY!
PROMISE ME THAT WE WILL KILL OURSELVES IF WE BECOME ORDINARY.
I PROMISE.
I'M NOT KIDDING, YOU KNOW! I'M REALLY SERIOUS, SWEAR IT.
I SWEAR IT AND I'LL WEAR OUR RING ON THIS FINGER.

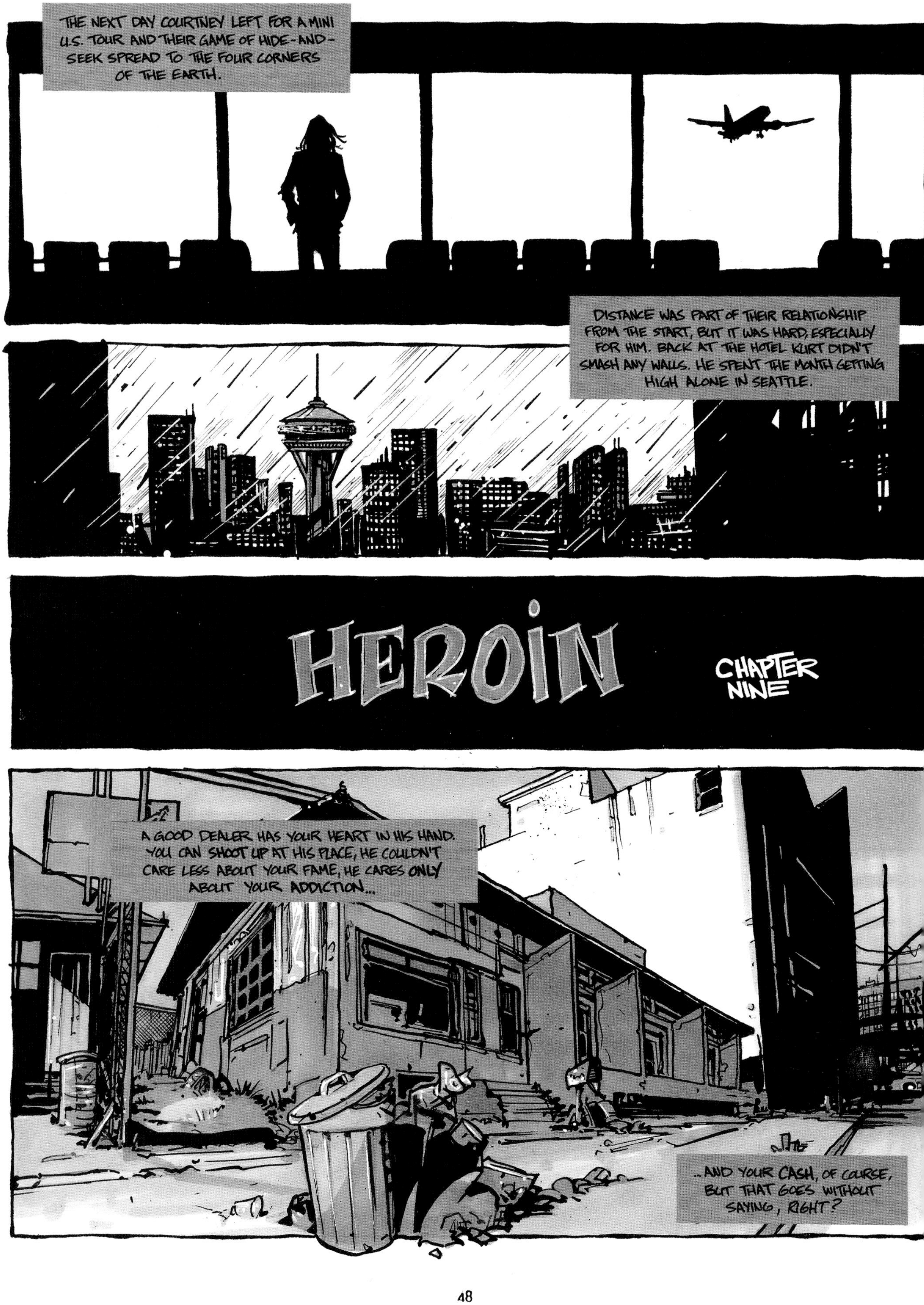

THE NEXT DAY COURTNEY LEFT FOR A MINI U.S. TOUR AND THEIR GAME OF HIDE-AND-SEEK SPREAD TO THE FOUR CORNERS OF THE EARTH.
DISTANCE WAS PART OF THEIR RELATIONSHIP FROM THE START, BUT IT WAS HARD, ESPECIALLY FOR HIM. BACK AT THE HOTEL KURT DIDN'T SMASH ANY WALLS. HE SPENT THE MONTH GETTING HIGH ALONE IN SEATTLE.
HEROIN
CHAPTER NINE
A GOOD DEALER HAS YOUR HEART IN HIS HAND. YOU CAN SHOOT UP AT HIS PLACE, HE COULDN'T CARE LESS ABOUT YOUR FAME, HE CARES ONLY ABOUT YOUR ADDICTION...
...AND YOUR CASH, OF COURSE, BUT THAT GOES WITHOUT SAYING, RIGHT?

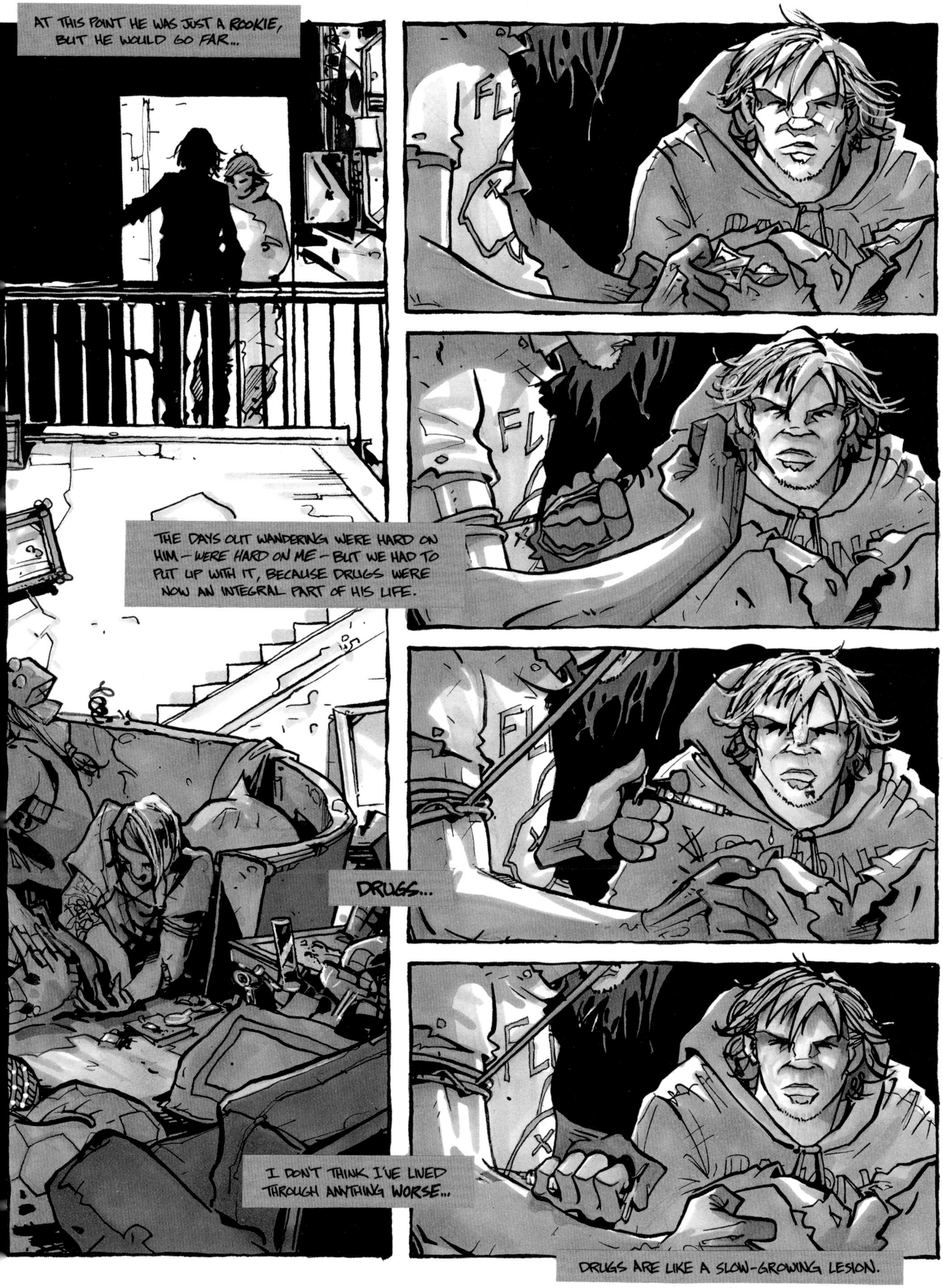
AT THIS POINT HE WAS JUST A ROOKIE, BUT HE WOULD GO FAR...
THE DAYS OUT WANDERING WERE HARD ON HIM — WERE HARD ON ME — BUT WE HAD TO PUT UP WITH IT, BECAUSE DRUGS WERE NOW AN INTEGRAL PART OF HIS LIFE.
DRUGS...
I DON'T THINK I'VE LIVED THROUGH ANYTHING WORSE...
DRUGS ARE LIKE A SLOW-GROWING LESION.

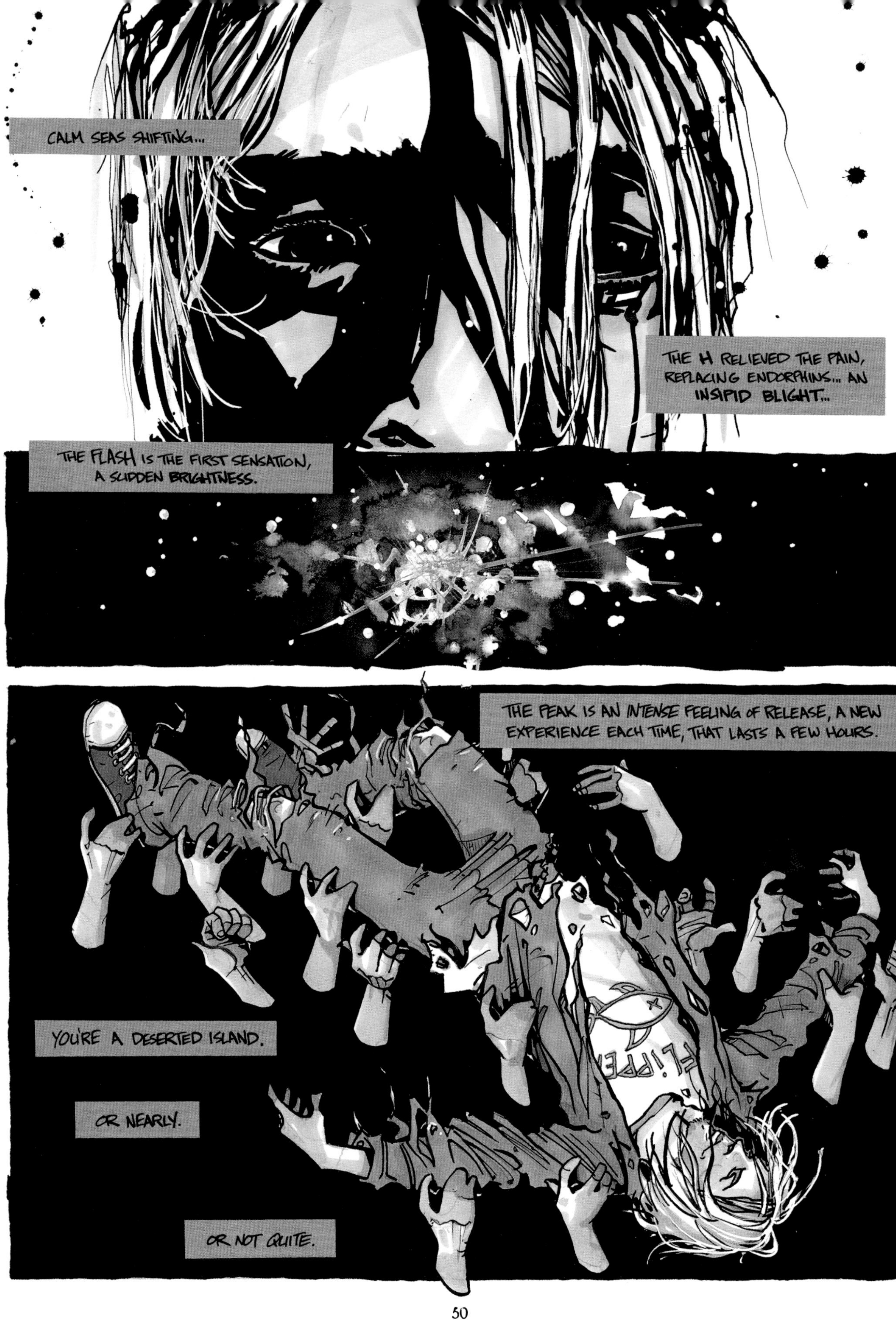
CALM SEAS SHIFTING...
THE H RELIEVED THE PAIN, REPLACING ENDORPHINS... AN INSIPID BLIGHT...
THE FLASH IS THE FIRST SENSATION, A SUDDEN BRIGHTNESS.
THE PEAK IS AN INTENSE FEELING OF RELEASE, A NEW EXPERIENCE EACH TIME, THAT LASTS A FEW HOURS.
YOU'RE A DESERTED ISLAND.
OR NEARLY.
OR NOT QUITE.

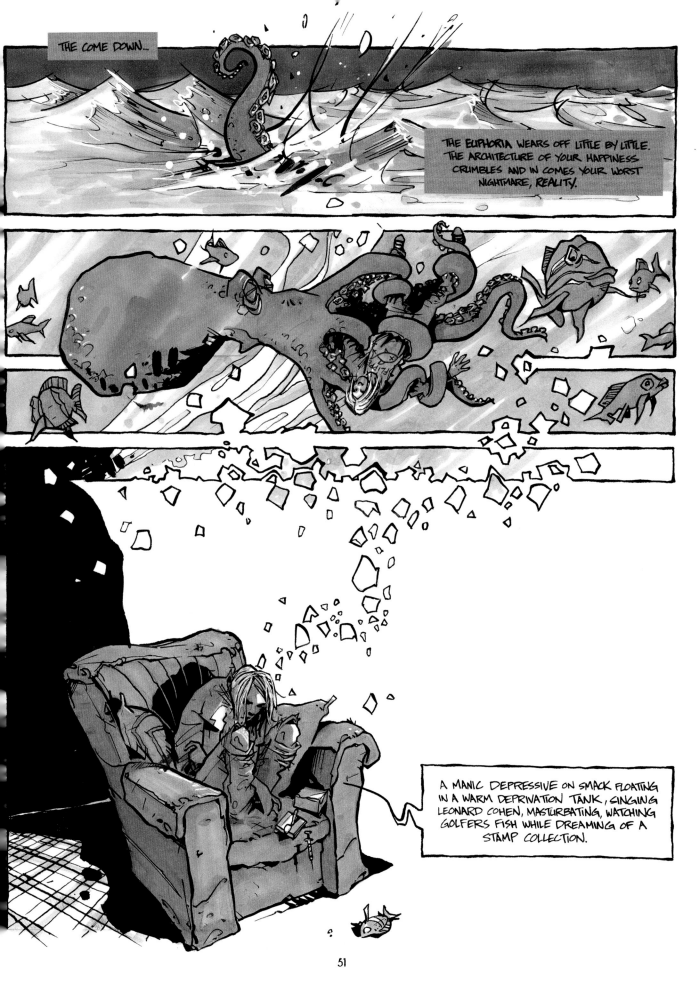

THE COME DOWN...

THE EUPHORIA WEARS OFF LITTLE BY LITTLE. THE ARCHITECTURE OF YOUR HAPPINESS CRUMBLES AND IN COMES YOUR WORST NIGHTMARE, REALITY.

A MANIC DEPRESSIVE ON SMACK FLOATING IN A WARM DEPRIVATION TANK, SINGING LEONARD COHEN, MASTURBATING, WATCHING GOLFERS FISH WHILE DREAMING OF A STAMP COLLECTION.

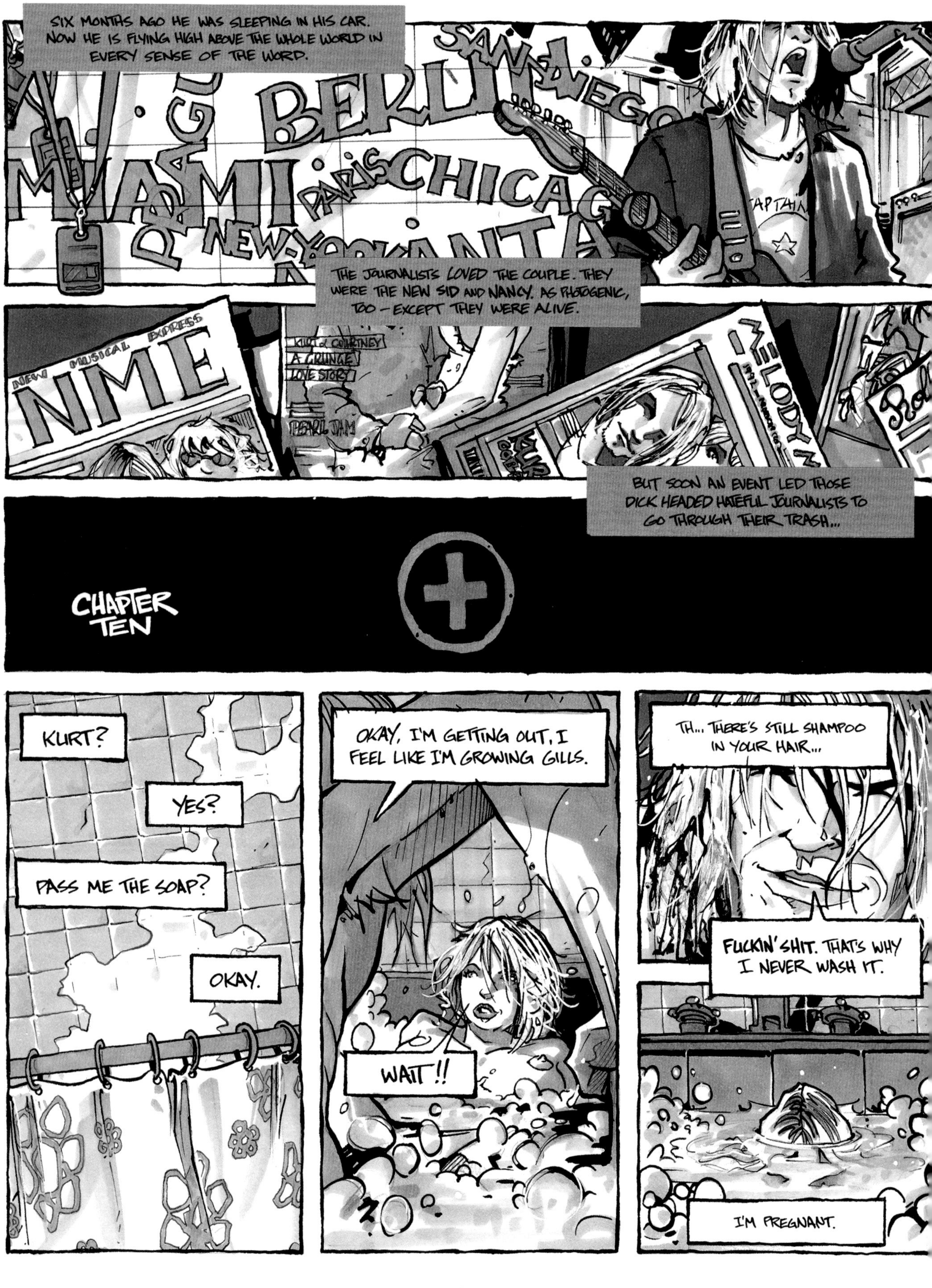
SIX MONTHS AGO HE WAS SLEEPING IN HIS CAR. NOW HE IS FLYING HIGH ABOVE THE WHOLE WORLD IN EVERY SENSE OF THE WORD.
BERLIN
MIAMI
PARIS
CHICAGO
NEW-YORK
THE JOURNALISTS LOVED THE COUPLE. THEY WERE THE NEW SID AND NANCY. AS PHOTOGENIC, TOO – EXCEPT THEY WERE ALIVE.
NEW MUSICAL EXPRESS
NME
KURT & COURTNEY
A GRUNGE
LOVE STORY
PEARL JAM
MELODY MAKER
BUT SOON AN EVENT LED THOSE DICK HEADED HATEFUL JOURNALISTS TO GO THROUGH THEIR TRASH...
CHAPTER TEN
KURT?
YES?
PASS ME THE SOAP?
OKAY.
OKAY, I'M GETTING OUT, I FEEL LIKE I'M GROWING GILLS.
WAIT!!
TH... THERE'S STILL SHAMPOO IN YOUR HAIR...
FUCKIN' SHIT. THAT'S WHY I NEVER WASH IT.
I'M PREGNANT.

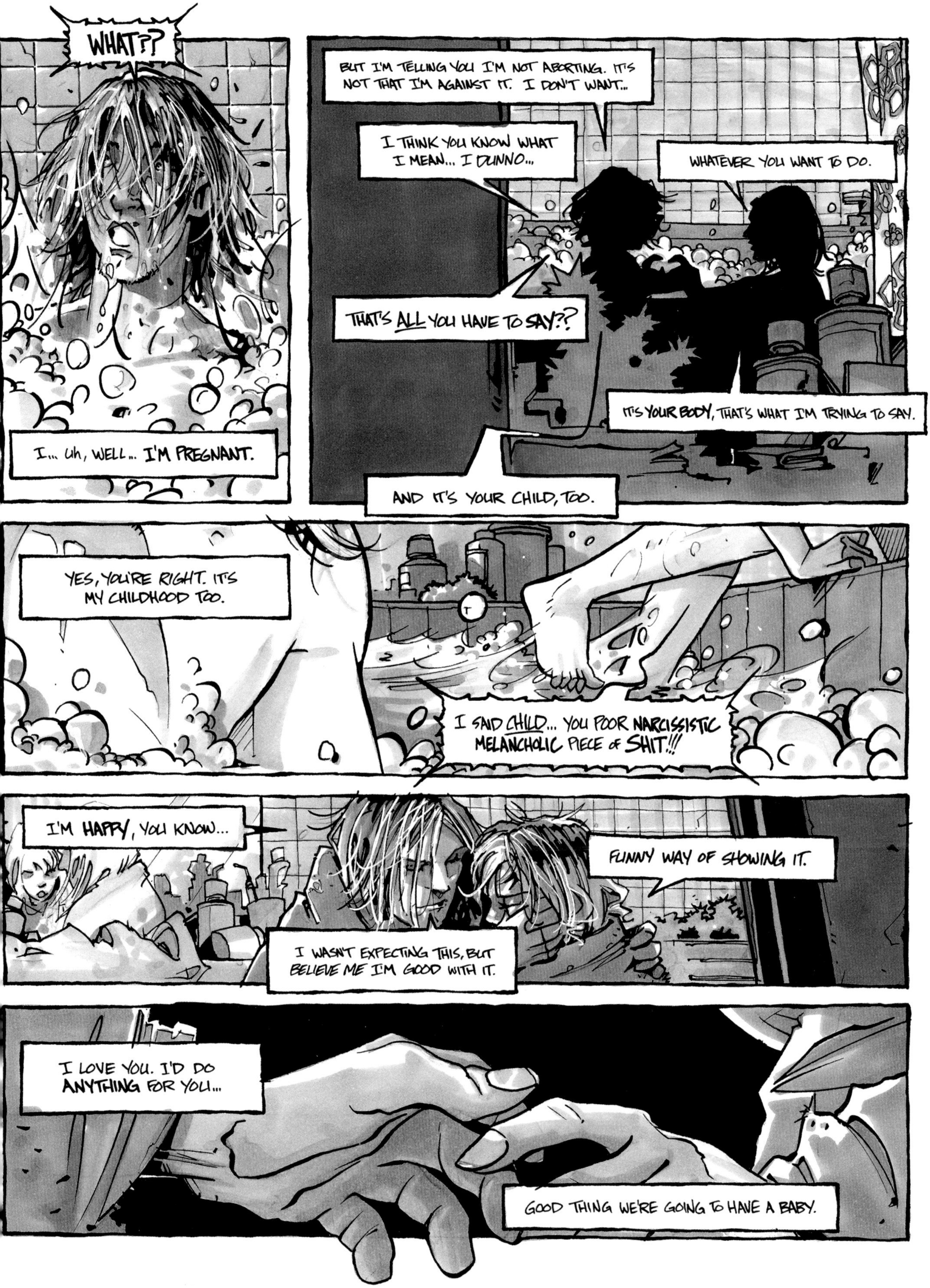
WHAT??
I... Uh, WELL... I'M PREGNANT.
BUT I'M TELLING YOU I'M NOT ABORTING. IT'S NOT THAT I'M AGAINST IT. I DON'T WANT...
I THINK YOU KNOW WHAT I MEAN... I DUNNO...
WHATEVER YOU WANT TO DO.
THAT'S ALL YOU HAVE TO SAY??
IT'S YOUR BODY, THAT'S WHAT I'M TRYING TO SAY.
AND IT'S YOUR CHILD, TOO.
YES, YOU'RE RIGHT. IT'S MY CHILDHOOD TOO.
I SAID CHILD... YOU POOR NARCISSISTIC MELANCHOLIC PIECE OF SHIT!!!
I'M HAPPY, YOU KNOW...
FUNNY WAY OF SHOWING IT.
I WASN'T EXPECTING THIS, BUT BELIEVE ME I'M GOOD WITH IT.
I LOVE YOU. I'D DO ANYTHING FOR YOU...
GOOD THING WE'RE GOING TO HAVE A BABY.

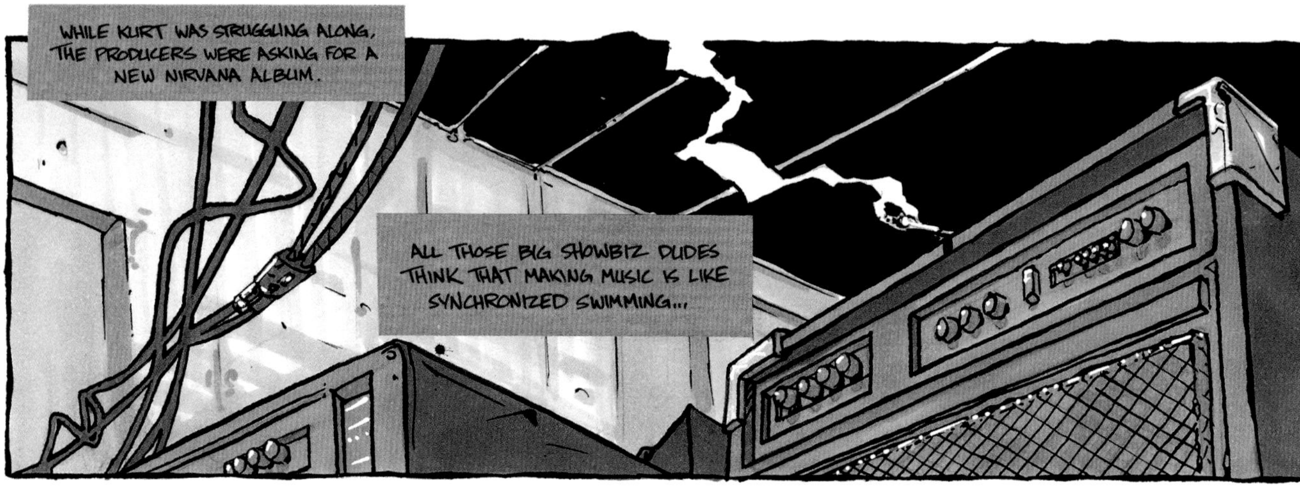
WHILE KURT WAS STRUGGLING ALONG, THE PRODUCERS WERE ASKING FOR A NEW NIRVANA ALBUM.
ALL THOSE BIG SHOWBIZ DUDES THINK THAT MAKING MUSIC IS LIKE SYNCHRONIZED SWIMMING...

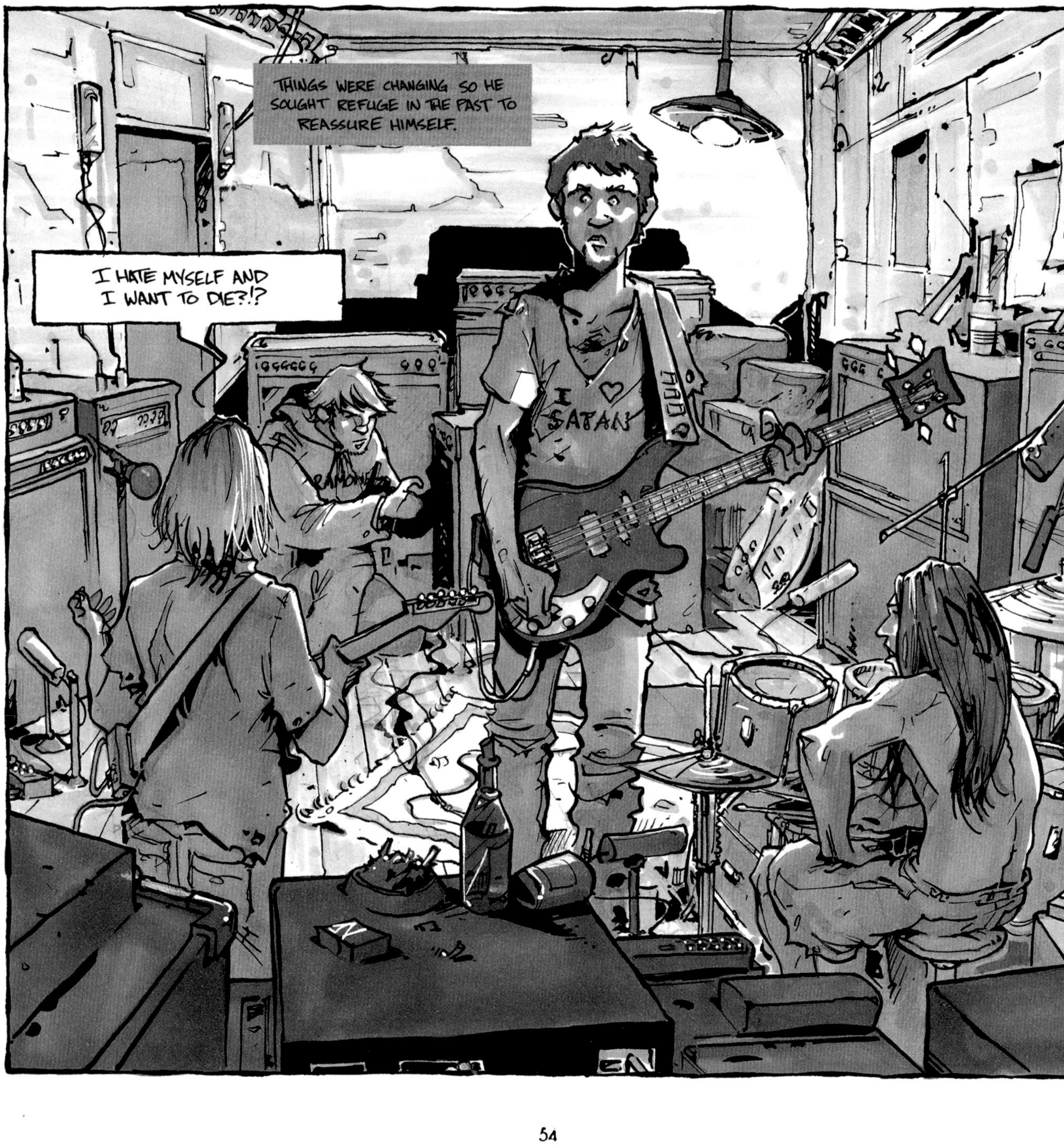
THINGS WERE CHANGING SO HE SOUGHT REFUGE IN THE PAST TO REASSURE HIMSELF.
I HATE MYSELF AND I WANT TO DIE?!?
I ♡ SATAN
RAMONES

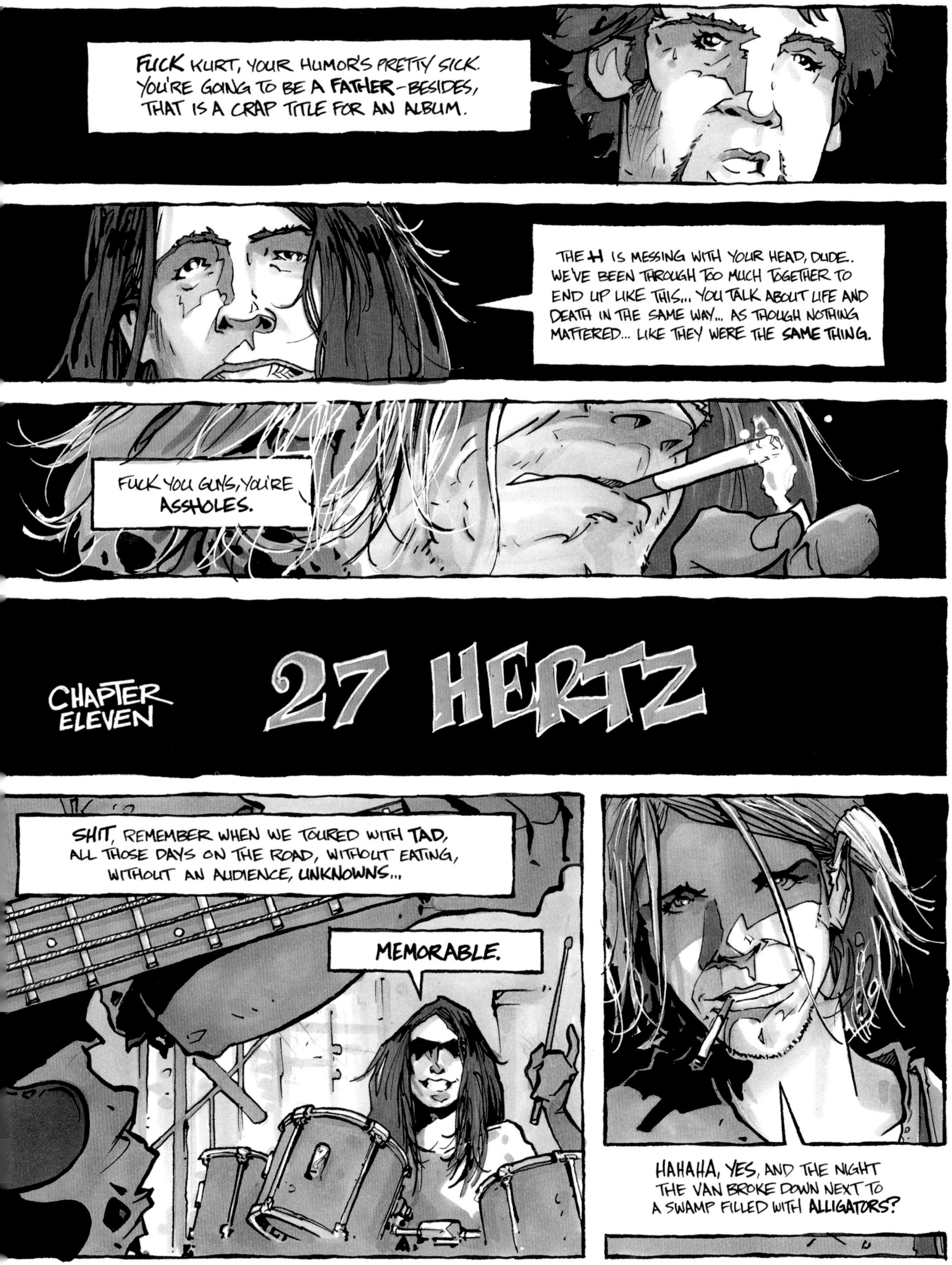
FUCK KURT, YOUR HUMOR'S PRETTY SICK. YOU'RE GOING TO BE A FATHER-BESIDES, THAT IS A CRAP TITLE FOR AN ALBUM.
THE H IS MESSING WITH YOUR HEAD, DUDE. WE'VE BEEN THROUGH TOO MUCH TOGETHER TO END UP LIKE THIS... YOU TALK ABOUT LIFE AND DEATH IN THE SAME WAY... AS THOUGH NOTHING MATTERED... LIKE THEY WERE THE SAME THING.
FUCK YOU GUYS, YOU'RE ASSHOLES.
CHAPTER ELEVEN
27 HERTZ
SHIT, REMEMBER WHEN WE TOURED WITH TAD, ALL THOSE DAYS ON THE ROAD, WITHOUT EATING, WITHOUT AN AUDIENCE, UNKNOWNS...
MEMORABLE.
HAHAHA, YES, AND THE NIGHT THE VAN BROKE DOWN NEXT TO A SWAMP FILLED WITH ALLIGATORS?

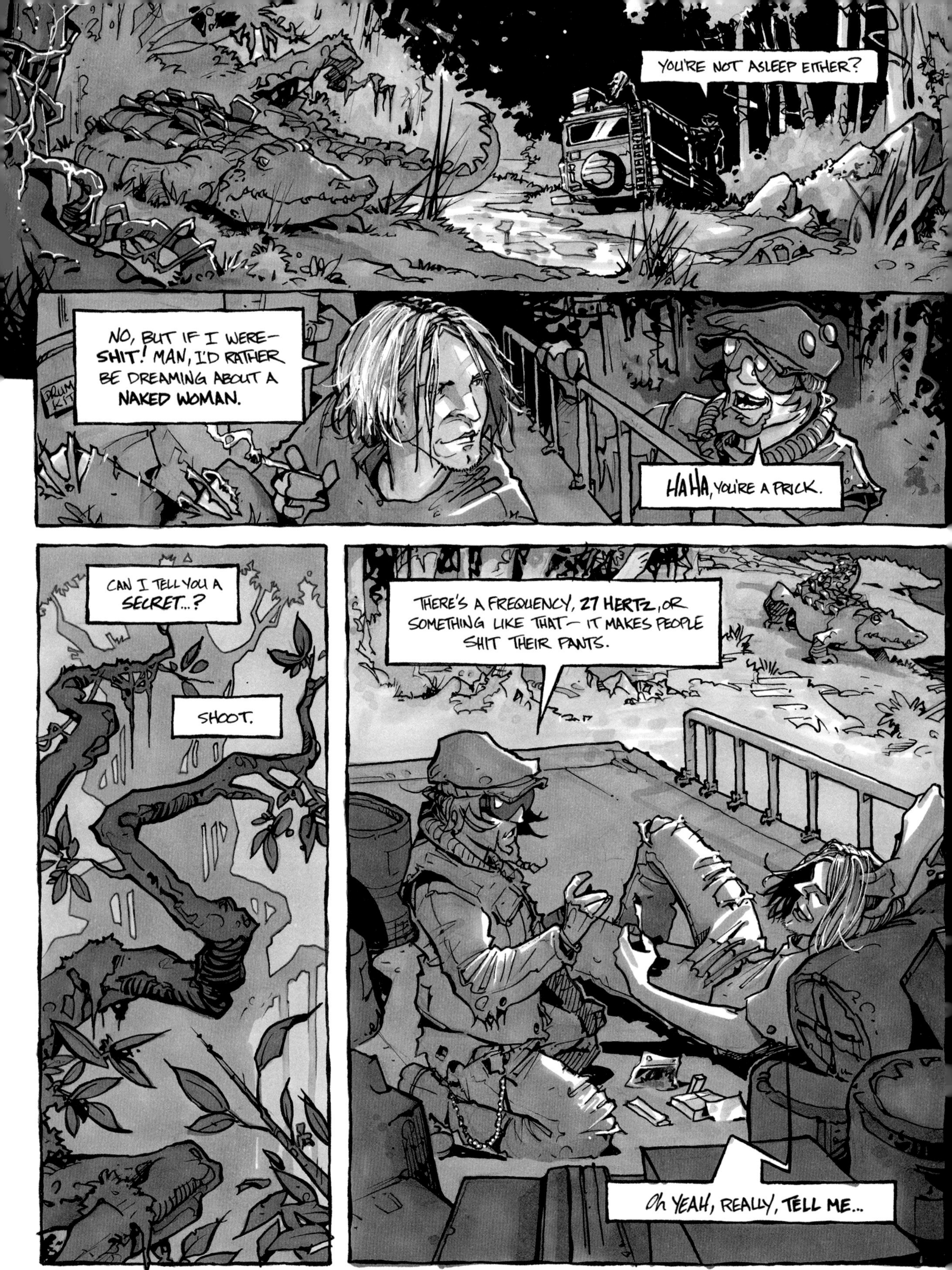
YOU'RE NOT ASLEEP EITHER?
NO, BUT IF I WERE- SHIT! MAN, I'D RATHER BE DREAMING ABOUT A NAKED WOMAN.
HAHA, YOU'RE A PRICK.
CAN I TELL YOU A SECRET...?
SHOOT.
THERE'S A FREQUENCY, 27 HERTZ, OR SOMETHING LIKE THAT- IT MAKES PEOPLE SHIT THEIR PANTS.
Oh YEAH, REALLY, TELL ME...

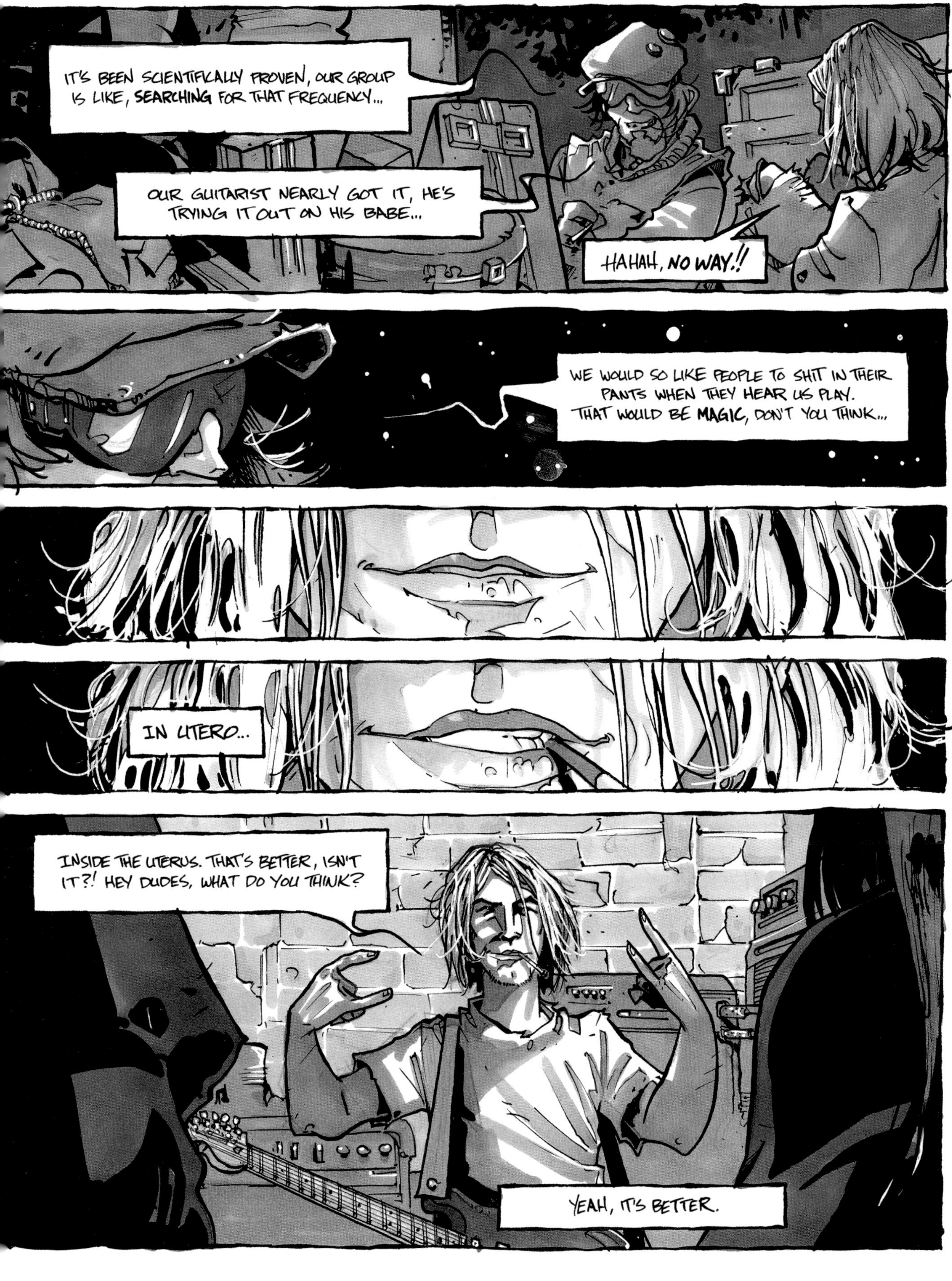
IT'S BEEN SCIENTIFICALLY PROVEN, OUR GROUP IS LIKE, **SEARCHING** FOR THAT FREQUENCY...
OUR GUITARIST NEARLY GOT IT, HE'S TRYING IT OUT ON HIS BABE...
HAHAH, **NO WAY**!!
WE WOULD SO LIKE PEOPLE TO SHIT IN THEIR PANTS WHEN THEY **HEAR** US PLAY. THAT WOULD BE **MAGIC**, DON'T YOU THINK...
IN UTERO...
INSIDE THE UTERUS. THAT'S BETTER, ISN'T IT?! HEY DUDES, WHAT DO YOU THINK?
YEAH, IT'S BETTER.

I DON'T LIKE THE SMELL OF KIDS.

HUH?!

THEY SMELL LIKE MILDEW, LIKE OLD PEOPLE. THAT'S WHY I ALWAYS CARRY DEODORANT, JUST IN CASE...

CHAPTER TWELVE — BODDAH II

YOU THINK I SMELL BAD?

NO, NOT YOU, YOU IDIOT, YOU'RE NOT A KID ANYMORE, REMEMBER... EVEN AS A KID YOU SMELLED GOOD, LIKE KINDNESS and SULFUR.

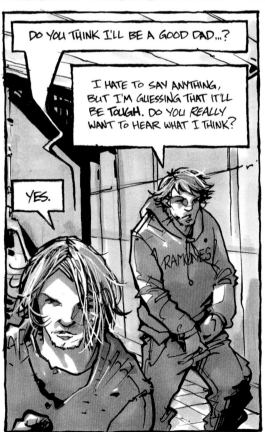

DO YOU THINK I'LL BE A GOOD DAD...?

I HATE TO SAY ANYTHING, BUT I'M GUESSING THAT IT'LL BE TOUGH. DO YOU REALLY WANT TO HEAR WHAT I THINK?

YES.

I WONDER IF YOU'RE NOT DOING IT TO GET REVENGE ON YOURSELF...

THAT'S A HORRIBLE THING TO SAY!!

YOU ASKED ME A QUESTION, I ANSWERED IT!

SOMETIMES I HATE YOU. WHY ARE YOU SUCH A DICK TO ME, WHAT'S YOUR PROBLEM? ARE YOU TRYING TO DESTROY ME?!

YOU DON'T NEED ME FOR THAT...

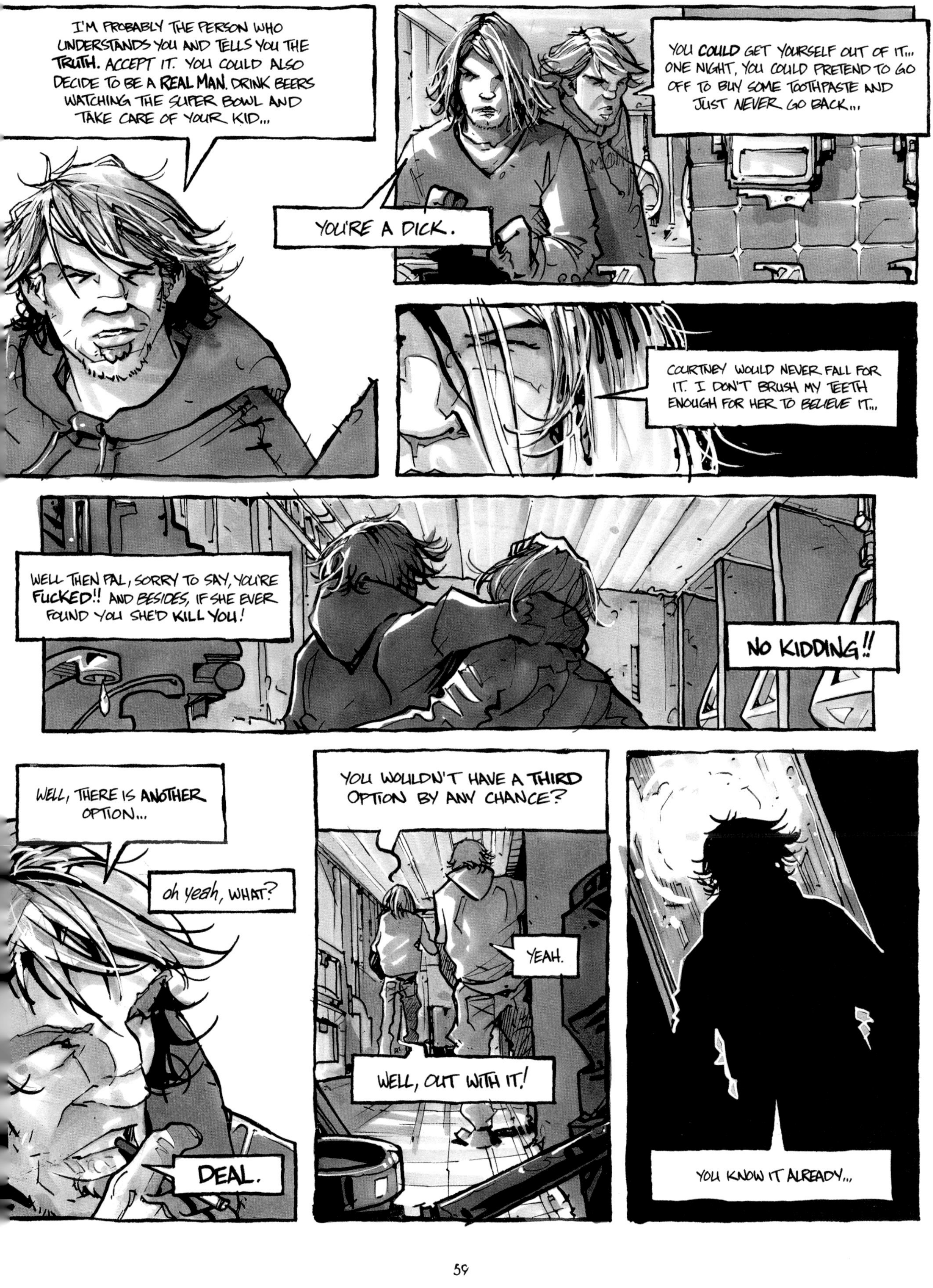
I'M PROBABLY THE PERSON WHO UNDERSTANDS YOU AND TELLS YOU THE TRUTH. ACCEPT IT. YOU COULD ALSO DECIDE TO BE A REAL MAN. DRINK BEERS WATCHING THE SUPER BOWL AND TAKE CARE OF YOUR KID...
YOU'RE A DICK.
YOU COULD GET YOURSELF OUT OF IT... ONE NIGHT, YOU COULD PRETEND TO GO OFF TO BUY SOME TOOTHPASTE AND JUST NEVER GO BACK...
COURTNEY WOULD NEVER FALL FOR IT. I DON'T BRUSH MY TEETH ENOUGH FOR HER TO BELIEVE IT...
WELL THEN PAL, SORRY TO SAY, YOU'RE FUCKED!! AND BESIDES, IF SHE EVER FOUND YOU SHE'D KILL YOU!
NO KIDDING!!
WELL, THERE IS ANOTHER OPTION...
oh yeah, WHAT?
DEAL.
YOU WOULDN'T HAVE A THIRD OPTION BY ANY CHANCE?
YEAH.
WELL, OUT WITH IT!
YOU KNOW IT ALREADY...

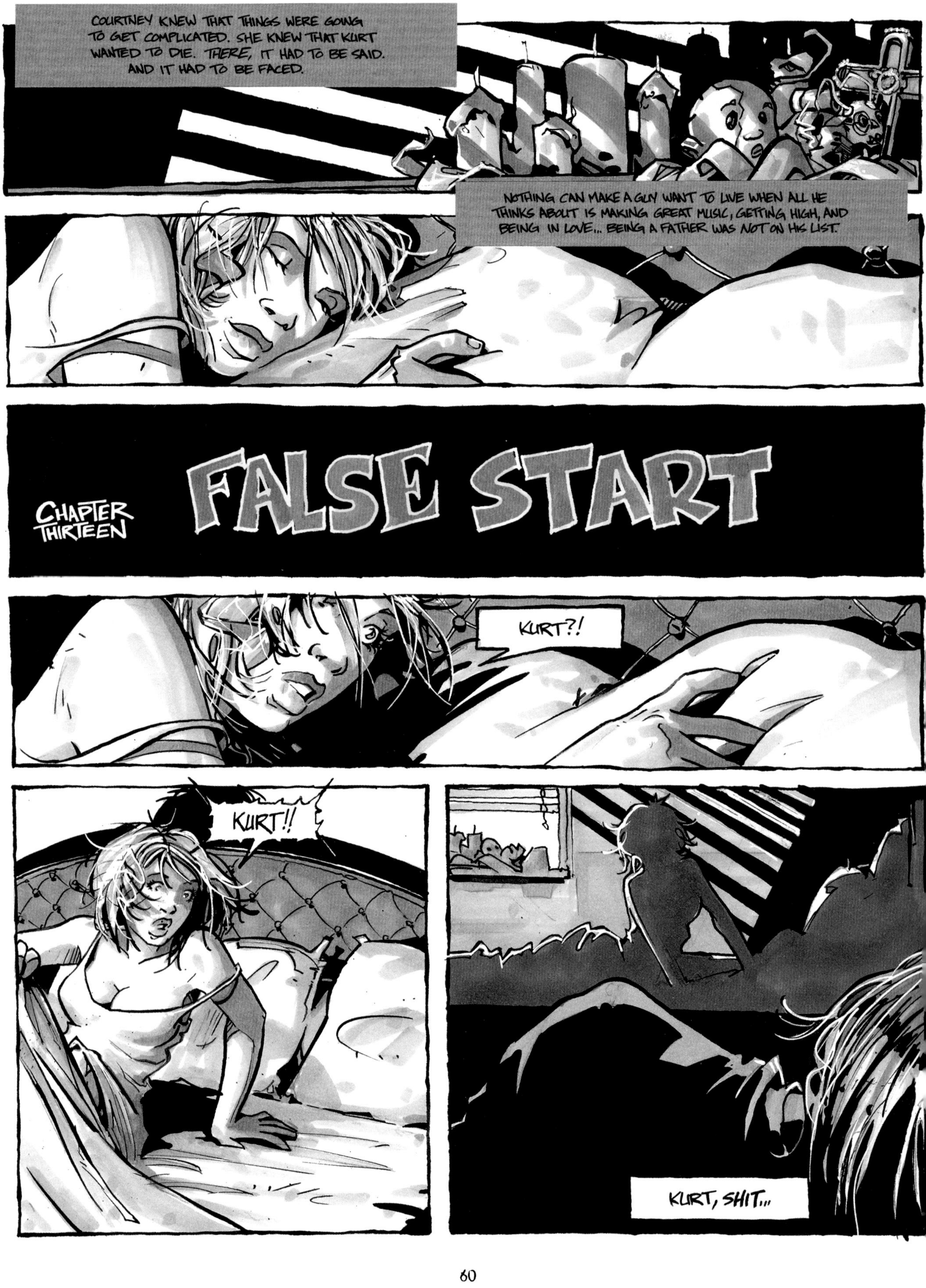
COURTNEY KNEW THAT THINGS WERE GOING TO GET COMPLICATED. SHE KNEW THAT KURT WANTED TO DIE. THERE, IT HAD TO BE SAID. AND IT HAD TO BE FACED.
NOTHING CAN MAKE A GUY WANT TO LIVE WHEN ALL HE THINKS ABOUT IS MAKING GREAT MUSIC, GETTING HIGH, AND BEING IN LOVE... BEING A FATHER WAS NOT ON HIS LIST.
CHAPTER THIRTEEN
FALSE START
KURT?!
KURT!!
KURT, SHIT...

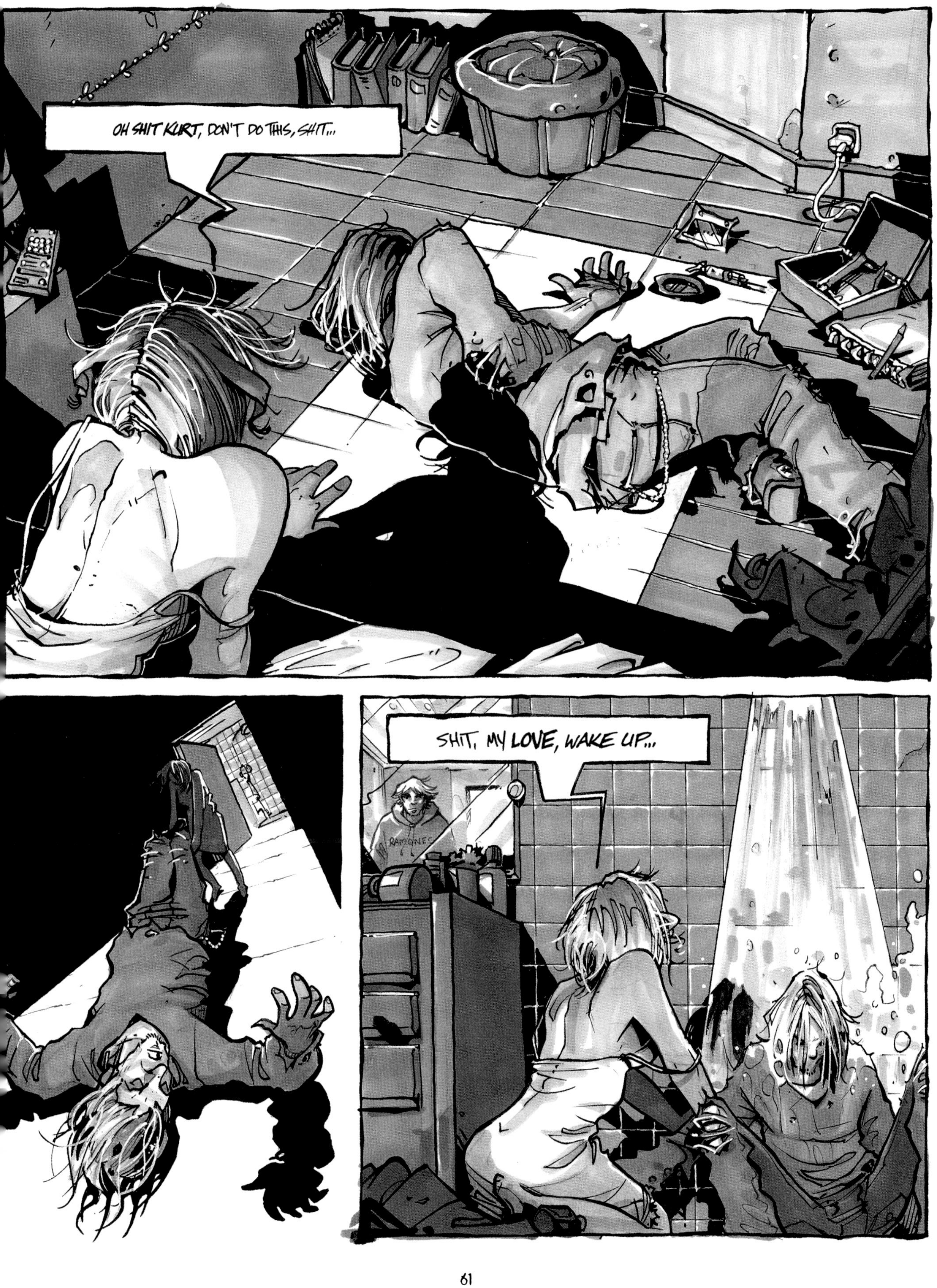
OH SHIT KURT, DON'T DO THIS, SHIT...
SHIT, MY LOVE, WAKE UP...
RAMONES

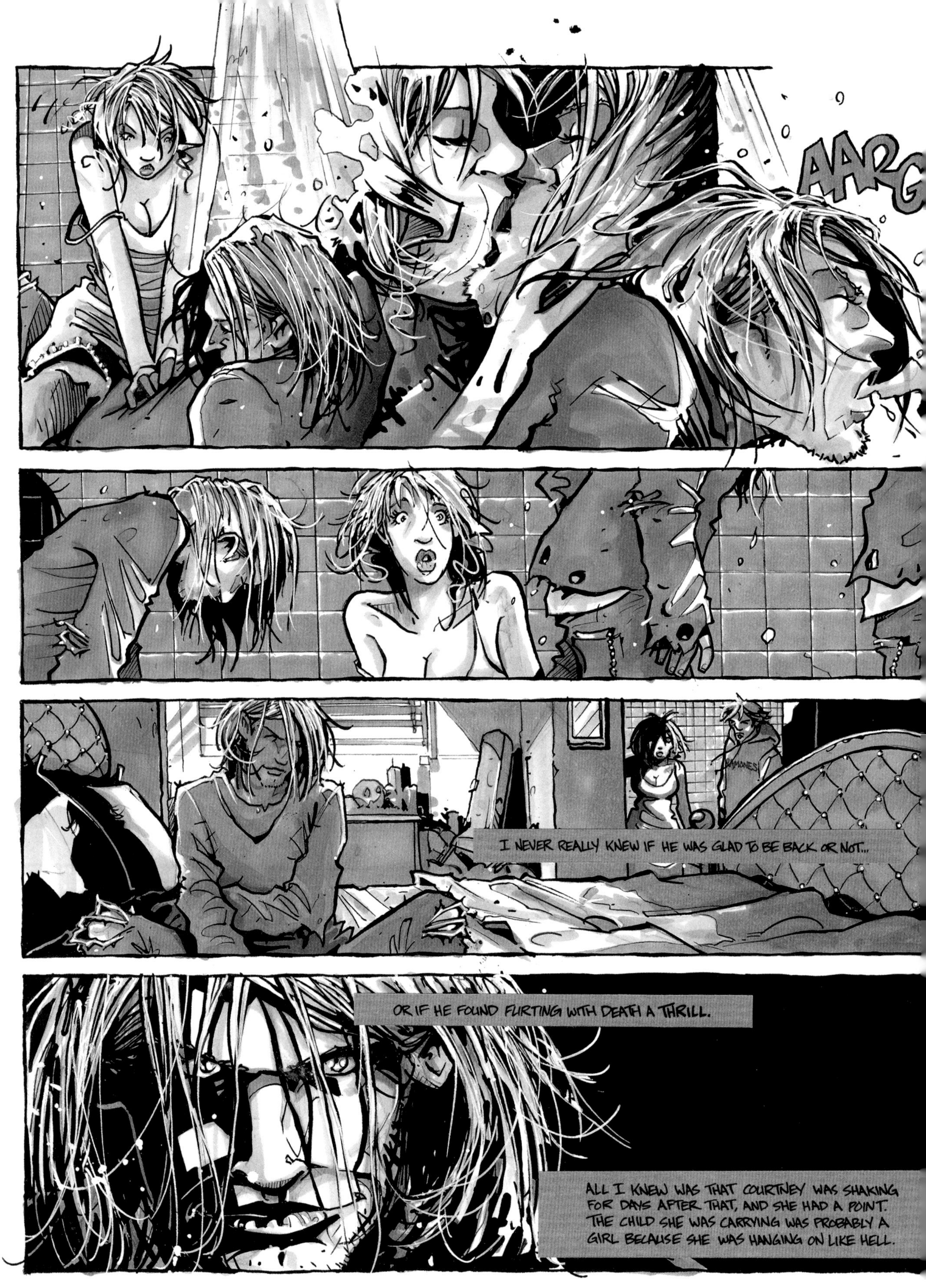
AARG
RAMONES
I NEVER REALLY KNEW IF HE WAS GLAD TO BE BACK OR NOT...
OR IF HE FOUND FLIRTING WITH DEATH A THRILL.
ALL I KNEW WAS THAT COURTNEY WAS SHAKING FOR DAYS AFTER THAT, AND SHE HAD A POINT. THE CHILD SHE WAS CARRYING WAS PROBABLY A GIRL BECAUSE SHE WAS HANGING ON LIKE HELL.

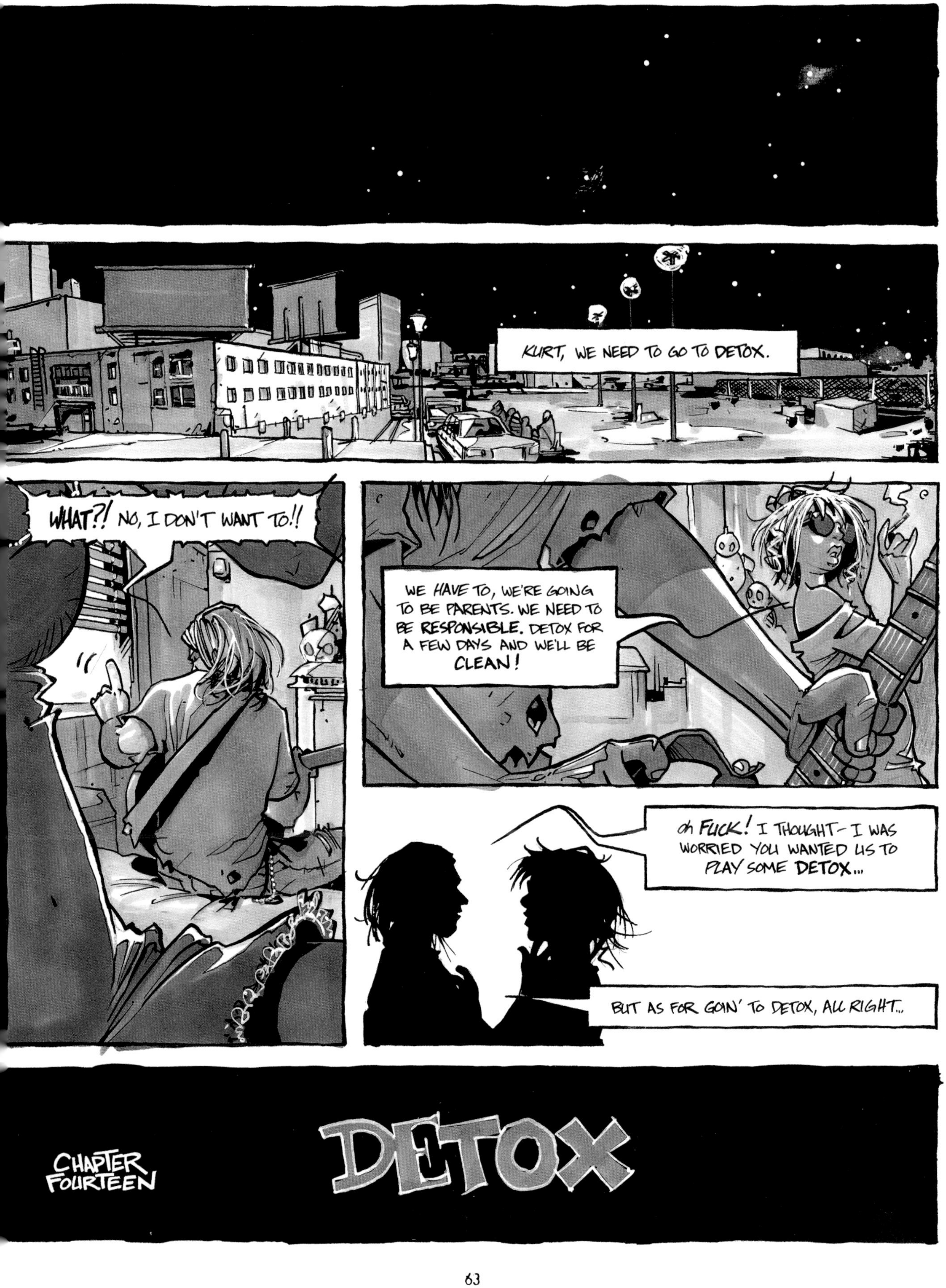
KURT, WE NEED TO GO TO DETOX.
WHAT?! NO, I DON'T WANT TO!!
WE HAVE TO, WE'RE GOING TO BE PARENTS. WE NEED TO BE RESPONSIBLE. DETOX FOR A FEW DAYS AND WE'LL BE CLEAN!
oh FUCK! I THOUGHT- I WAS WORRIED YOU WANTED US TO PLAY SOME DETOX...
BUT AS FOR GOIN' TO DETOX, ALL RIGHT...
CHAPTER FOURTEEN
DETOX

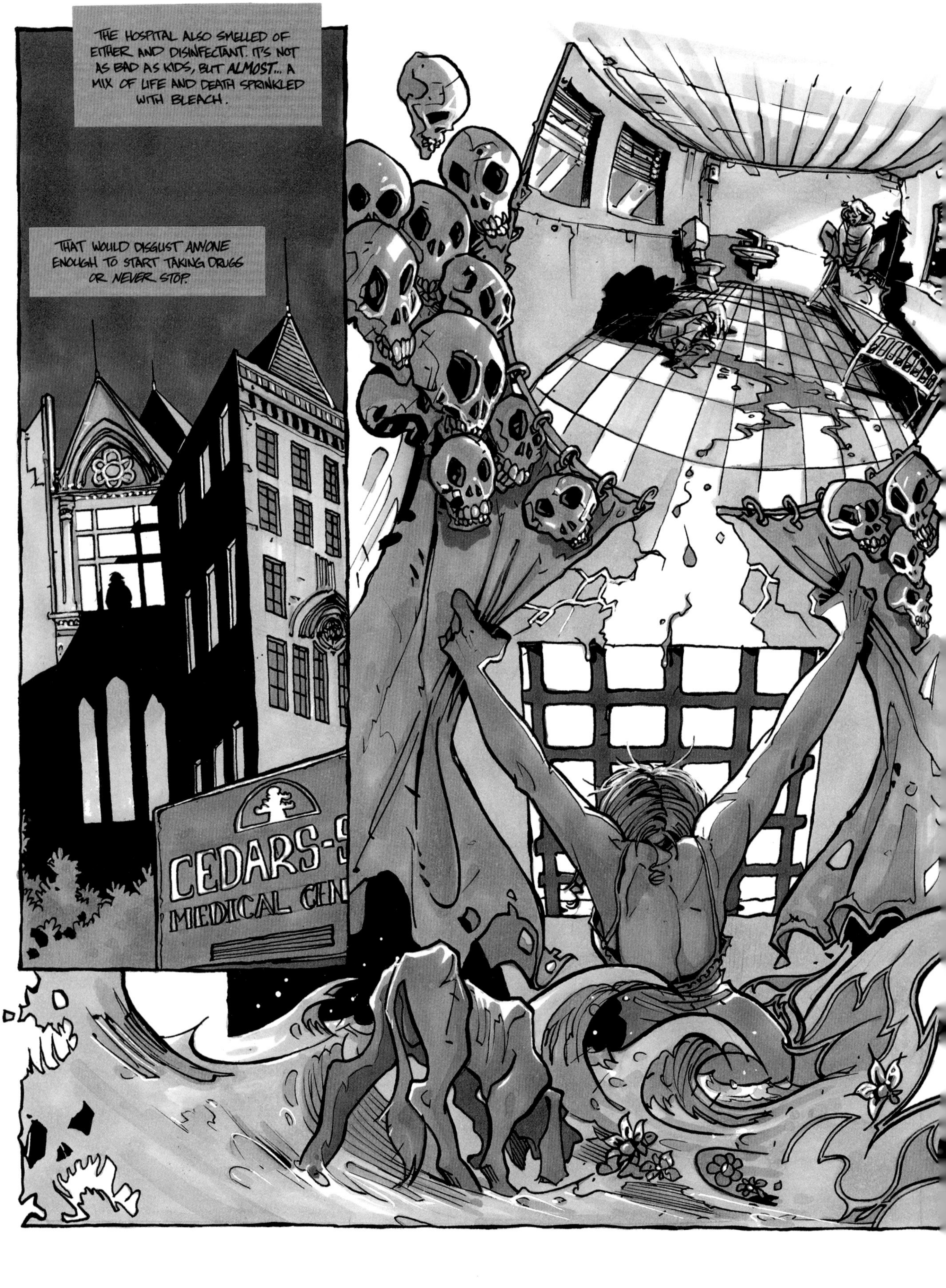
THE HOSPITAL ALSO SMELLED OF EITHER AND DISINFECTANT. IT'S NOT AS BAD AS KIDS, BUT ALMOST... A MIX OF LIFE AND DEATH SPRINKLED WITH BLEACH.
THAT WOULD DISGUST ANYONE ENOUGH TO START TAKING DRUGS OR NEVER STOP.
CEDARS-S
MEDICAL CEN

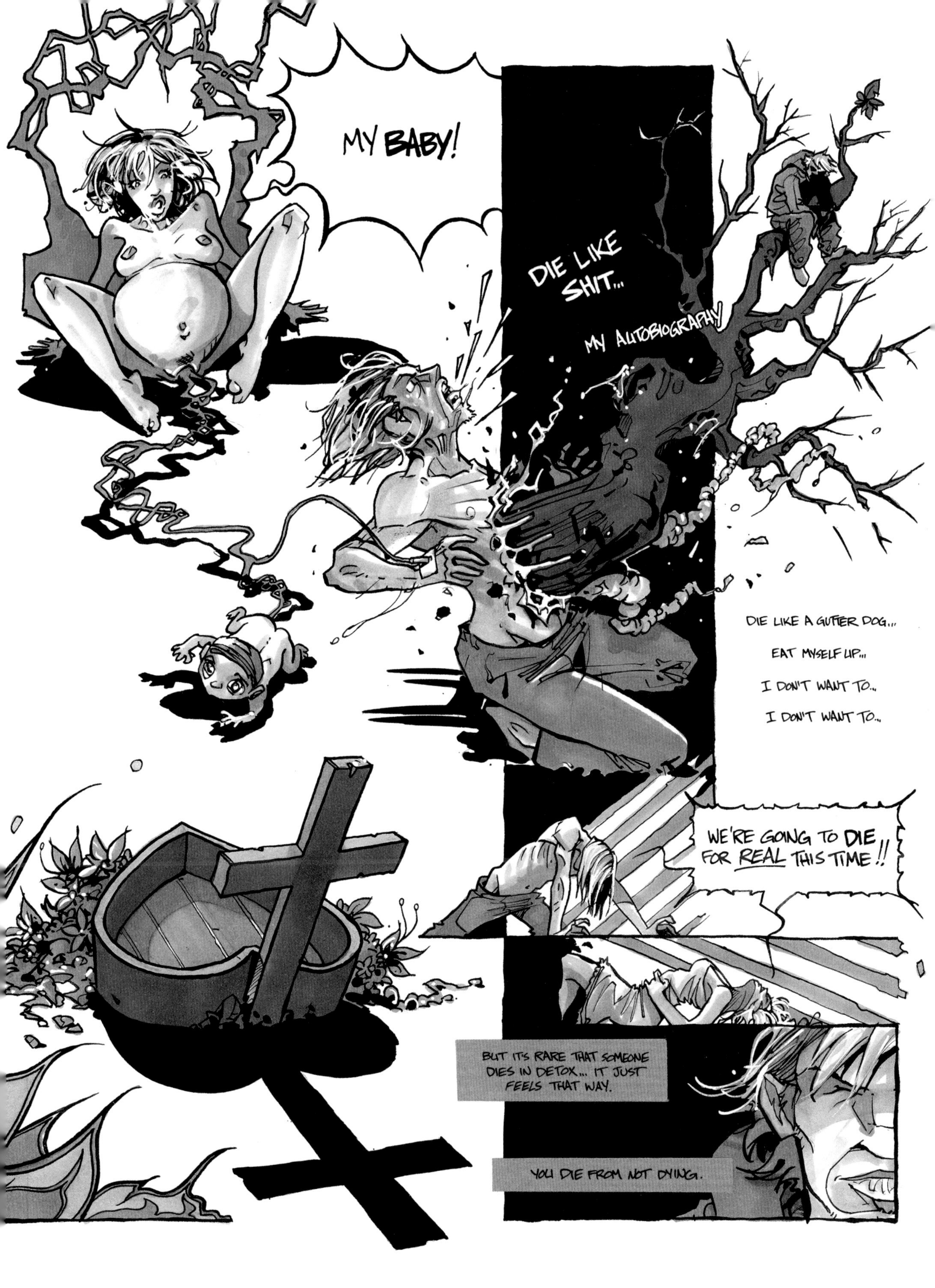
MY BABY!
DIE LIKE SHIT...
MY AUTOBIOGRAPHY
DIE LIKE A GUTTER DOG...
EAT MYSELF UP...
I DON'T WANT TO...
I DON'T WANT TO...
WE'RE GOING TO DIE FOR REAL THIS TIME!!
BUT IT'S RARE THAT SOMEONE DIES IN DETOX... IT JUST FEELS THAT WAY.
YOU DIE FROM NOT DYING.

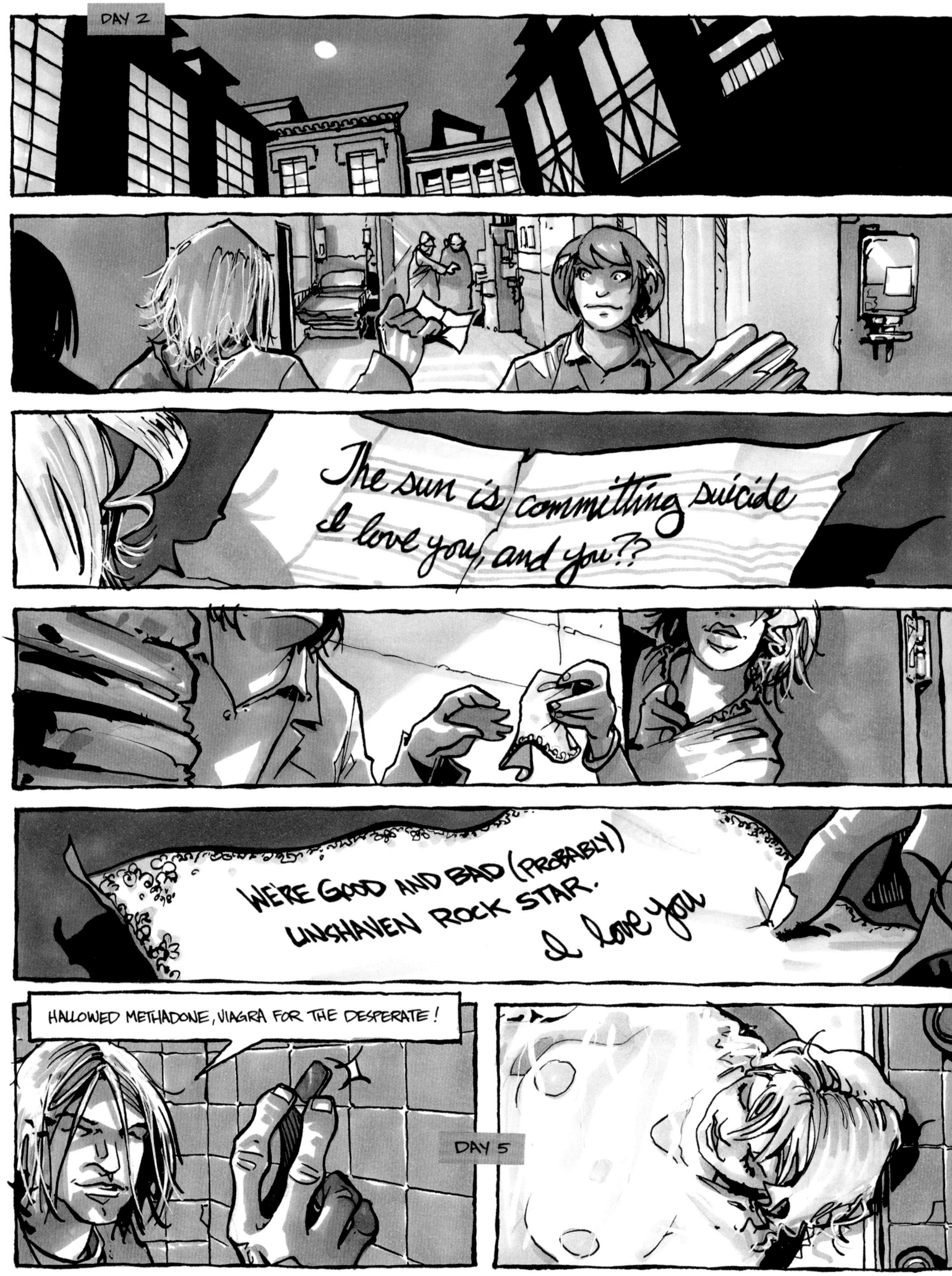
DAY 2
The sun is committing suicide
I love you, and you??
WE'RE GOOD AND BAD (PROBABLY)
UNSHAVEN ROCK STAR.
I love you
HALLOWED METHADONE, VIAGRA FOR THE DESPERATE!
DAY 5

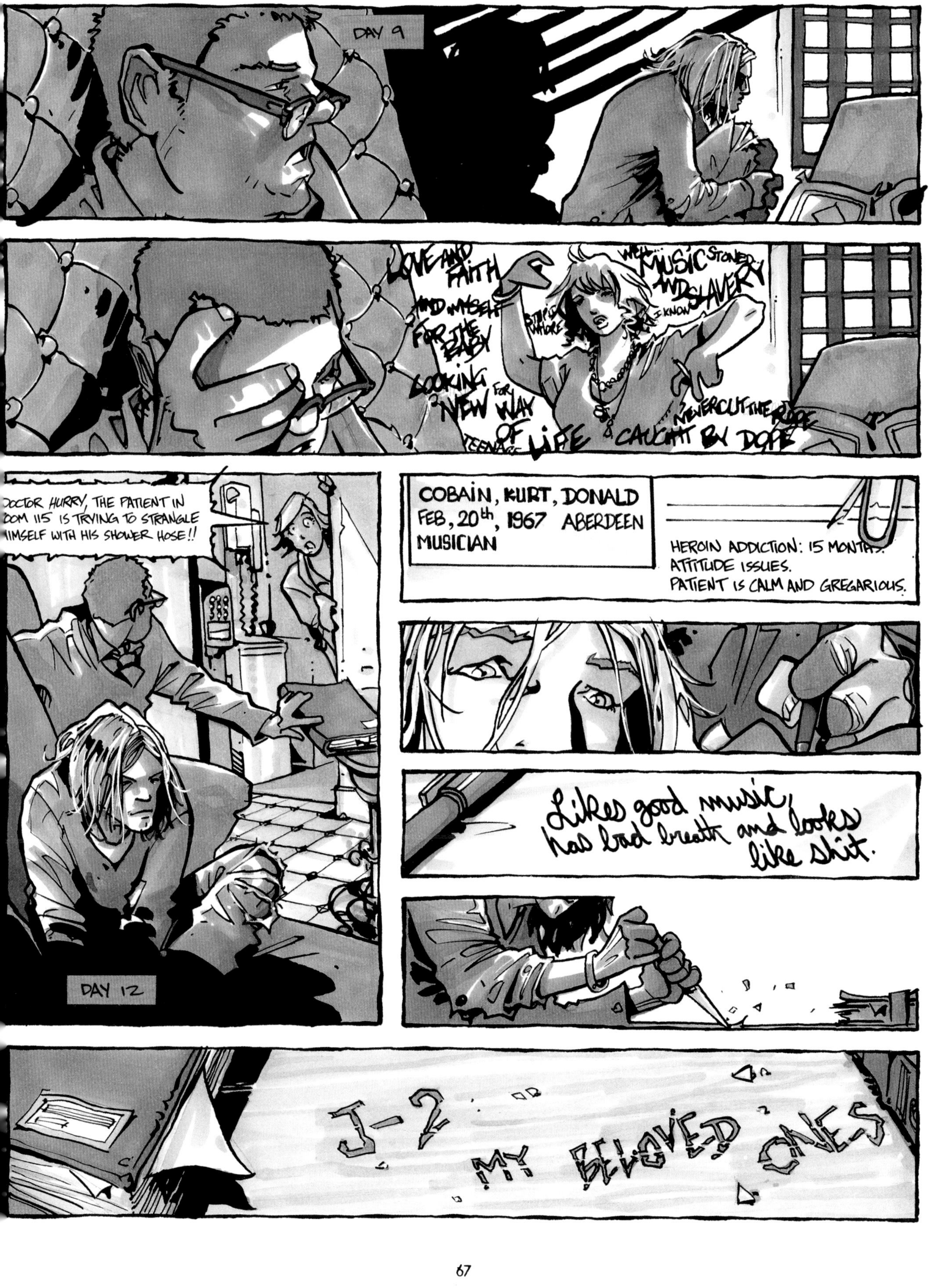

DAY 9
LOVE AND FAITH
AND MYSELF
FOR THE BABY
LOOKING FOR NEW WAY OF LIFE
TEENAGE
STUPID WHORE
WITH MUSIC STONED
AND SLAVERY
I KNOW
NEVER CUT THE ROPE
CAUGHT BY DOPE
DOCTOR HURRY, THE PATIENT IN
OOM 115 IS TRYING TO STRANGLE
IMSELF WITH HIS SHOWER HOSE!!
COBAIN, KURT, DONALD
FEB, 20th, 1967 ABERDEEN
MUSICIAN
HEROIN ADDICTION: 15 MONTHS.
ATTITUDE ISSUES.
PATIENT IS CALM AND GREGARIOUS.
Likes good music, has bad breath and looks like shit.
DAY 12
J-2
MY BELOVED ONES

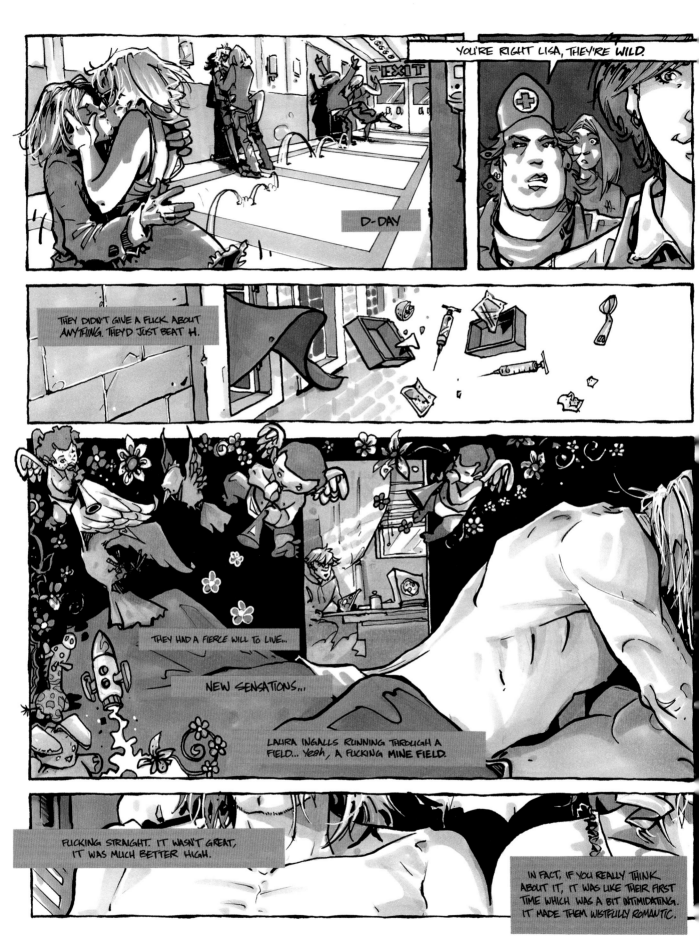

YOU'RE RIGHT LISA, THEY'RE WILD.

D-DAY

THEY DIDN'T GIVE A FUCK ABOUT ANYTHING. THEY'D JUST BEAT H.

THEY HAD A FIERCE WILL TO LIVE...

NEW SENSATIONS...

LAURA INGALLS RUNNING THROUGH A FIELD... Yeah, A FUCKING MINE FIELD.

FUCKING STRAIGHT. IT WASN'T GREAT, IT WAS MUCH BETTER HIGH.

IN FACT, IF YOU REALLY THINK ABOUT IT, IT WAS LIKE THEIR FIRST TIME WHICH WAS A BIT INTIMIDATING. IT MADE THEM WISTFULLY ROMANTIC.

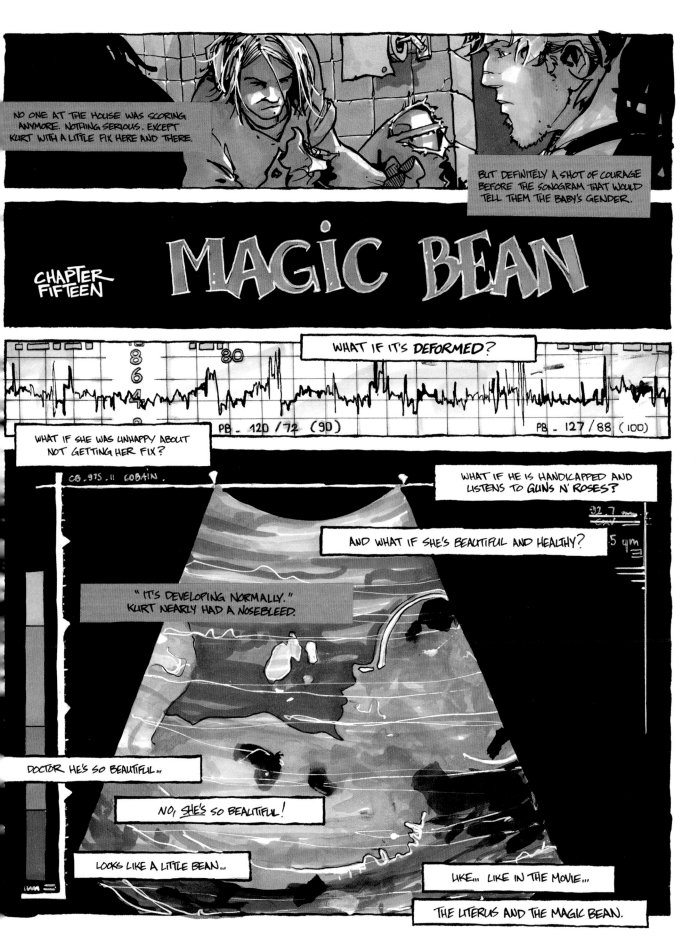

NO ONE AT THE HOUSE WAS SCORING ANYMORE. NOTHING SERIOUS. EXCEPT KURT WITH A LITTLE FIX HERE AND THERE.

BUT DEFINITELY A SHOT OF COURAGE BEFORE THE SONOGRAM THAT WOULD TELL THEM THE BABY'S GENDER.

CHAPTER FIFTEEN MAGIC BEAN

WHAT IF IT'S **DEFORMED?**

WHAT IF SHE WAS UNHAPPY ABOUT NOT GETTING HER FIX?

WHAT IF HE IS HANDICAPPED AND LISTENS TO GUNS N' ROSES?

AND WHAT IF SHE'S BEAUTIFUL AND HEALTHY?

"IT'S DEVELOPING NORMALLY." KURT NEARLY HAD A NOSEBLEED.

DOCTOR HE'S SO BEAUTIFUL...

NO, _SHE'S_ SO BEAUTIFUL!

LOOKS LIKE A LITTLE BEAN...

LIKE... LIKE IN THE MOVIE...

THE UTERUS AND THE MAGIC BEAN.

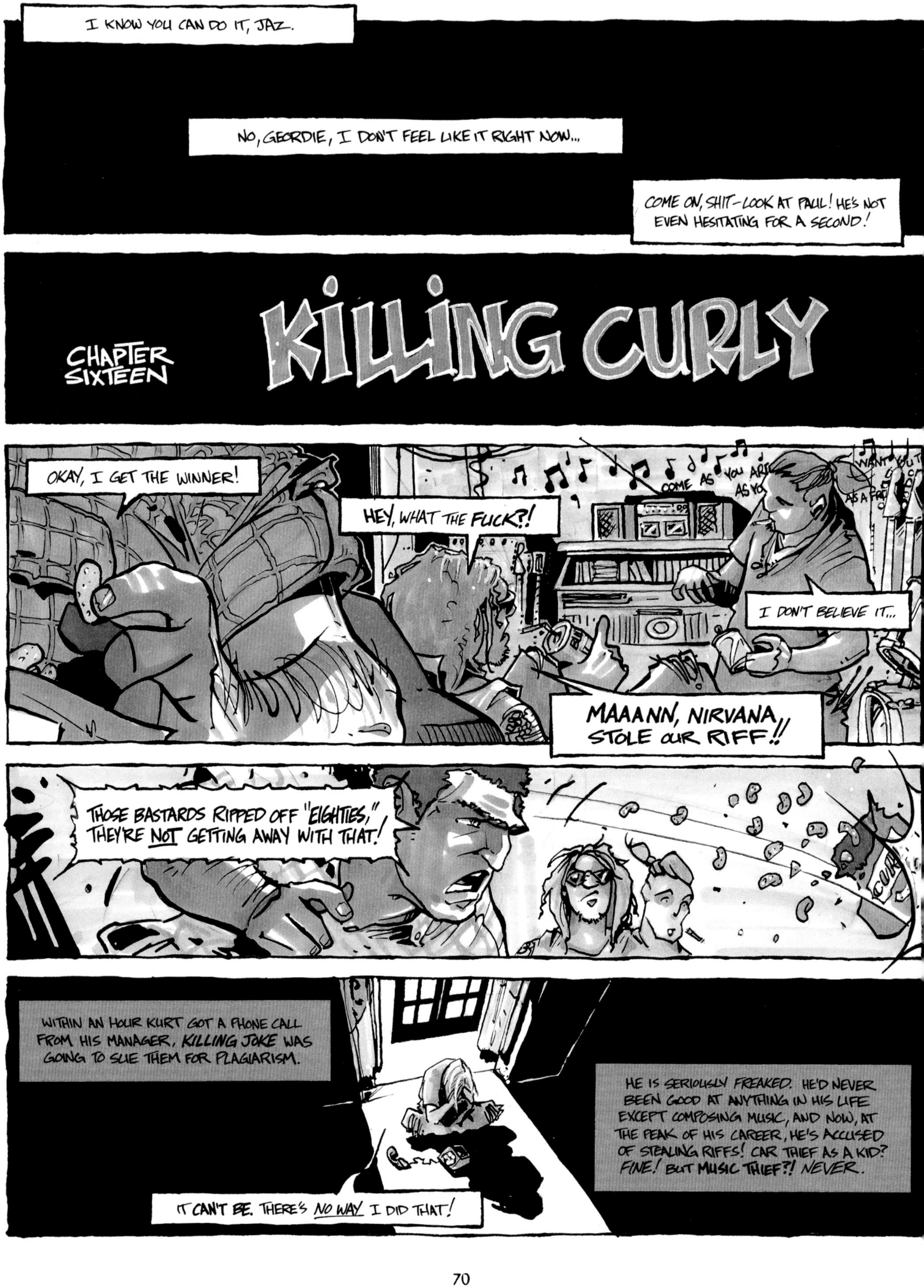
I KNOW YOU CAN DO IT, JAZ.
NO, GEORDIE, I DON'T FEEL LIKE IT RIGHT NOW...
COME ON, SHIT—LOOK AT PAUL! HE'S NOT EVEN HESITATING FOR A SECOND!
CHAPTER SIXTEEN
KILLING CURLY
OKAY, I GET THE WINNER!
HEY, WHAT THE FUCK?!
I DON'T BELIEVE IT...
MAAANN, NIRVANA, STOLE OUR RIFF!!
THOSE BASTARDS RIPPED OFF "EIGHTIES," THEY'RE NOT GETTING AWAY WITH THAT!
WITHIN AN HOUR KURT GOT A PHONE CALL FROM HIS MANAGER. KILLING JOKE WAS GOING TO SUE THEM FOR PLAGIARISM.
HE IS SERIOUSLY FREAKED. HE'D NEVER BEEN GOOD AT ANYTHING IN HIS LIFE EXCEPT COMPOSING MUSIC, AND NOW, AT THE PEAK OF HIS CAREER, HE'S ACCUSED OF STEALING RIFFS! CAR THIEF AS A KID? FINE! BUT MUSIC THIEF?! NEVER.
IT CAN'T BE. THERE'S NO WAY I DID THAT!

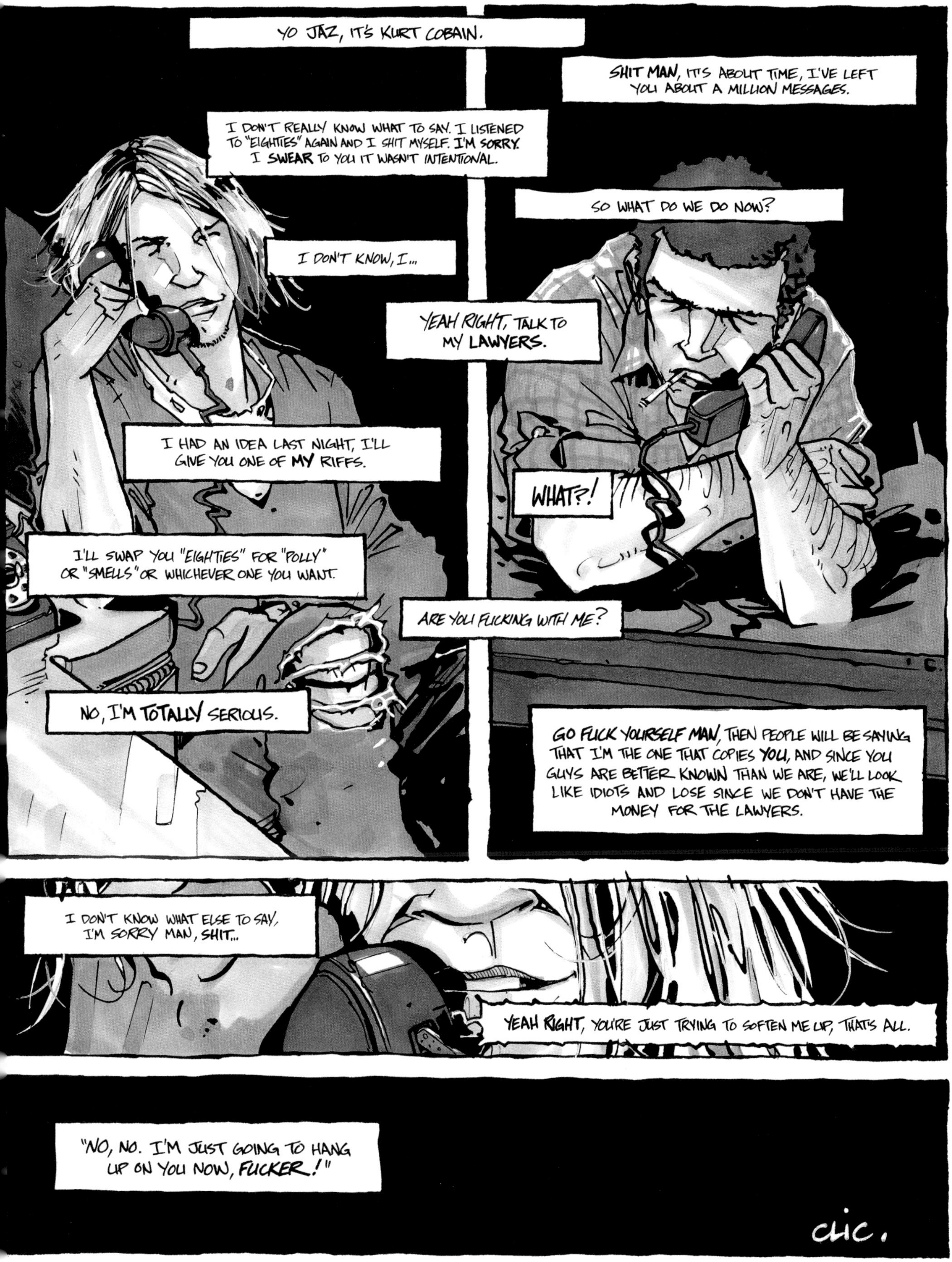
YO JAZ, IT'S KURT COBAIN.
SHIT MAN, IT'S ABOUT TIME, I'VE LEFT YOU ABOUT A MILLION MESSAGES.
I DON'T REALLY KNOW WHAT TO SAY. I LISTENED TO "EIGHTIES" AGAIN AND I SHIT MYSELF. I'M SORRY. I SWEAR TO YOU IT WASN'T INTENTIONAL.
SO WHAT DO WE DO NOW?
I DON'T KNOW, I...
YEAH RIGHT, TALK TO MY LAWYERS.
I HAD AN IDEA LAST NIGHT, I'LL GIVE YOU ONE OF MY RIFFS.
WHAT?!
I'LL SWAP YOU "EIGHTIES" FOR "POLLY" OR "SMELLS" OR WHICHEVER ONE YOU WANT.
ARE YOU FUCKING WITH ME?
NO, I'M TOTALLY SERIOUS.
GO FUCK YOURSELF MAN, THEN PEOPLE WILL BE SAYING THAT I'M THE ONE THAT COPIES YOU, AND SINCE YOU GUYS ARE BETTER KNOWN THAN WE ARE, WE'LL LOOK LIKE IDIOTS AND LOSE SINCE WE DON'T HAVE THE MONEY FOR THE LAWYERS.
I DON'T KNOW WHAT ELSE TO SAY, I'M SORRY MAN, SHIT...
YEAH RIGHT, YOU'RE JUST TRYING TO SOFTEN ME UP, THAT'S ALL.
"NO, NO. I'M JUST GOING TO HANG UP ON YOU NOW, FUCKER!"
CLIC.

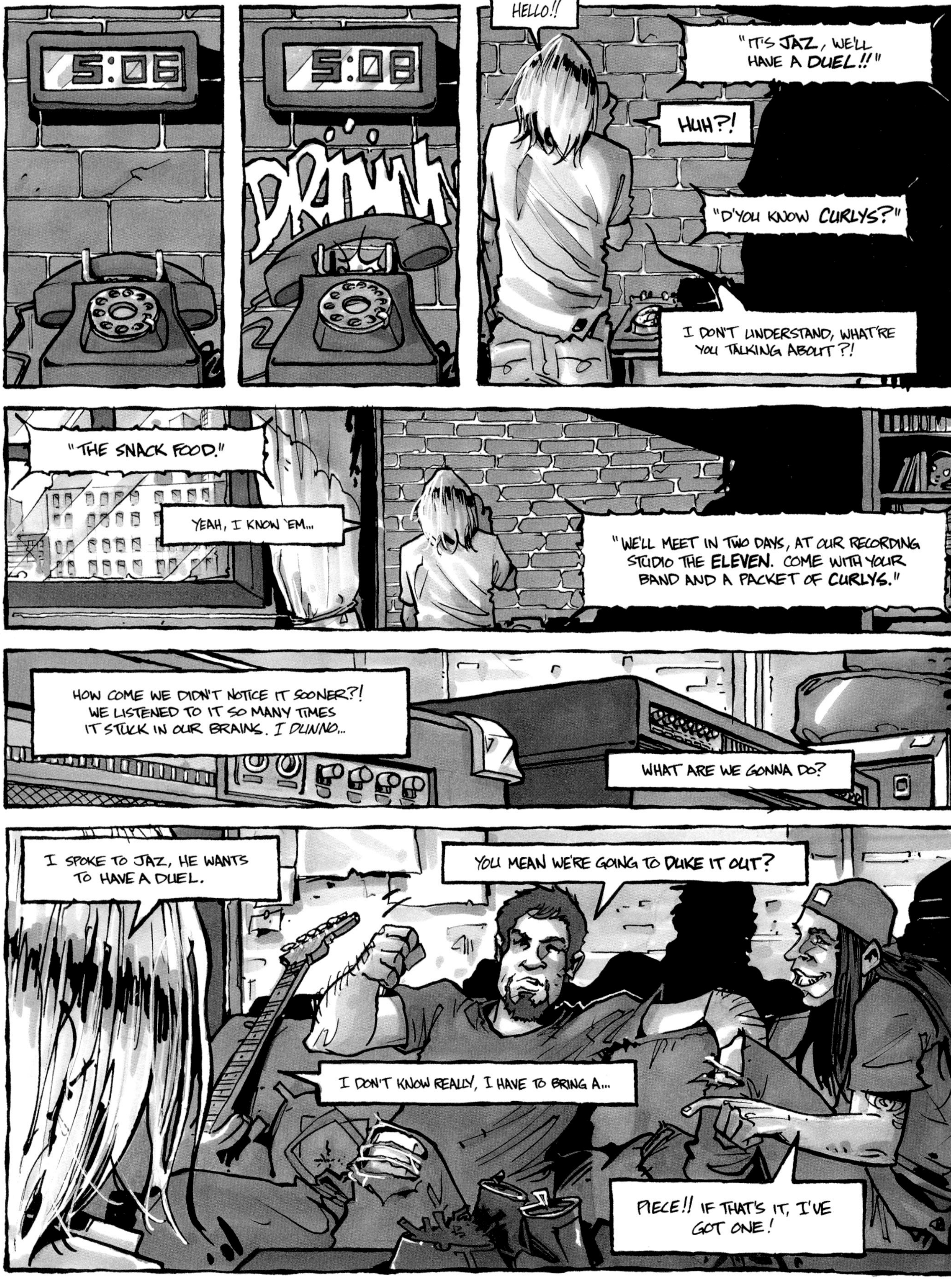
5:06
5:08
DRIIINN
HELLO!!
"IT'S JAZ, WE'LL HAVE A DUEL!!"
HUH?!
"D'YOU KNOW CURLYS?"
I DON'T UNDERSTAND, WHAT'RE YOU TALKING ABOUT?!
"THE SNACK FOOD."
YEAH, I KNOW 'EM...
"WE'LL MEET IN TWO DAYS, AT OUR RECORDING STUDIO THE ELEVEN. COME WITH YOUR BAND AND A PACKET OF CURLYS."
HOW COME WE DIDN'T NOTICE IT SOONER?! WE LISTENED TO IT SO MANY TIMES IT STUCK IN OUR BRAINS. I DUNNO...
WHAT ARE WE GONNA DO?
I SPOKE TO JAZ, HE WANTS TO HAVE A DUEL.
YOU MEAN WE'RE GOING TO DUKE IT OUT?
I DON'T KNOW REALLY, I HAVE TO BRING A...
PIECE!! IF THAT'S IT, I'VE GOT ONE!

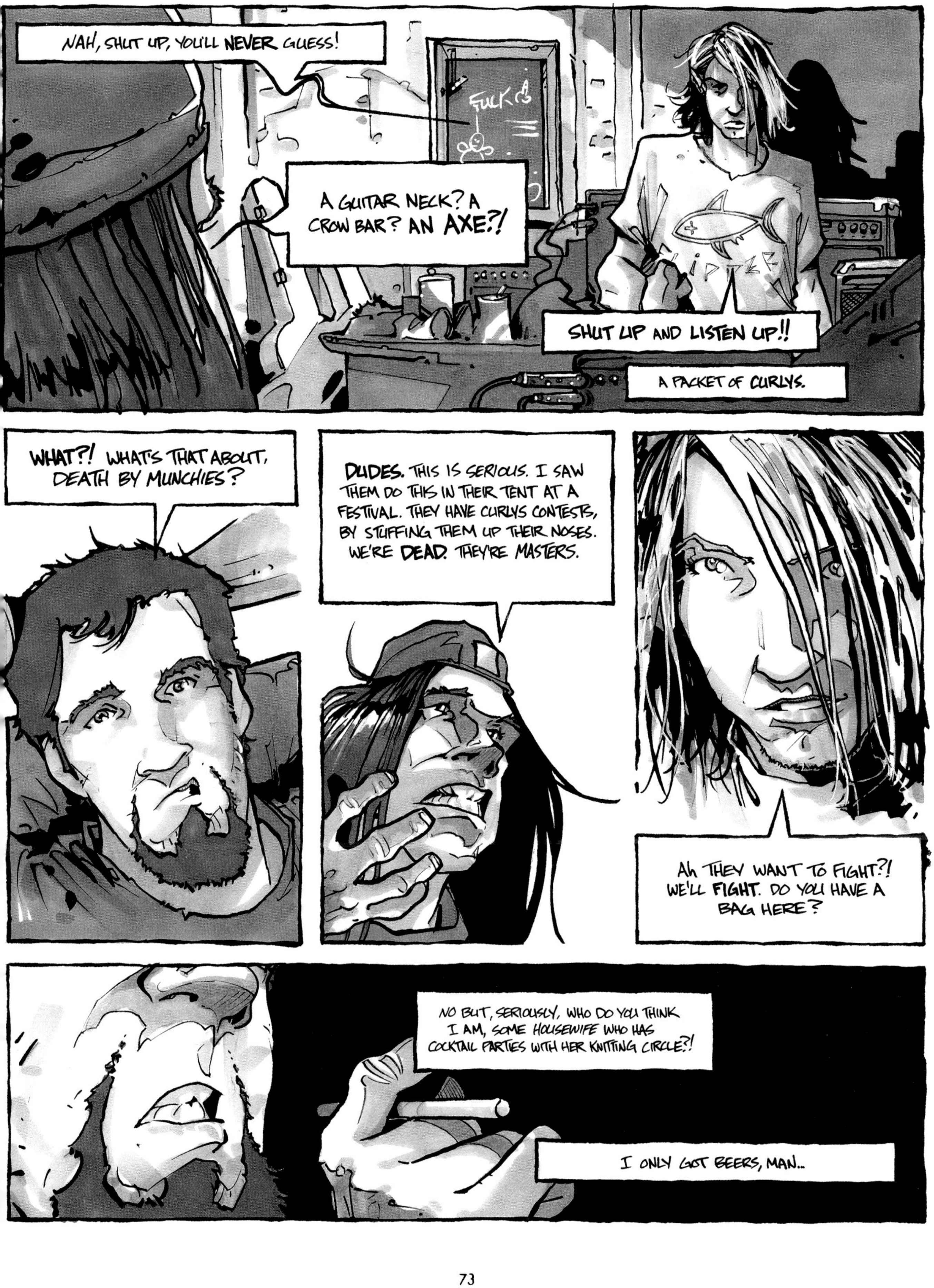
NAH, SHUT UP, YOU'LL NEVER GUESS!
FUCK
A GUITAR NECK? A CROW BAR? AN AXE?!
SHUT UP AND LISTEN UP!!
A PACKET OF CURLYS.
WHAT?! WHAT'S THAT ABOUT, DEATH BY MUNCHIES?
DUDES. THIS IS SERIOUS. I SAW THEM DO THIS IN THEIR TENT AT A FESTIVAL. THEY HAVE CURLYS CONTESTS, BY STUFFING THEM UP THEIR NOSES. WE'RE DEAD. THEY'RE MASTERS.
Ah THEY WANT TO FIGHT?! WE'LL FIGHT. DO YOU HAVE A BAG HERE?
NO BUT, SERIOUSLY, WHO DO YOU THINK I AM, SOME HOUSEWIFE WHO HAS COCKTAIL PARTIES WITH HER KNITTING CIRCLE?!
I ONLY GOT BEERS, MAN...

FOR THE NEXT TWO DAYS THEY HID OUT AT KRIST'S HOUSE. HE DIDN'T WANT COURTNEY TO FIND OUT THE TRUTH. THEY TOLD HER THEY WERE DOING SOME INTENSE REHEARSING.

LOOK GUYS, A CURLY HAS THE SHAPE OF A TINY PIECE OF **INTESTINE** OR A **CATERPILLAR**, RIGHT?

IT HAD BEEN A LONG TIME SINCE THEY'D HAD THAT MUCH FUN...

IT SHOULD WEIGH ABOUT THE SAME AS HALF A BALL OF HASH. IF YOU'RE AIMING FOR AN ORIFICE YOU HAVE TO BE ABOVE IT AND AT A BIT OF AN ANGLE, BECAUSE OF ITS NATURAL BOOMERANG FORM...

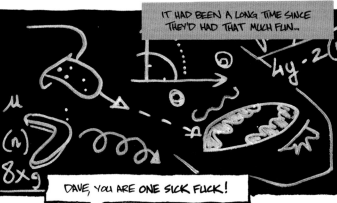

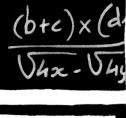

DAVE, YOU ARE ONE SICK FUCK!

I'M SERIOUS, KURT, WE CAN'T LET THEM DO THIS TO US. WE **DID** RIP THEIR RIFF BUT NOT ON PURPOSE. IT'S NO REASON TO LET THEM WIN...

...THEY WANT A MUNCHIES WAR, THEY'LL GET ONE.

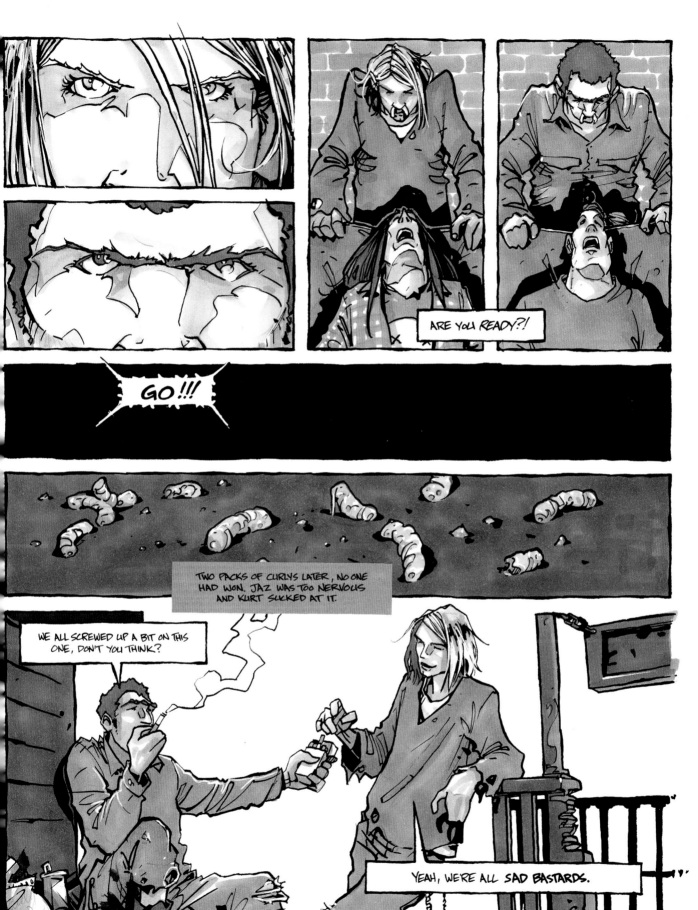

ARE YOU READY?!

GO!!!

TWO PACKS OF CURLYS LATER, NO ONE HAD WON. JAZ WAS TOO NERVOUS AND KURT SUCKED AT IT.

WE ALL SCREWED UP A BIT ON THIS ONE, DON'T YOU THINK?

YEAH, WE'RE ALL SAD BASTARDS.

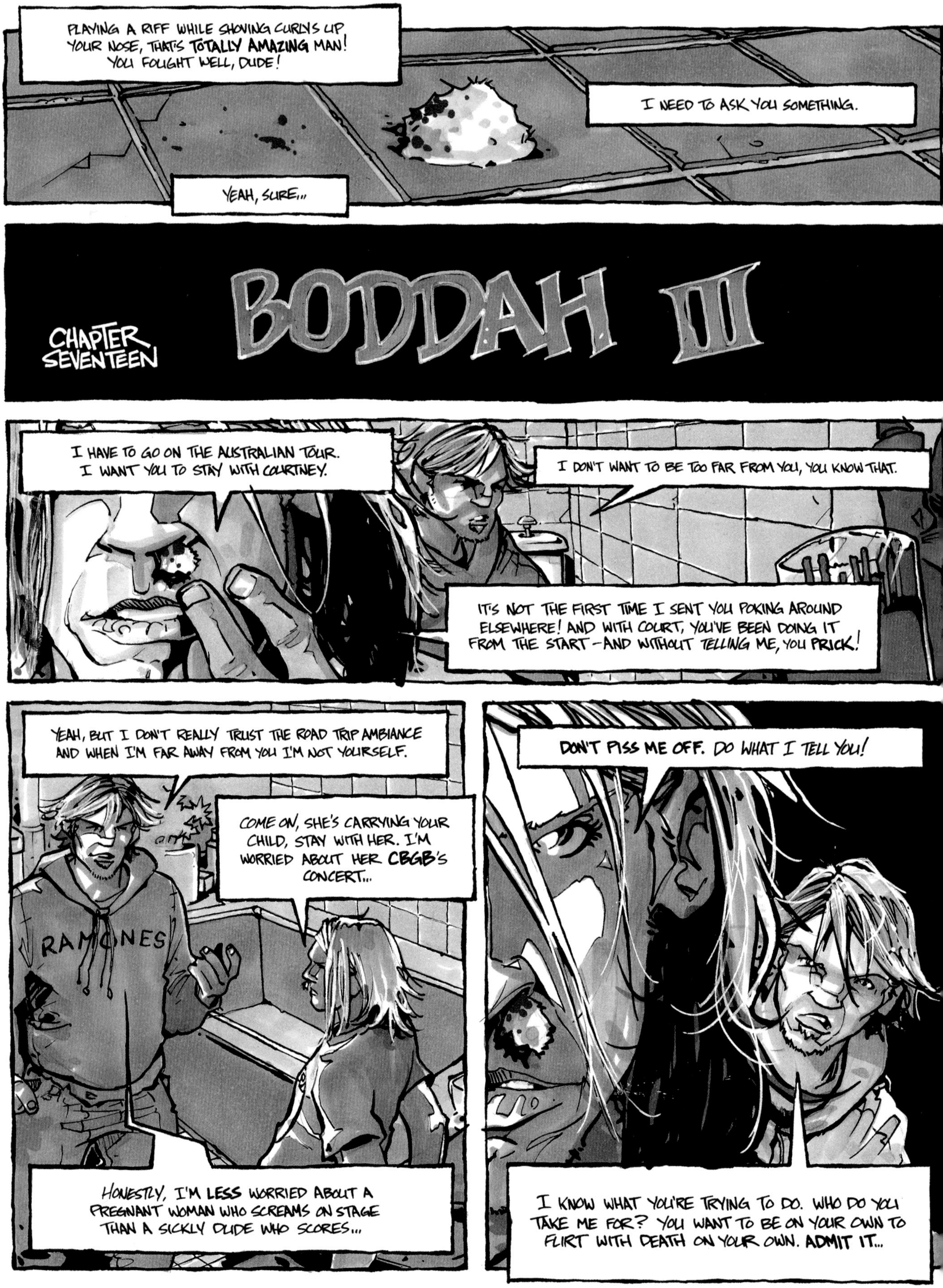
PLAYING A RIFF WHILE SHOVING CURLYS UP YOUR NOSE, THAT'S TOTALLY AMAZING MAN! YOU FOUGHT WELL, DUDE!
I NEED TO ASK YOU SOMETHING.
YEAH, SURE...
CHAPTER SEVENTEEN
BODDAH III
I HAVE TO GO ON THE AUSTRALIAN TOUR. I WANT YOU TO STAY WITH COURTNEY.
I DON'T WANT TO BE TOO FAR FROM YOU, YOU KNOW THAT.
IT'S NOT THE FIRST TIME I SENT YOU POKING AROUND ELSEWHERE! AND WITH COURT, YOU'VE BEEN DOING IT FROM THE START—AND WITHOUT TELLING ME, YOU PRICK!
YEAH, BUT I DON'T REALLY TRUST THE ROAD TRIP AMBIANCE AND WHEN I'M FAR AWAY FROM YOU I'M NOT YOURSELF.
COME ON, SHE'S CARRYING YOUR CHILD, STAY WITH HER. I'M WORRIED ABOUT HER CBGB'S CONCERT...
RAMONES
HONESTLY, I'M LESS WORRIED ABOUT A PREGNANT WOMAN WHO SCREAMS ON STAGE THAN A SICKLY DUDE WHO SCORES...
DON'T PISS ME OFF. DO WHAT I TELL YOU!
I KNOW WHAT YOU'RE TRYING TO DO. WHO DO YOU TAKE ME FOR? YOU WANT TO BE ON YOUR OWN TO FLIRT WITH DEATH ON YOUR OWN. ADMIT IT...

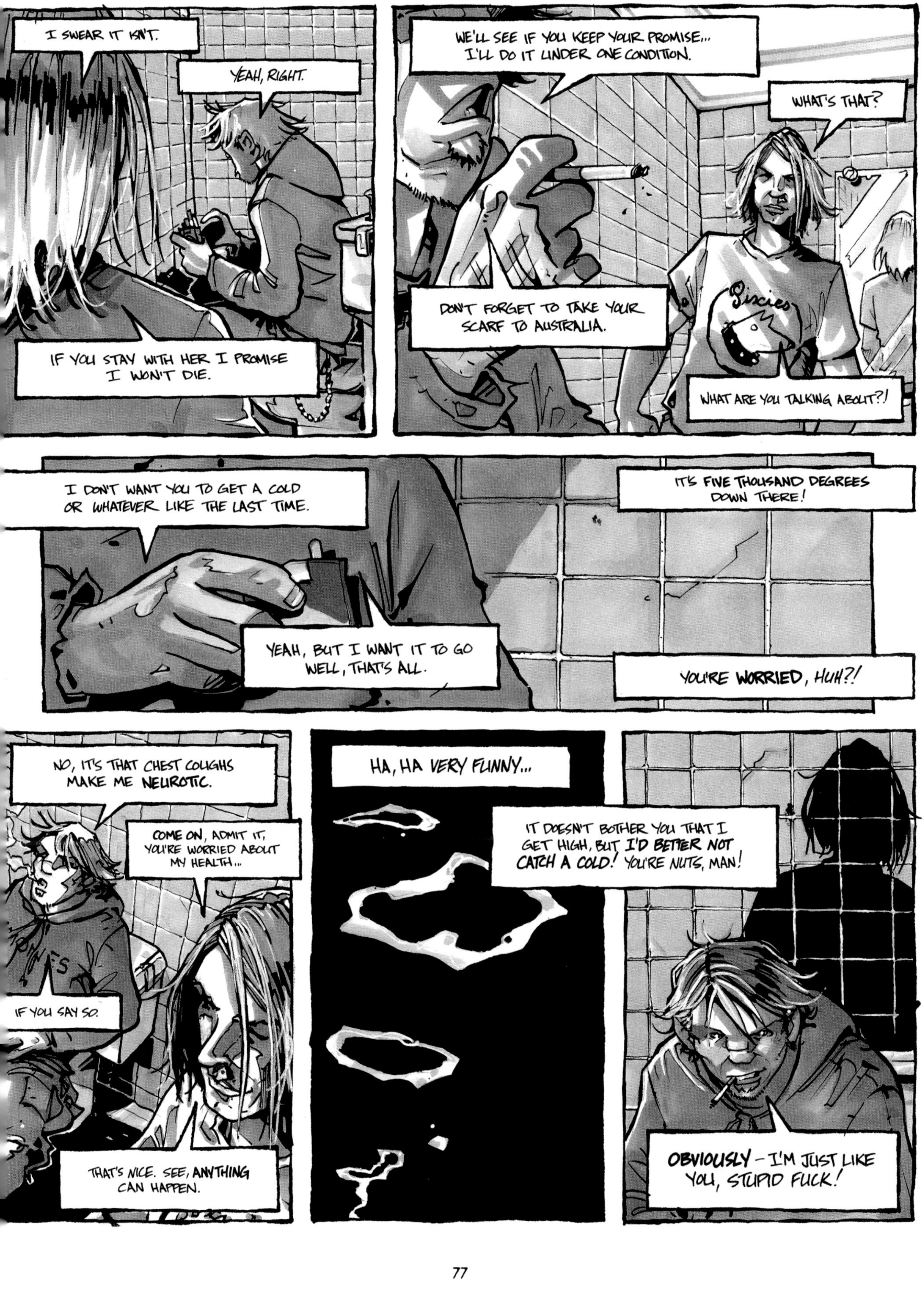
I SWEAR IT ISN'T.
YEAH, RIGHT.
IF YOU STAY WITH HER I PROMISE I WON'T DIE.
WE'LL SEE IF YOU KEEP YOUR PROMISE... I'LL DO IT UNDER ONE CONDITION.
WHAT'S THAT?
DON'T FORGET TO TAKE YOUR SCARF TO AUSTRALIA.
WHAT ARE YOU TALKING ABOUT?!
I DON'T WANT YOU TO GET A COLD OR WHATEVER LIKE THE LAST TIME.
IT'S FIVE THOUSAND DEGREES DOWN THERE!
YEAH, BUT I WANT IT TO GO WELL, THAT'S ALL.
YOU'RE WORRIED, HUH?!
NO, IT'S THAT CHEST COUGHS MAKE ME NEUROTIC.
COME ON, ADMIT IT, YOU'RE WORRIED ABOUT MY HEALTH...
IF YOU SAY SO.
THAT'S NICE. SEE, ANYTHING CAN HAPPEN.
HA, HA VERY FUNNY...
IT DOESN'T BOTHER YOU THAT I GET HIGH, BUT I'D BETTER NOT CATCH A COLD! YOU'RE NUTS, MAN!
OBVIOUSLY – I'M JUST LIKE YOU, STUPID FUCK!

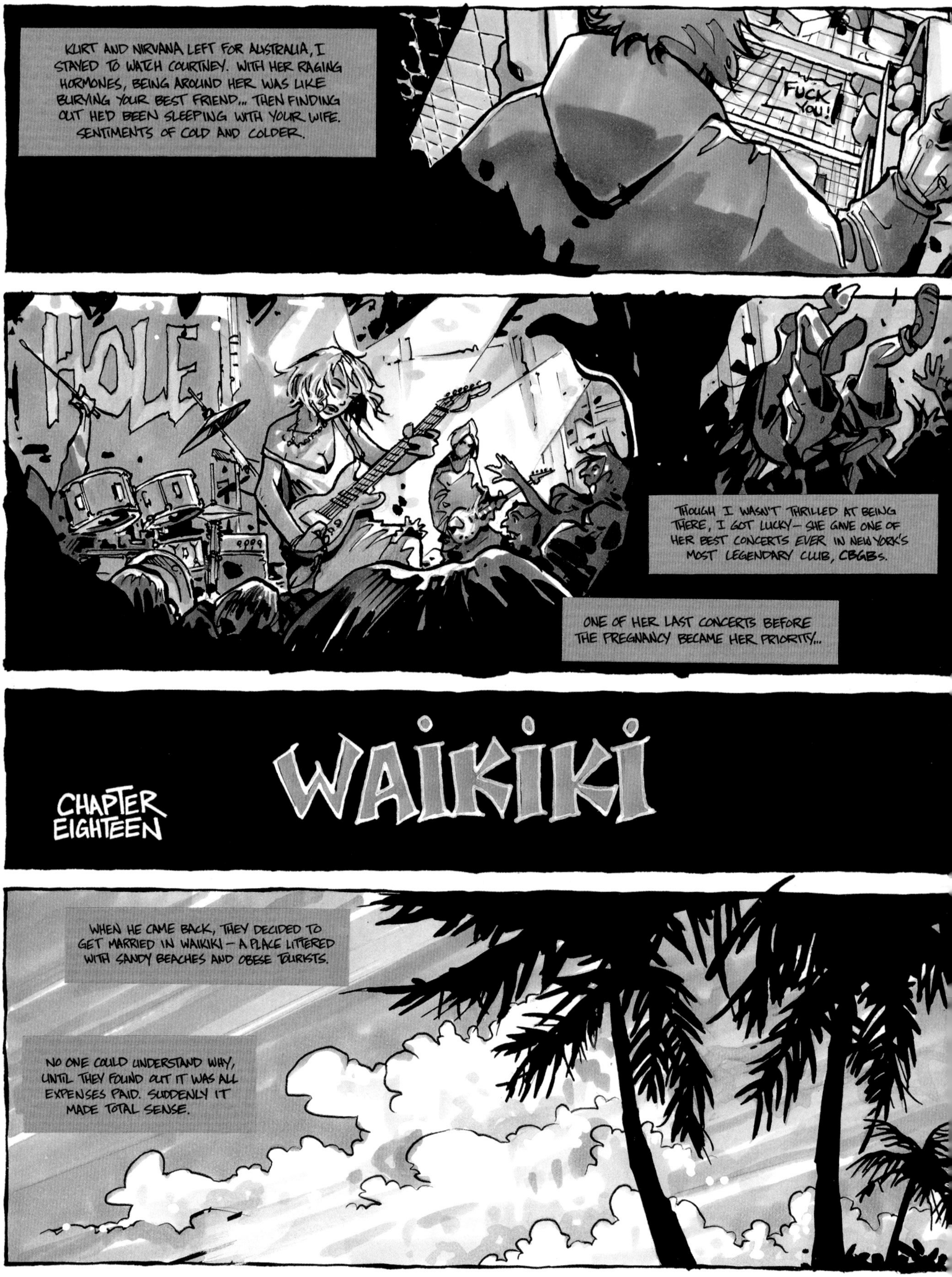
KURT AND NIRVANA LEFT FOR AUSTRALIA, I STAYED TO WATCH COURTNEY. WITH HER RAGING HORMONES, BEING AROUND HER WAS LIKE BURYING YOUR BEST FRIEND... THEN FINDING OUT HE'D BEEN SLEEPING WITH YOUR WIFE. SENTIMENTS OF COLD AND COLDER.
FUCK YOU!
HOLE
THOUGH I WASN'T THRILLED AT BEING THERE, I GOT LUCKY— SHE GAVE ONE OF HER BEST CONCERTS EVER IN NEW YORK'S MOST LEGENDARY CLUB, CBGBs.
ONE OF HER LAST CONCERTS BEFORE THE PREGNANCY BECAME HER PRIORITY...
CHAPTER EIGHTEEN
WAIKIKI
WHEN HE CAME BACK, THEY DECIDED TO GET MARRIED IN WAIKIKI — A PLACE LITTERED WITH SANDY BEACHES AND OBESE TOURISTS.
NO ONE COULD UNDERSTAND WHY, UNTIL THEY FOUND OUT IT WAS ALL EXPENSES PAID. SUDDENLY IT MADE TOTAL SENSE.

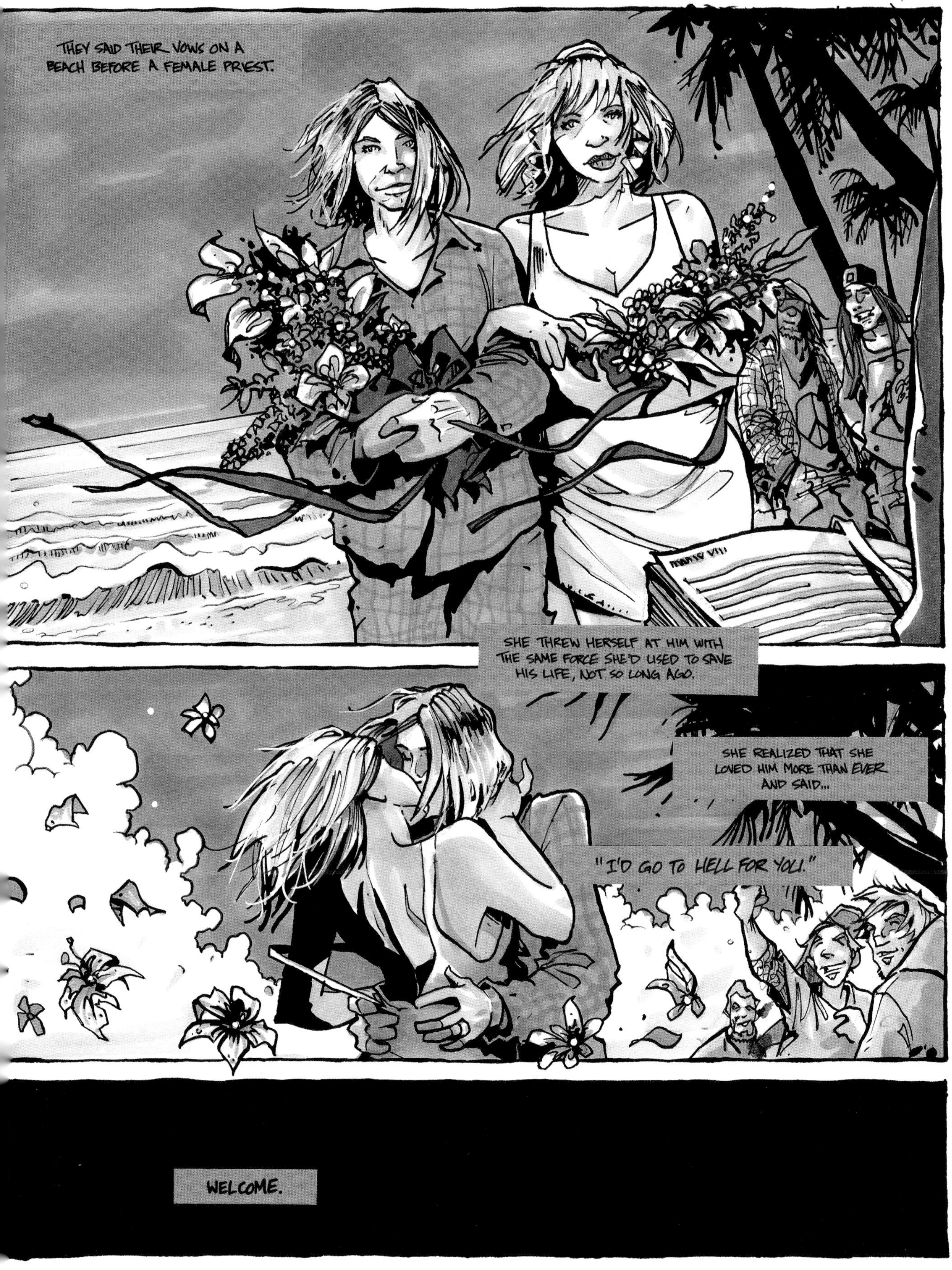
THEY SAID THEIR VOWS ON A BEACH BEFORE A FEMALE PRIEST.
SHE THREW HERSELF AT HIM WITH THE SAME FORCE SHE'D USED TO SAVE HIS LIFE, NOT SO LONG AGO.
SHE REALIZED THAT SHE LOVED HIM MORE THAN EVER AND SAID...
"I'D GO TO HELL FOR YOU."
WELCOME.

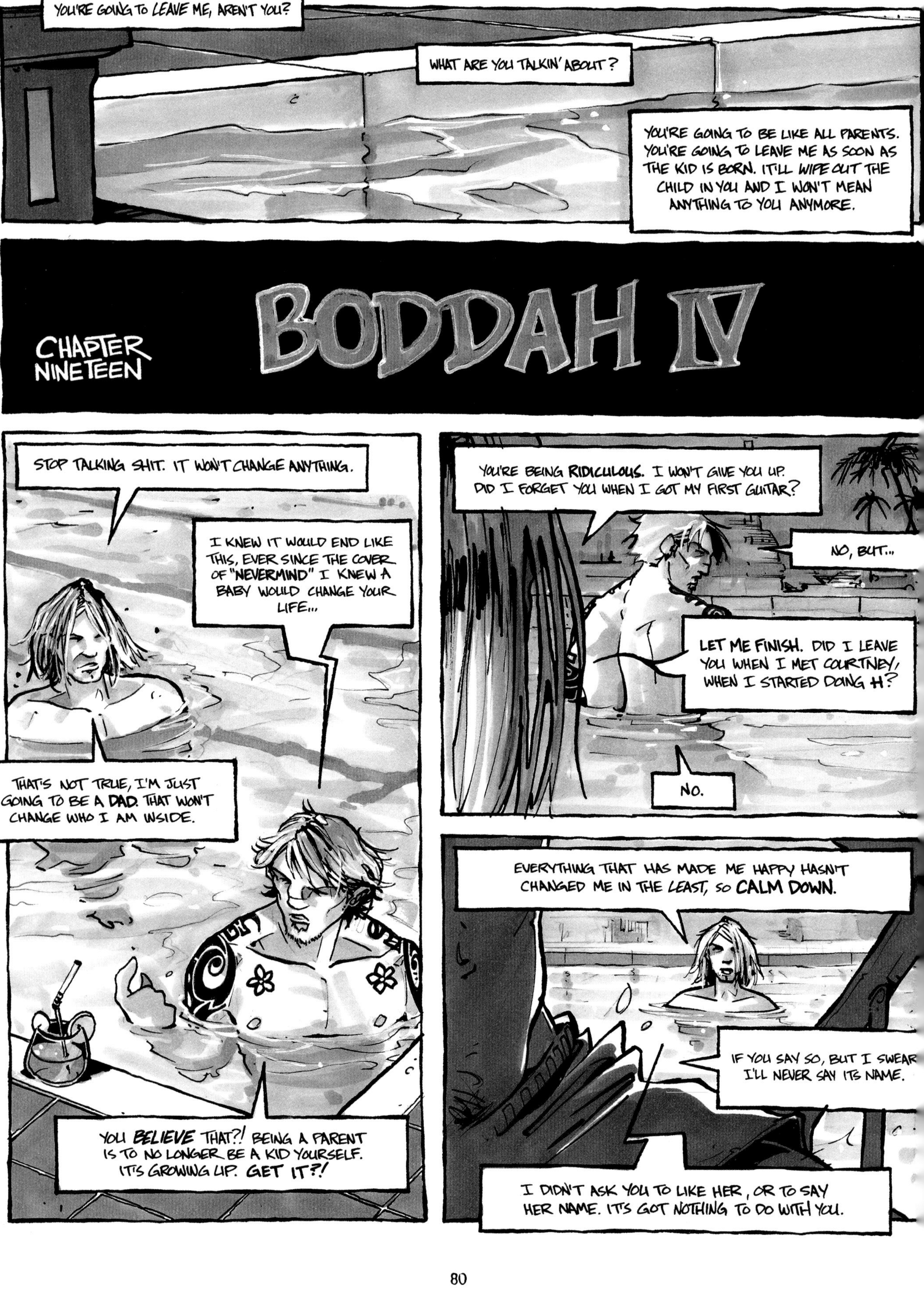
YOU'RE GOING TO LEAVE ME, AREN'T YOU?
WHAT ARE YOU TALKIN' ABOUT?
YOU'RE GOING TO BE LIKE ALL PARENTS. YOU'RE GOING TO LEAVE ME AS SOON AS THE KID IS BORN. IT'LL WIFE OUT THE CHILD IN YOU AND I WON'T MEAN ANYTHING TO YOU ANYMORE.
CHAPTER NINETEEN
BODDAH IV
STOP TALKING SHIT. IT WON'T CHANGE ANYTHING.
I KNEW IT WOULD END LIKE THIS, EVER SINCE THE COVER OF "NEVERMIND" I KNEW A BABY WOULD CHANGE YOUR LIFE...
THAT'S NOT TRUE, I'M JUST GOING TO BE A DAD. THAT WON'T CHANGE WHO I AM INSIDE.
YOU BELIEVE THAT?! BEING A PARENT IS TO NO LONGER BE A KID YOURSELF. IT'S GROWING UP. GET IT?!
YOU'RE BEING RIDICULOUS. I WON'T GIVE YOU UP. DID I FORGET YOU WHEN I GOT MY FIRST GUITAR?
NO, BUT...
LET ME FINISH. DID I LEAVE YOU WHEN I MET COURTNEY, WHEN I STARTED DOING H?
NO.
EVERYTHING THAT HAS MADE ME HAPPY HASN'T CHANGED ME IN THE LEAST, SO CALM DOWN.
IF YOU SAY SO, BUT I SWEAR I'LL NEVER SAY ITS NAME.
I DIDN'T ASK YOU TO LIKE HER, OR TO SAY HER NAME. IT'S GOT NOTHING TO DO WITH YOU.

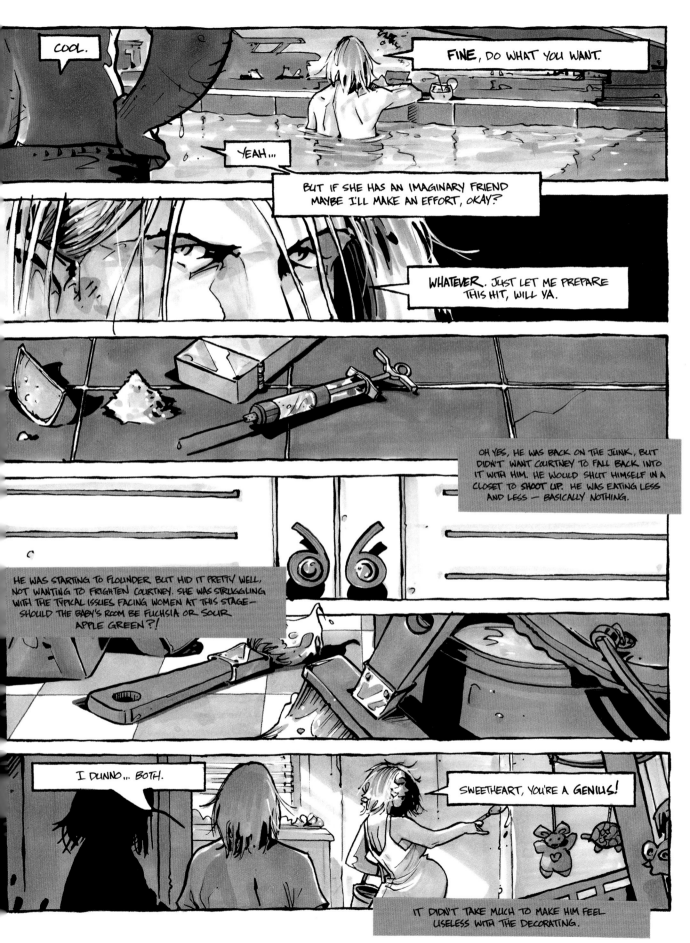

COOL.

FINE, DO WHAT YOU WANT.

YEAH...

BUT IF SHE HAS AN IMAGINARY FRIEND MAYBE I'LL MAKE AN EFFORT, OKAY?

WHATEVER. JUST LET ME PREPARE THIS HIT, WILL YA.

OH YES, HE WAS BACK ON THE JUNK, BUT DIDN'T WANT COURTNEY TO FALL BACK INTO IT WITH HIM. HE WOULD SHUT HIMSELF IN A CLOSET TO SHOOT UP. HE WAS EATING LESS AND LESS — BASICALLY NOTHING.

HE WAS STARTING TO FLOUNDER BUT HID IT PRETTY WELL, NOT WANTING TO FRIGHTEN COURTNEY. SHE WAS STRUGGLING WITH THE TYPICAL ISSUES FACING WOMEN AT THIS STAGE— SHOULD THE BABY'S ROOM BE FUCHSIA OR SOUR APPLE GREEN?!

I DUNNO... BOTH.

SWEETHEART, YOU'RE A GENIUS!

IT DIDN'T TAKE MUCH TO MAKE HIM FEEL USELESS WITH THE DECORATING.

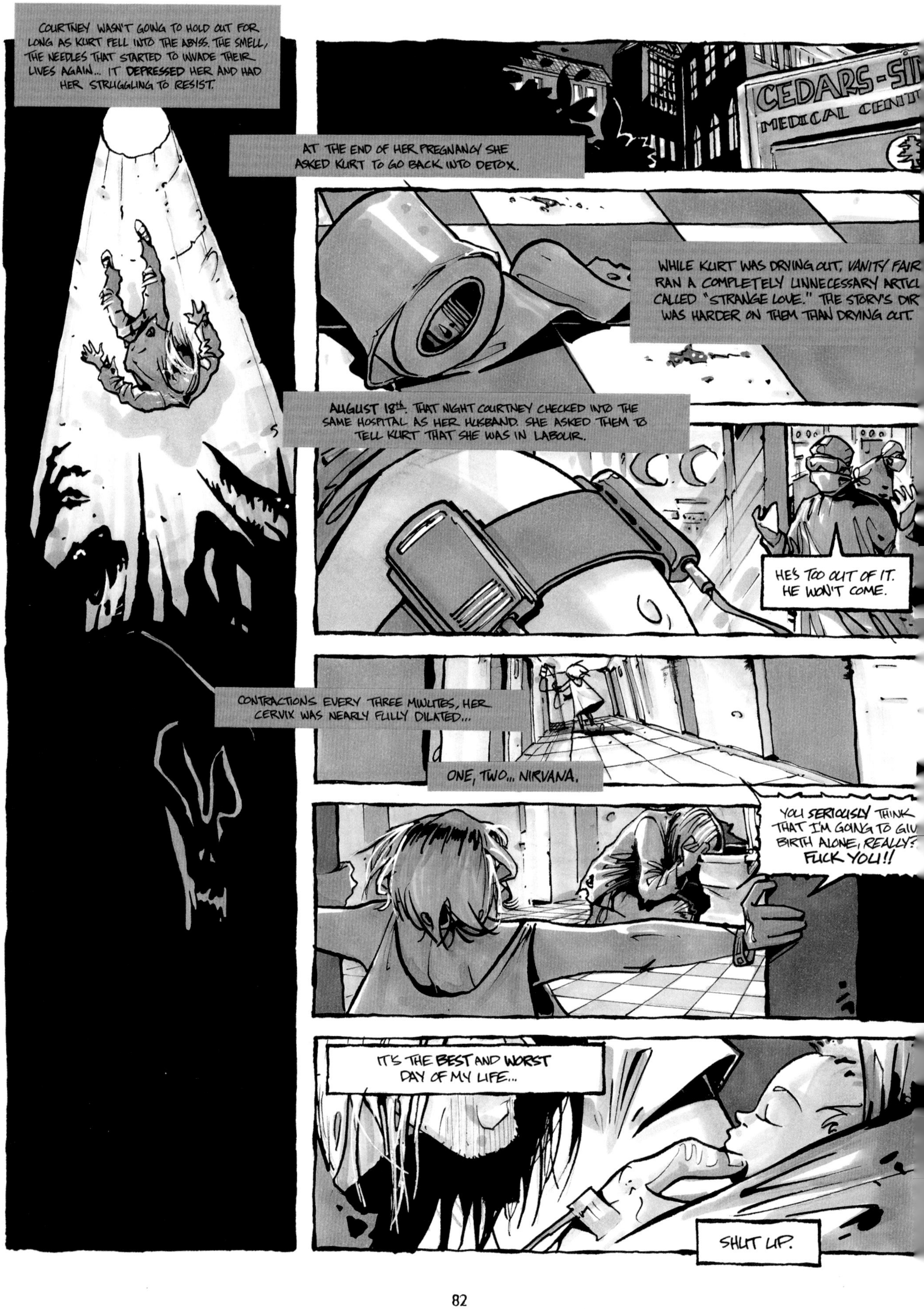

COURTNEY WASN'T GOING TO HOLD OUT FOR LONG AS KURT FELL INTO THE ABYSS. THE SMELL, THE NEEDLES THAT STARTED TO INVADE THEIR LIVES AGAIN... IT DEPRESSED HER AND HAD HER STRUGGLING TO RESIST.
CEDARS-SI
MEDICAL CENT
AT THE END OF HER PREGNANCY SHE ASKED KURT TO GO BACK INTO DETOX.
WHILE KURT WAS DRYING OUT, VANITY FAIR RAN A COMPLETELY UNNECESSARY ARTICL CALLED "STRANGE LOVE." THE STORY'S DIR WAS HARDER ON THEM THAN DRYING OUT.
AUGUST 18TH. THAT NIGHT COURTNEY CHECKED INTO THE SAME HOSPITAL AS HER HUSBAND. SHE ASKED THEM TO TELL KURT THAT SHE WAS IN LABOUR.
HE'S TOO OUT OF IT. HE WON'T COME.
CONTRACTIONS EVERY THREE MINUTES, HER CERVIX WAS NEARLY FULLY DILATED...
ONE, TWO... NIRVANA.
YOU SERIOUSLY THINK THAT I'M GOING TO GIV BIRTH ALONE, REALLY? FUCK YOU!!
IT'S THE BEST AND WORST DAY OF MY LIFE...
SHUT UP.

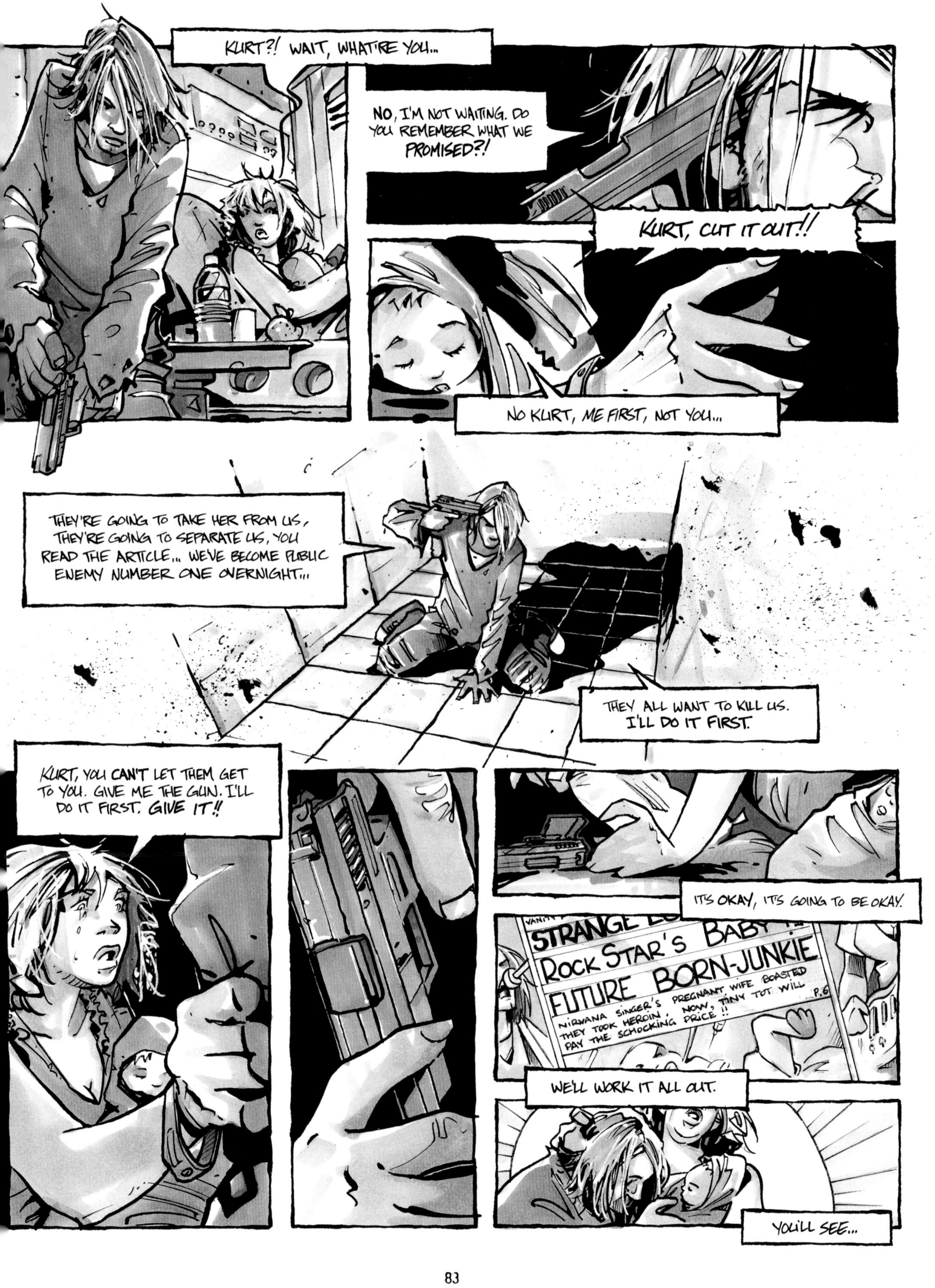
KURT?! WAIT, WHAT'RE YOU...
NO, I'M NOT WAITING. DO YOU REMEMBER WHAT WE PROMISED?!
KURT, CUT IT OUT!!
NO KURT, ME FIRST, NOT YOU...
THEY'RE GOING TO TAKE HER FROM US, THEY'RE GOING TO SEPARATE US, YOU READ THE ARTICLE... WE'VE BECOME PUBLIC ENEMY NUMBER ONE OVERNIGHT...
THEY ALL WANT TO KILL US. I'LL DO IT FIRST.
KURT, YOU CAN'T LET THEM GET TO YOU. GIVE ME THE GUN. I'LL DO IT FIRST. GIVE IT!!
IT'S OKAY, IT'S GOING TO BE OKAY.
STRANGE
ROCK STAR'S BABY
FUTURE BORN-JUNKIE
NIRVANA SINGER'S PREGNANT WIFE BOASTED THEY TOOK HEROIN, NOW, TINY TOT WILL PAY THE SCHOCKING PRICE !!
P. 6
WE'LL WORK IT ALL OUT.
YOU'LL SEE...

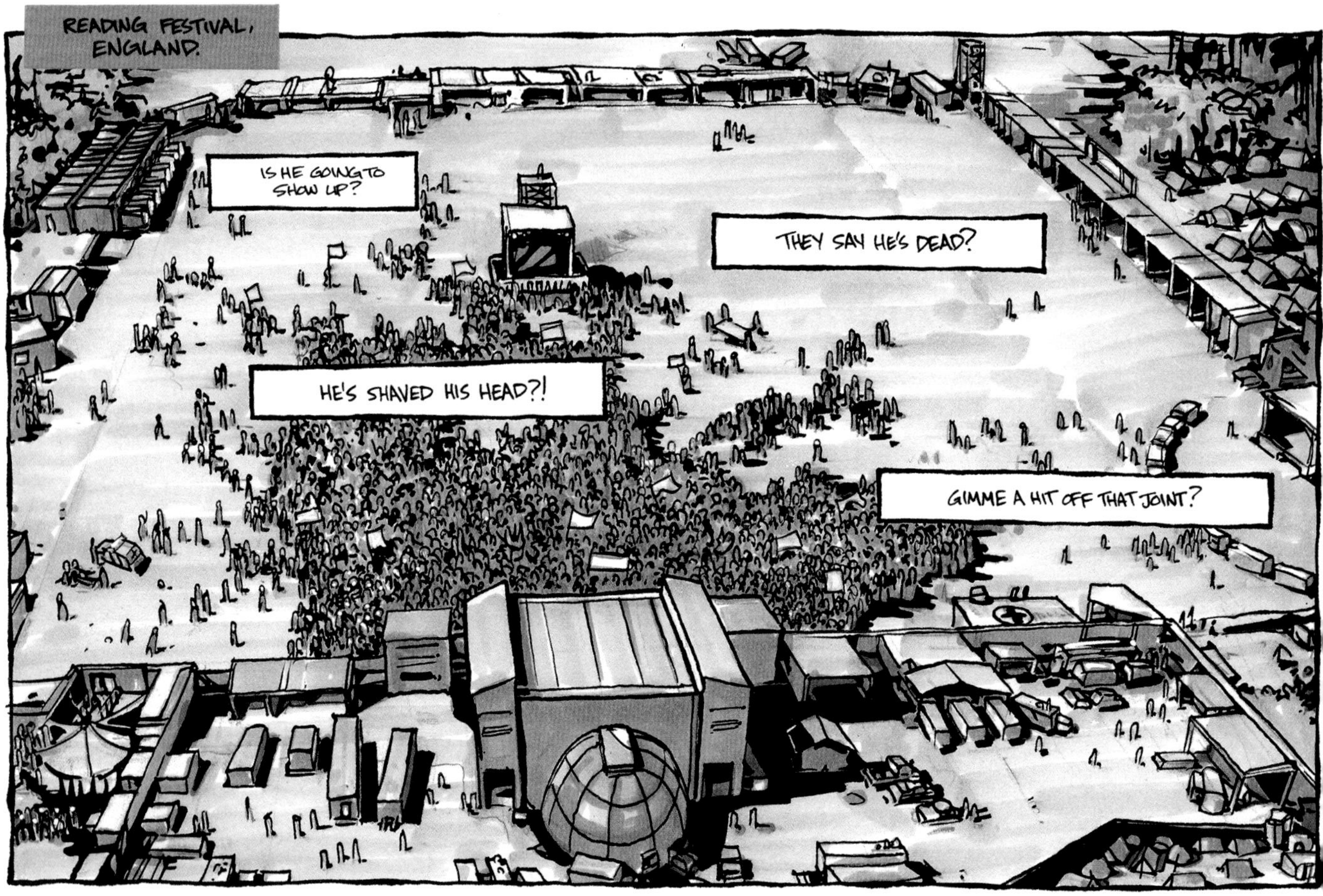
READING FESTIVAL, ENGLAND.
IS HE GOING TO SHOW UP?
THEY SAY HE'S DEAD?
HE'S SHAVED HIS HEAD?!
GIMME A HIT OFF THAT JOINT?

CHAPTER TWENTY READING SHIT

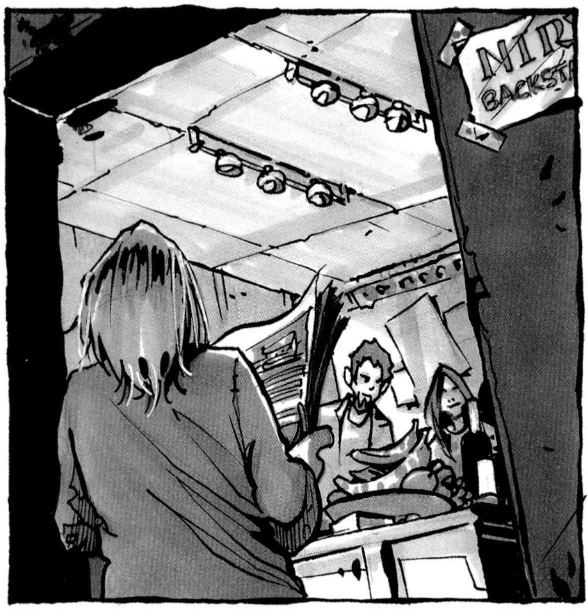

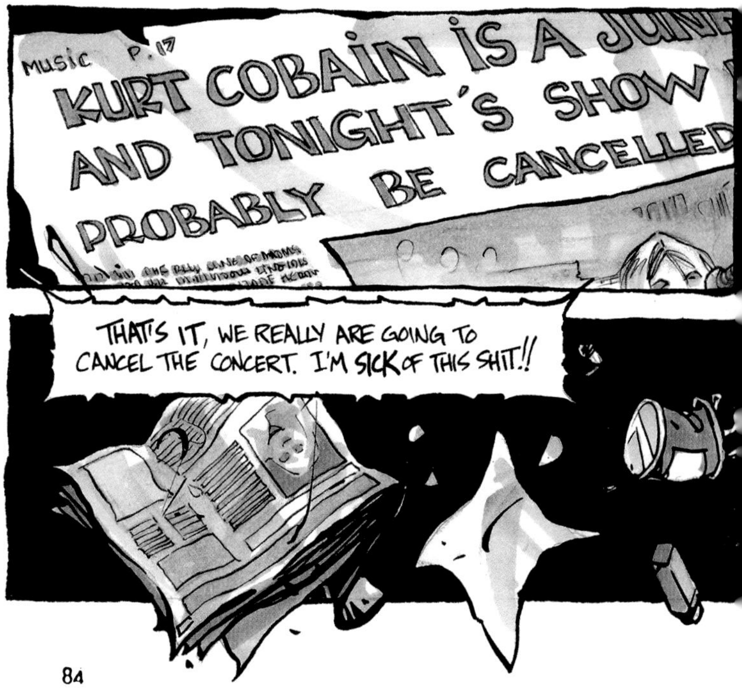
MUSIC P. 17
KURT COBAIN IS A
AND TONIGHT'S SHOW
PROBABLY BE CANCELLED
THAT'S IT, WE REALLY ARE GOING TO CANCEL THE CONCERT. I'M SICK OF THIS SHIT!!

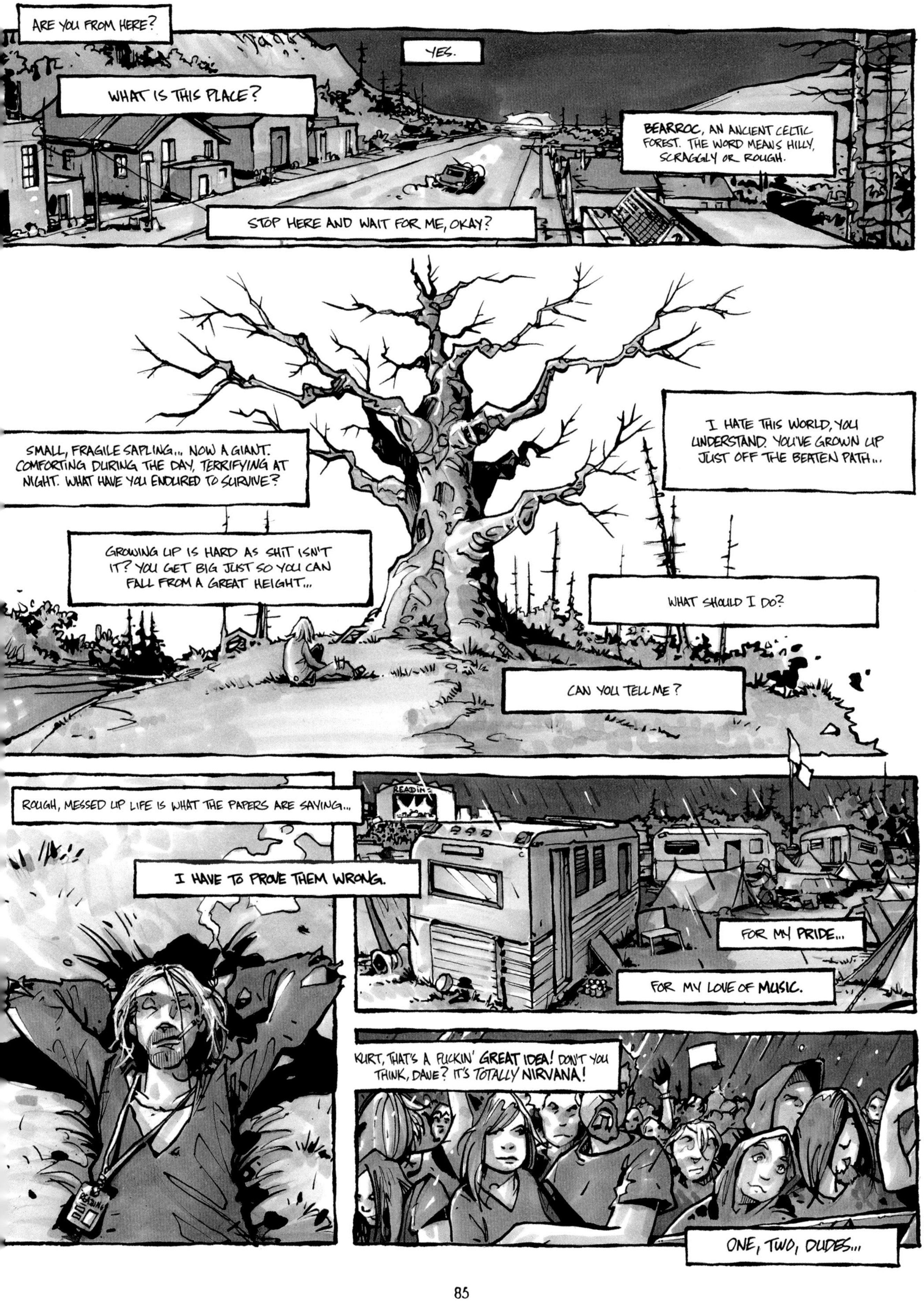
ARE YOU FROM HERE?
YES.
WHAT IS THIS PLACE?
BEARROC, AN ANCIENT CELTIC FOREST. THE WORD MEANS HILLY, SCRAGGLY OR ROUGH.
STOP HERE AND WAIT FOR ME, OKAY?
SMALL, FRAGILE SAPLING... NOW A GIANT. COMFORTING DURING THE DAY, TERRIFYING AT NIGHT. WHAT HAVE YOU ENDURED TO SURVIVE?
GROWING UP IS HARD AS SHIT ISN'T IT? YOU GET BIG JUST SO YOU CAN FALL FROM A GREAT HEIGHT...
I HATE THIS WORLD, YOU UNDERSTAND. YOU'VE GROWN UP JUST OFF THE BEATEN PATH...
WHAT SHOULD I DO?
CAN YOU TELL ME?
ROUGH, MESSED UP LIFE IS WHAT THE PAPERS ARE SAYING...
I HAVE TO PROVE THEM WRONG.
READING
FOR MY PRIDE...
FOR MY LOVE OF MUSIC.
KURT, THAT'S A FUCKIN' GREAT IDEA! DON'T YOU THINK, DAVE? IT'S TOTALLY NIRVANA!
ONE, TWO, DUDES...

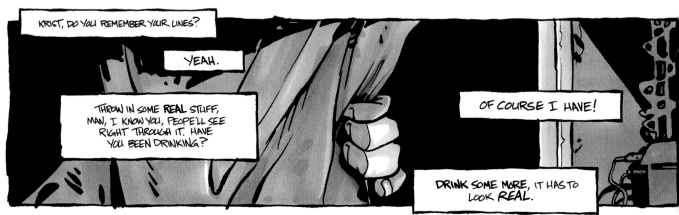

KRIST, DO YOU REMEMBER YOUR LINES?

YEAH.

THROW IN SOME **REAL** STUFF, MAN, I KNOW YOU, PEOPLE'LL SEE RIGHT THROUGH IT. HAVE YOU BEEN DRINKING?

OF COURSE I HAVE!

DRINK SOME MORE, IT HAS TO LOOK **REAL**.

IT'S SO... I CAN SEE... THIS. IT'S TOO **PAINFUL**. THIS IS TOO **PAINFUL**. YOU'RE GONNA MAKE IT MAN! YOU'RE GONNA MAKE IT.

I HAVE TO PROVE THEM WRONG.

WITH THE SUPPORT OF HIS FRIENDS AND FAMILY, HE'S GONNA MAKE IT....

IS IT HIM?!

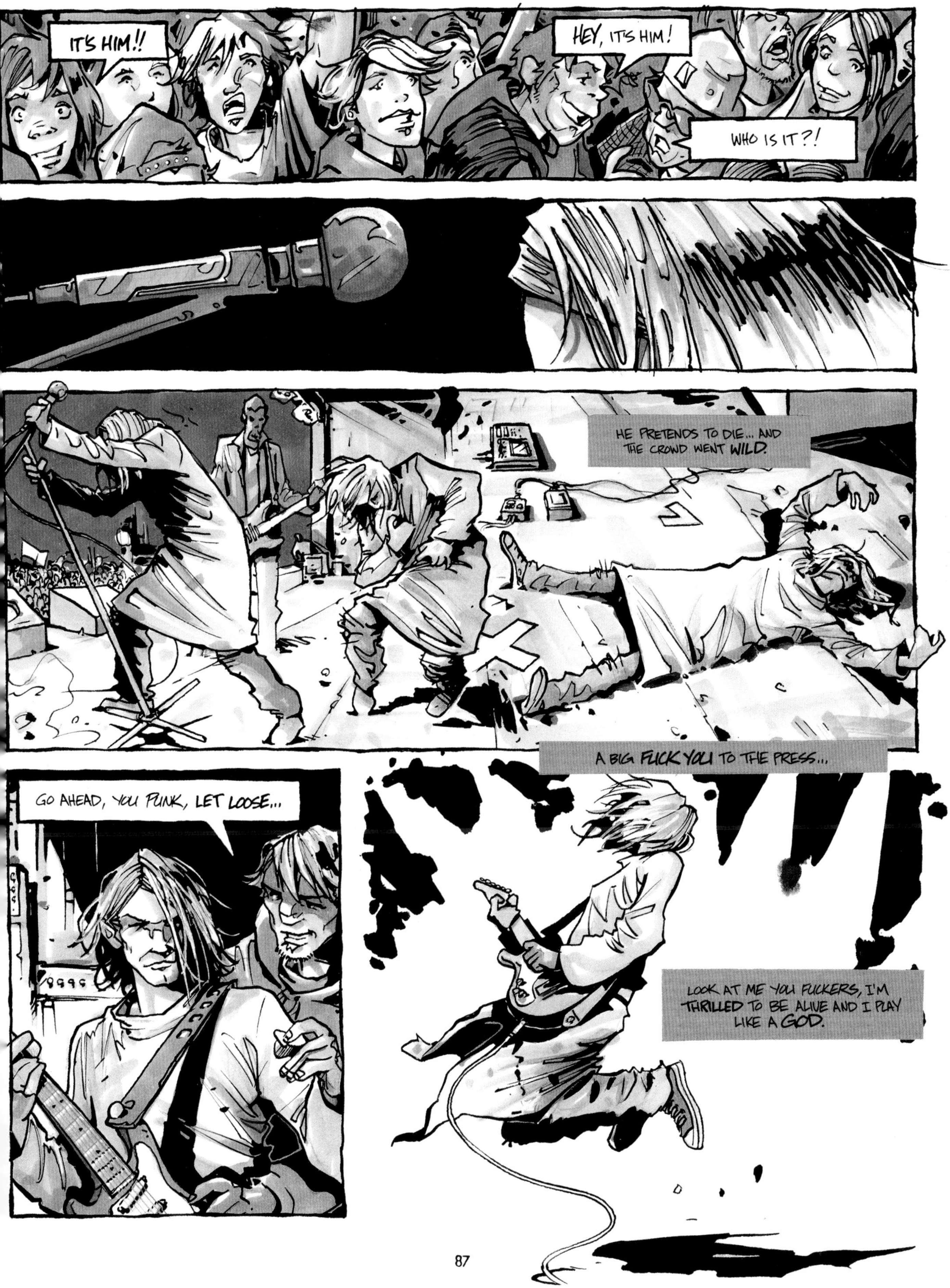
IT'S HIM!!
HEY, IT'S HIM!
WHO IS IT?!
HE PRETENDS TO DIE... AND THE CROWD WENT WILD.
A BIG FUCK YOU TO THE PRESS...
GO AHEAD, YOU PUNK, LET LOOSE...
LOOK AT ME YOU FUCKERS, I'M THRILLED TO BE ALIVE AND I PLAY LIKE A GOD.

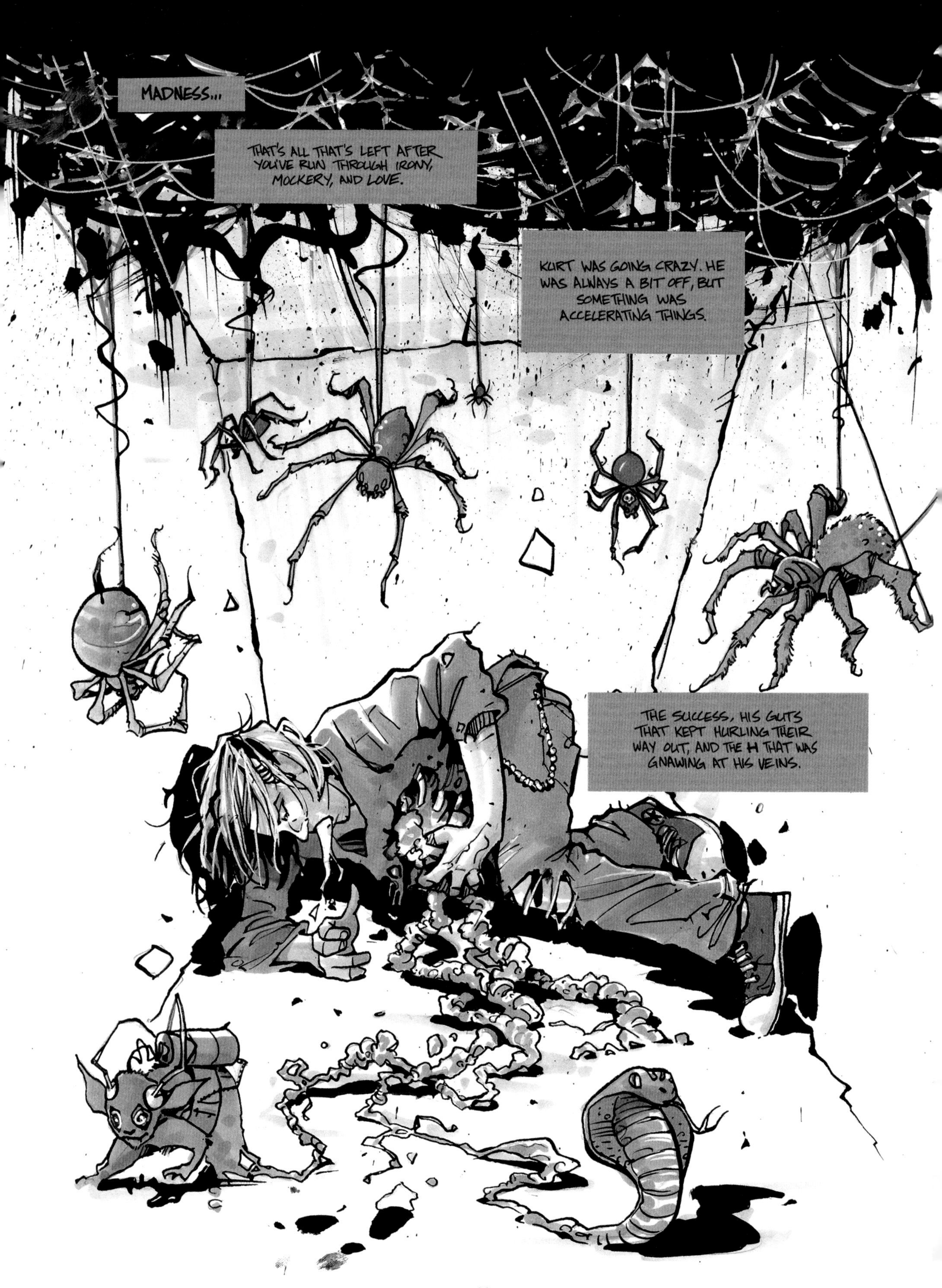
MADNESS...
THAT'S ALL THAT'S LEFT AFTER YOU'VE RUN THROUGH IRONY, MOCKERY, AND LOVE.
KURT WAS GOING CRAZY. HE WAS ALWAYS A BIT OFF, BUT SOMETHING WAS ACCELERATING THINGS.
THE SUCCESS, HIS GUTS THAT KEPT HURLING THEIR WAY OUT, AND THE H THAT WAS GNAWING AT HIS VEINS.

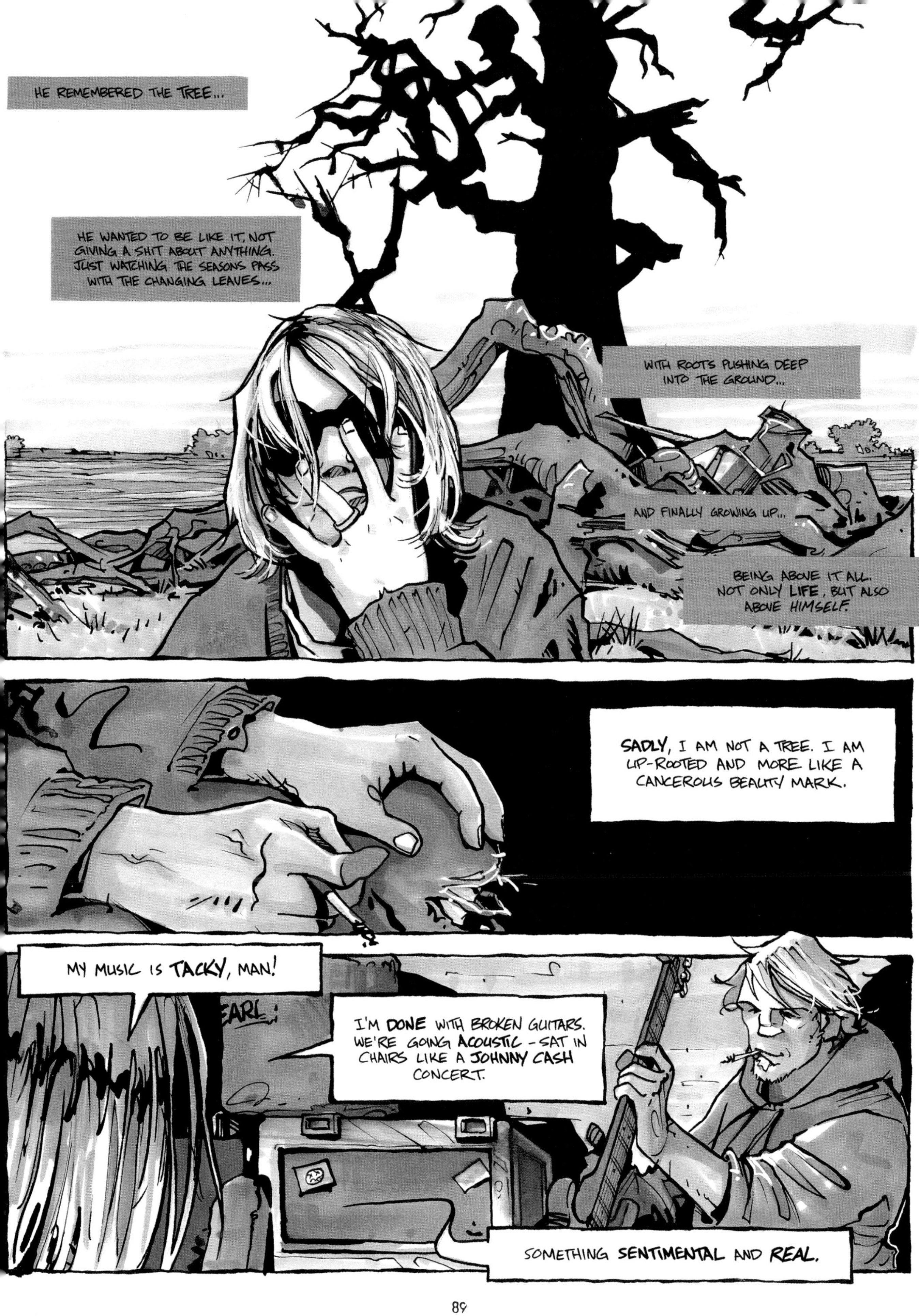
HE REMEMBERED THE TREE...
HE WANTED TO BE LIKE IT, NOT GIVING A SHIT ABOUT ANYTHING. JUST WATCHING THE SEASONS PASS WITH THE CHANGING LEAVES...
WITH ROOTS PUSHING DEEP INTO THE GROUND...
AND FINALLY GROWING UP...
BEING ABOVE IT ALL. NOT ONLY LIFE, BUT ALSO ABOVE HIMSELF.
SADLY, I AM NOT A TREE. I AM UP-ROOTED AND MORE LIKE A CANCEROUS BEAUTY MARK.
MY MUSIC IS TACKY, MAN!
I'M DONE WITH BROKEN GUITARS. WE'RE GOING ACOUSTIC - SAT IN CHAIRS LIKE A JOHNNY CASH CONCERT.
SOMETHING SENTIMENTAL AND REAL.

"HELLO, MY HUSBAND'S LOCKED HIMSELF IN THE BATHROOM WITH HIS GUNS. **PLEASE** COME, HE'S THREATENING TO COMMIT **SUICIDE.**"

CHAPTER TWENTY ONE
911

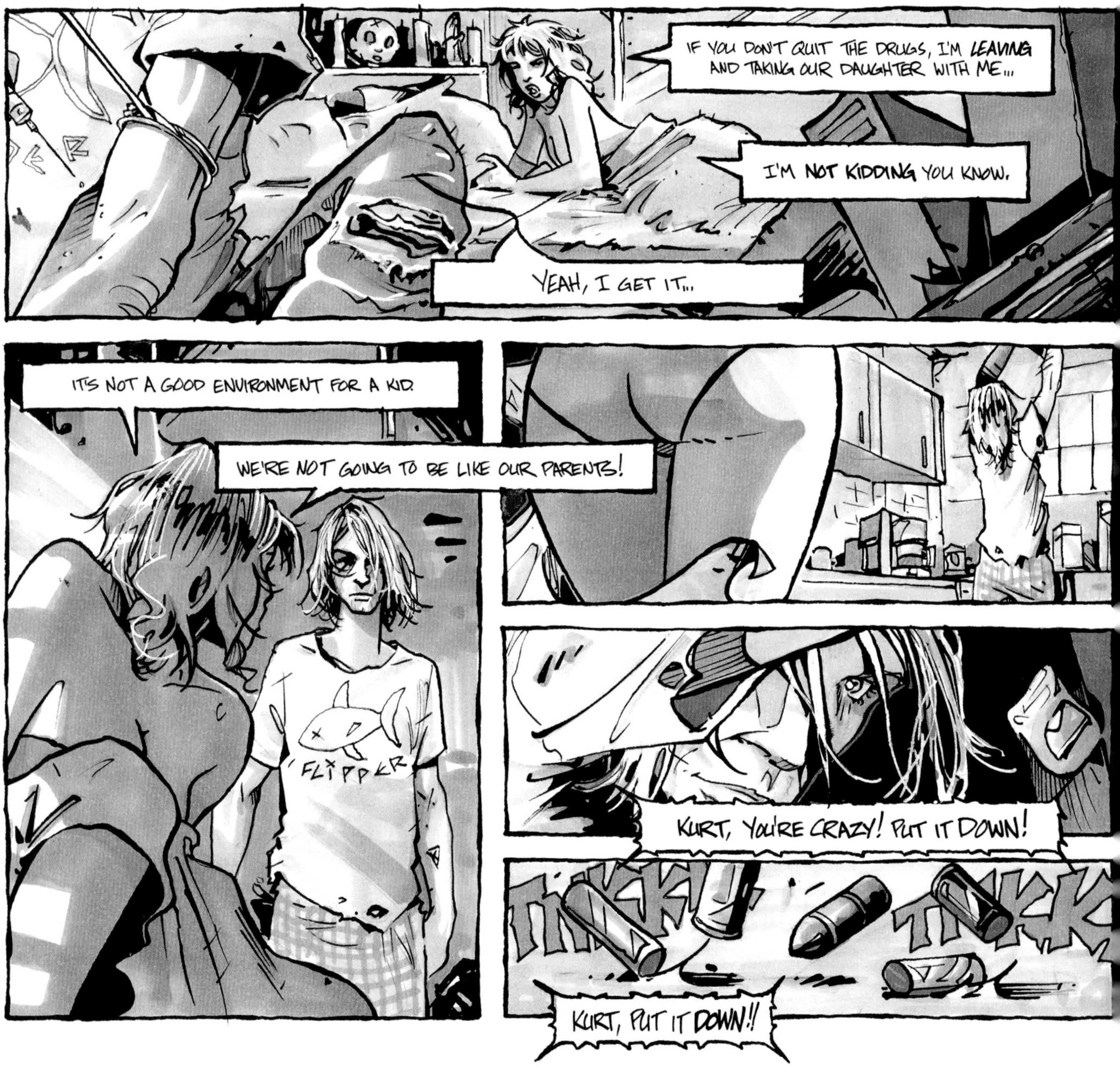

IF YOU DON'T QUIT THE DRUGS, I'M LEAVING AND TAKING OUR DAUGHTER WITH ME...
I'M NOT KIDDING YOU KNOW.
YEAH, I GET IT...
IT'S NOT A GOOD ENVIRONMENT FOR A KID.
WE'RE NOT GOING TO BE LIKE OUR PARENTS!
FLIPPER
KURT, YOU'RE CRAZY! PUT IT DOWN!
TIKK!
TIKK
KURT, PUT IT DOWN!!

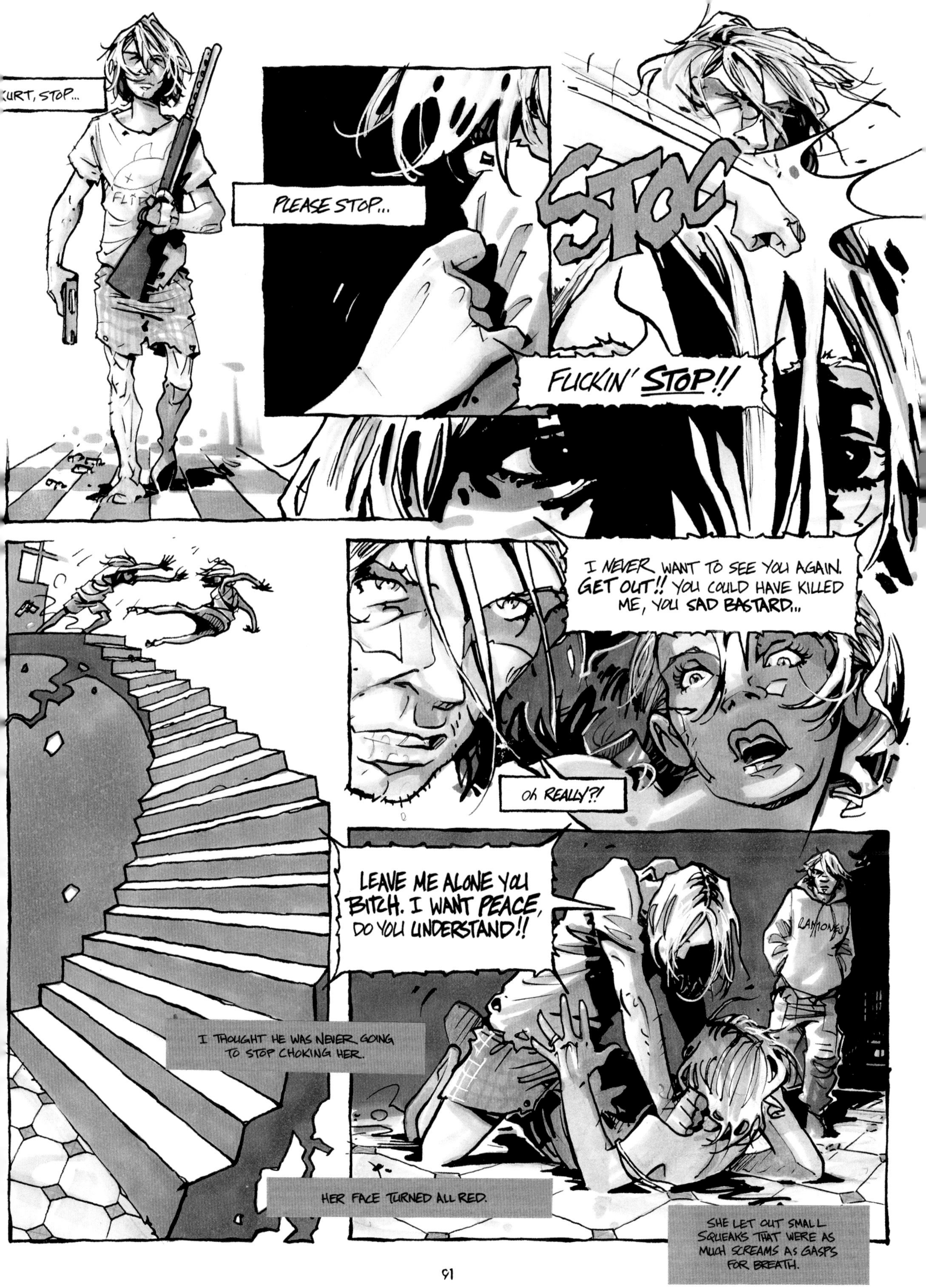
KURT, STOP...
PLEASE STOP...
STOC
FUCKIN' STOP!!
I NEVER WANT TO SEE YOU AGAIN. GET OUT!! YOU COULD HAVE KILLED ME, YOU SAD BASTARD...
Oh REALLY?!
LEAVE ME ALONE YOU BITCH. I WANT PEACE, DO YOU UNDERSTAND!!
I THOUGHT HE WAS NEVER GOING TO STOP CHOKING HER.
HER FACE TURNED ALL RED.
SHE LET OUT SMALL SQUEAKS THAT WERE AS MUCH SCREAMS AS GASPS FOR BREATH.

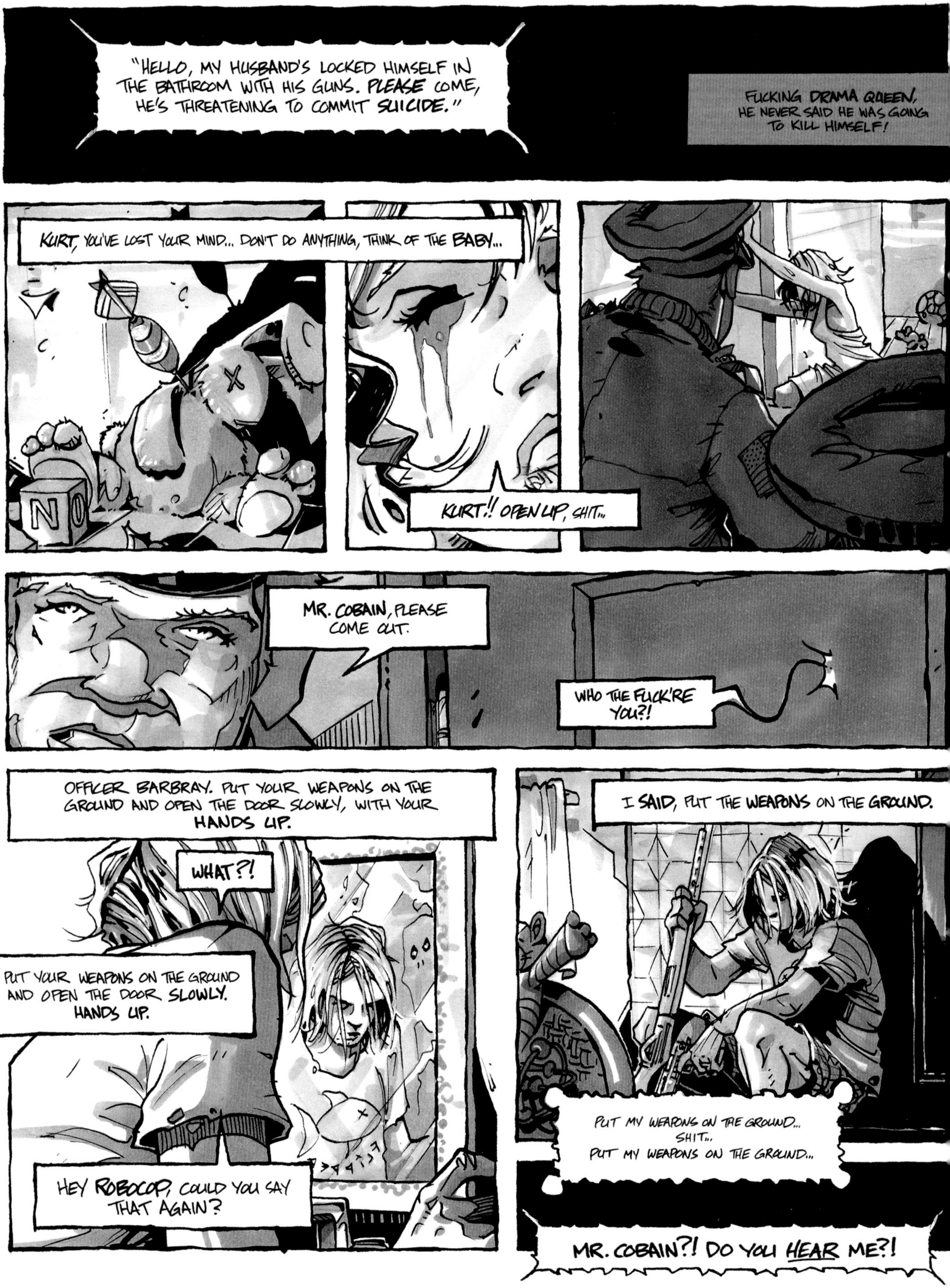

"HELLO, MY HUSBAND'S LOCKED HIMSELF IN THE BATHROOM WITH HIS GUNS. PLEASE COME, HE'S THREATENING TO COMMIT SUICIDE."
FUCKING DRAMA QUEEN, HE NEVER SAID HE WAS GOING TO KILL HIMSELF!
KURT, YOU'VE LOST YOUR MIND... DON'T DO ANYTHING, THINK OF THE BABY...
NO
KURT!! OPEN UP, SHIT...
MR. COBAIN, PLEASE COME OUT.
WHO THE FUCK'RE YOU?!
OFFICER BARBRAY. PUT YOUR WEAPONS ON THE GROUND AND OPEN THE DOOR SLOWLY, WITH YOUR HANDS UP.
WHAT?!
PUT YOUR WEAPONS ON THE GROUND AND OPEN THE DOOR SLOWLY. HANDS UP.
HEY ROBOCOP, COULD YOU SAY THAT AGAIN?
I SAID, PUT THE WEAPONS ON THE GROUND.
PUT MY WEAPONS ON THE GROUND... SHIT... PUT MY WEAPONS ON THE GROUND...
MR. COBAIN?! DO YOU HEAR ME?!

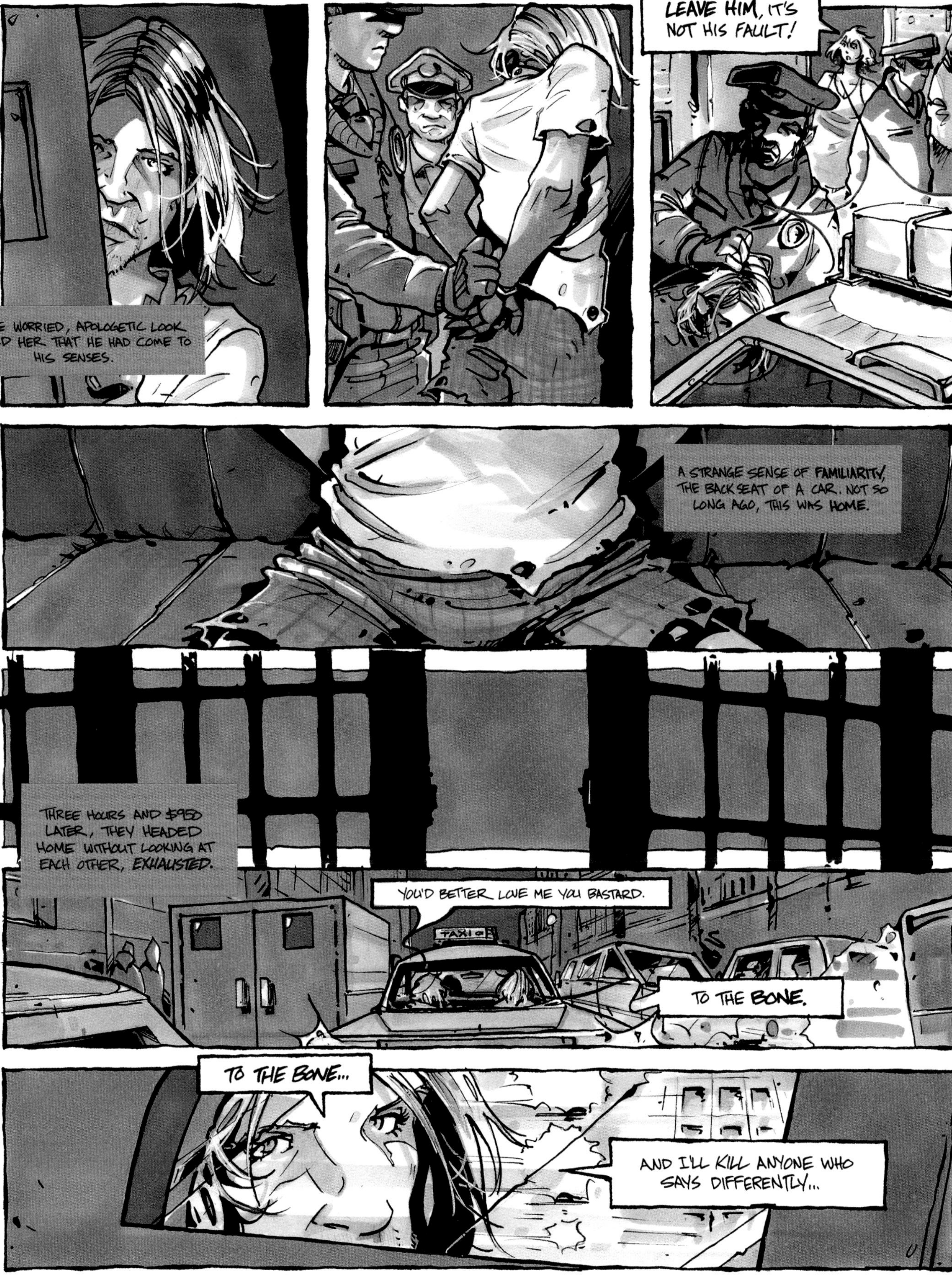
THE WORRIED, APOLOGETIC LOOK TOLD HER THAT HE HAD COME TO HIS SENSES.
LEAVE HIM, IT'S NOT HIS FAULT!
A STRANGE SENSE OF FAMILIARITY, THE BACK SEAT OF A CAR. NOT SO LONG AGO, THIS WAS HOME.
THREE HOURS AND $950 LATER, THEY HEADED HOME WITHOUT LOOKING AT EACH OTHER, EXHAUSTED.
YOU'D BETTER LOVE ME YOU BASTARD.
TAXI
TO THE BONE.
TO THE BONE...
AND I'LL KILL ANYONE WHO SAYS DIFFERENTLY...

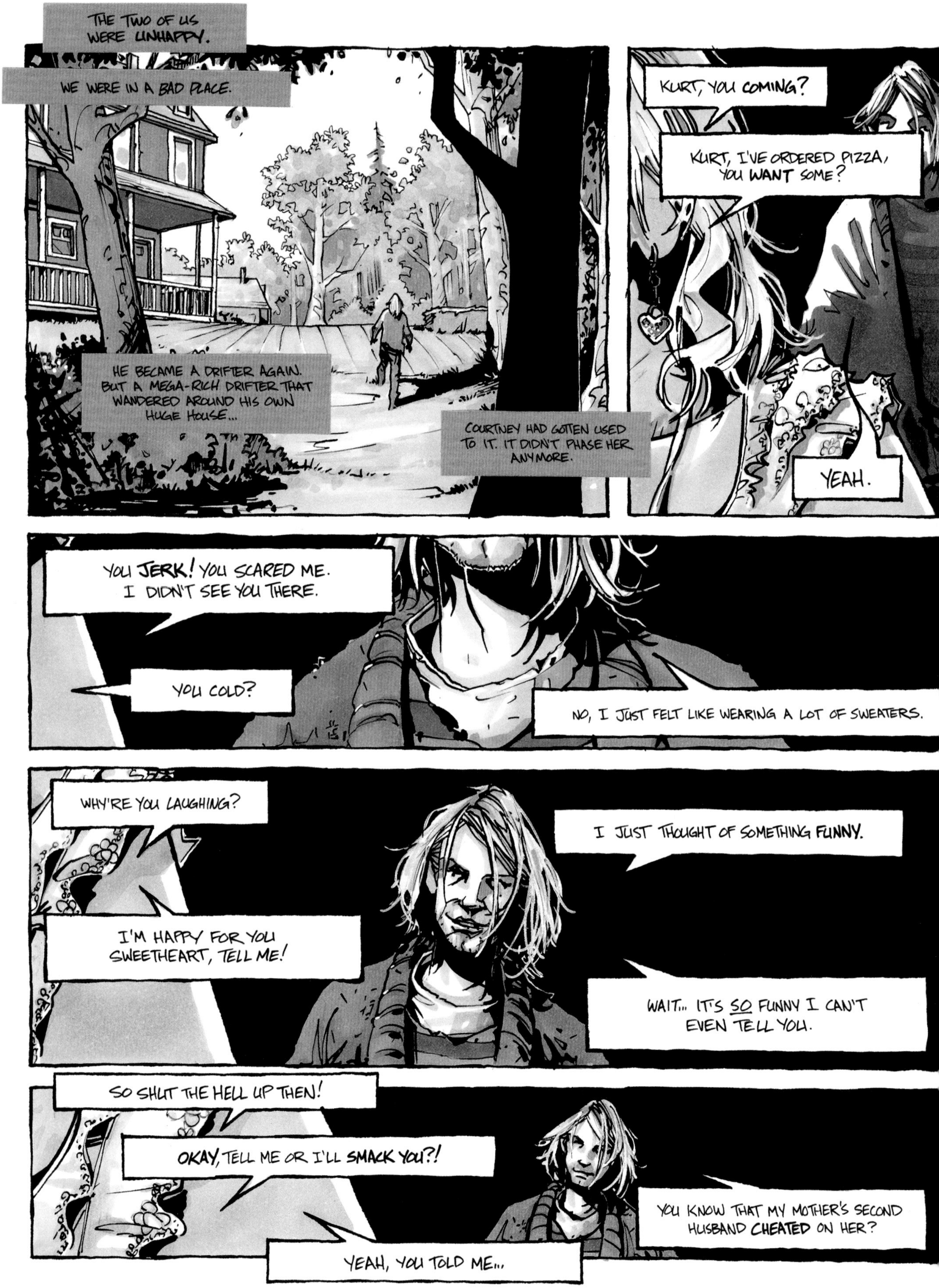

THE TWO OF US WERE UNHAPPY.
WE WERE IN A BAD PLACE.
HE BECAME A DRIFTER AGAIN. BUT A MEGA-RICH DRIFTER THAT WANDERED AROUND HIS OWN HUGE HOUSE...
COURTNEY HAD GOTTEN USED TO IT. IT DIDN'T PHASE HER ANYMORE.
KURT, YOU COMING?
KURT, I'VE ORDERED PIZZA, YOU WANT SOME?
YEAH.
YOU JERK! YOU SCARED ME. I DIDN'T SEE YOU THERE.
YOU COLD?
NO, I JUST FELT LIKE WEARING A LOT OF SWEATERS.
WHY'RE YOU LAUGHING?
I JUST THOUGHT OF SOMETHING FUNNY.
I'M HAPPY FOR YOU SWEETHEART, TELL ME!
WAIT... IT'S SO FUNNY I CAN'T EVEN TELL YOU.
SO SHUT THE HELL UP THEN!
OKAY, TELL ME OR I'LL SMACK YOU?!
YOU KNOW THAT MY MOTHER'S SECOND HUSBAND CHEATED ON HER?
YEAH, YOU TOLD ME...

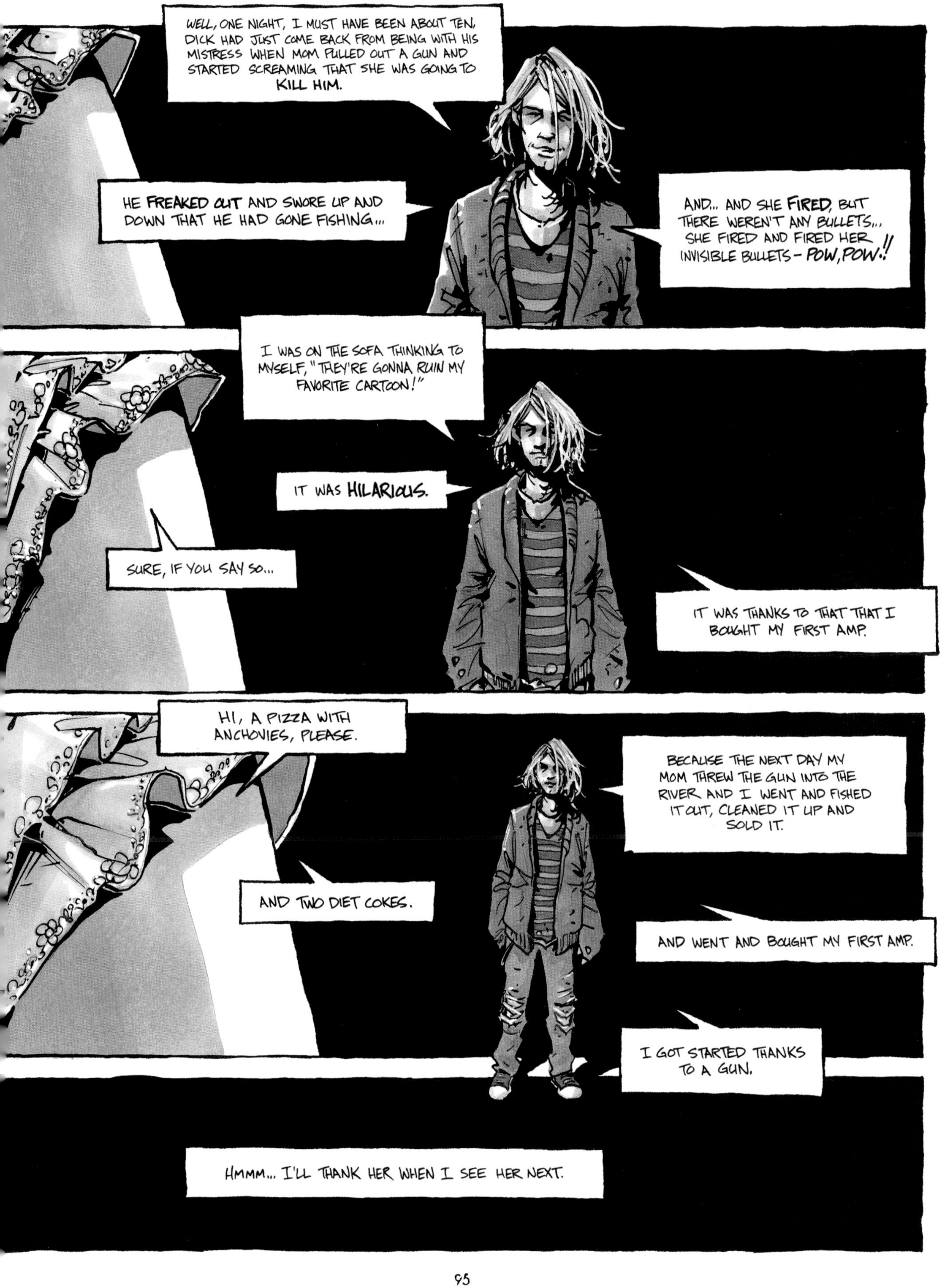
WELL, ONE NIGHT, I MUST HAVE BEEN ABOUT TEN, DICK HAD JUST COME BACK FROM BEING WITH HIS MISTRESS WHEN MOM PULLED OUT A GUN AND STARTED SCREAMING THAT SHE WAS GOING TO **KILL HIM.**
HE **FREAKED OUT** AND SWORE UP AND DOWN THAT HE HAD GONE FISHING...
AND... AND SHE **FIRED**, BUT THERE WEREN'T ANY BULLETS... SHE FIRED AND FIRED HER INVISIBLE BULLETS- **POW, POW!!**
I WAS ON THE SOFA THINKING TO MYSELF, "THEY'RE GONNA RUIN MY FAVORITE CARTOON!"
IT WAS **HILARIOUS.**
SURE, IF YOU SAY SO...
IT WAS THANKS TO THAT THAT I BOUGHT MY FIRST AMP.
HI, A PIZZA WITH ANCHOVIES, PLEASE.
BECAUSE THE NEXT DAY MY MOM THREW THE GUN INTO THE RIVER AND I WENT AND FISHED IT OUT, CLEANED IT UP AND SOLD IT.
AND TWO DIET COKES.
AND WENT AND BOUGHT MY FIRST AMP.
I GOT STARTED THANKS TO A GUN.
HMMM... I'LL THANK HER WHEN I SEE HER NEXT.

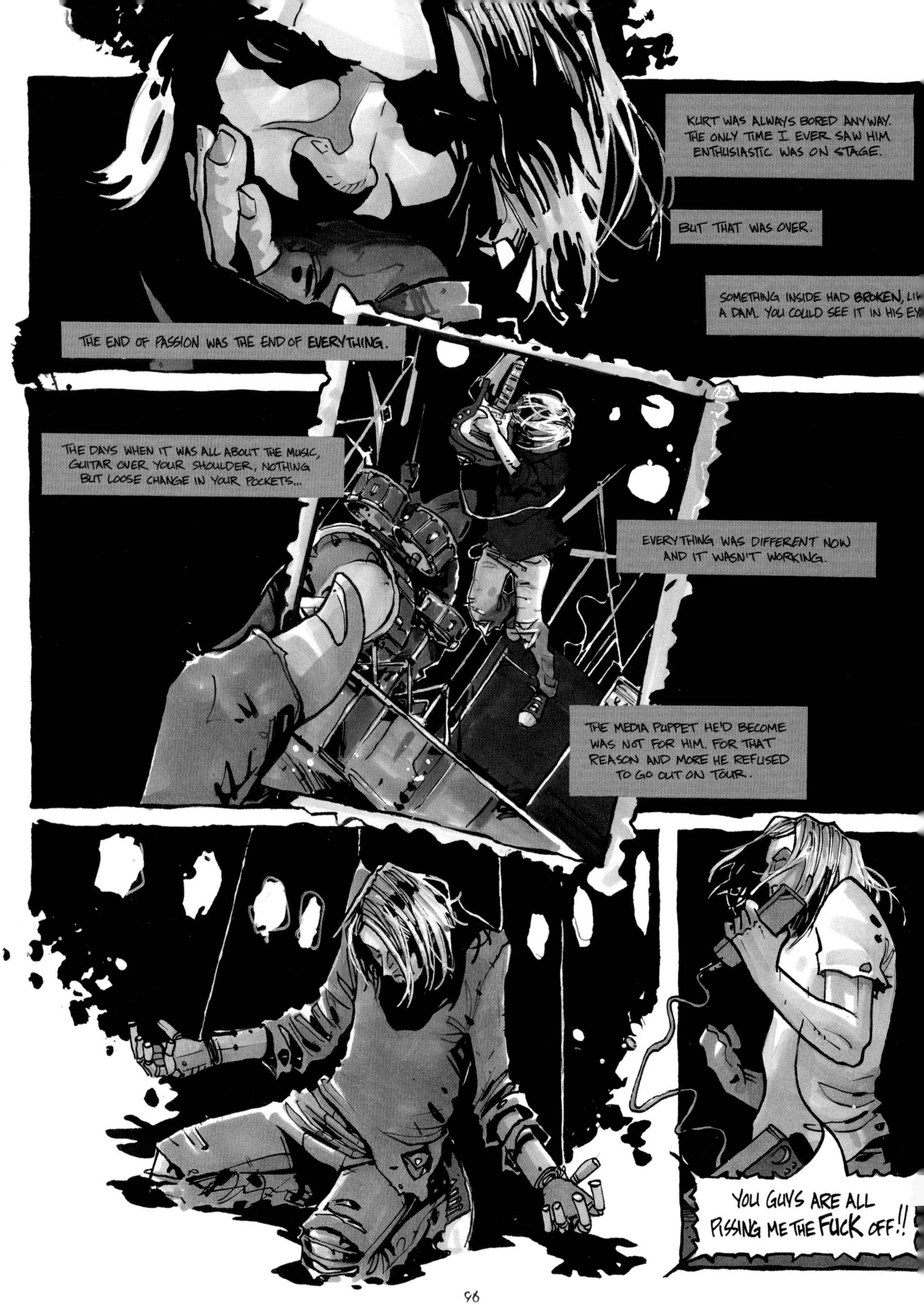
KURT WAS ALWAYS BORED ANYWAY. THE ONLY TIME I EVER SAW HIM ENTHUSIASTIC WAS ON STAGE.
BUT THAT WAS OVER.
SOMETHING INSIDE HAD BROKEN, LIK
A DAM. YOU COULD SEE IT IN HIS EY
THE END OF PASSION WAS THE END OF EVERYTHING.
THE DAYS WHEN IT WAS ALL ABOUT THE MUSIC, GUITAR OVER YOUR SHOULDER, NOTHING BUT LOOSE CHANGE IN YOUR POCKETS...
EVERYTHING WAS DIFFERENT NOW AND IT WASN'T WORKING.
THE MEDIA PUPPET HE'D BECOME WAS NOT FOR HIM. FOR THAT REASON AND MORE HE REFUSED TO GO OUT ON TOUR.
YOU GUYS ARE ALL PISSING ME THE FUCK OFF!!

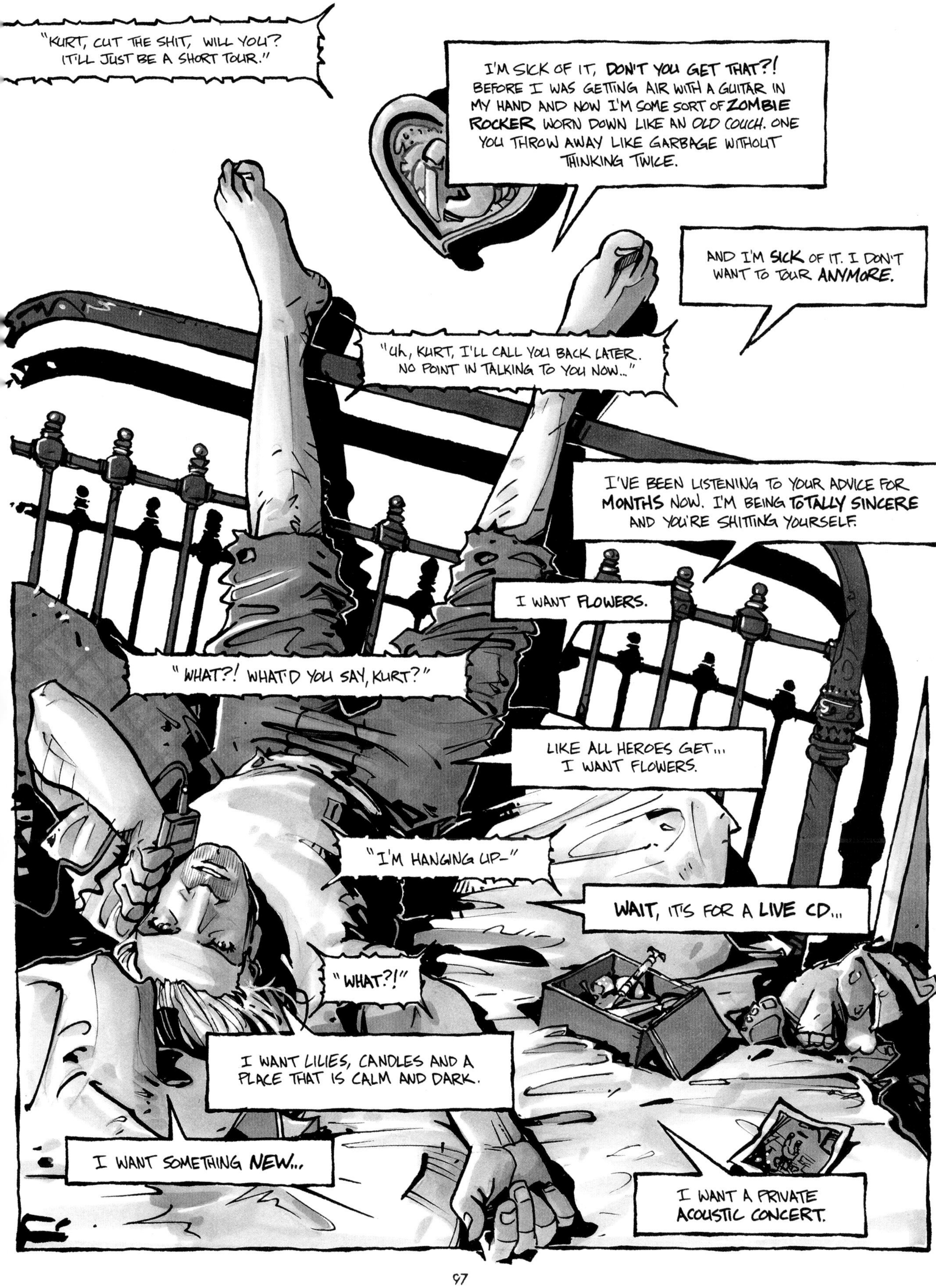
"KURT, CUT THE SHIT, WILL YOU? IT'LL JUST BE A SHORT TOUR."
I'M SICK OF IT, DON'T YOU GET THAT?! BEFORE I WAS GETTING AIR WITH A GUITAR IN MY HAND AND NOW I'M SOME SORT OF ZOMBIE ROCKER WORN DOWN LIKE AN OLD COUCH. ONE YOU THROW AWAY LIKE GARBAGE WITHOUT THINKING TWICE.
AND I'M SICK OF IT. I DON'T WANT TO TOUR ANYMORE.
"UH, KURT, I'LL CALL YOU BACK LATER. NO POINT IN TALKING TO YOU NOW..."
I'VE BEEN LISTENING TO YOUR ADVICE FOR MONTHS NOW. I'M BEING TOTALLY SINCERE AND YOU'RE SHITTING YOURSELF.
I WANT FLOWERS.
"WHAT?! WHAT'D YOU SAY, KURT?"
LIKE ALL HEROES GET... I WANT FLOWERS.
"I'M HANGING UP-"
WAIT, IT'S FOR A LIVE CD...
"WHAT?!"
I WANT LILIES, CANDLES AND A PLACE THAT IS CALM AND DARK.
I WANT SOMETHING NEW...
I WANT A PRIVATE ACOUSTIC CONCERT.

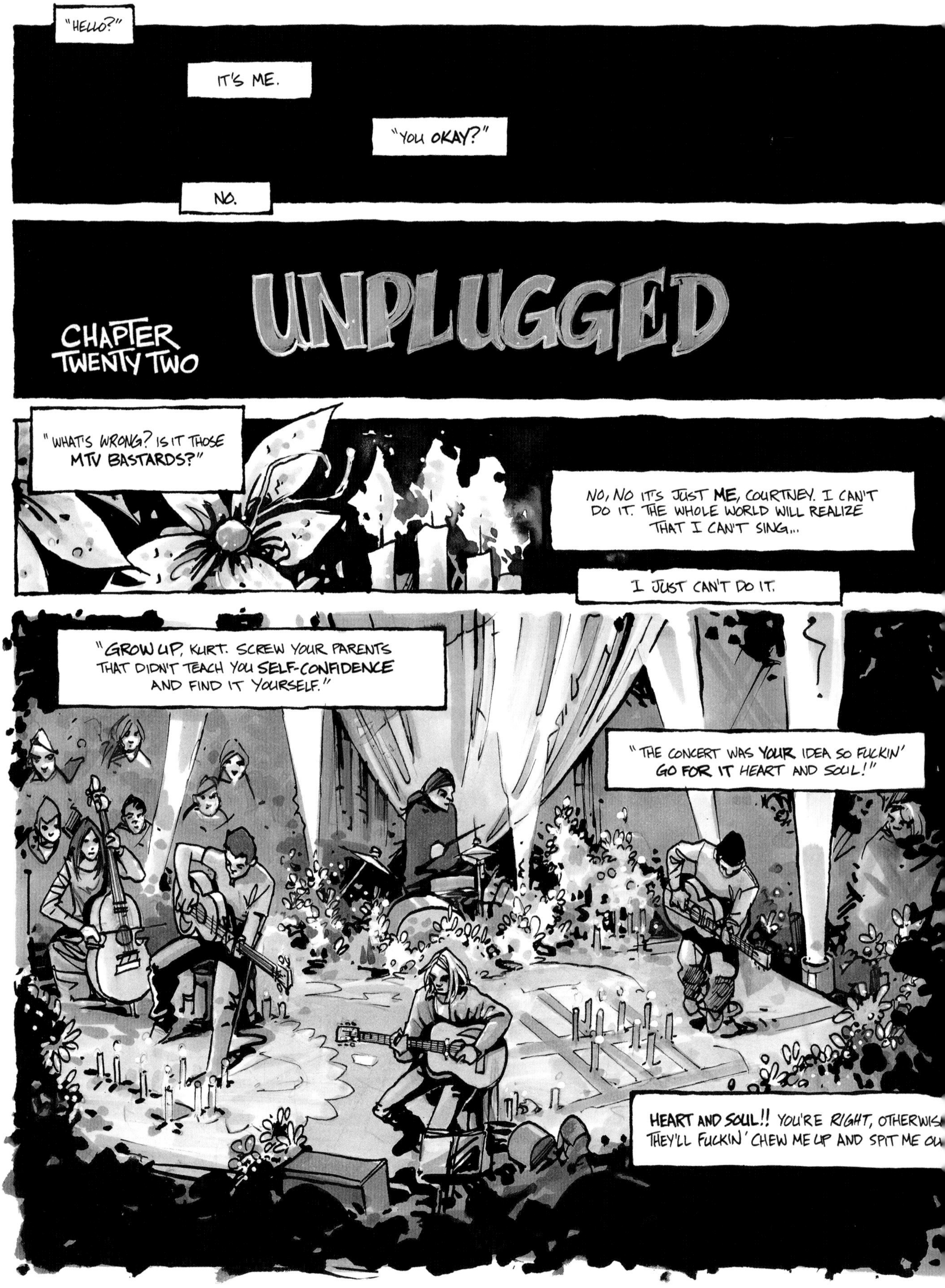
"HELLO?"
IT'S ME.
"YOU OKAY?"
NO.
CHAPTER TWENTY TWO
UNPLUGGED
"WHAT'S WRONG? IS IT THOSE MTV BASTARDS?"
NO, NO IT'S JUST ME, COURTNEY. I CAN'T DO IT. THE WHOLE WORLD WILL REALIZE THAT I CAN'T SING...
I JUST CAN'T DO IT.
"GROW UP, KURT. SCREW YOUR PARENTS THAT DIDN'T TEACH YOU SELF-CONFIDENCE AND FIND IT YOURSELF."
"THE CONCERT WAS YOUR IDEA SO FUCKIN' GO FOR IT HEART AND SOUL!"
HEART AND SOUL!! YOU'RE RIGHT, OTHERWIS
THEY'LL FUCKIN' CHEW ME UP AND SPIT ME OU

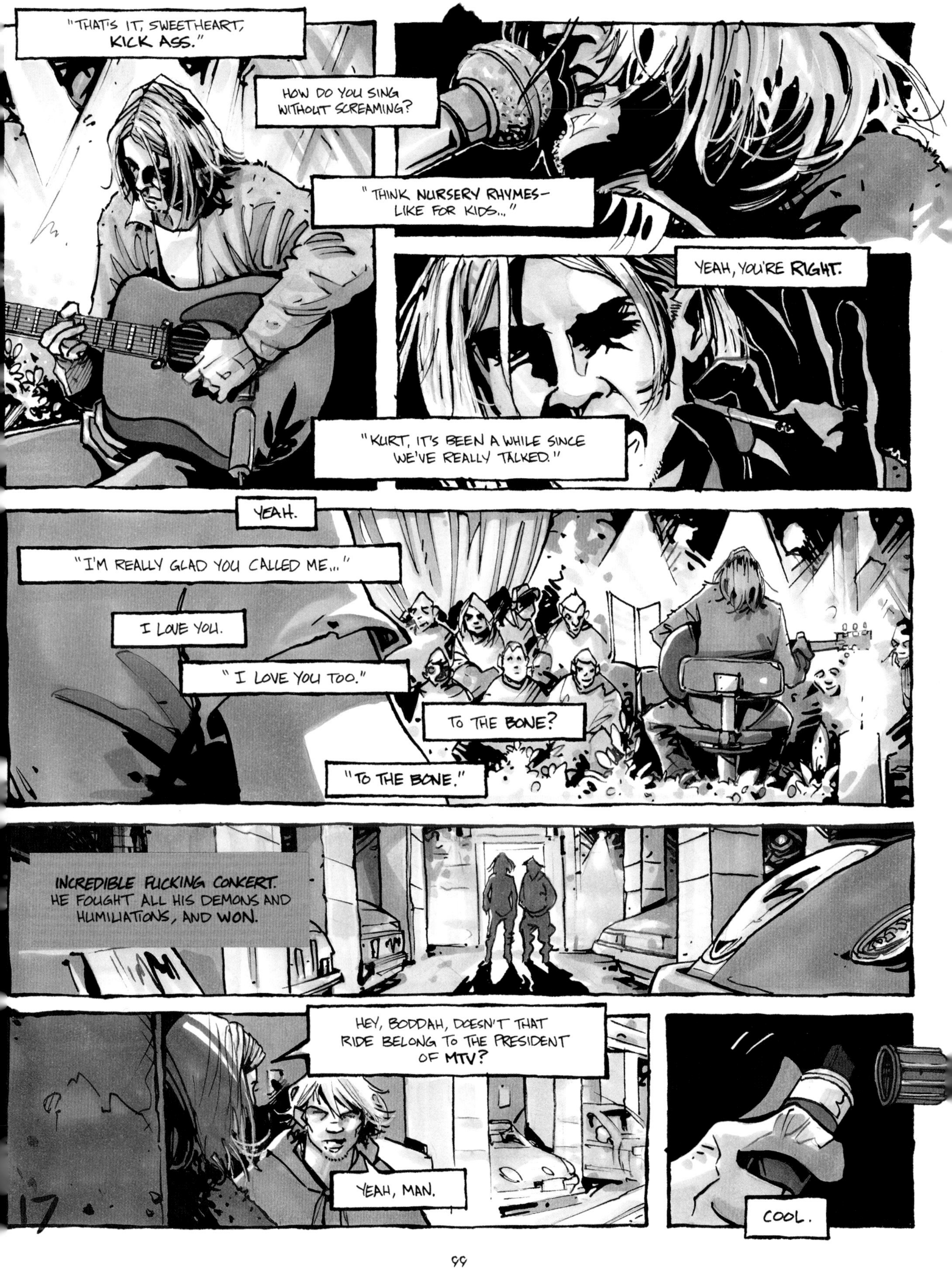
"THAT'S IT, SWEETHEART, KICK ASS."
HOW DO YOU SING WITHOUT SCREAMING?
"THINK NURSERY RHYMES- LIKE FOR KIDS..."
YEAH, YOU'RE RIGHT.
"KURT, IT'S BEEN A WHILE SINCE WE'VE REALLY TALKED."
YEAH.
"I'M REALLY GLAD YOU CALLED ME..."
I LOVE YOU.
"I LOVE YOU TOO."
TO THE BONE?
"TO THE BONE."
INCREDIBLE FUCKING CONCERT. HE FOUGHT ALL HIS DEMONS AND HUMILIATIONS, AND WON.
HEY, BODDAH, DOESN'T THAT RIDE BELONG TO THE PRESIDENT OF MTV?
YEAH, MAN.
COOL.

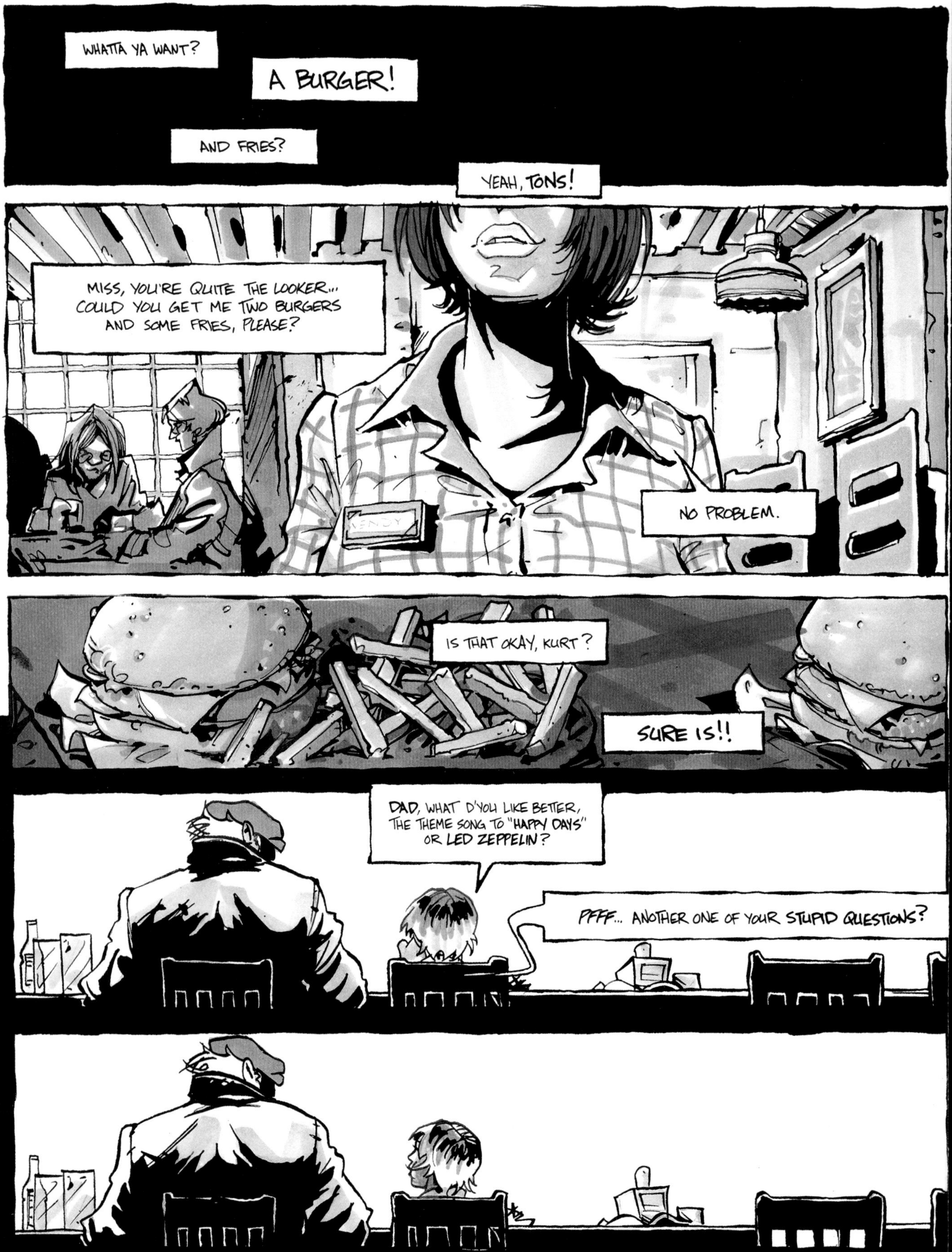
WHATTA YA WANT?
A BURGER!
AND FRIES?
YEAH, TONS!
MISS, YOU'RE QUITE THE LOOKER... COULD YOU GET ME TWO BURGERS AND SOME FRIES, PLEASE?
NO PROBLEM.
IS THAT OKAY, KURT?
SURE IS!!
DAD, WHAT D'YOU LIKE BETTER, THE THEME SONG TO "HAPPY DAYS" OR LED ZEPPELIN?
PFFF... ANOTHER ONE OF YOUR STUPID QUESTIONS?

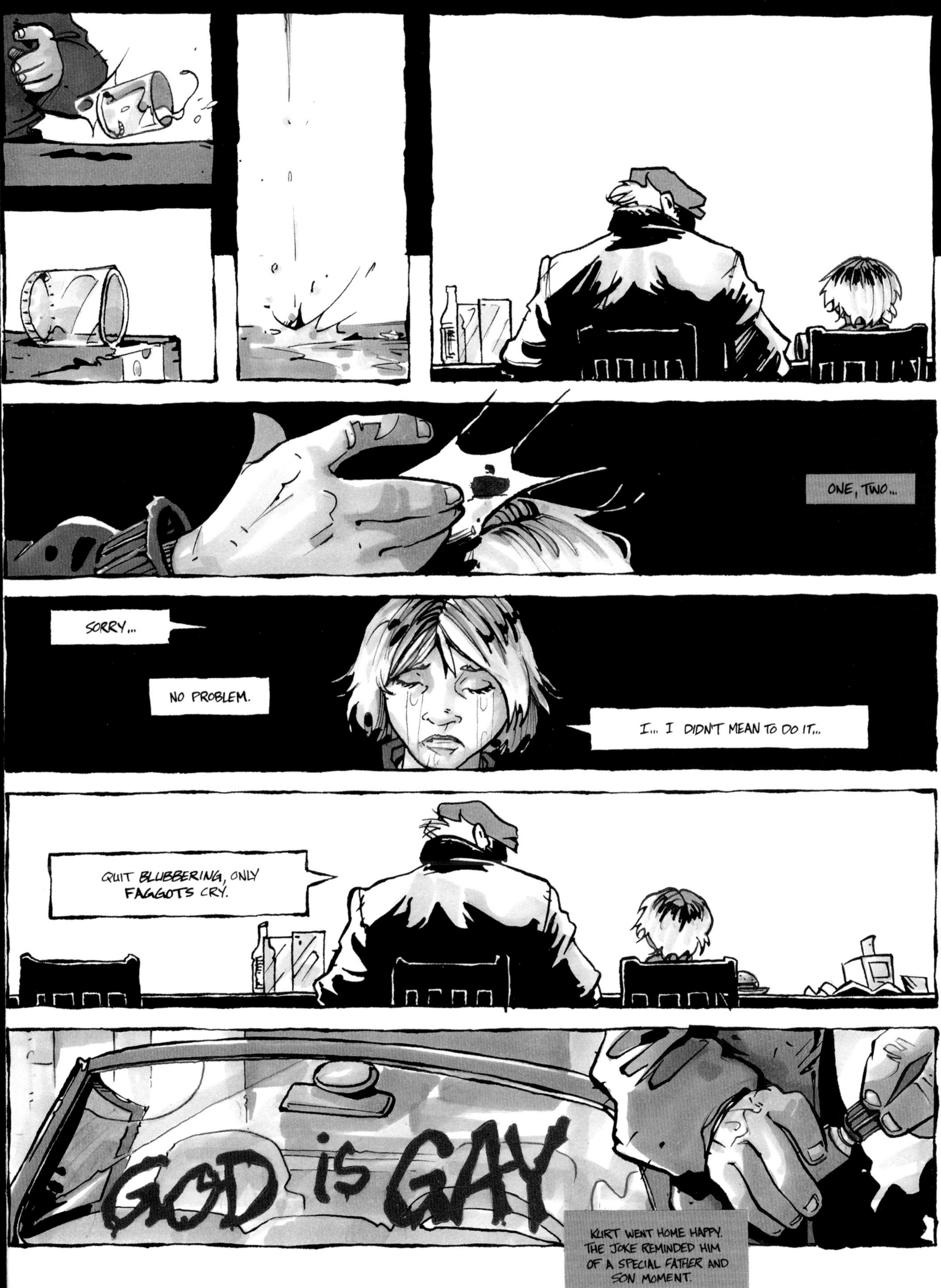
ONE, TWO...
SORRY...
NO PROBLEM.
I... I DIDN'T MEAN TO DO IT...
QUIT BLUBBERING, ONLY FAGGOTS CRY.
GOD IS GAY
KURT WENT HOME HAPPY. THE JOKE REMINDED HIM OF A SPECIAL FATHER AND SON MOMENT.

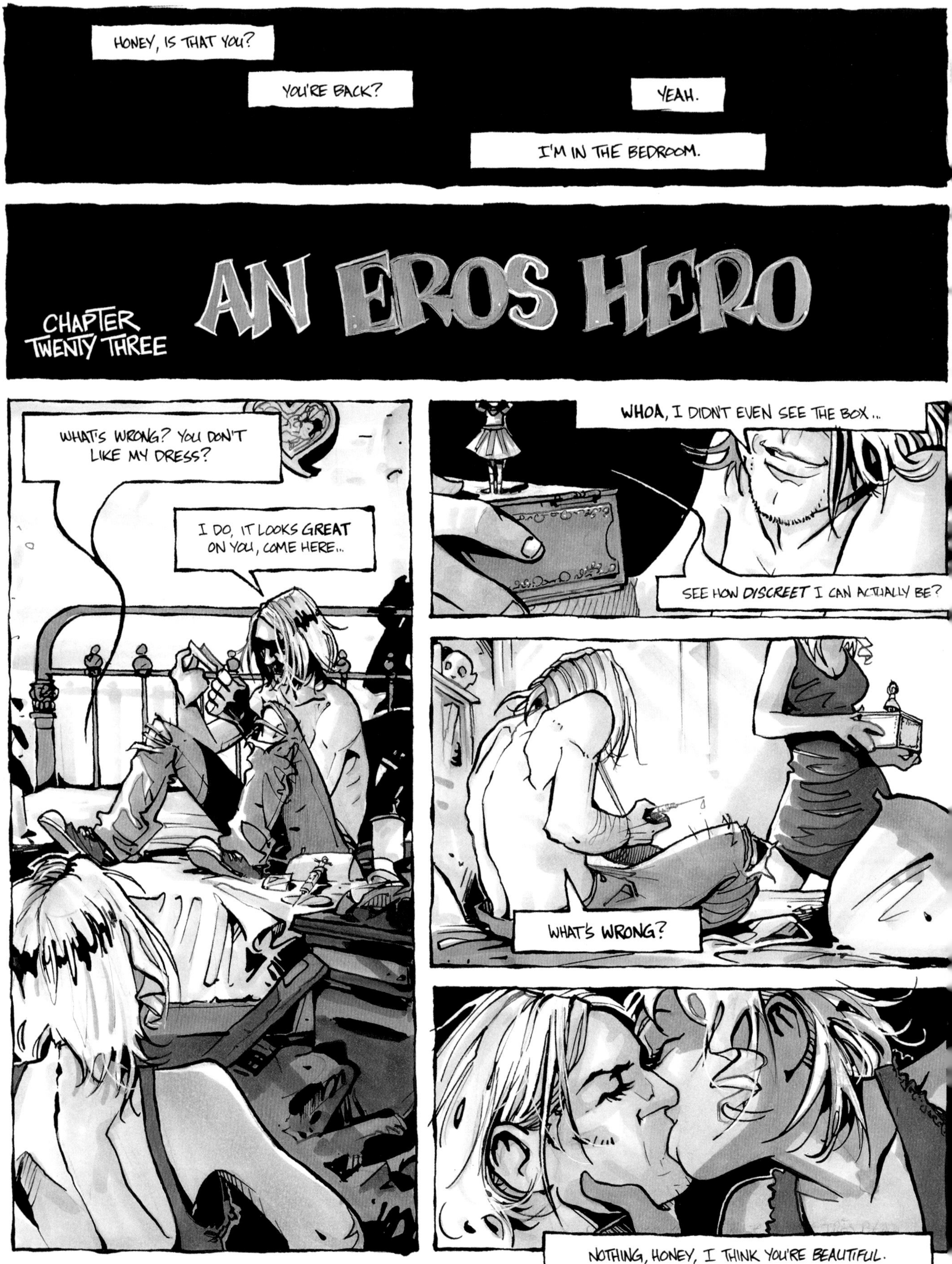
HONEY, IS THAT YOU?
YOU'RE BACK?
YEAH.
I'M IN THE BEDROOM.
CHAPTER TWENTY THREE
AN EROS HERO
WHAT'S WRONG? YOU DON'T LIKE MY DRESS?
I DO, IT LOOKS GREAT ON YOU, COME HERE...
WHOA, I DIDN'T EVEN SEE THE BOX...
SEE HOW DISCREET I CAN ACTUALLY BE?
WHAT'S WRONG?
NOTHING, HONEY, I THINK YOU'RE BEAUTIFUL.

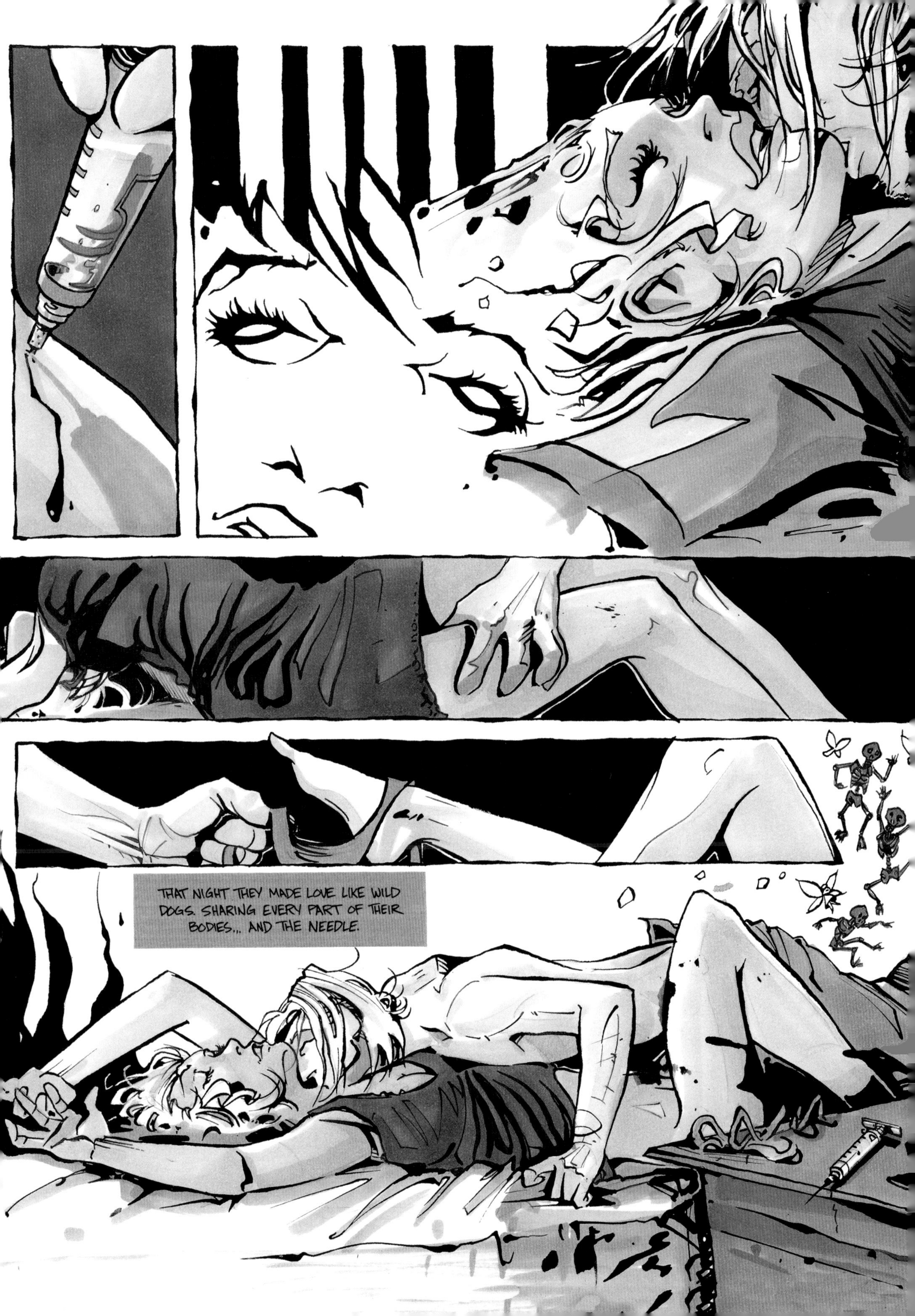
THAT NIGHT THEY MADE LOVE LIKE WILD DOGS. SHARING EVERY PART OF THEIR BODIES... AND THE NEEDLE.

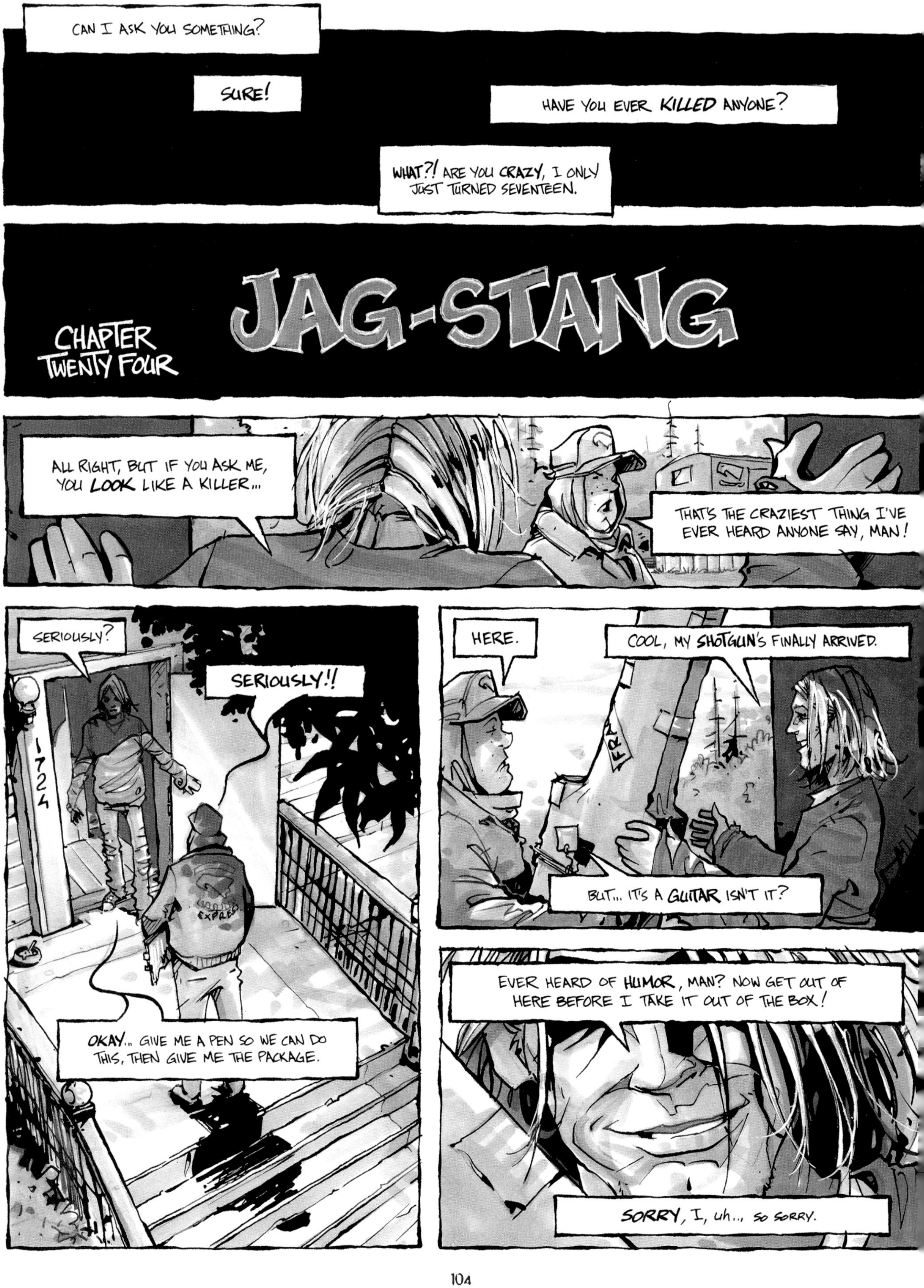
CAN I ASK YOU SOMETHING?
SURE!
HAVE YOU EVER KILLED ANYONE?
WHAT?! ARE YOU CRAZY, I ONLY JUST TURNED SEVENTEEN.
CHAPTER TWENTY FOUR
JAG-STANG
ALL RIGHT, BUT IF YOU ASK ME, YOU LOOK LIKE A KILLER...
THAT'S THE CRAZIEST THING I'VE EVER HEARD ANYONE SAY, MAN!
SERIOUSLY?
SERIOUSLY!!
1724
OKAY... GIVE ME A PEN SO WE CAN DO THIS, THEN GIVE ME THE PACKAGE.
HERE.
COOL, MY SHOTGUN'S FINALLY ARRIVED.
BUT... IT'S A GUITAR ISN'T IT?
EVER HEARD OF HUMOR, MAN? NOW GET OUT OF HERE BEFORE I TAKE IT OUT OF THE BOX!
SORRY, I, uh... SO SORRY.

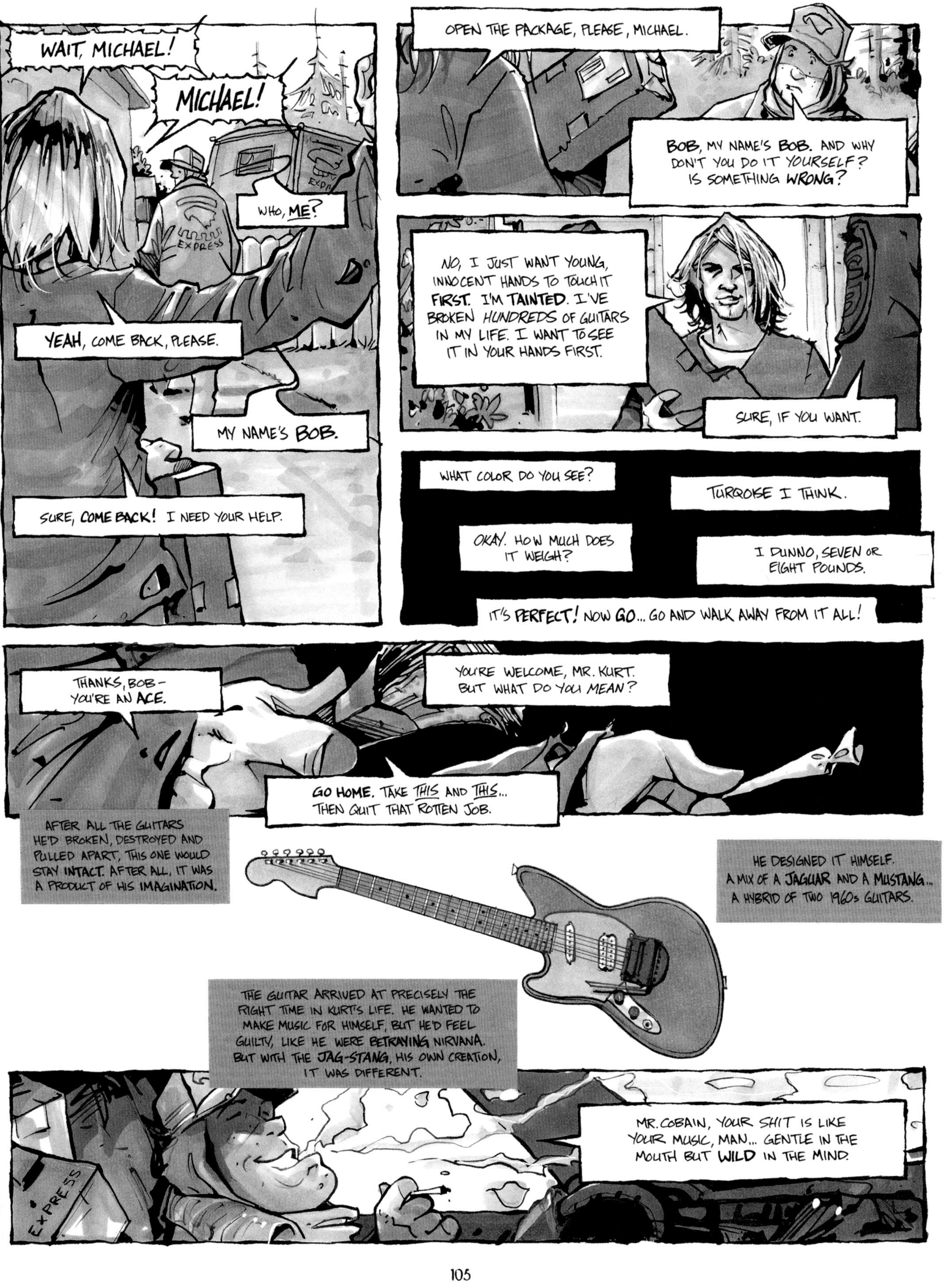
WAIT, MICHAEL!
MICHAEL!
EXPRESS
WHO, ME?
YEAH, COME BACK, PLEASE.
MY NAME'S BOB.
SURE, COME BACK! I NEED YOUR HELP.
OPEN THE PACKAGE, PLEASE, MICHAEL.
BOB, MY NAME'S BOB. AND WHY DON'T YOU DO IT YOURSELF? IS SOMETHING WRONG?
NO, I JUST WANT YOUNG, INNOCENT HANDS TO TOUCH IT FIRST. I'M TAINTED. I'VE BROKEN HUNDREDS OF GUITARS IN MY LIFE. I WANT TO SEE IT IN YOUR HANDS FIRST.
SURE, IF YOU WANT.
WHAT COLOR DO YOU SEE?
TURQOISE I THINK.
OKAY. HOW MUCH DOES IT WEIGH?
I DUNNO, SEVEN OR EIGHT POUNDS.
IT'S PERFECT! NOW GO... GO AND WALK AWAY FROM IT ALL!
THANKS, BOB - YOU'RE AN ACE.
YOU'RE WELCOME, MR. KURT. BUT WHAT DO YOU MEAN?
GO HOME. TAKE THIS AND THIS... THEN QUIT THAT ROTTEN JOB.
AFTER ALL THE GUITARS HE'D BROKEN, DESTROYED AND PULLED APART, THIS ONE WOULD STAY INTACT. AFTER ALL, IT WAS A PRODUCT OF HIS IMAGINATION.
HE DESIGNED IT HIMSELF. A MIX OF A JAGUAR AND A MUSTANG... A HYBRID OF TWO 1960s GUITARS.
THE GUITAR ARRIVED AT PRECISELY THE RIGHT TIME IN KURT'S LIFE. HE WANTED TO MAKE MUSIC FOR HIMSELF, BUT HE'D FEEL GUILTY, LIKE HE WERE BETRAYING NIRVANA. BUT WITH THE JAG-STANG, HIS OWN CREATION, IT WAS DIFFERENT.
MR. COBAIN, YOUR SHIT IS LIKE YOUR MUSIC, MAN... GENTLE IN THE MOUTH BUT WILD IN THE MIND.
EXPRESS

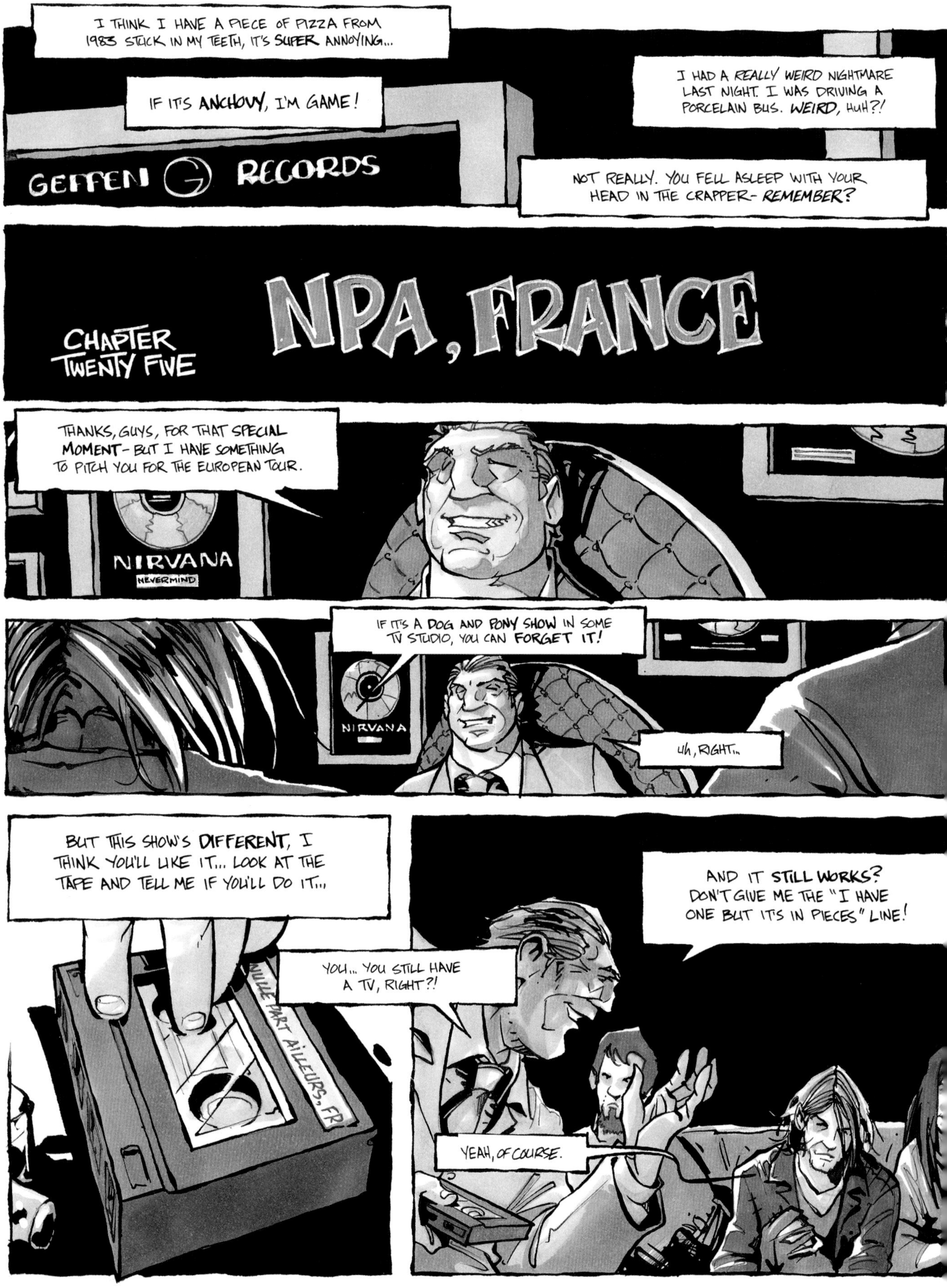

I THINK I HAVE A PIECE OF PIZZA FROM 1983 STUCK IN MY TEETH, IT'S SUPER ANNOYING...
IF IT'S ANCHOVY, I'M GAME!
I HAD A REALLY WEIRD NIGHTMARE LAST NIGHT. I WAS DRIVING A PORCELAIN BUS. WEIRD, HUH?!
NOT REALLY. YOU FELL ASLEEP WITH YOUR HEAD IN THE CRAPPER- REMEMBER?
GEFFEN RECORDS
CHAPTER TWENTY FIVE
NPA, FRANCE
THANKS, GUYS, FOR THAT SPECIAL MOMENT- BUT I HAVE SOMETHING TO PITCH YOU FOR THE EUROPEAN TOUR.
NIRVANA
NEVERMIND
IF IT'S A DOG AND PONY SHOW IN SOME TV STUDIO, YOU CAN FORGET IT!
NIRVANA
UH, RIGHT...
BUT THIS SHOW'S DIFFERENT, I THINK YOU'LL LIKE IT... LOOK AT THE TAPE AND TELL ME IF YOU'LL DO IT...
NULLE PART AILLEURS, FR
YOU... YOU STILL HAVE A TV, RIGHT?!
AND IT STILL WORKS? DON'T GIVE ME THE "I HAVE ONE BUT IT'S IN PIECES" LINE!
YEAH, OF COURSE.

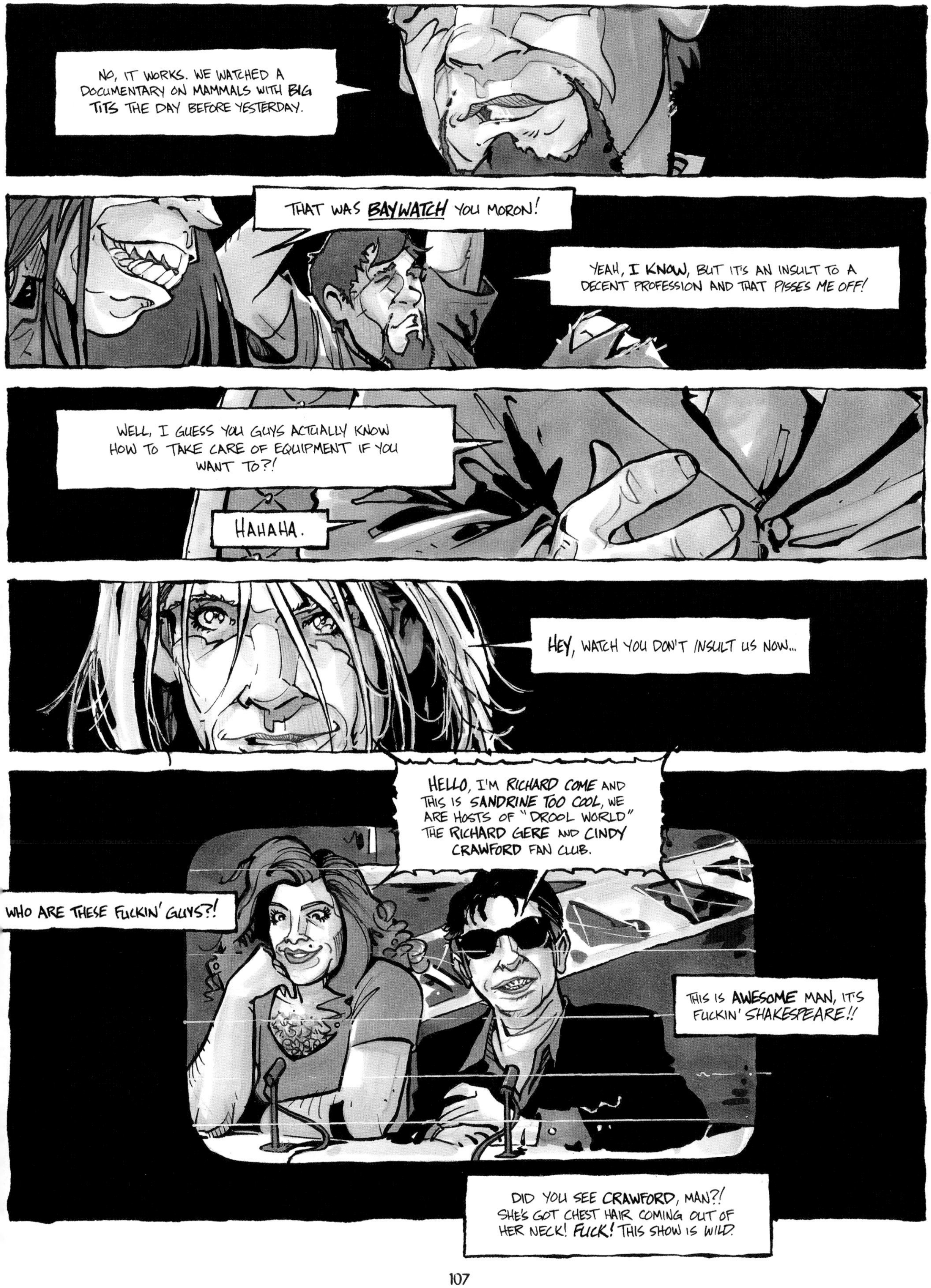

NO, IT WORKS. WE WATCHED A DOCUMENTARY ON MAMMALS WITH BIG TITS THE DAY BEFORE YESTERDAY.
THAT WAS BAYWATCH YOU MORON!
YEAH, I KNOW, BUT IT'S AN INSULT TO A DECENT PROFESSION AND THAT PISSES ME OFF!
WELL, I GUESS YOU GUYS ACTUALLY KNOW HOW TO TAKE CARE OF EQUIPMENT IF YOU WANT TO?!
HAHAHA.
HEY, WATCH YOU DON'T INSULT US NOW...
HELLO, I'M RICHARD COME AND THIS IS SANDRINE TOO COOL, WE ARE HOSTS OF "DROOL WORLD" THE RICHARD GERE AND CINDY CRAWFORD FAN CLUB.
WHO ARE THESE FUCKIN' GUYS?!
THIS IS AWESOME MAN, IT'S FUCKIN' SHAKESPEARE!!
DID YOU SEE CRAWFORD, MAN?! SHE'S GOT CHEST HAIR COMING OUT OF HER NECK! FUCK! THIS SHOW IS WILD.

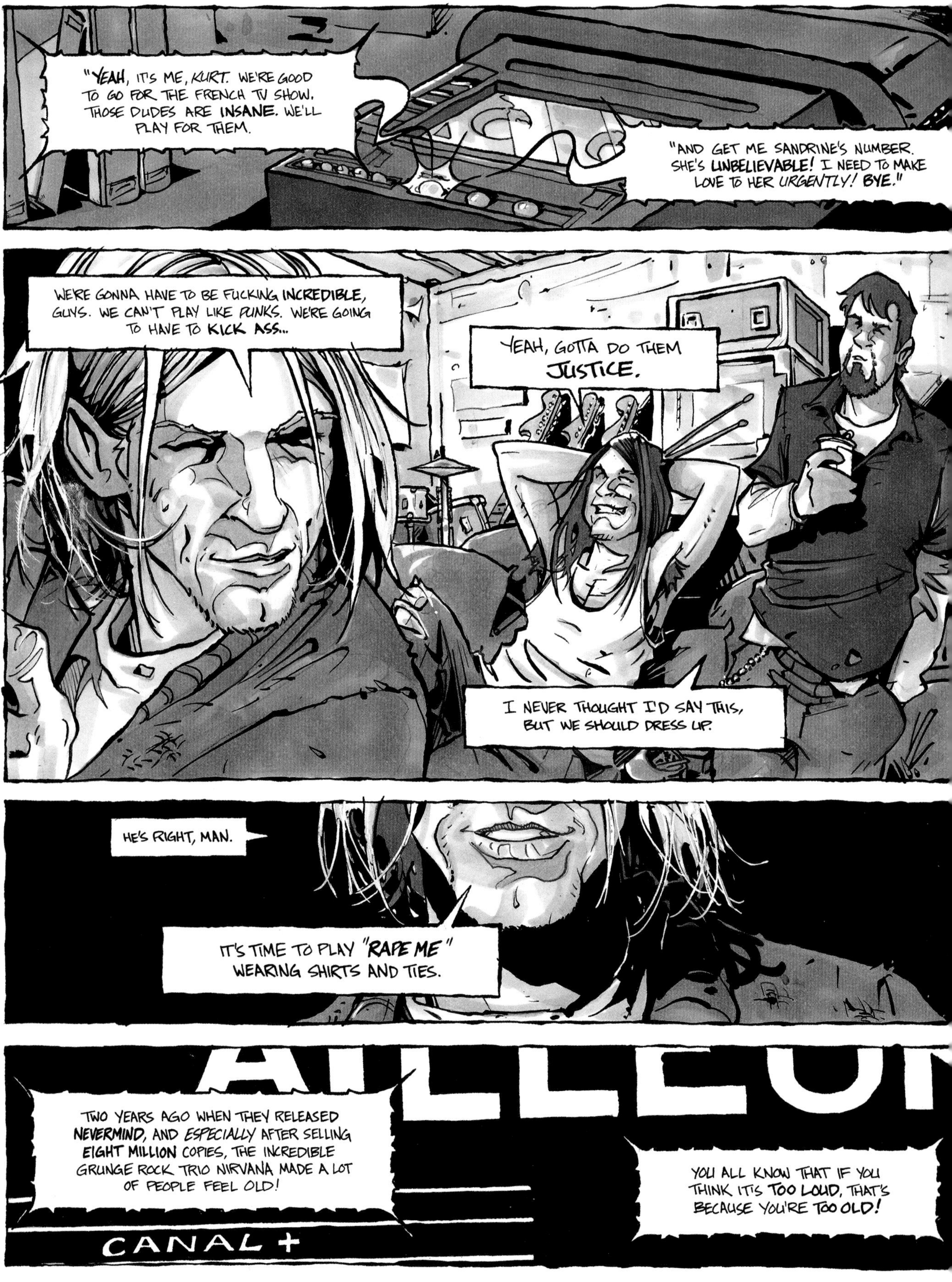
"YEAH, IT'S ME, KURT. WE'RE GOOD TO GO FOR THE FRENCH TV SHOW. THOSE DUDES ARE INSANE. WE'LL PLAY FOR THEM.
"AND GET ME SANDRINE'S NUMBER. SHE'S UNBELIEVABLE! I NEED TO MAKE LOVE TO HER URGENTLY! BYE."
WE'RE GONNA HAVE TO BE FUCKING INCREDIBLE, GUYS. WE CAN'T PLAY LIKE PUNKS. WE'RE GOING TO HAVE TO KICK ASS...
YEAH, GOTTA DO THEM JUSTICE.
I NEVER THOUGHT I'D SAY THIS, BUT WE SHOULD DRESS UP.
HE'S RIGHT, MAN.
IT'S TIME TO PLAY "RAPE ME" WEARING SHIRTS AND TIES.
TWO YEARS AGO WHEN THEY RELEASED NEVERMIND, AND ESPECIALLY AFTER SELLING EIGHT MILLION COPIES, THE INCREDIBLE GRUNGE ROCK TRIO NIRVANA MADE A LOT OF PEOPLE FEEL OLD!
YOU ALL KNOW THAT IF YOU THINK IT'S TOO LOUD, THAT'S BECAUSE YOU'RE TOO OLD!
CANAL +

THE CROWD LOVES NIRVANA!

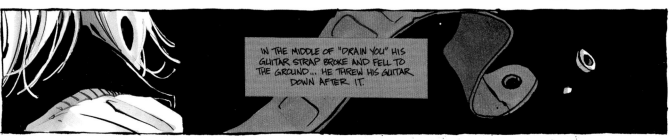

IN THE MIDDLE OF "DRAIN YOU" HIS GUITAR STRAP BROKE AND FELL TO THE GROUND... HE THREW HIS GUITAR DOWN AFTER IT.

THEN LET OUT AN OTHERWORLDLY SCREAM.

A PURE, UNADULTERATED SCREAM.

AN ABYSMAL SCREAM THAT INVADED THE STAGE AND RAFTERS AND FELL DOWN LIKE RAIN.

PIECES OF THE CEILING FELL DOWN WITH IT.

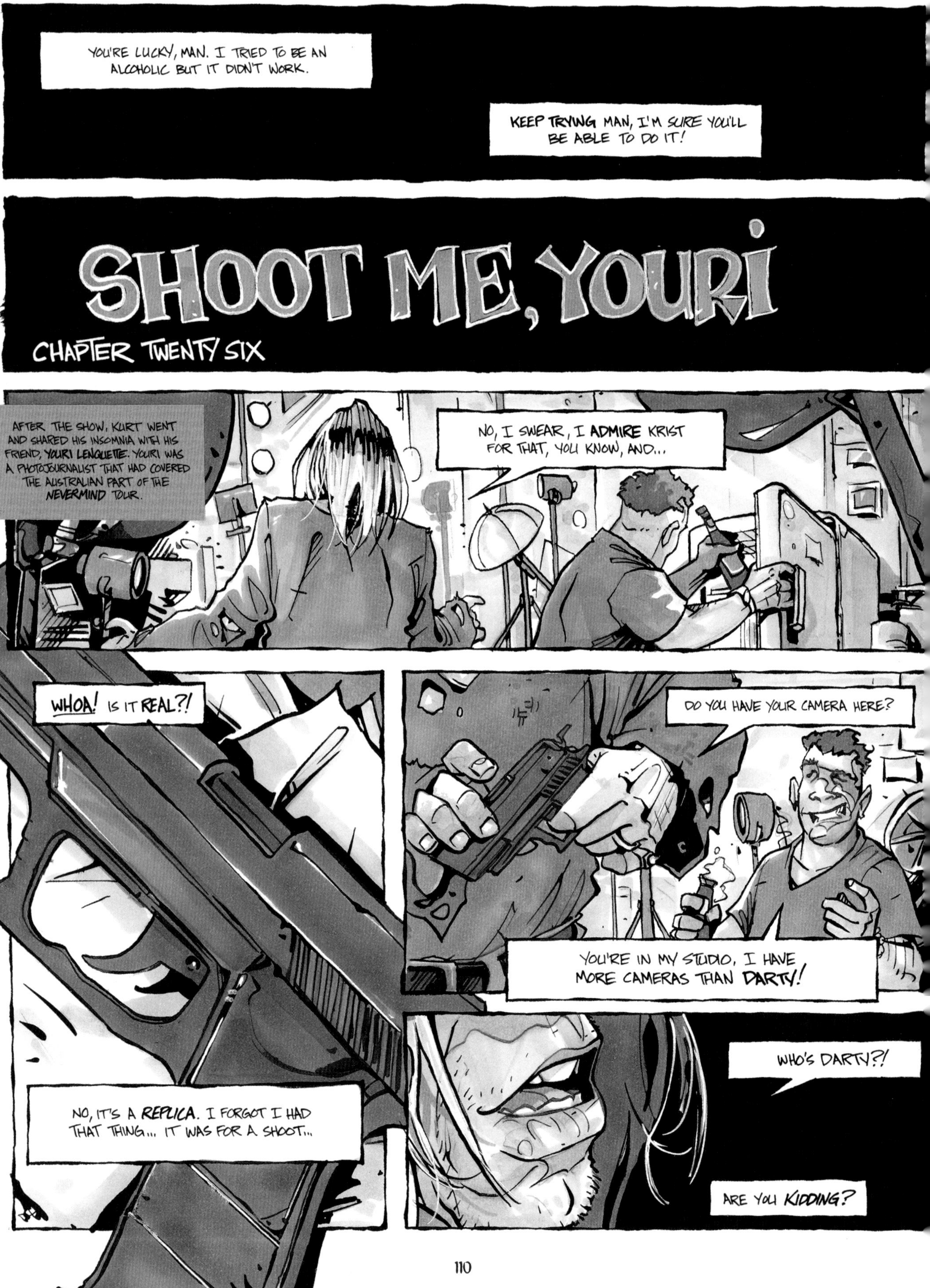

YOU'RE LUCKY, MAN. I TRIED TO BE AN ALCOHOLIC BUT IT DIDN'T WORK.
KEEP TRYING MAN, I'M SURE YOU'LL BE ABLE TO DO IT!
SHOOT ME, YOURI
CHAPTER TWENTY SIX
AFTER THE SHOW, KURT WENT AND SHARED HIS INSOMNIA WITH HIS FRIEND, YOURI LENQUETTE. YOURI WAS A PHOTOJOURNALIST THAT HAD COVERED THE AUSTRALIAN PART OF THE NEVERMIND TOUR.
NO, I SWEAR, I ADMIRE KRIST FOR THAT, YOU KNOW, AND...
WHOA! IS IT REAL?!
DO YOU HAVE YOUR CAMERA HERE?
YOU'RE IN MY STUDIO, I HAVE MORE CAMERAS THAN DARTY!
NO, IT'S A REPLICA. I FORGOT I HAD THAT THING... IT WAS FOR A SHOOT...
WHO'S DARTY?!
ARE YOU KIDDING?

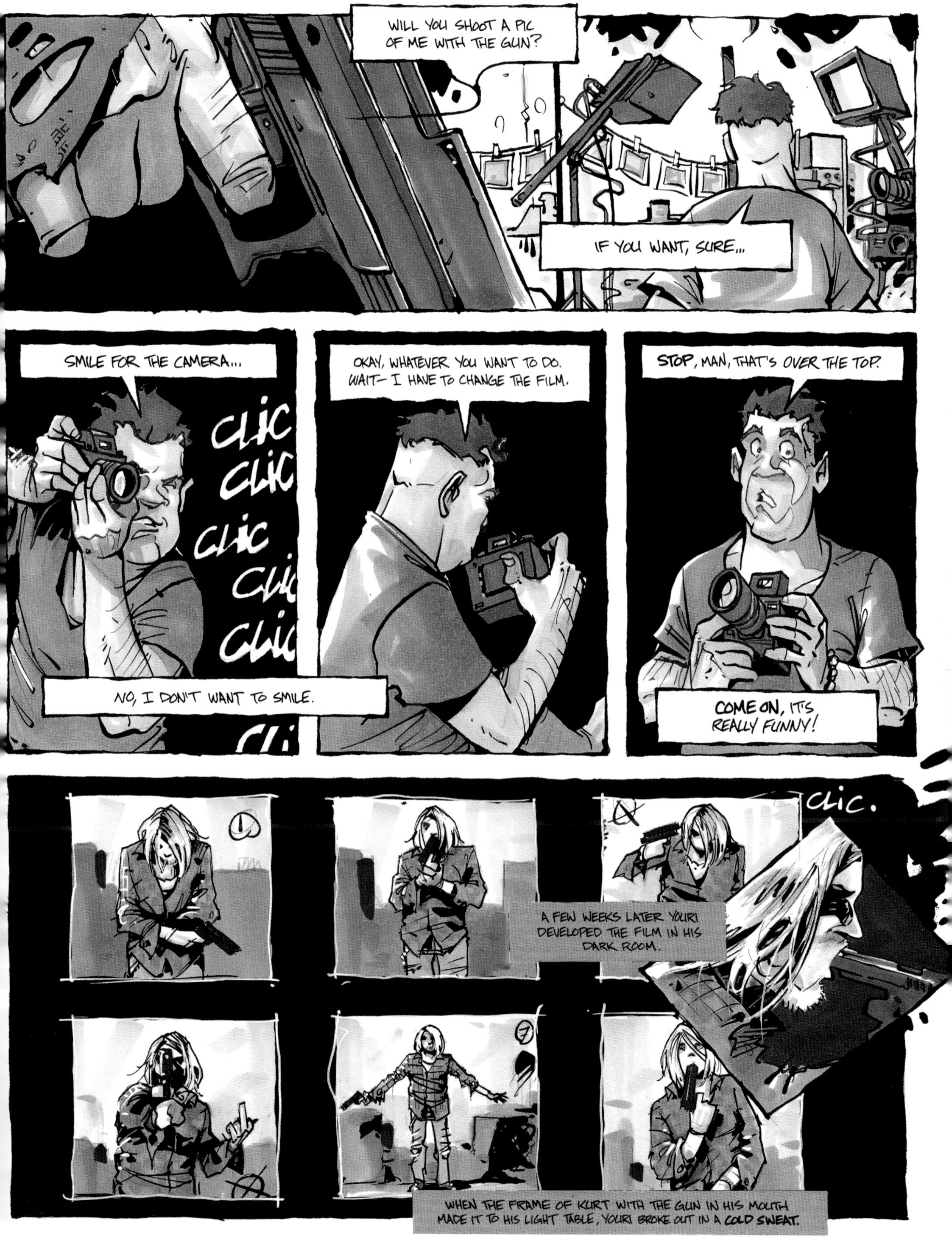

WILL YOU SHOOT A PIC OF ME WITH THE GUN?
IF YOU WANT, SURE...
SMILE FOR THE CAMERA...
CLIC CLIC CLIC CLIC CLIC
NO, I DON'T WANT TO SMILE.
OKAY, WHATEVER YOU WANT TO DO. WAIT- I HAVE TO CHANGE THE FILM.
STOP, MAN, THAT'S OVER THE TOP.
COME ON, IT'S REALLY FUNNY!
CLIC.
A FEW WEEKS LATER YOURI DEVELOPED THE FILM IN HIS DARK ROOM.
WHEN THE FRAME OF KURT WITH THE GUN IN HIS MOUTH MADE IT TO HIS LIGHT TABLE, YOURI BROKE OUT IN A COLD SWEAT.

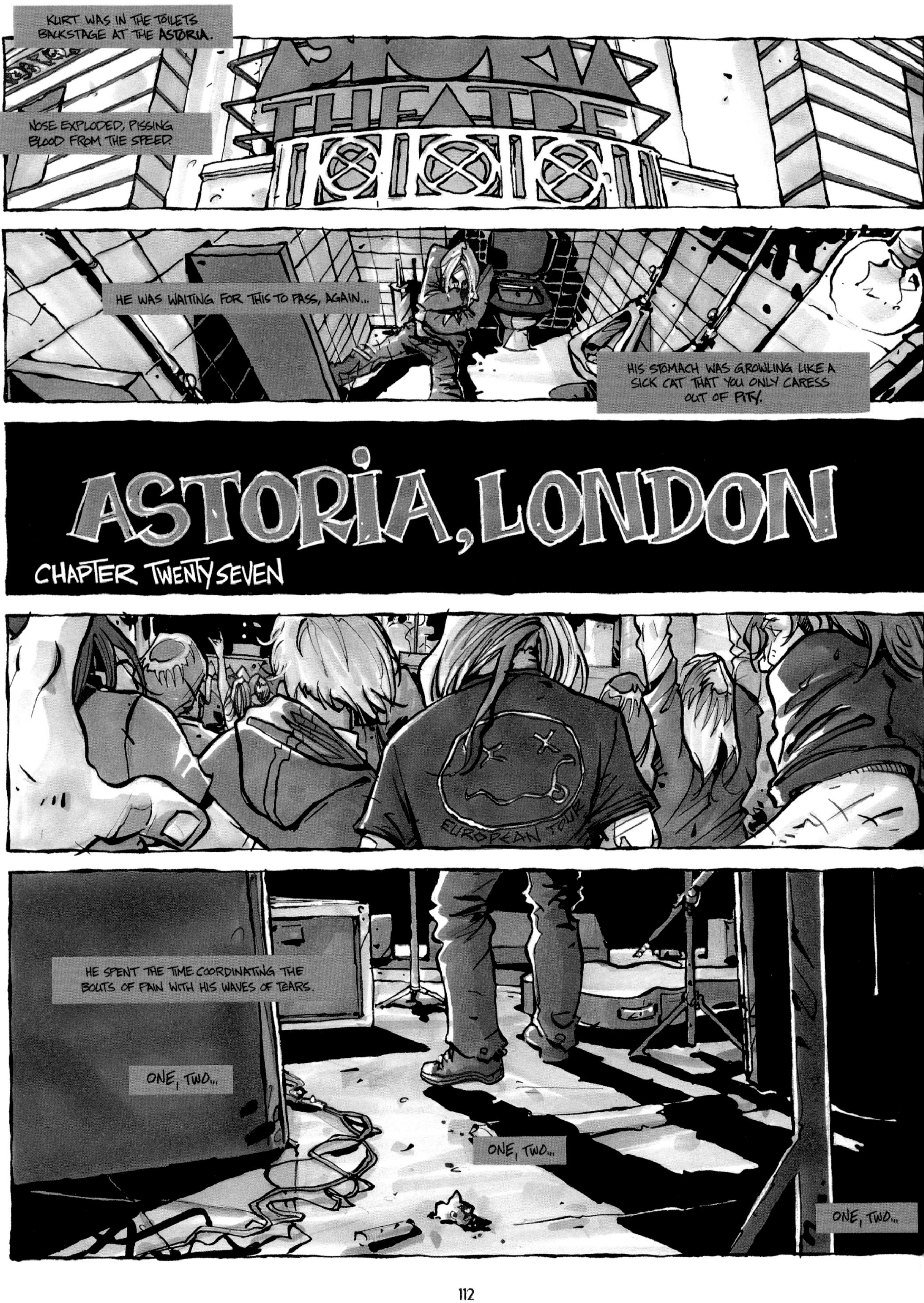
KURT WAS IN THE TOILETS BACKSTAGE AT THE ASTORIA.
THEATRE
NOSE EXPLODED, PISSING BLOOD FROM THE SPEED.
HE WAS WAITING FOR THIS TO PASS, AGAIN...
HIS STOMACH WAS GROWLING LIKE A SICK CAT THAT YOU ONLY CARESS OUT OF PITY.
ASTORIA, LONDON
CHAPTER TWENTY SEVEN
EUROPEAN TOUR
HE SPENT THE TIME COORDINATING THE BOUTS OF PAIN WITH HIS WAVES OF TEARS.
ONE, TWO...
ONE, TWO...
ONE, TWO...

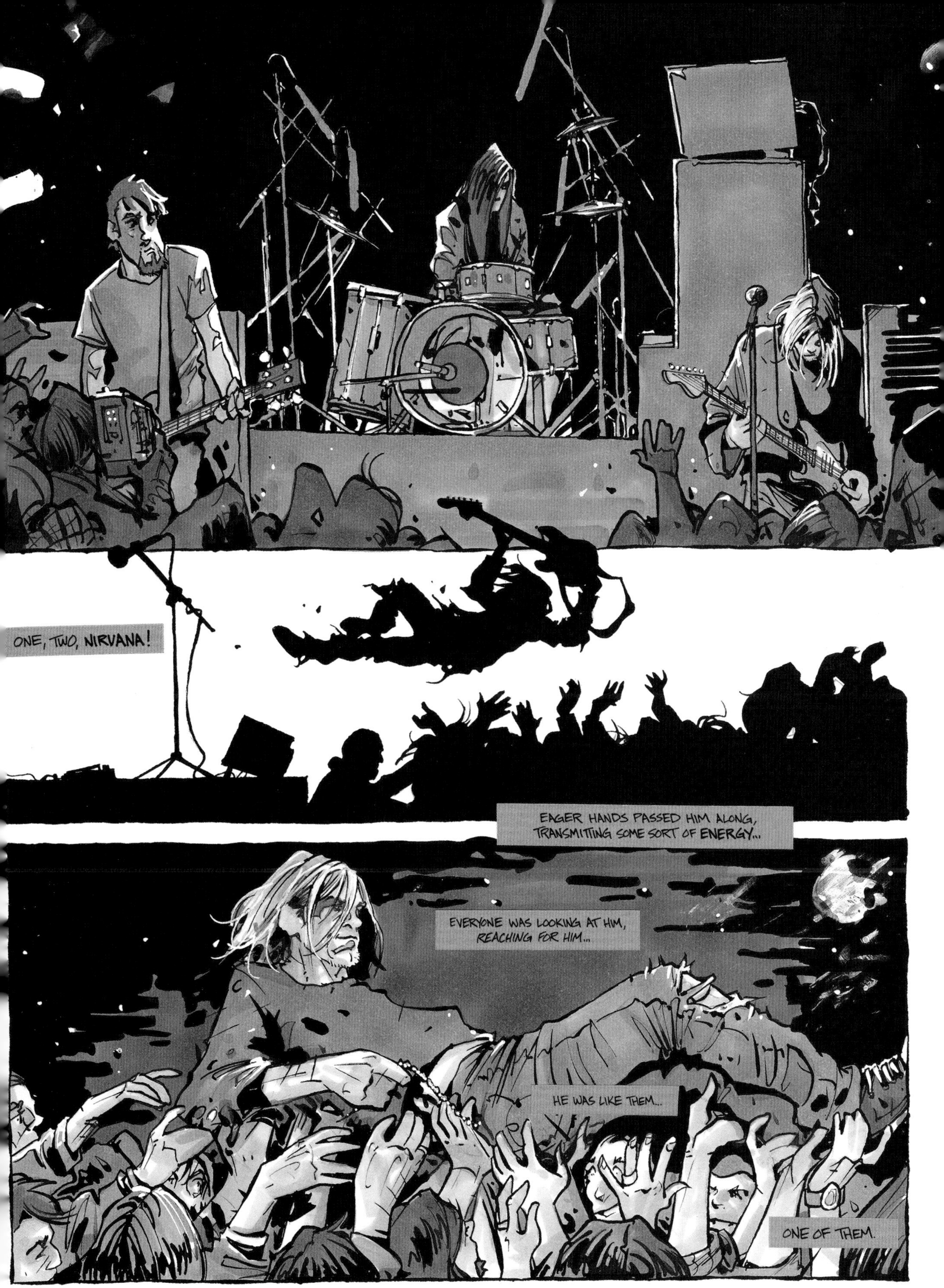

ONE, TWO, NIRVANA!
EAGER HANDS PASSED HIM ALONG, TRANSMITTING SOME SORT OF ENERGY...
EVERYONE WAS LOOKING AT HIM, REACHING FOR HIM...
HE WAS LIKE THEM...
ONE OF THEM.

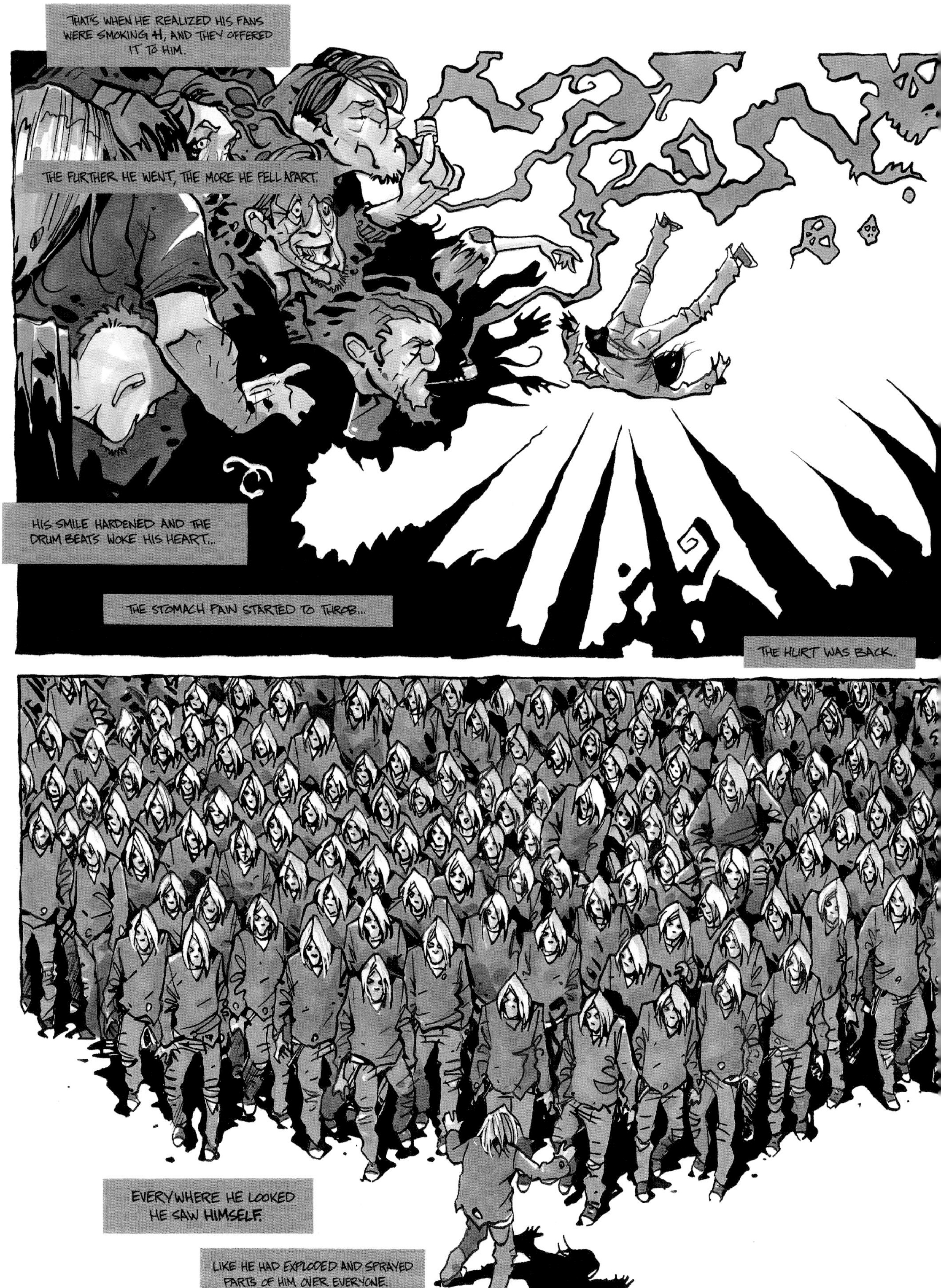
THAT'S WHEN HE REALIZED HIS FANS WERE SMOKING H, AND THEY OFFERED IT TO HIM.
THE FURTHER HE WENT, THE MORE HE FELL APART.
HIS SMILE HARDENED AND THE DRUM BEATS WOKE HIS HEART...
THE STOMACH PAIN STARTED TO THROB...
THE HURT WAS BACK.
EVERYWHERE HE LOOKED HE SAW **HIMSELF**.
LIKE HE HAD EXPLODED AND SPRAYED PARTS OF HIM OVER EVERYONE.

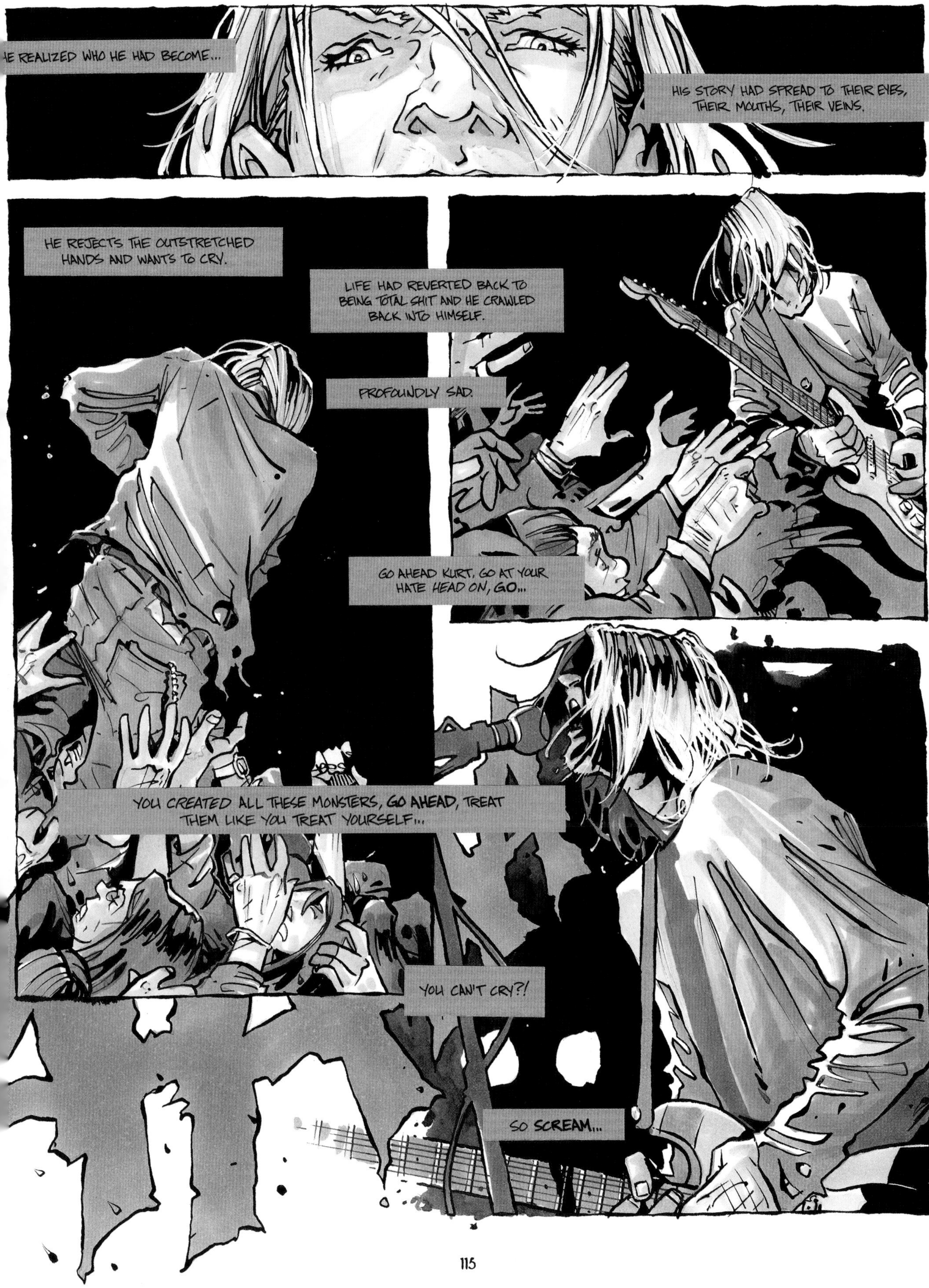
HE REALIZED WHO HE HAD BECOME...
HIS STORY HAD SPREAD TO THEIR EYES, THEIR MOUTHS, THEIR VEINS.
HE REJECTS THE OUTSTRETCHED HANDS AND WANTS TO CRY.
LIFE HAD REVERTED BACK TO BEING TOTAL SHIT AND HE CRAWLED BACK INTO HIMSELF.
PROFOUNDLY SAD.
GO AHEAD KURT, GO AT YOUR HATE HEAD ON, GO...
YOU CREATED ALL THESE MONSTERS, GO AHEAD, TREAT THEM LIKE YOU TREAT YOURSELF...
YOU CAN'T CRY?!
SO SCREAM...

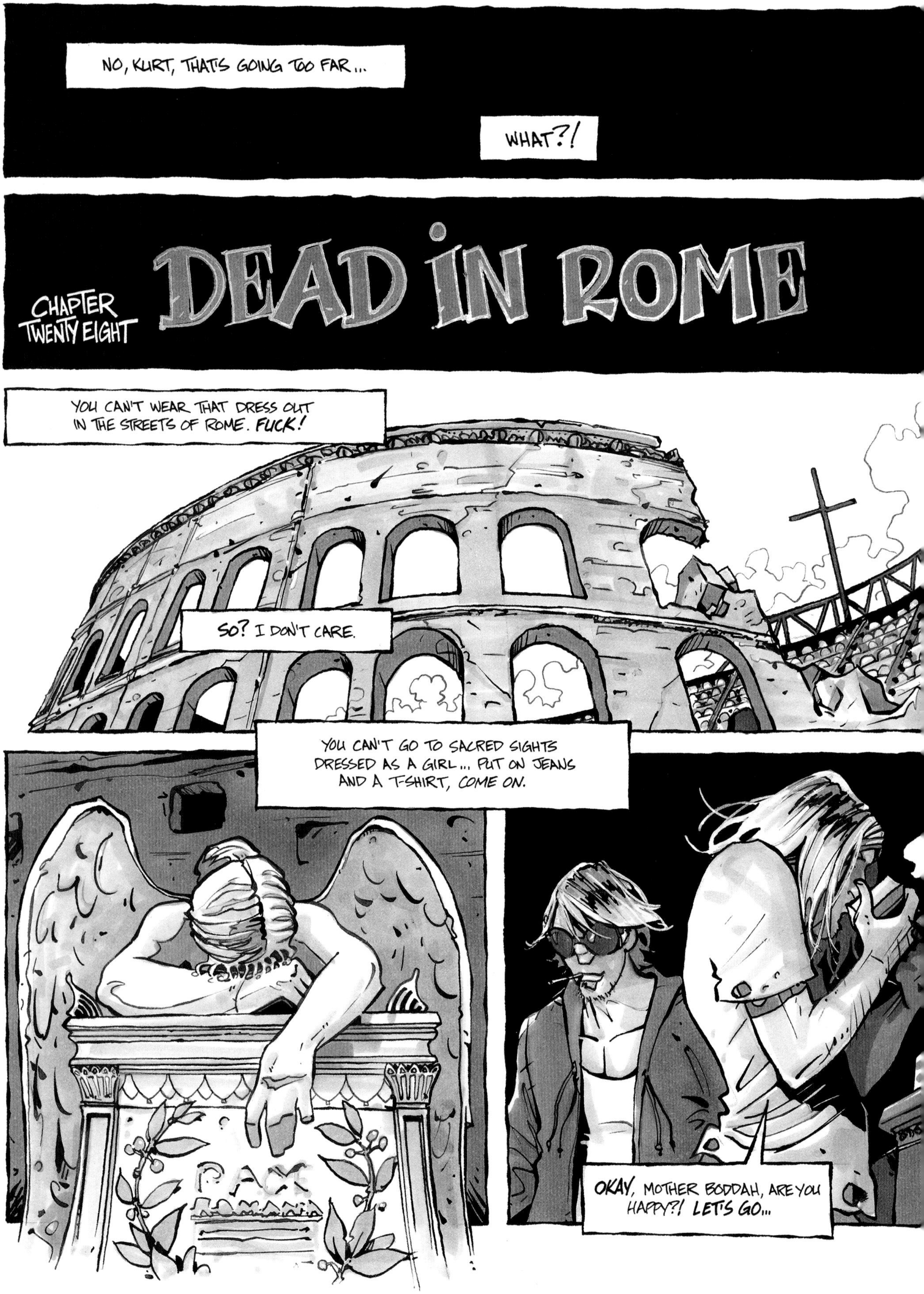
NO, KURT, THAT'S GOING TOO FAR...
WHAT?!
CHAPTER TWENTY EIGHT
DEAD IN ROME
YOU CAN'T WEAR THAT DRESS OUT IN THE STREETS OF ROME. FUCK!
SO? I DON'T CARE.
YOU CAN'T GO TO SACRED SIGHTS DRESSED AS A GIRL... PUT ON JEANS AND A T-SHIRT, COME ON.
OKAY, MOTHER BODDAH, ARE YOU HAPPY?! LET'S GO...

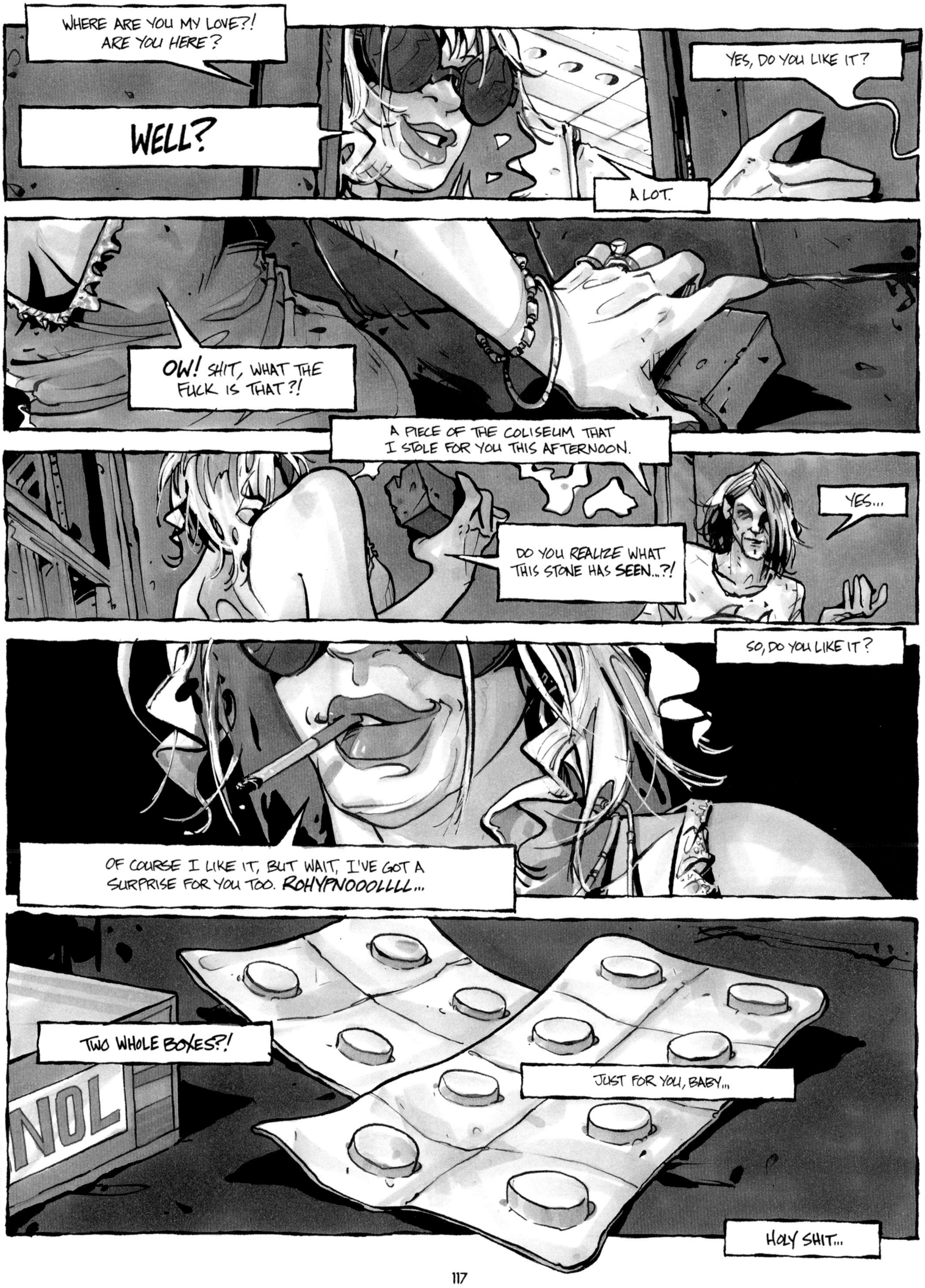
WHERE ARE YOU MY LOVE?! ARE YOU HERE?
WELL?
YES, DO YOU LIKE IT?
A LOT.
OW! SHIT, WHAT THE FUCK IS THAT?!
A PIECE OF THE COLISEUM THAT I STOLE FOR YOU THIS AFTERNOON.
DO YOU REALIZE WHAT THIS STONE HAS SEEN...?!
YES...
SO, DO YOU LIKE IT?
OF COURSE I LIKE IT, BUT WAIT, I'VE GOT A SURPRISE FOR YOU TOO. ROHYPNOOOLLLL...
NOL
TWO WHOLE BOXES?!
JUST FOR YOU, BABY...
HOLY SHIT...

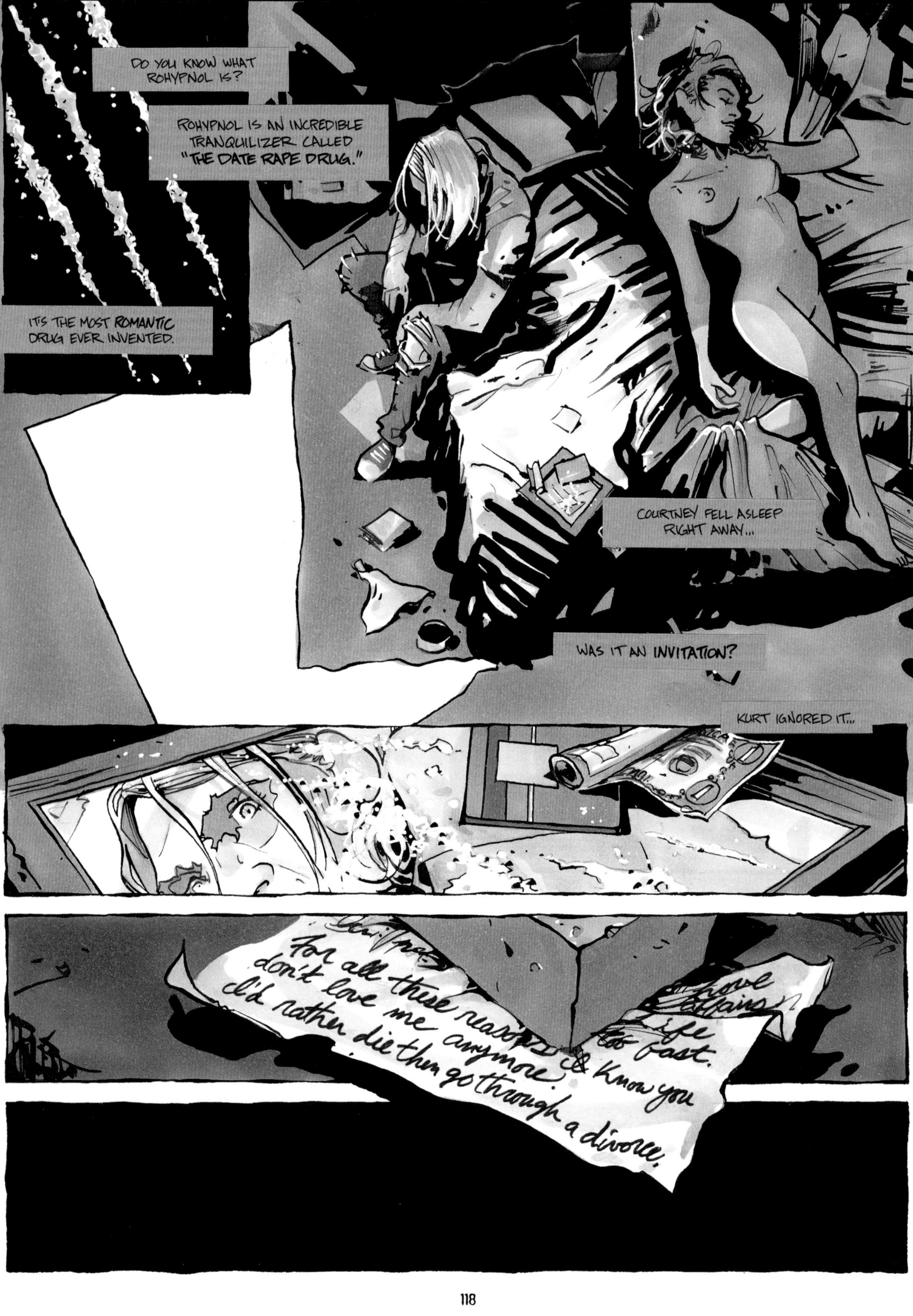
DO YOU KNOW WHAT ROHYPNOL IS?
ROHYPNOL IS AN INCREDIBLE TRANQUILIZER CALLED "THE DATE RAPE DRUG."
IT'S THE MOST ROMANTIC DRUG EVER INVENTED.
COURTNEY FELL ASLEEP RIGHT AWAY...
WAS IT AN INVITATION?
KURT IGNORED IT...
For all these reasons I know you
don't love me anymore.
I'd rather die then go through a divorce.

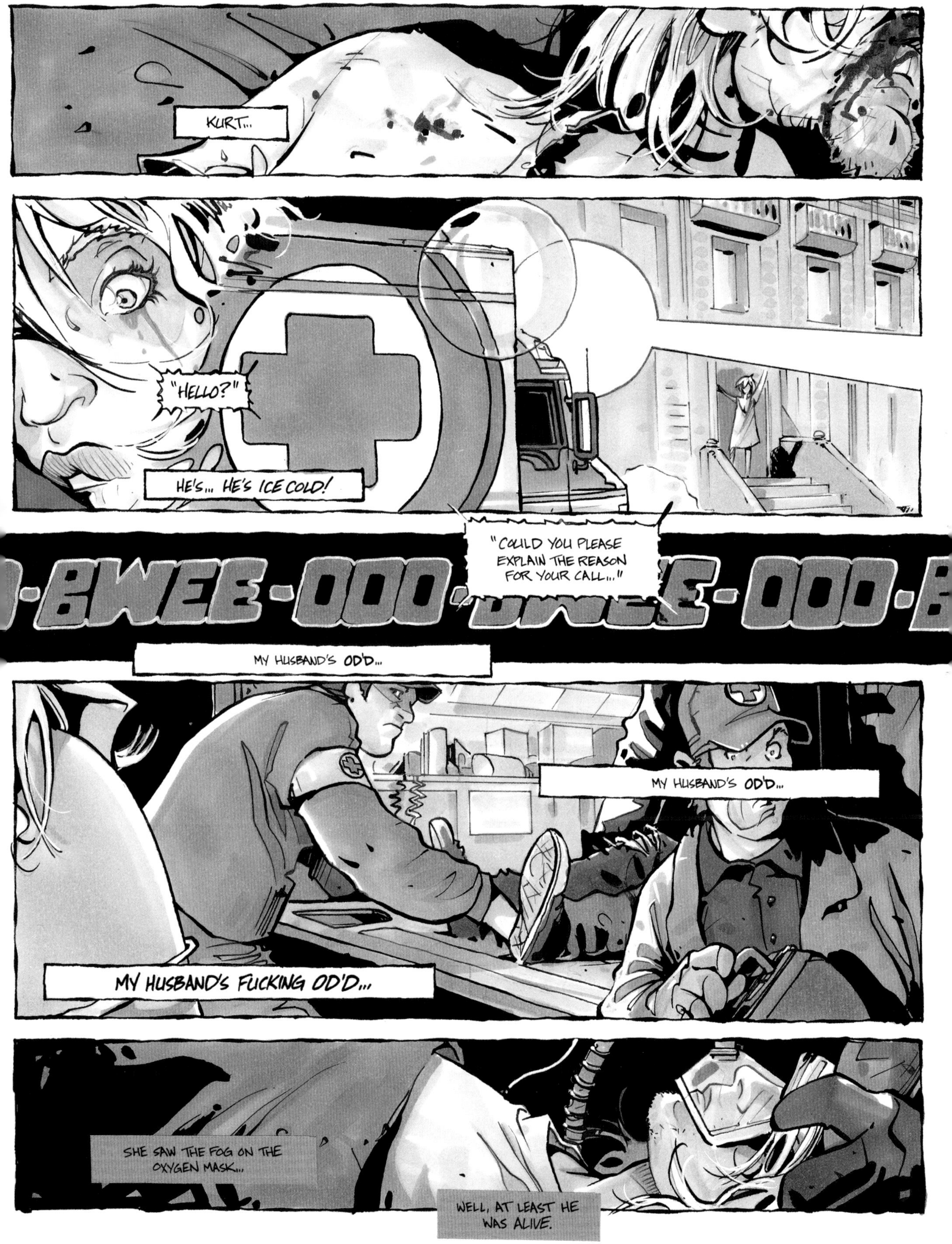

KURT...
"HELLO?"
HE'S... HE'S ICE COLD!
"COULD YOU PLEASE EXPLAIN THE REASON FOR YOUR CALL..."
BWEE-OOO-BWEE-OOO-B
MY HUSBAND'S OD'D...
MY HUSBAND'S OD'D...
MY HUSBAND'S FUCKING OD'D...
SHE SAW THE FOG ON THE OXYGEN MASK...
WELL, AT LEAST HE WAS ALIVE.

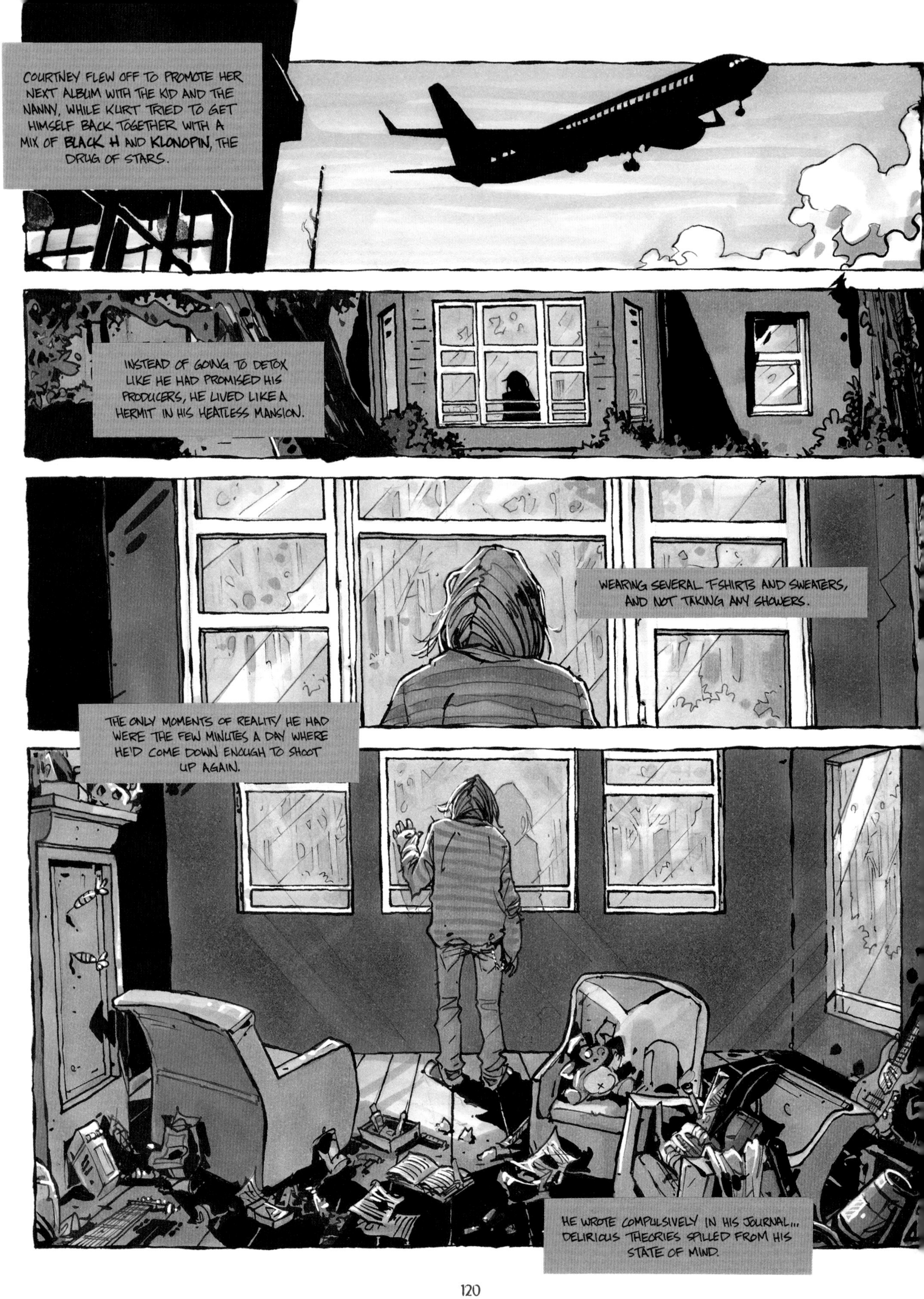
COURTNEY FLEW OFF TO PROMOTE HER NEXT ALBUM WITH THE KID AND THE NANNY, WHILE KURT TRIED TO GET HIMSELF BACK TOGETHER WITH A MIX OF BLACK H AND KLONOPIN, THE DRUG OF STARS.
INSTEAD OF GOING TO DETOX LIKE HE HAD PROMISED HIS PRODUCERS, HE LIVED LIKE A HERMIT IN HIS HEATLESS MANSION.
WEARING SEVERAL T-SHIRTS AND SWEATERS, AND NOT TAKING ANY SHOWERS.
THE ONLY MOMENTS OF REALITY HE HAD WERE THE FEW MINUTES A DAY WHERE HE'D COME DOWN ENOUGH TO SHOOT UP AGAIN.
HE WROTE COMPULSIVELY IN HIS JOURNAL... DELIRIOUS THEORIES SPILLED FROM HIS STATE OF MIND.

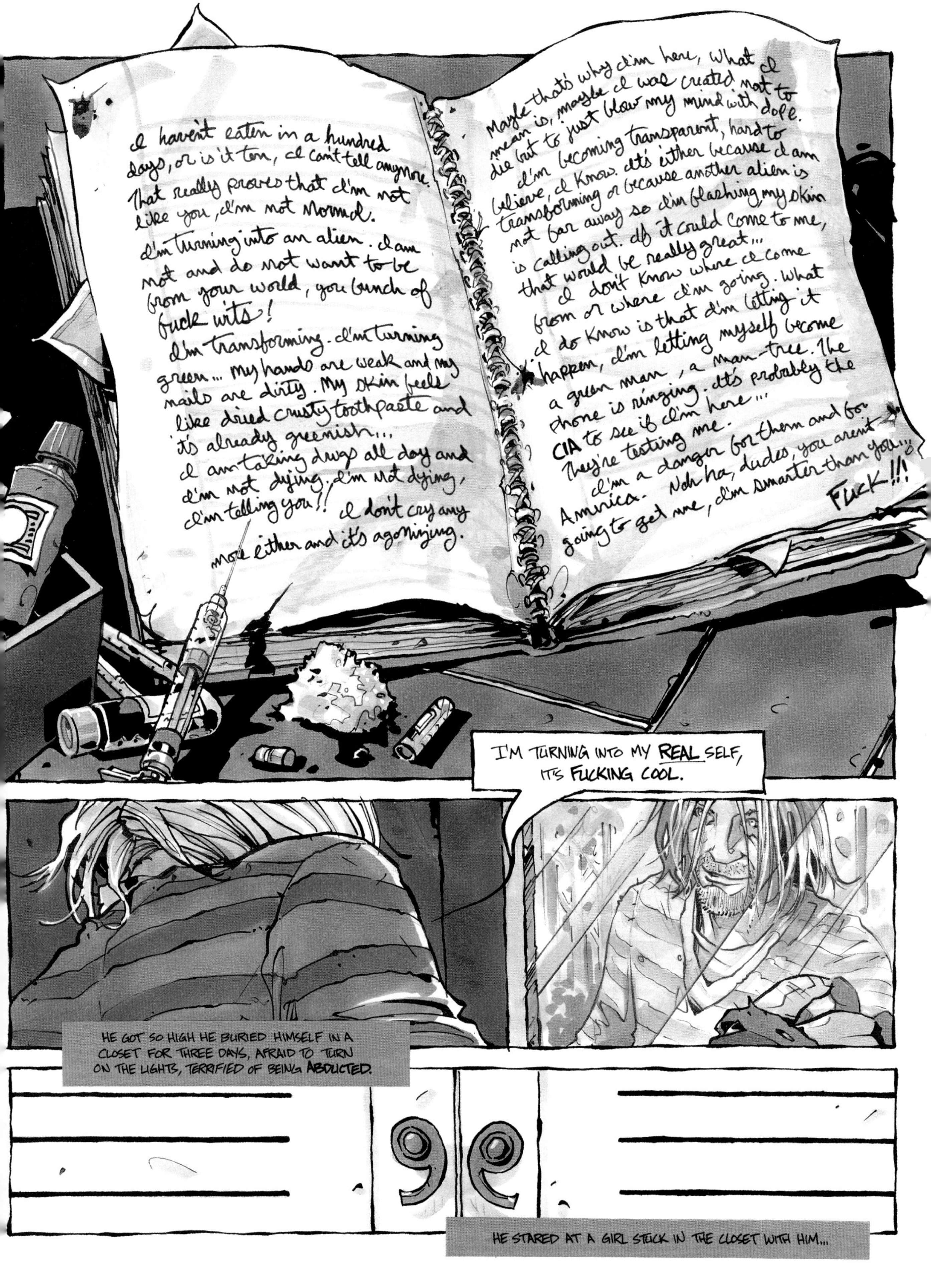
I haven't eaten in a hundred days, or is it ten, I can't tell anymore. That really proves that I'm not like you, I'm not normal.
I'm turning into an alien. I am not and do not want to be from your world, you bunch of fuck wits!
I'm transforming. I'm turning green... My hands are weak and my nails are dirty. My skin feels like dried crusty toothpaste and it's already greenish...
I am taking drugs all day and I'm not dying, I'm not dying, I'm telling you!! I don't cry any more either and it's agonizing.
Maybe that's why I'm here, What I mean is, maybe I was created not to die but to just blow my mind with dope.
I'm becoming transparent, hard to believe, I know. It's either because I am transforming or because another alien is not far away so I'm flashing my skin is calling out. If it could come to me, that would be really great...
I don't know where I come from or where I'm going. What I do know is that I'm letting it happen, I'm letting myself become a green man, a man-tree. The phone is ringing. It's probably the CIA to see if I'm here...
They're testing me.
I'm a danger for them and for America. Nah ha, dudes, you aren't going to get me, I'm smarter than you...
FUCK!!!
I'M TURNING INTO MY REAL SELF, IT'S FUCKING COOL.
HE GOT SO HIGH HE BURIED HIMSELF IN A CLOSET FOR THREE DAYS, AFRAID TO TURN ON THE LIGHTS, TERRIFIED OF BEING ABDUCTED.
HE STARED AT A GIRL STUCK IN THE CLOSET WITH HIM...

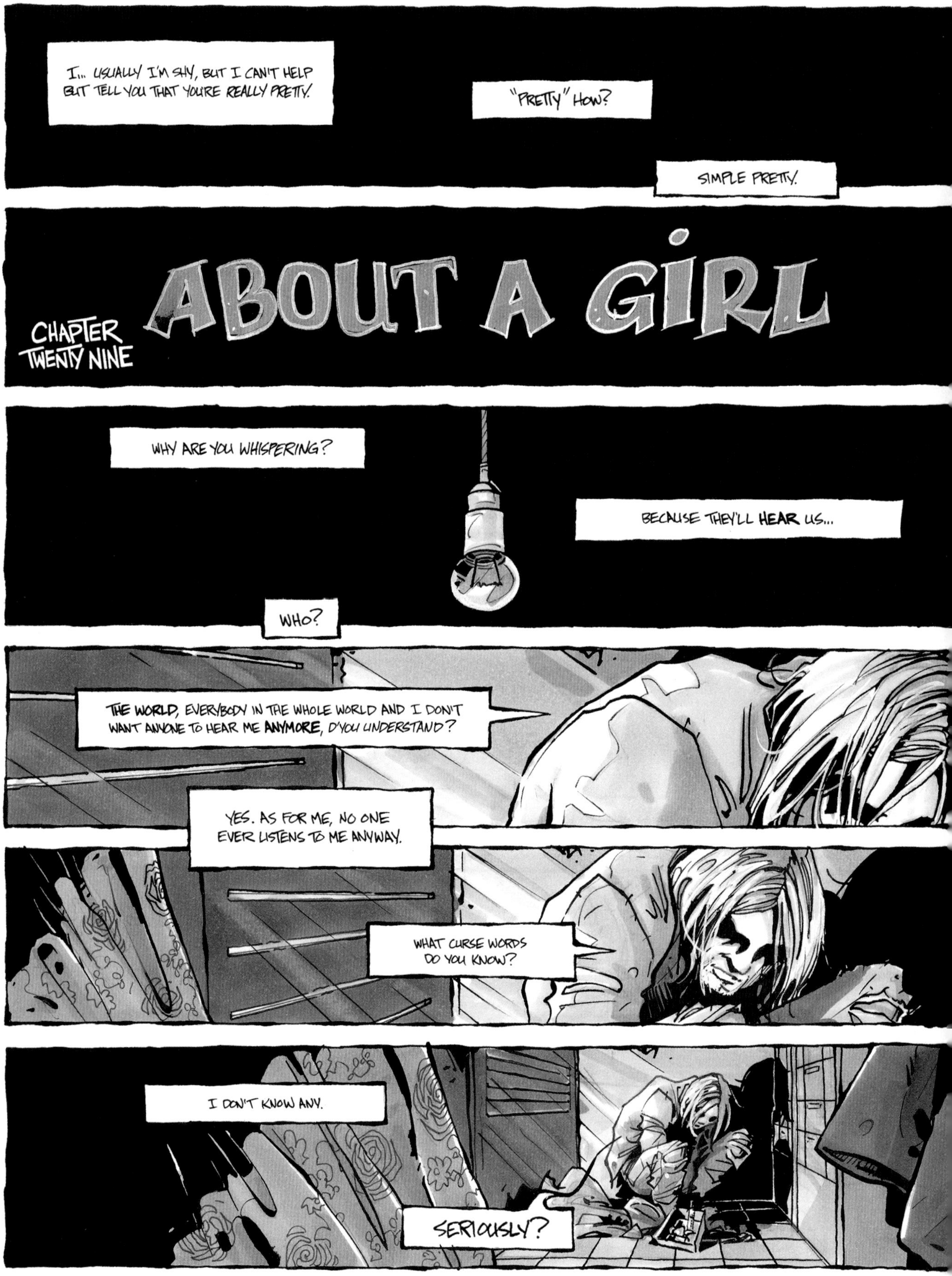
I... USUALLY I'M SHY, BUT I CAN'T HELP BUT TELL YOU THAT YOU'RE REALLY PRETTY.
"PRETTY" HOW?
SIMPLE PRETTY.
CHAPTER TWENTY NINE
ABOUT A GIRL
WHY ARE YOU WHISPERING?
BECAUSE THEY'LL **HEAR** US...
WHO?
THE WORLD, EVERYBODY IN THE WHOLE WORLD AND I DON'T WANT ANYONE TO HEAR ME **ANYMORE**, D'YOU UNDERSTAND?
YES. AS FOR ME, NO ONE EVER LISTENS TO ME ANYWAY.
WHAT CURSE WORDS DO YOU KNOW?
I DON'T KNOW ANY.
SERIOUSLY?

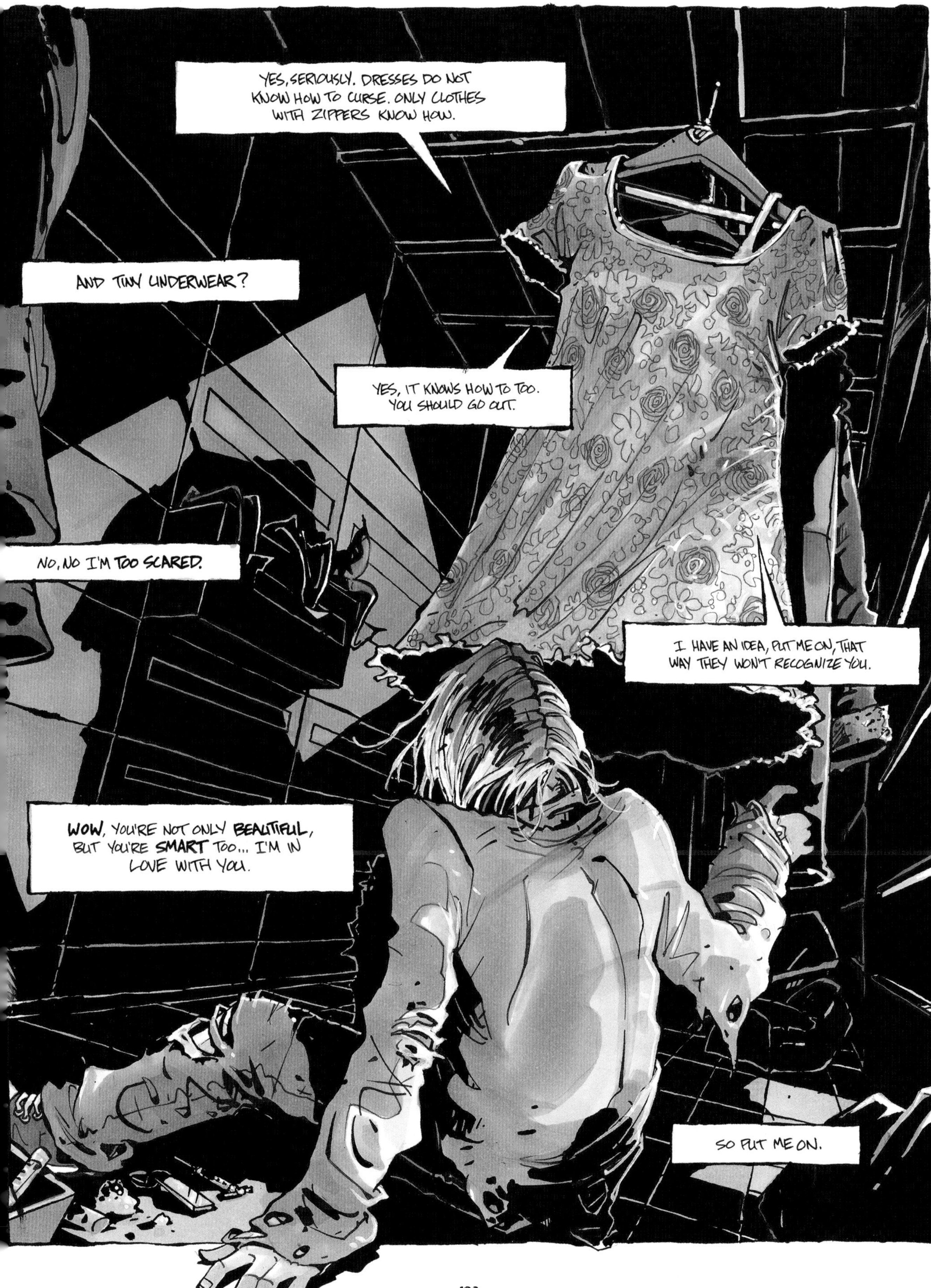

YES, SERIOUSLY. DRESSES DO NOT KNOW HOW TO CURSE. ONLY CLOTHES WITH ZIPPERS KNOW HOW.
AND TINY UNDERWEAR?
YES, IT KNOWS HOW TO TOO. YOU SHOULD GO OUT.
NO, NO I'M TOO SCARED.
I HAVE AN IDEA, PUT ME ON, THAT WAY THEY WON'T RECOGNIZE YOU.
WOW, YOU'RE NOT ONLY BEAUTIFUL, BUT YOU'RE SMART TOO... I'M IN LOVE WITH YOU.
SO PUT ME ON.

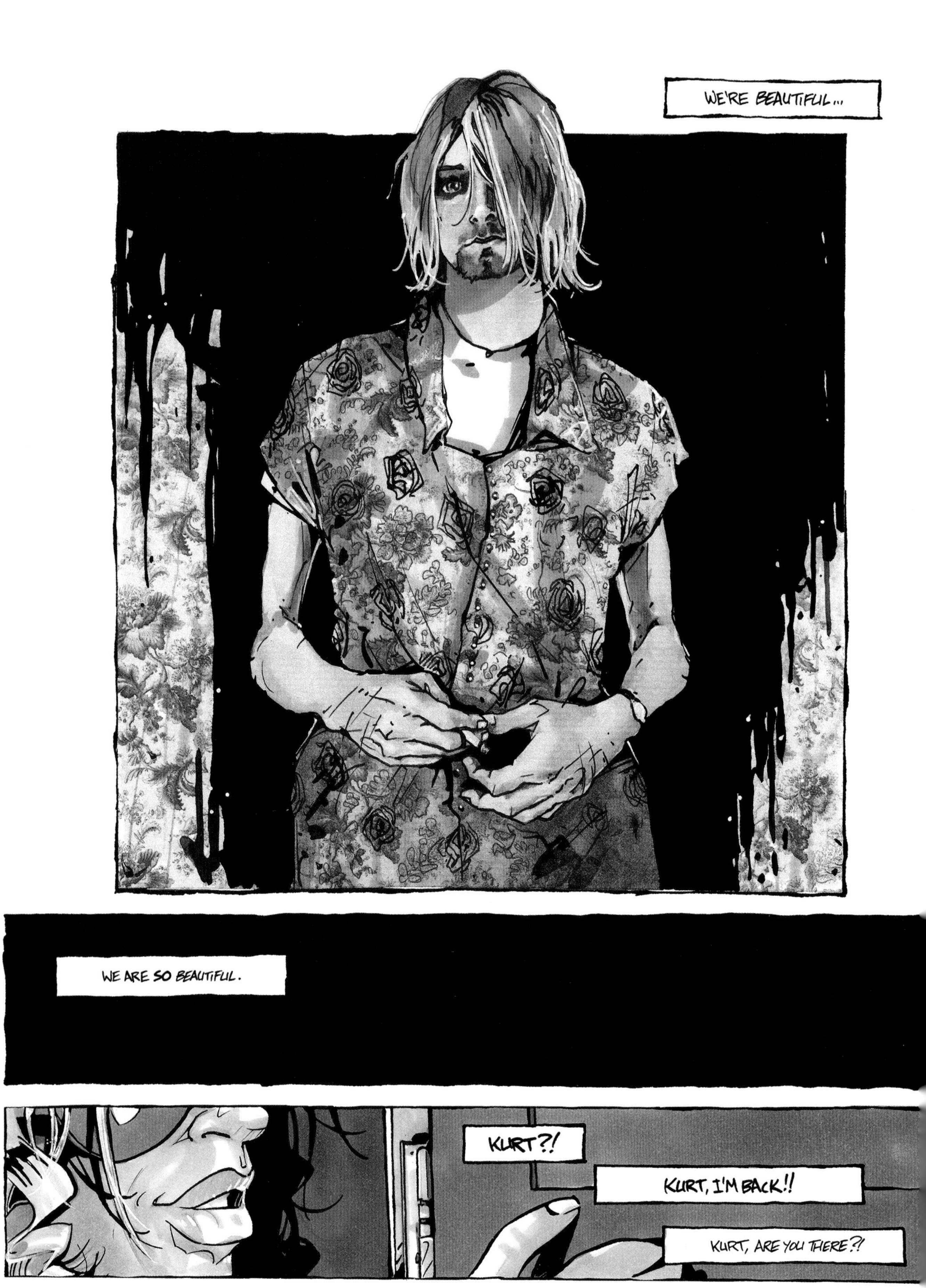
WE'RE BEAUTIFUL...
WE ARE SO BEAUTIFUL.
KURT?!
KURT, I'M BACK!!
KURT, ARE YOU THERE?!

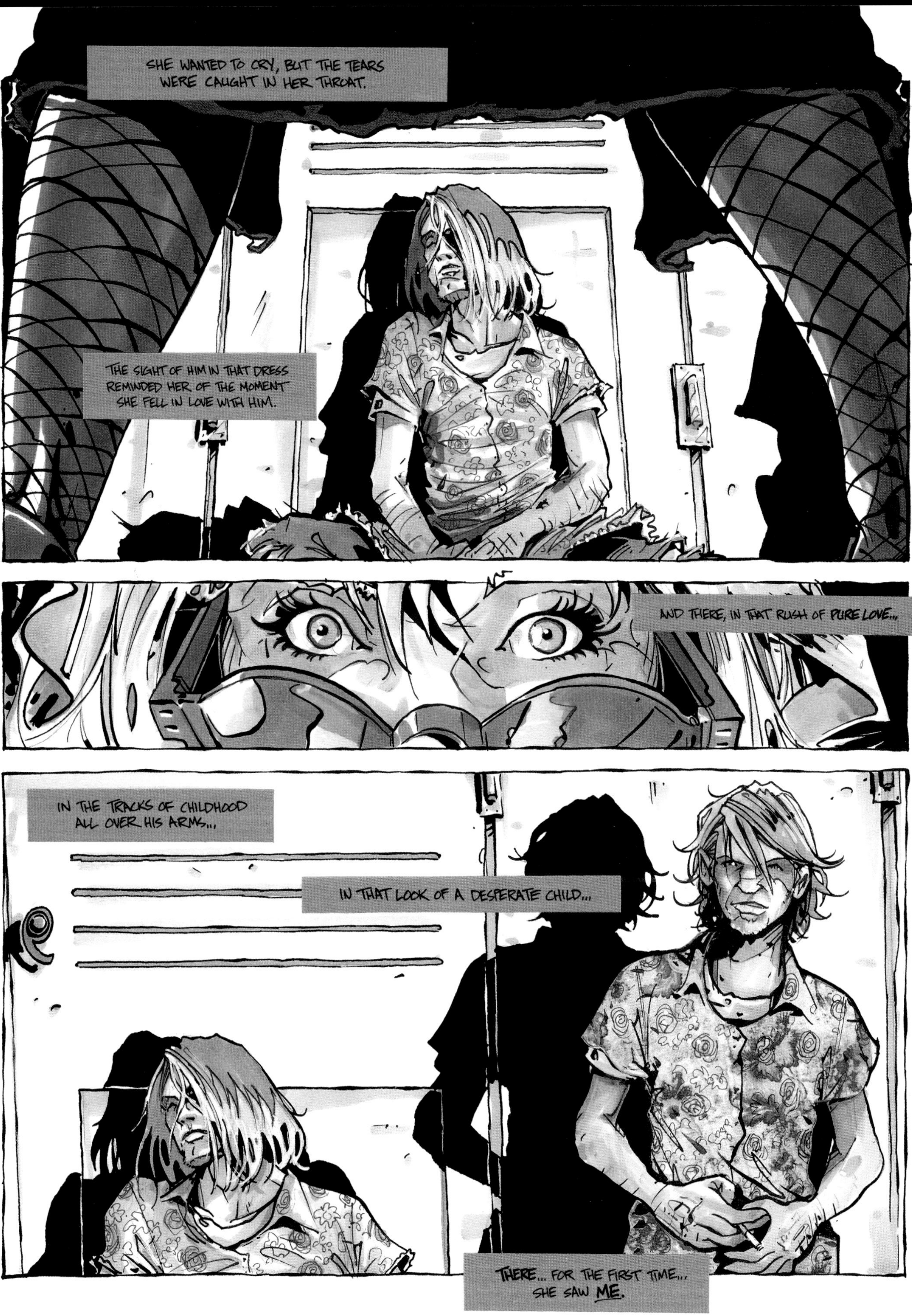
SHE WANTED TO CRY, BUT THE TEARS WERE CAUGHT IN HER THROAT.
THE SIGHT OF HIM IN THAT DRESS REMINDED HER OF THE MOMENT SHE FELL IN LOVE WITH HIM.
AND THERE, IN THAT RUSH OF PURE LOVE...
IN THE TRACKS OF CHILDHOOD ALL OVER HIS ARMS...
IN THAT LOOK OF A DESPERATE CHILD...
THERE... FOR THE FIRST TIME... SHE SAW ME.

I DON'T FEEL WELL.

ARE YOU FEELING *NAUSEOUS*?

I MUST BE ANEMIC SINCE I'VE NEVER EATEN.

OR, *I DON'T KNOW*, I'VE GOT THE FLU, CANCER, A BLOW DRY, NASAL HERNIA.

BASICALLY, THE OTHER ONE HURTS, UNDERSTAND?

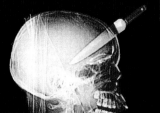

WILL YOU ANSWER, SHIT?

SORRY, I GOT CARRIED AWAY... I'M NOT MYSELF RIGHT NOW...

JUST TO BE CLEAR, DOCTOR, I DON'T EXIST, BUT I HAVE A NAME.

MY NAME IS *BODDAH*.

UNCLE CHUCK

CHAPTER THIRTY

YOU CAN ADMIT MY SITUATION IS PAINFUL.

HMM! SO KURT, YOU OKAY LITTLE MAN?

YUP.

I DON'T KNOW IF YOUR MOTHER TOLD YOU, BUT I'M OFF TO *VIETNAM*...

YUP.

MOOOMM!! WHERE'S *BODDAH'S* PLATE?!

OH, *SORRY* SWEETHEART...

THAT'S WHAT I WANTED TO TALK TO YOU ABOUT, KURT.

UH, I'M OFF TO VIETNAM SO I WONDER IF I COULD BRING *BODDAH* WITH ME.

YOU SEE, I'M GOING TO BE ALONE OUT THERE, AND THAT'S GOING TO BE *HARD*. SO I WAS WONDERING IF YOU WOULD *LEND* HIM TO ME?

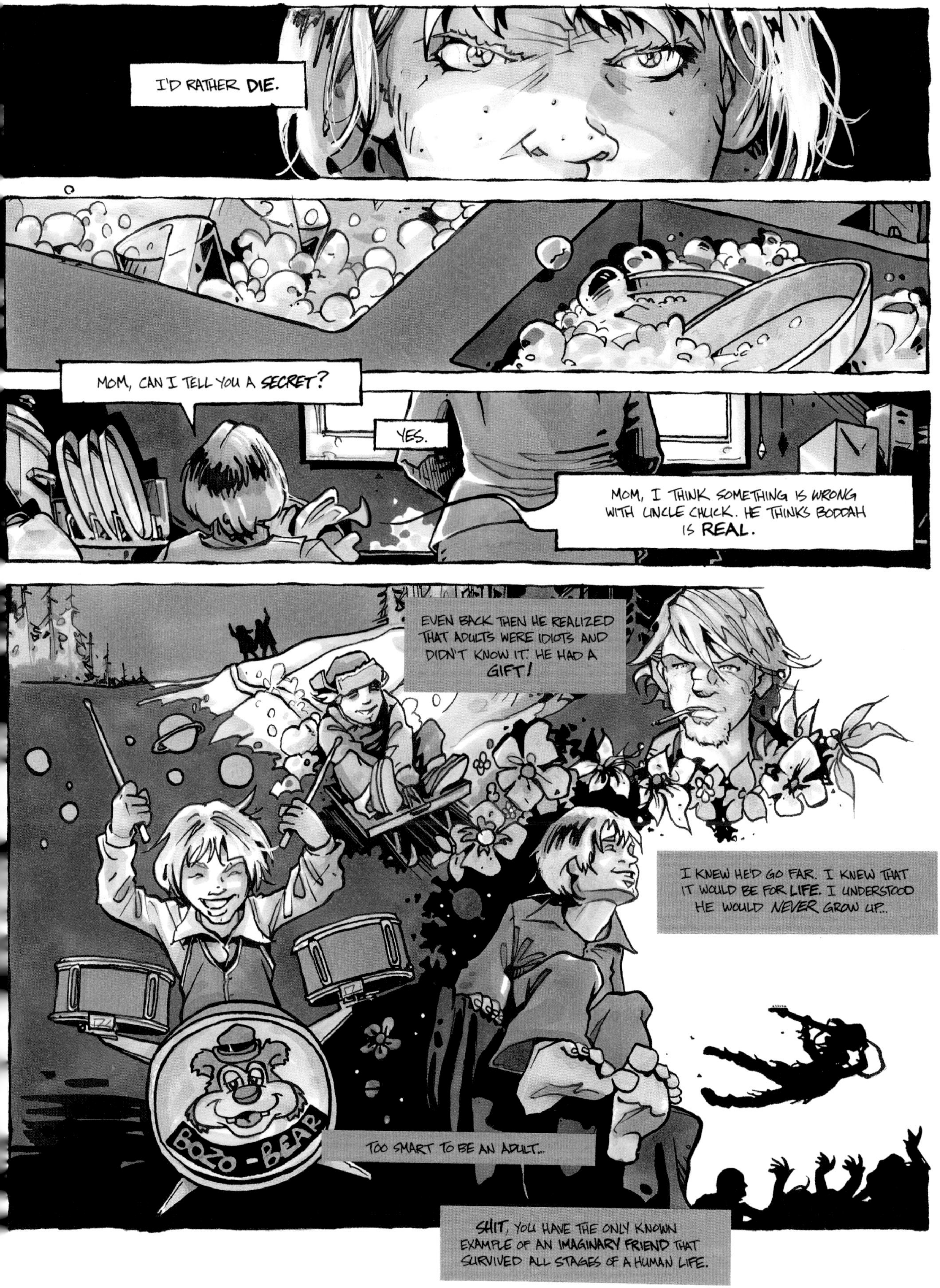

I'D RATHER DIE.
MOM, CAN I TELL YOU A SECRET?
YES.
MOM, I THINK SOMETHING IS WRONG WITH UNCLE CHUCK. HE THINKS BODDAH IS REAL.
EVEN BACK THEN HE REALIZED THAT ADULTS WERE IDIOTS AND DIDN'T KNOW IT. HE HAD A GIFT!
I KNEW HE'D GO FAR. I KNEW THAT IT WOULD BE FOR LIFE. I UNDERSTOOD HE WOULD NEVER GROW UP...
BOZO-BEAR
TOO SMART TO BE AN ADULT...
SHIT, YOU HAVE THE ONLY KNOWN EXAMPLE OF AN IMAGINARY FRIEND THAT SURVIVED ALL STAGES OF A HUMAN LIFE.

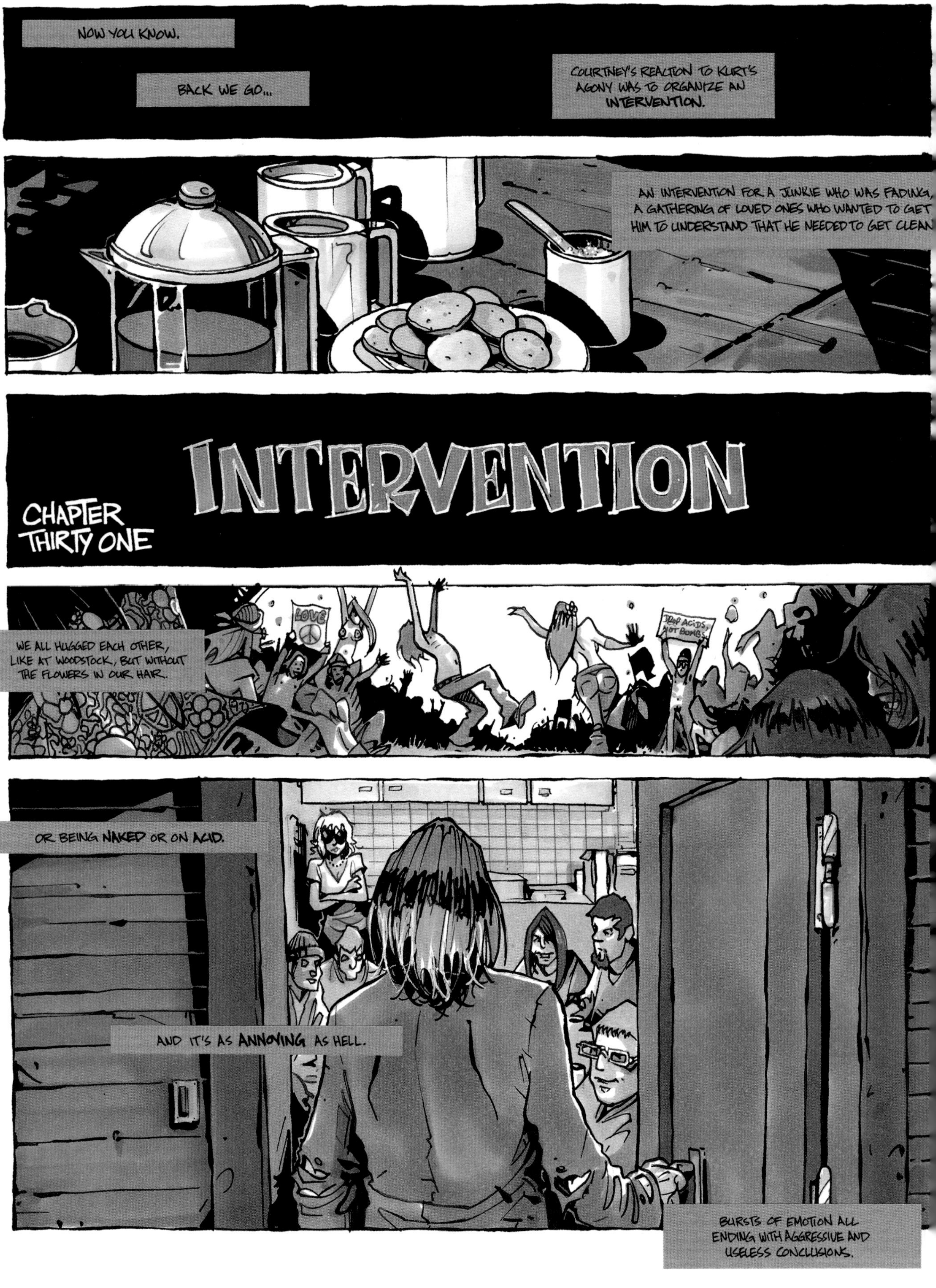
NOW YOU KNOW.
BACK WE GO...
COURTNEY'S REACTION TO KURT'S AGONY WAS TO ORGANIZE AN INTERVENTION.
AN INTERVENTION FOR A JUNKIE WHO WAS FADING, A GATHERING OF LOVED ONES WHO WANTED TO GET HIM TO UNDERSTAND THAT HE NEEDED TO GET CLEAN.
INTERVENTION
CHAPTER THIRTY ONE
WE ALL HUGGED EACH OTHER, LIKE AT WOODSTOCK, BUT WITHOUT THE FLOWERS IN OUR HAIR.
LOVE
DROP ACIDS, NOT BOMBS
OR BEING NAKED OR ON ACID.
AND IT'S AS ANNOYING AS HELL.
BURSTS OF EMOTION ALL ENDING WITH AGGRESSIVE AND USELESS CONCLUSIONS.

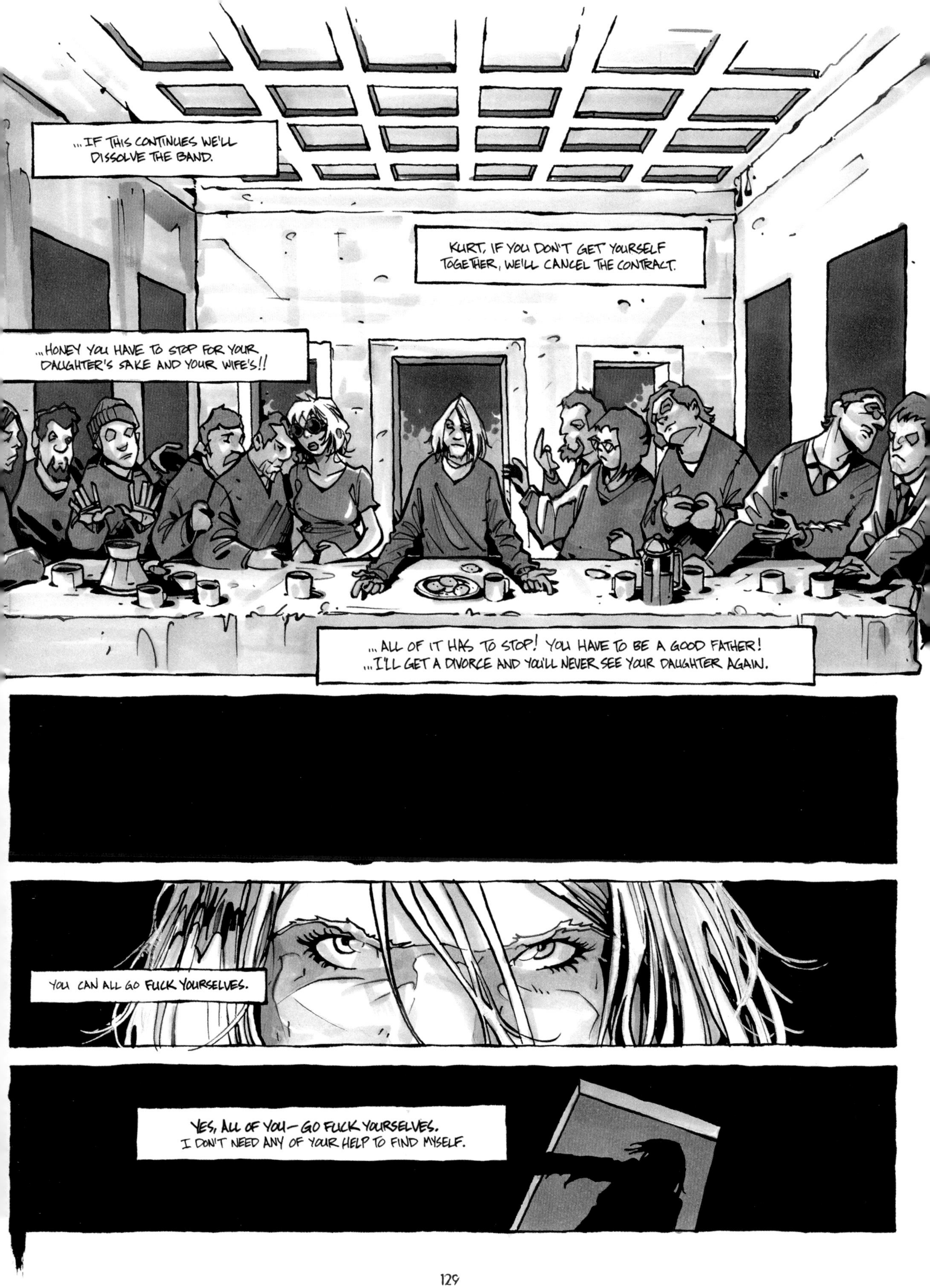
...IF THIS CONTINUES WE'LL DISSOLVE THE BAND.
KURT, IF YOU DON'T GET YOURSELF TOGETHER, WE'LL CANCEL THE CONTRACT.
...HONEY YOU HAVE TO STOP FOR YOUR DAUGHTER'S SAKE AND YOUR WIFE'S!!
...ALL OF IT HAS TO STOP! YOU HAVE TO BE A GOOD FATHER!
...I'LL GET A DIVORCE AND YOU'LL NEVER SEE YOUR DAUGHTER AGAIN.
YOU CAN ALL GO FUCK YOURSELVES.
YES, ALL OF YOU—GO FUCK YOURSELVES.
I DON'T NEED ANY OF YOUR HELP TO FIND MYSELF.

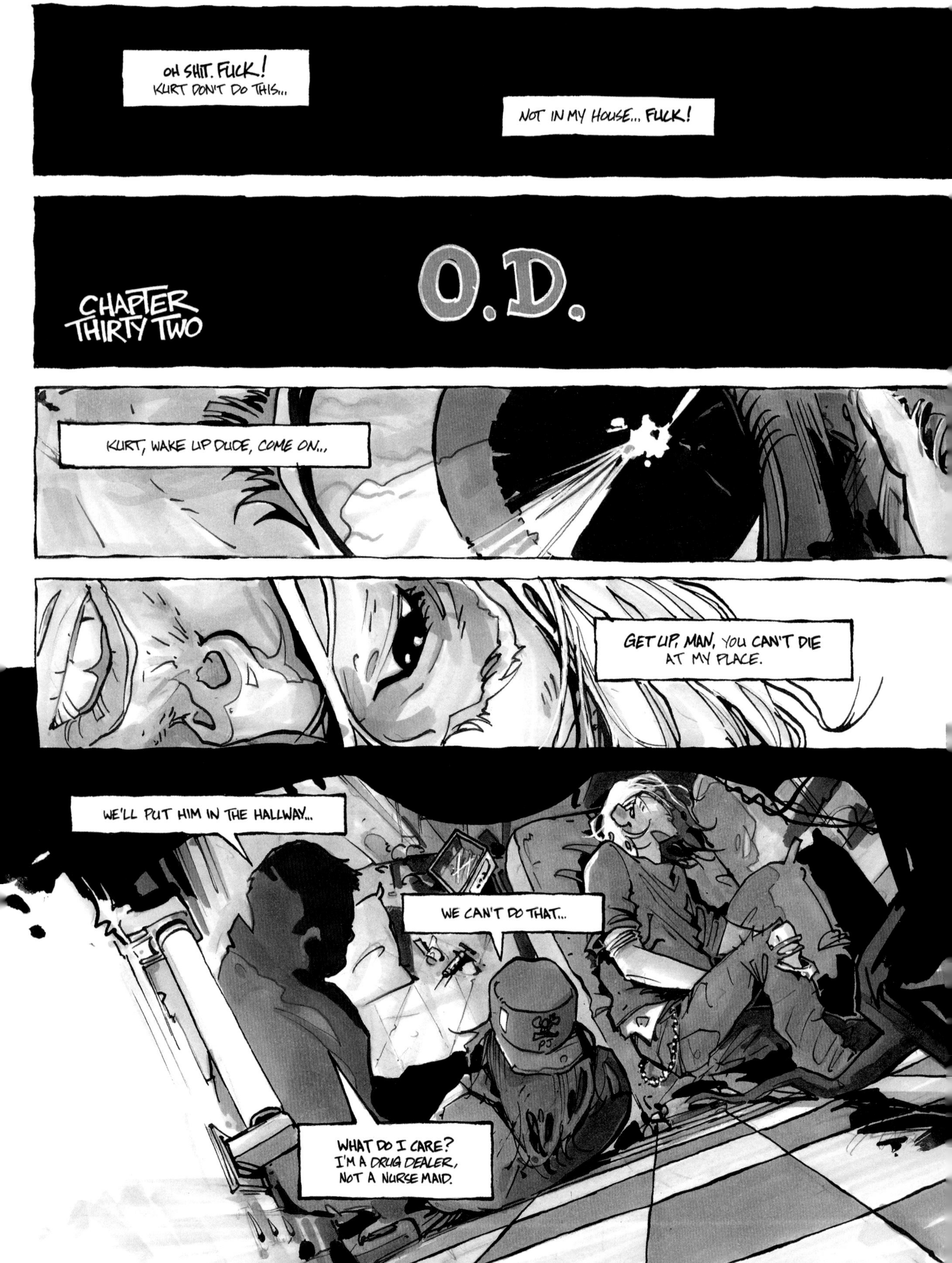
OH SHIT. FUCK! KURT DON'T DO THIS...
NOT IN MY HOUSE... FUCK!
CHAPTER THIRTY TWO
O.D.
KURT, WAKE UP DUDE, COME ON...
GET UP, MAN, YOU CAN'T DIE AT MY PLACE.
WE'LL PUT HIM IN THE HALLWAY...
WE CAN'T DO THAT...
WHAT DO I CARE? I'M A DRUG DEALER, NOT A NURSE MAID.

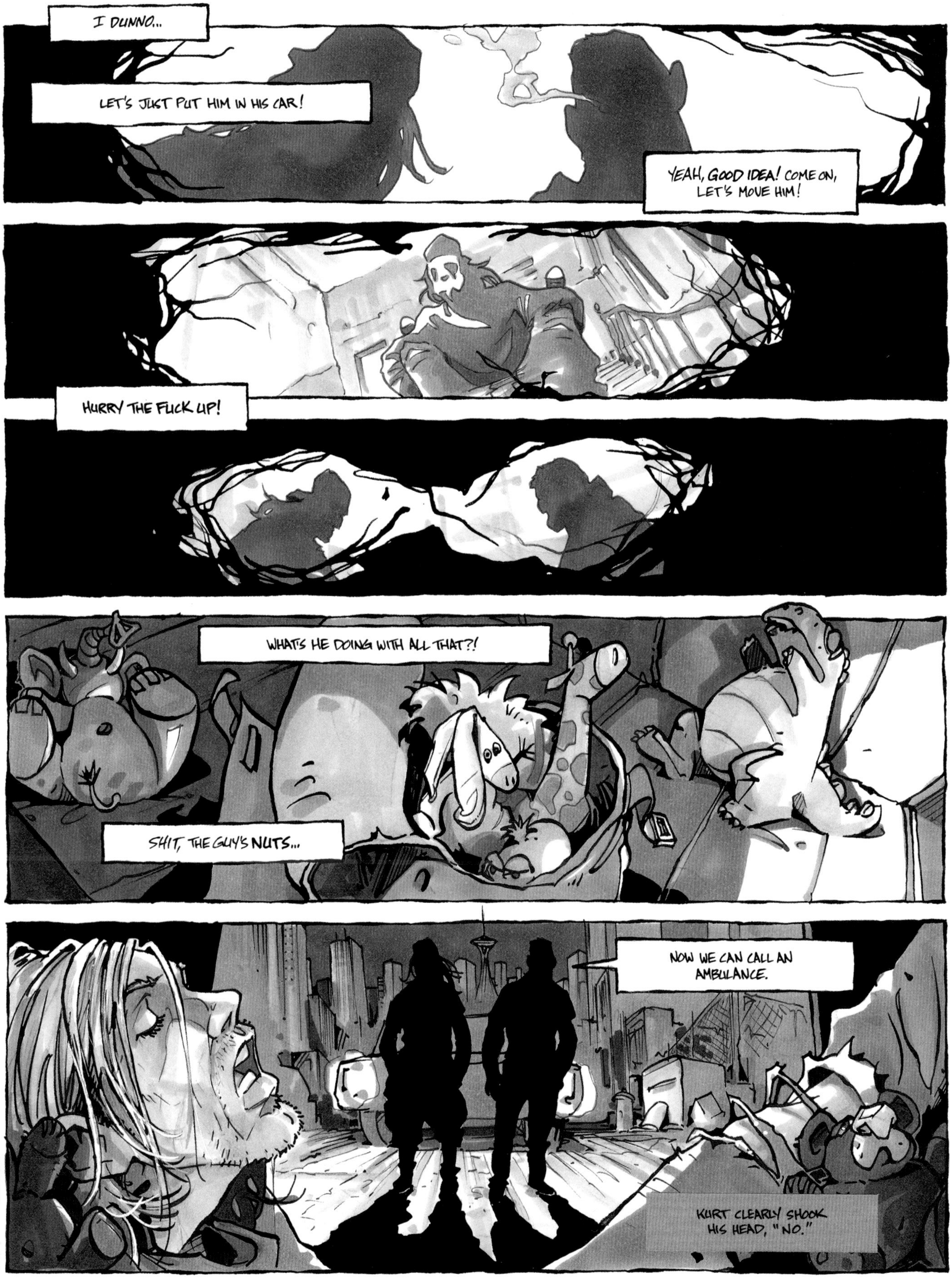
I DUNNO...
LET'S JUST PUT HIM IN HIS CAR!
YEAH, GOOD IDEA! COME ON, LET'S MOVE HIM!
HURRY THE FUCK UP!
WHAT'S HE DOING WITH ALL THAT?!
SHIT, THE GUY'S NUTS...
NOW WE CAN CALL AN AMBULANCE.
KURT CLEARLY SHOOK HIS HEAD, "NO."

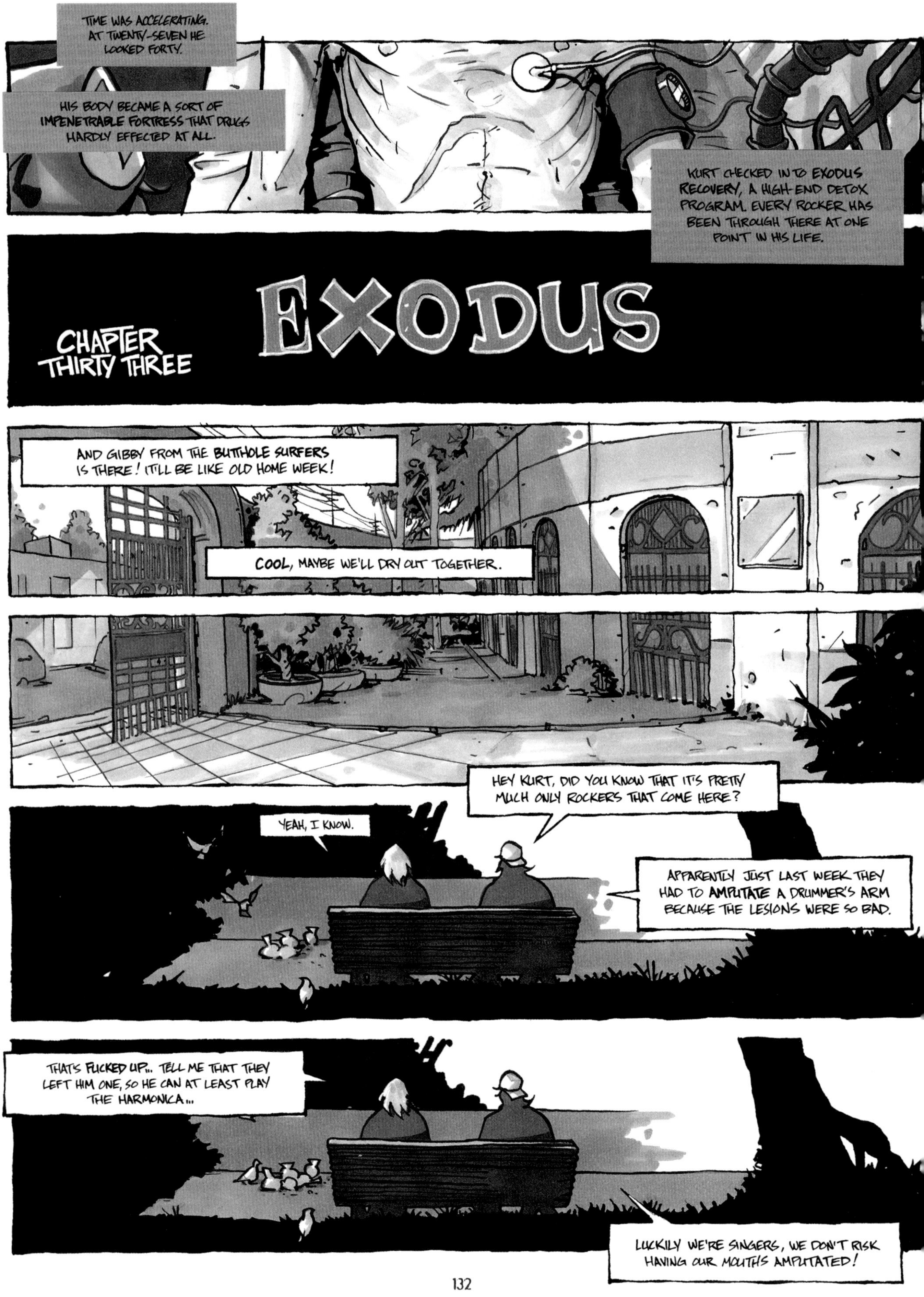
TIME WAS ACCELERATING. AT TWENTY-SEVEN HE LOOKED FORTY.
HIS BODY BECAME A SORT OF IMPENETRABLE FORTRESS THAT DRUGS HARDLY EFFECTED AT ALL.
KURT CHECKED IN TO EXODUS RECOVERY, A HIGH-END DETOX PROGRAM. EVERY ROCKER HAS BEEN THROUGH THERE AT ONE POINT IN HIS LIFE.
CHAPTER THIRTY THREE
EXODUS
AND GIBBY FROM THE BUTTHOLE SURFERS IS THERE! IT'LL BE LIKE OLD HOME WEEK!
COOL, MAYBE WE'LL DRY OUT TOGETHER.
HEY KURT, DID YOU KNOW THAT IT'S PRETTY MUCH ONLY ROCKERS THAT COME HERE?
YEAH, I KNOW.
APPARENTLY JUST LAST WEEK THEY HAD TO AMPUTATE A DRUMMER'S ARM BECAUSE THE LESIONS WERE SO BAD.
THAT'S FUCKED UP... TELL ME THAT THEY LEFT HIM ONE, SO HE CAN AT LEAST PLAY THE HARMONICA...
LUCKILY WE'RE SINGERS, WE DON'T RISK HAVING OUR MOUTHS AMPUTATED!

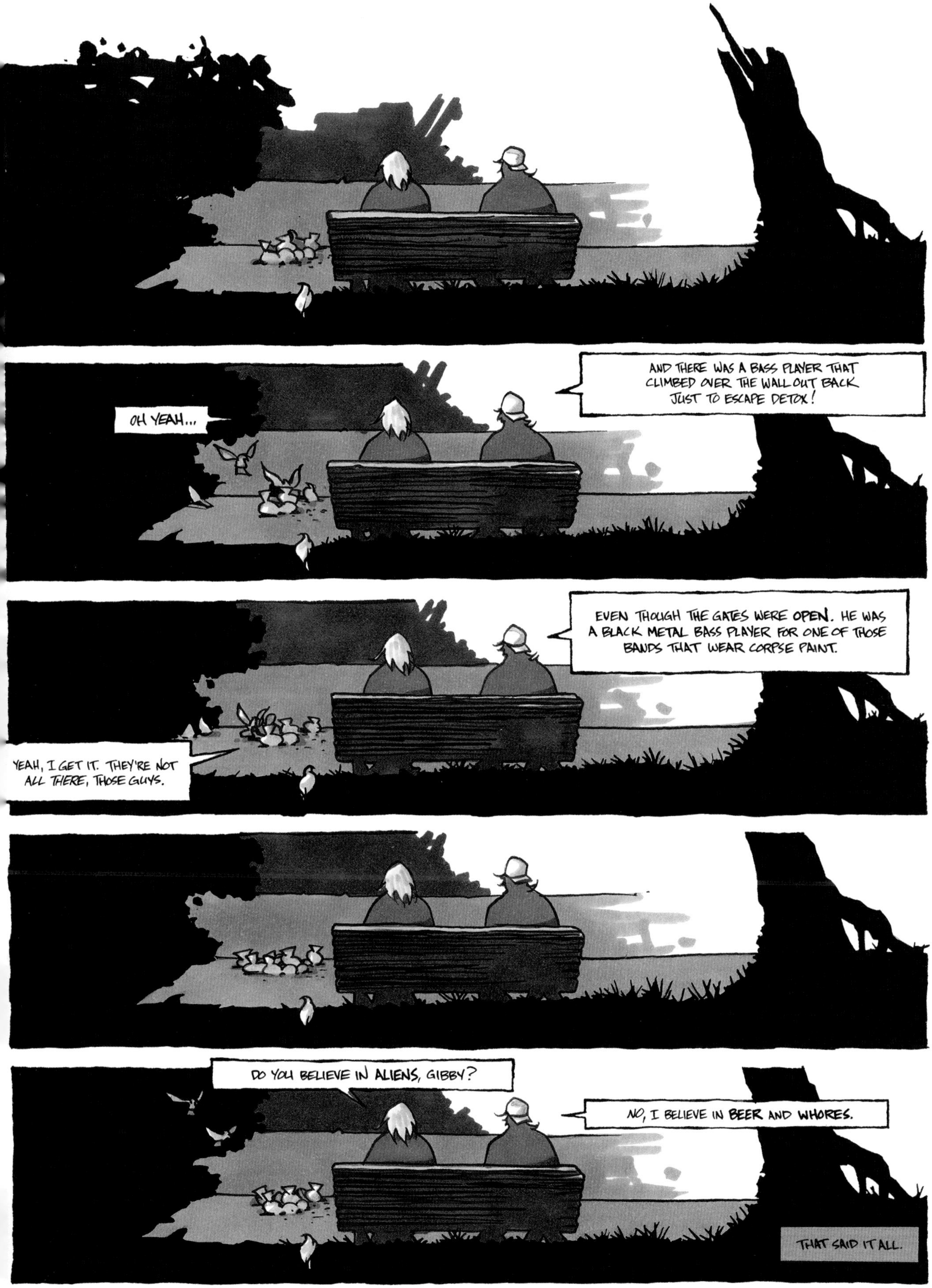
AND THERE WAS A BASS PLAYER THAT CLIMBED OVER THE WALL OUT BACK JUST TO ESCAPE DETOX!
OH YEAH...
EVEN THOUGH THE GATES WERE OPEN. HE WAS A BLACK METAL BASS PLAYER FOR ONE OF THOSE BANDS THAT WEAR CORPSE PAINT.
YEAH, I GET IT. THEY'RE NOT ALL THERE, THOSE GUYS.
DO YOU BELIEVE IN ALIENS, GIBBY?
NO, I BELIEVE IN BEER AND WHORES.
THAT SAID IT ALL.

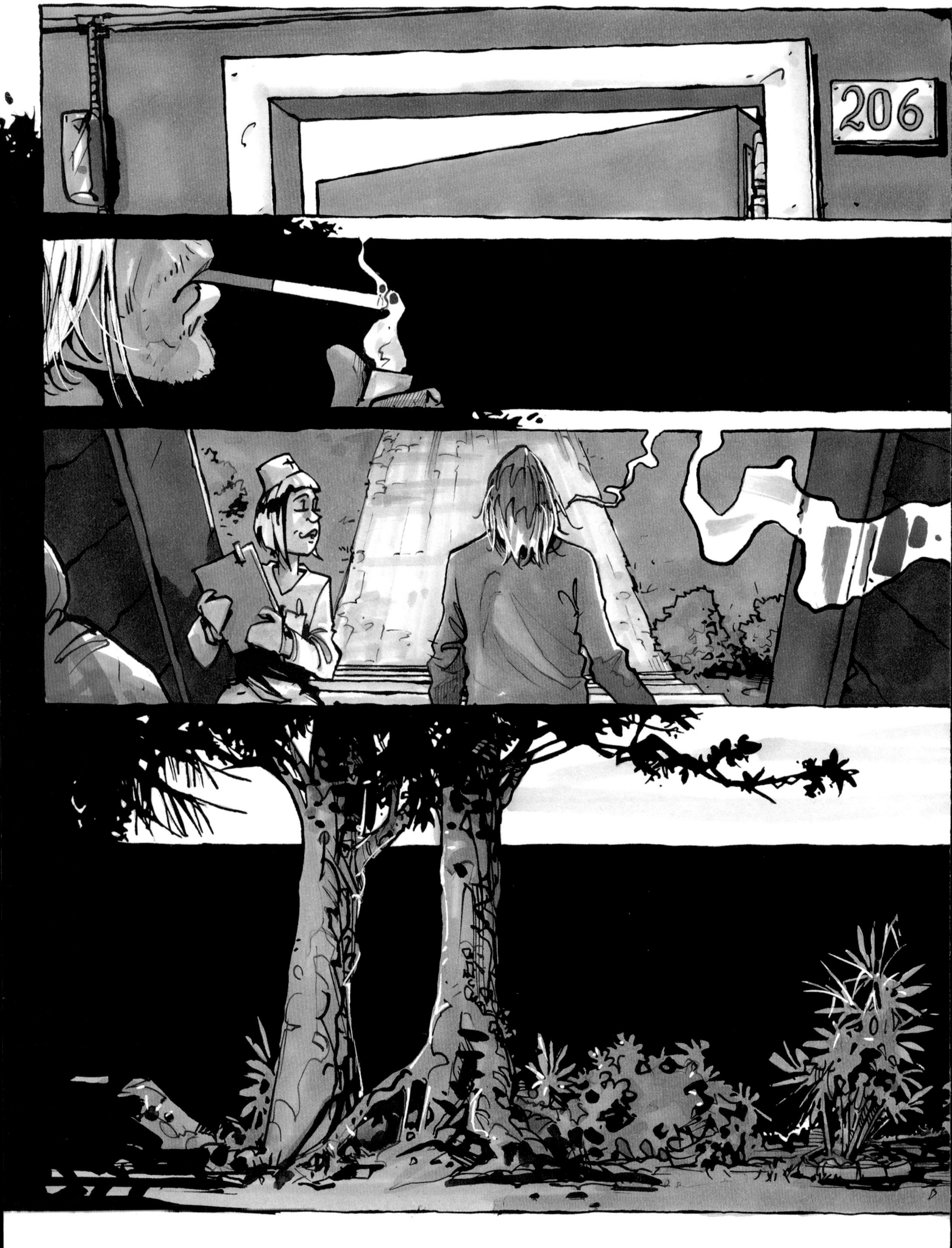
206

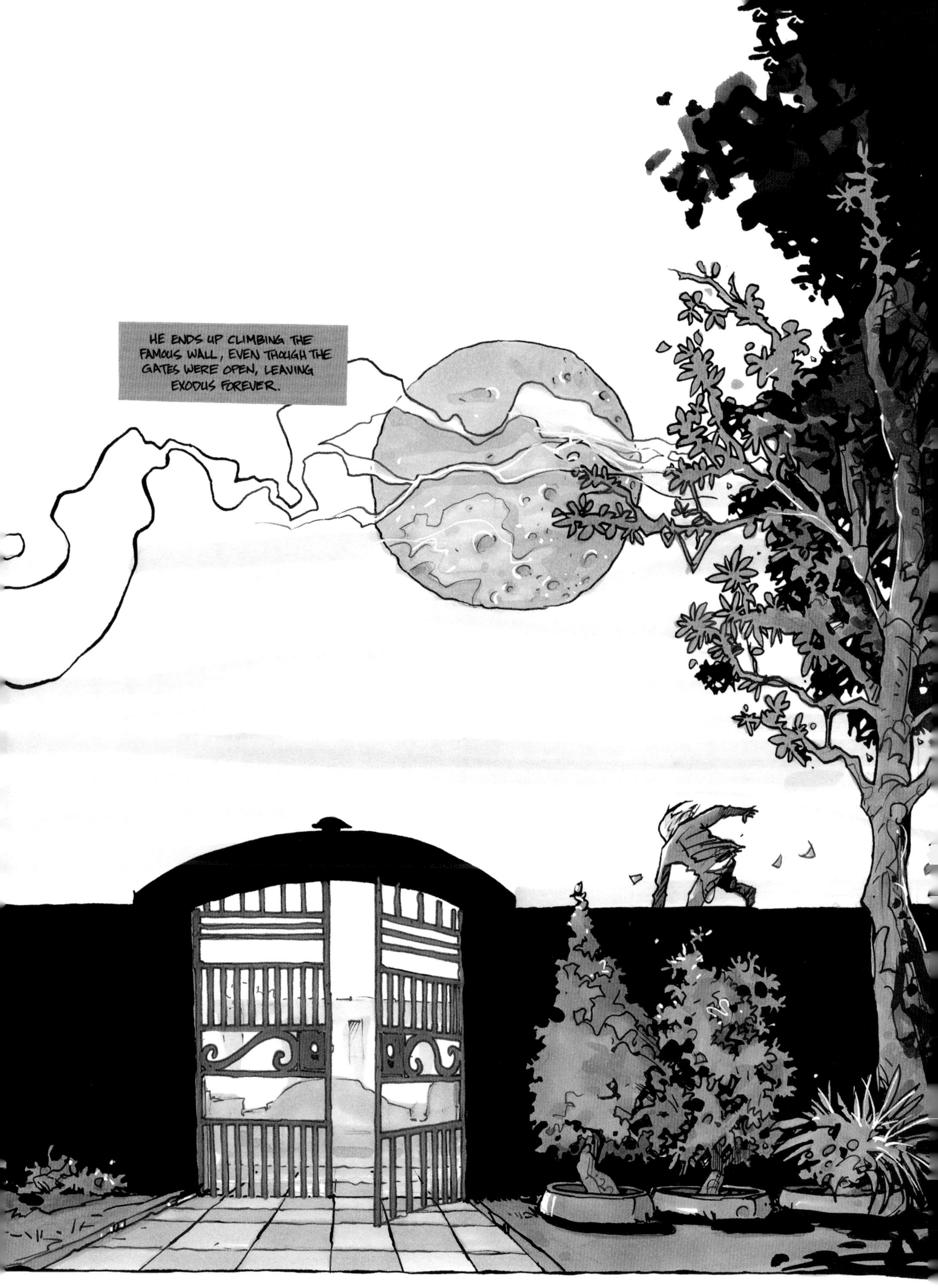
HE ENDS UP CLIMBING THE FAMOUS WALL, EVEN THOUGH THE GATES WERE OPEN, LEAVING EXODUS FOREVER.

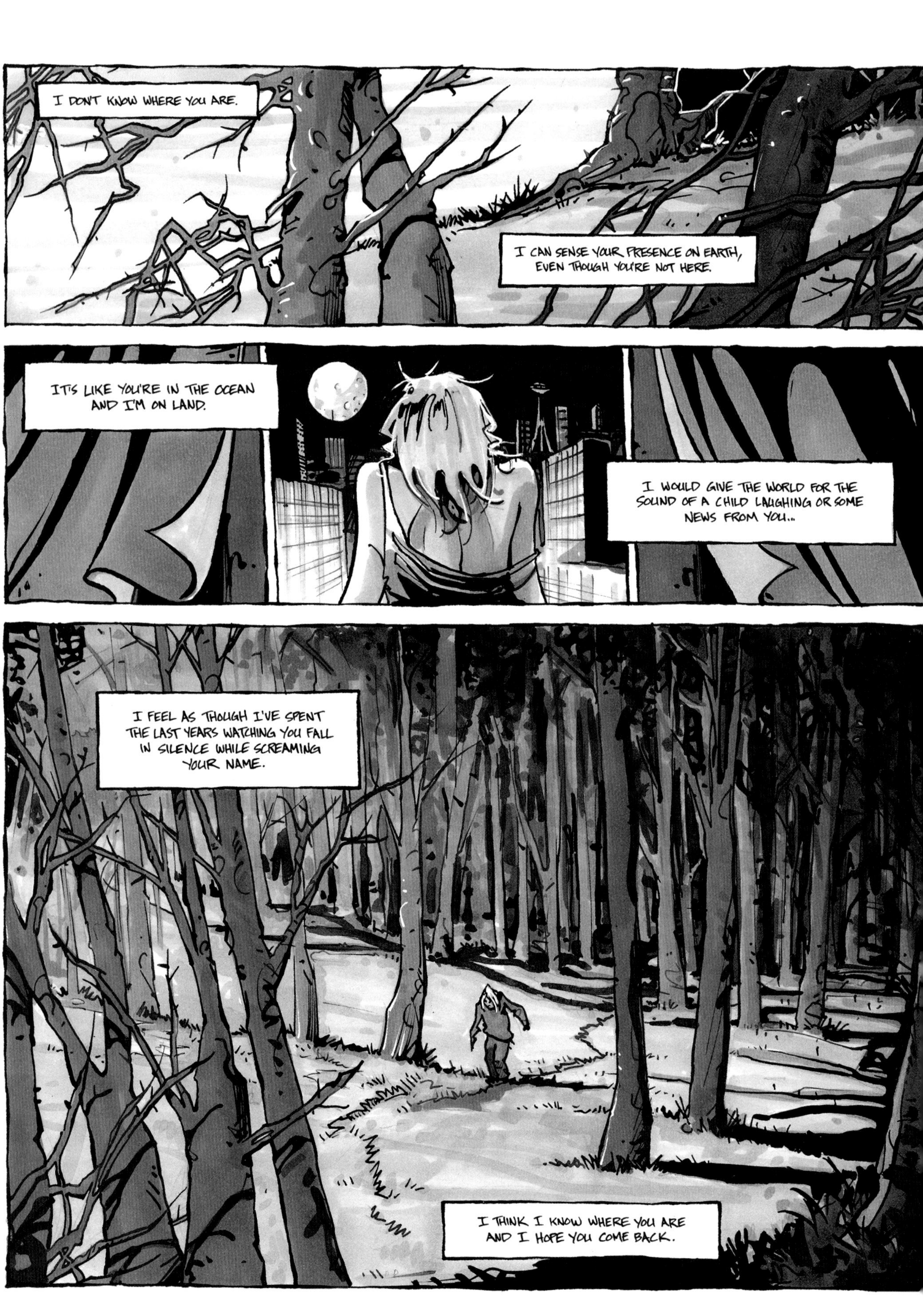
I DON'T KNOW WHERE YOU ARE.
I CAN SENSE YOUR PRESENCE ON EARTH, EVEN THOUGH YOU'RE NOT HERE.
IT'S LIKE YOU'RE IN THE OCEAN AND I'M ON LAND.
I WOULD GIVE THE WORLD FOR THE SOUND OF A CHILD LAUGHING OR SOME NEWS FROM YOU...
I FEEL AS THOUGH I'VE SPENT THE LAST YEARS WATCHING YOU FALL IN SILENCE WHILE SCREAMING YOUR NAME.
I THINK I KNOW WHERE YOU ARE AND I HOPE YOU COME BACK.

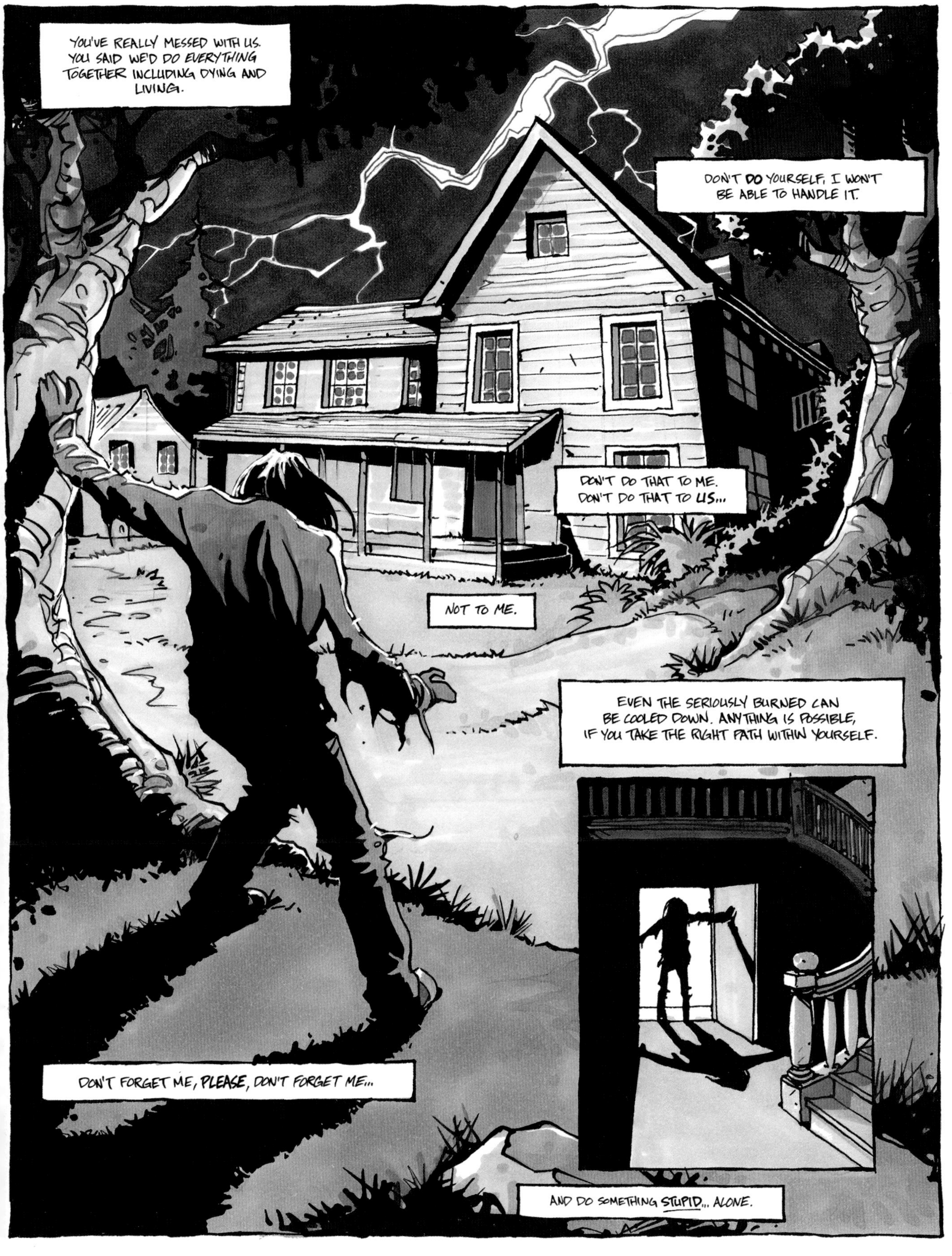
YOU'VE REALLY MESSED WITH US. YOU SAID WE'D DO EVERYTHING TOGETHER INCLUDING DYING AND LIVING.
DON'T DO YOURSELF, I WON'T BE ABLE TO HANDLE IT.
DON'T DO THAT TO ME. DON'T DO THAT TO US...
NOT TO ME.
EVEN THE SERIOUSLY BURNED CAN BE COOLED DOWN. ANYTHING IS POSSIBLE, IF YOU TAKE THE RIGHT PATH WITHIN YOURSELF.
DON'T FORGET ME, PLEASE, DON'T FORGET ME...
AND DO SOMETHING STUPID... ALONE.

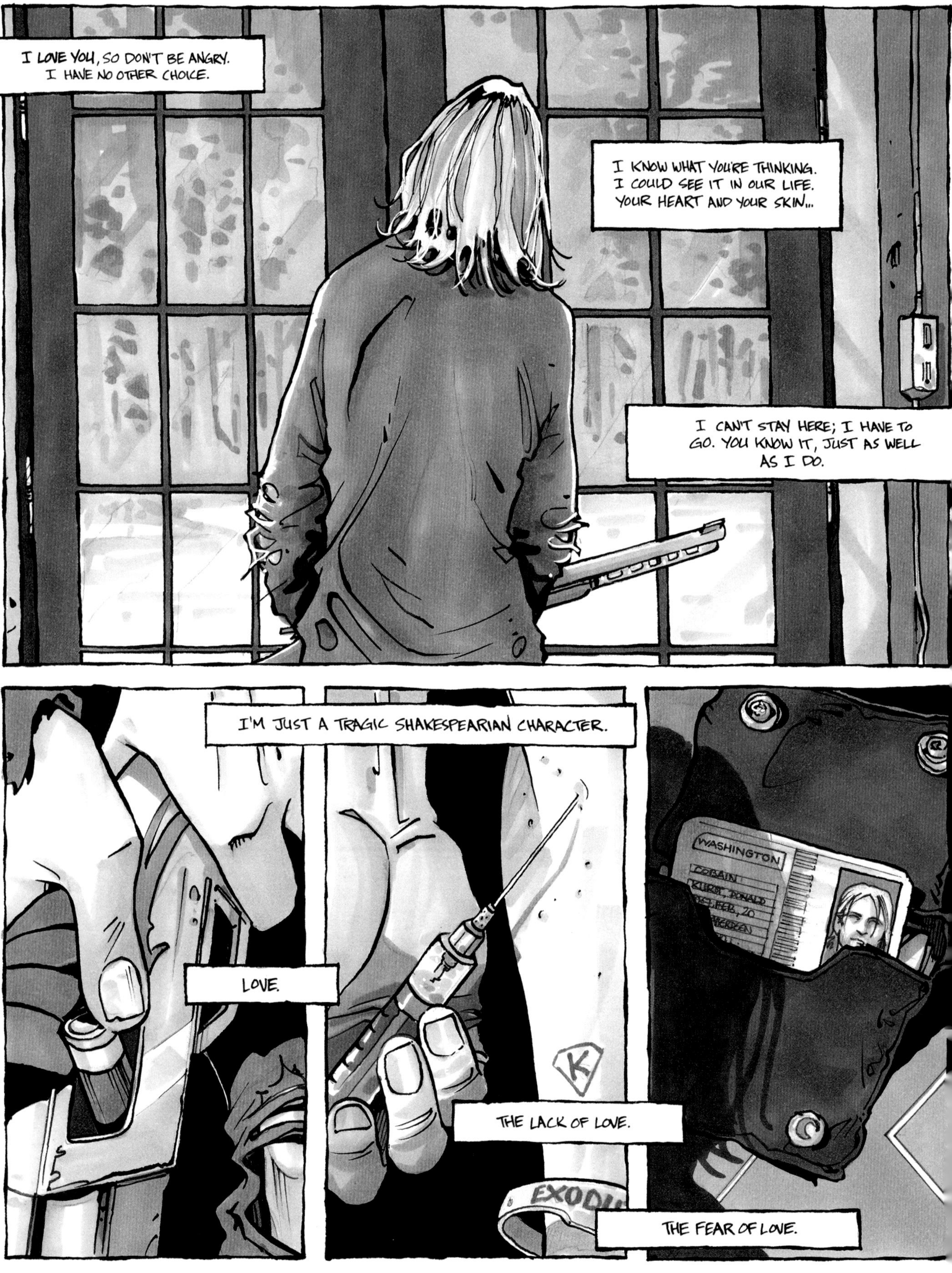
I LOVE YOU, SO DON'T BE ANGRY. I HAVE NO OTHER CHOICE.
I KNOW WHAT YOU'RE THINKING. I COULD SEE IT IN OUR LIFE. YOUR HEART AND YOUR SKIN...
I CAN'T STAY HERE; I HAVE TO GO. YOU KNOW IT, JUST AS WELL AS I DO.
I'M JUST A TRAGIC SHAKESPEARIAN CHARACTER.
LOVE.
THE LACK OF LOVE.
WASHINGTON
COBAIN
THE FEAR OF LOVE.

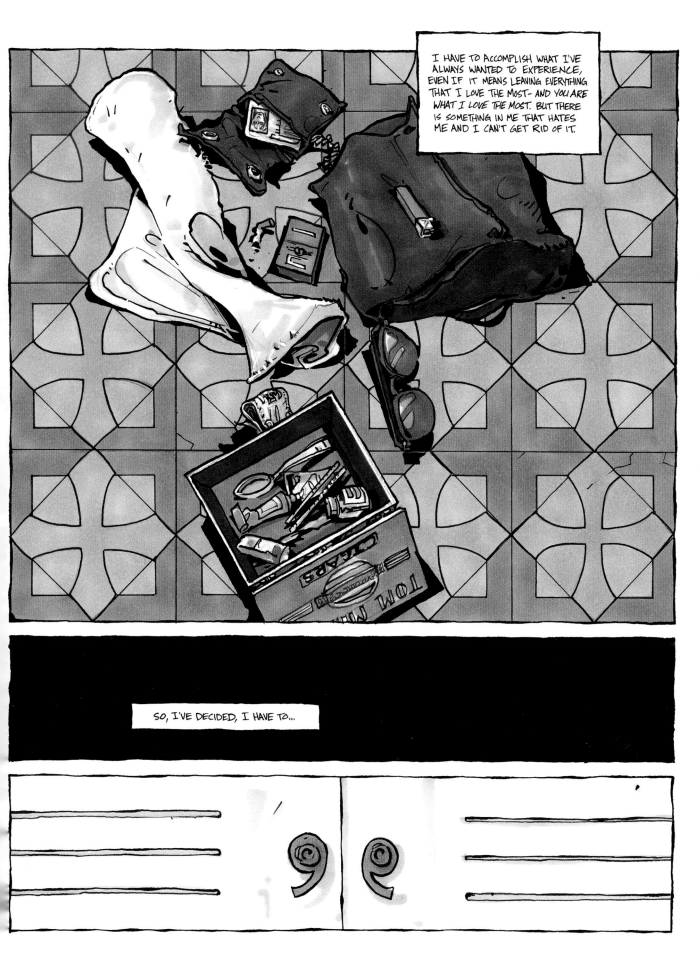

I HAVE TO ACCOMPLISH WHAT I'VE ALWAYS WANTED TO EXPERIENCE, EVEN IF IT MEANS LEAVING EVERYTHING THAT I LOVE THE MOST- AND YOU ARE WHAT I LOVE THE MOST. BUT THERE IS SOMETHING IN ME THAT HATES ME AND I CAN'T GET RID OF IT.

SO, I'VE DECIDED, I HAVE TO...

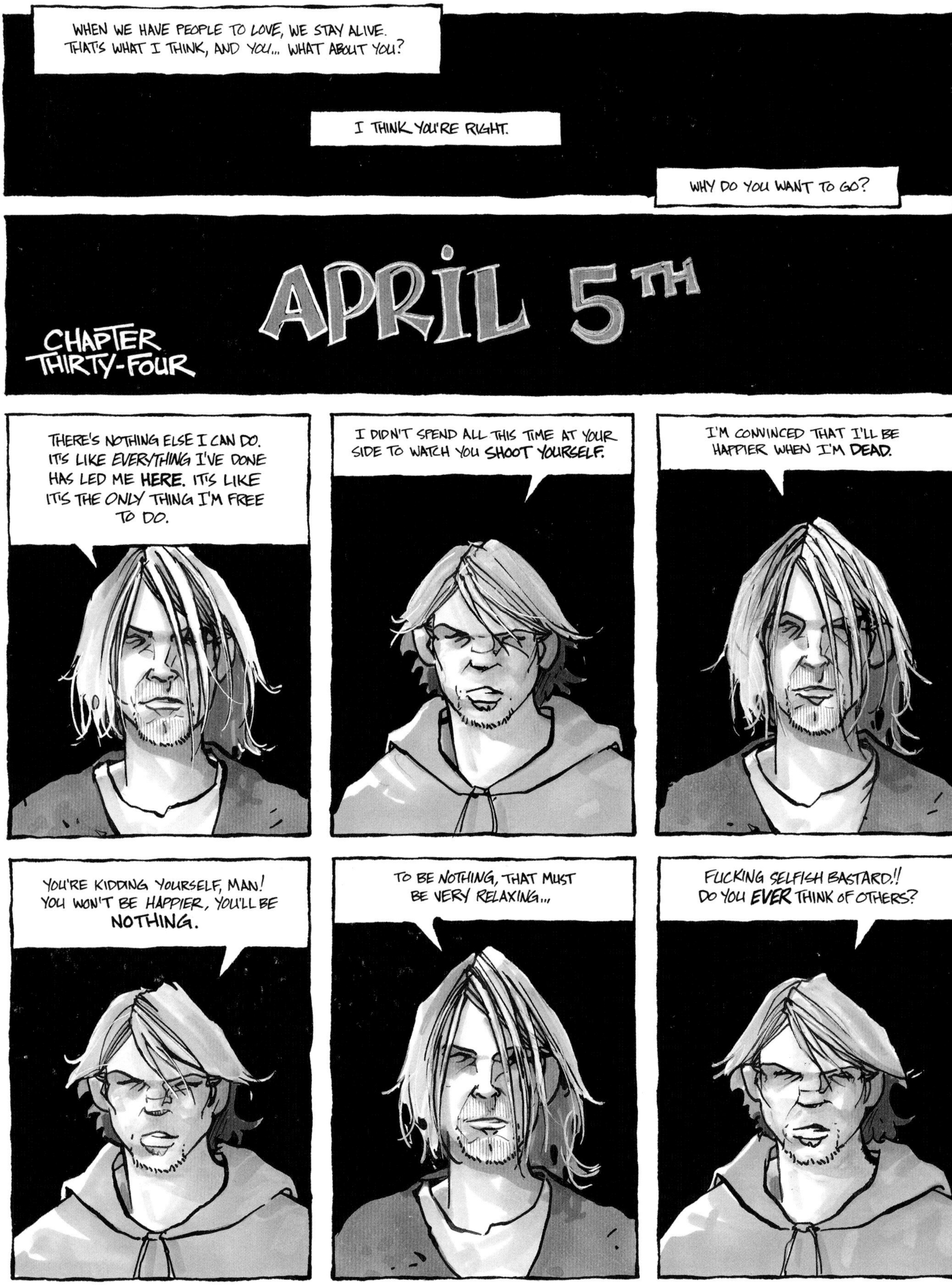
WHEN WE HAVE PEOPLE TO LOVE, WE STAY ALIVE. THAT'S WHAT I THINK, AND YOU... WHAT ABOUT YOU?
I THINK YOU'RE RIGHT.
WHY DO YOU WANT TO GO?
APRIL 5TH
CHAPTER THIRTY-FOUR
THERE'S NOTHING ELSE I CAN DO. IT'S LIKE EVERYTHING I'VE DONE HAS LED ME HERE. IT'S LIKE IT'S THE ONLY THING I'M FREE TO DO.
I DIDN'T SPEND ALL THIS TIME AT YOUR SIDE TO WATCH YOU SHOOT YOURSELF.
I'M CONVINCED THAT I'LL BE HAPPIER WHEN I'M DEAD.
YOU'RE KIDDING YOURSELF, MAN! YOU WON'T BE HAPPIER, YOU'LL BE NOTHING.
TO BE NOTHING, THAT MUST BE VERY RELAXING...
FUCKING SELFISH BASTARD!! DO YOU EVER THINK OF OTHERS?

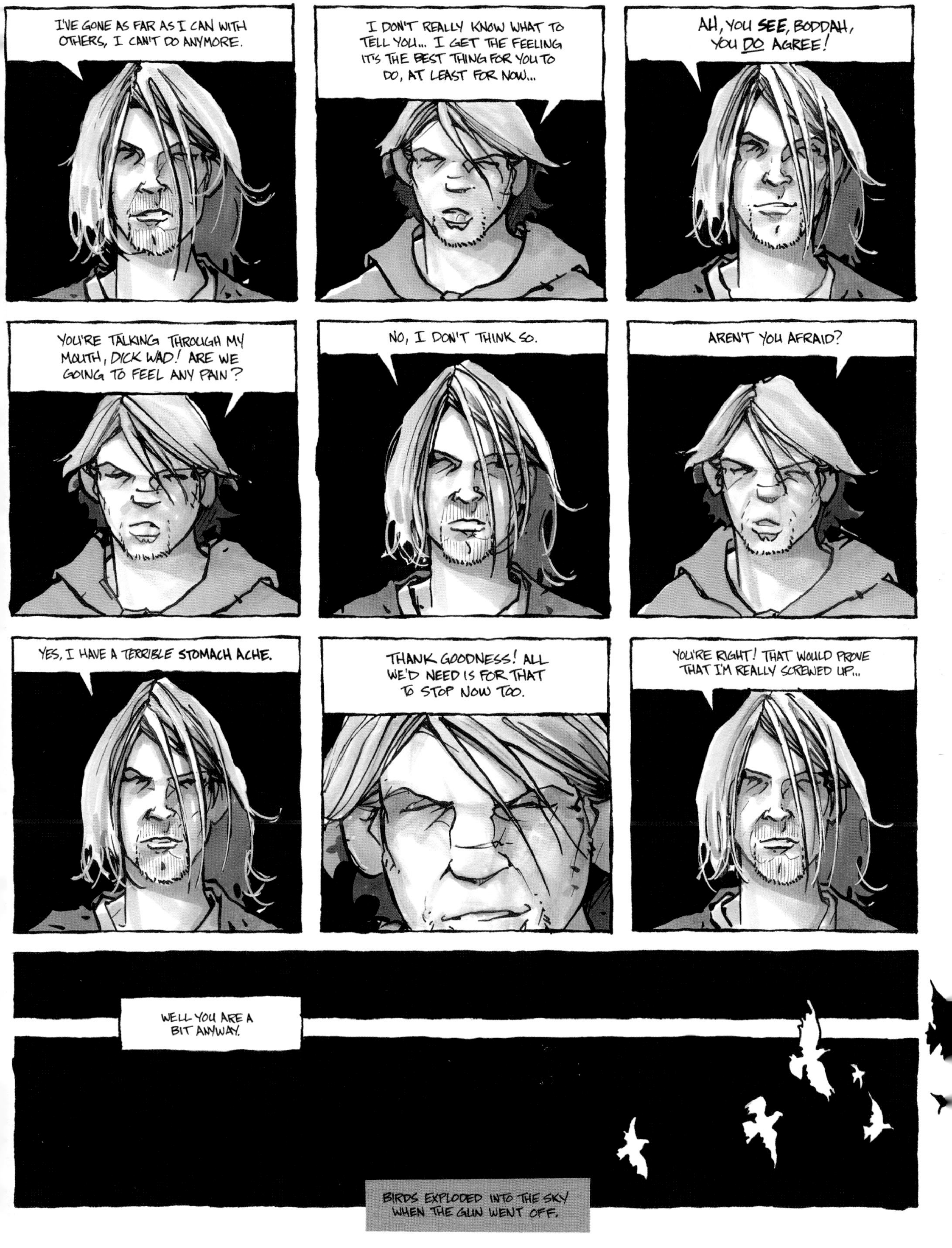
I'VE GONE AS FAR AS I CAN WITH OTHERS, I CAN'T DO ANYMORE.
I DON'T REALLY KNOW WHAT TO TELL YOU... I GET THE FEELING IT'S THE BEST THING FOR YOU TO DO, AT LEAST FOR NOW...
AH, YOU **SEE**, BODDAH, YOU DO AGREE!
YOU'RE TALKING THROUGH MY MOUTH, DICK WAD! ARE WE GOING TO FEEL ANY PAIN?
NO, I DON'T THINK SO.
AREN'T YOU AFRAID?
YES, I HAVE A TERRIBLE **STOMACH ACHE.**
THANK GOODNESS! ALL WE'D NEED IS FOR THAT TO STOP NOW TOO.
YOU'RE RIGHT! THAT WOULD PROVE THAT I'M REALLY SCREWED UP...
WELL YOU ARE A BIT ANYWAY.
BIRDS EXPLODED INTO THE SKY WHEN THE GUN WENT OFF.

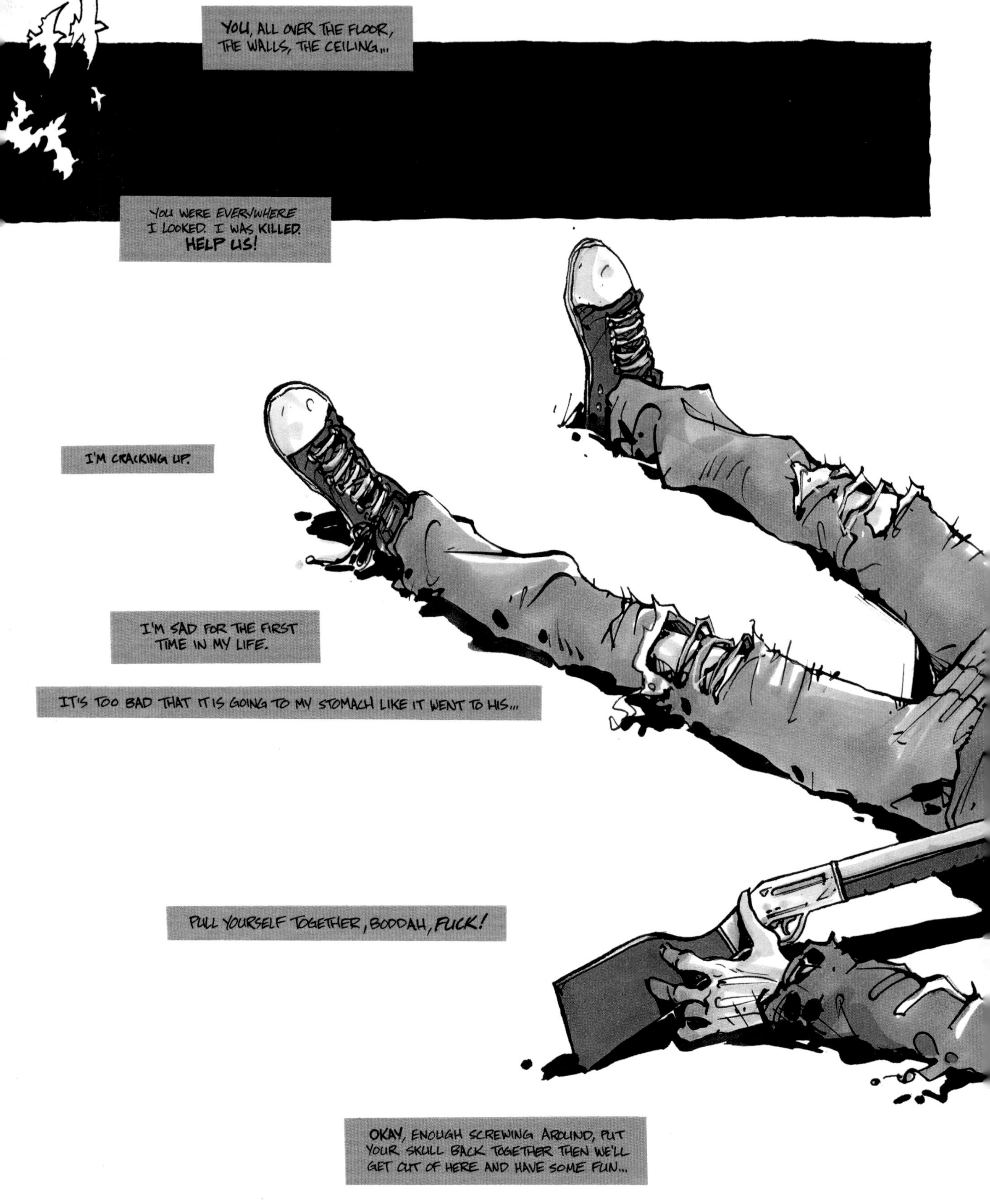
YOU, ALL OVER THE FLOOR, THE WALLS, THE CEILING...
YOU WERE EVERYWHERE I LOOKED. I WAS KILLED. HELP US!
I'M CRACKING UP.
I'M SAD FOR THE FIRST TIME IN MY LIFE.
IT'S TOO BAD THAT IT IS GOING TO MY STOMACH LIKE IT WENT TO HIS...
PULL YOURSELF TOGETHER, BODDAH, FUCK!
OKAY, ENOUGH SCREWING AROUND, PUT YOUR SKULL BACK TOGETHER THEN WE'LL GET OUT OF HERE AND HAVE SOME FUN...

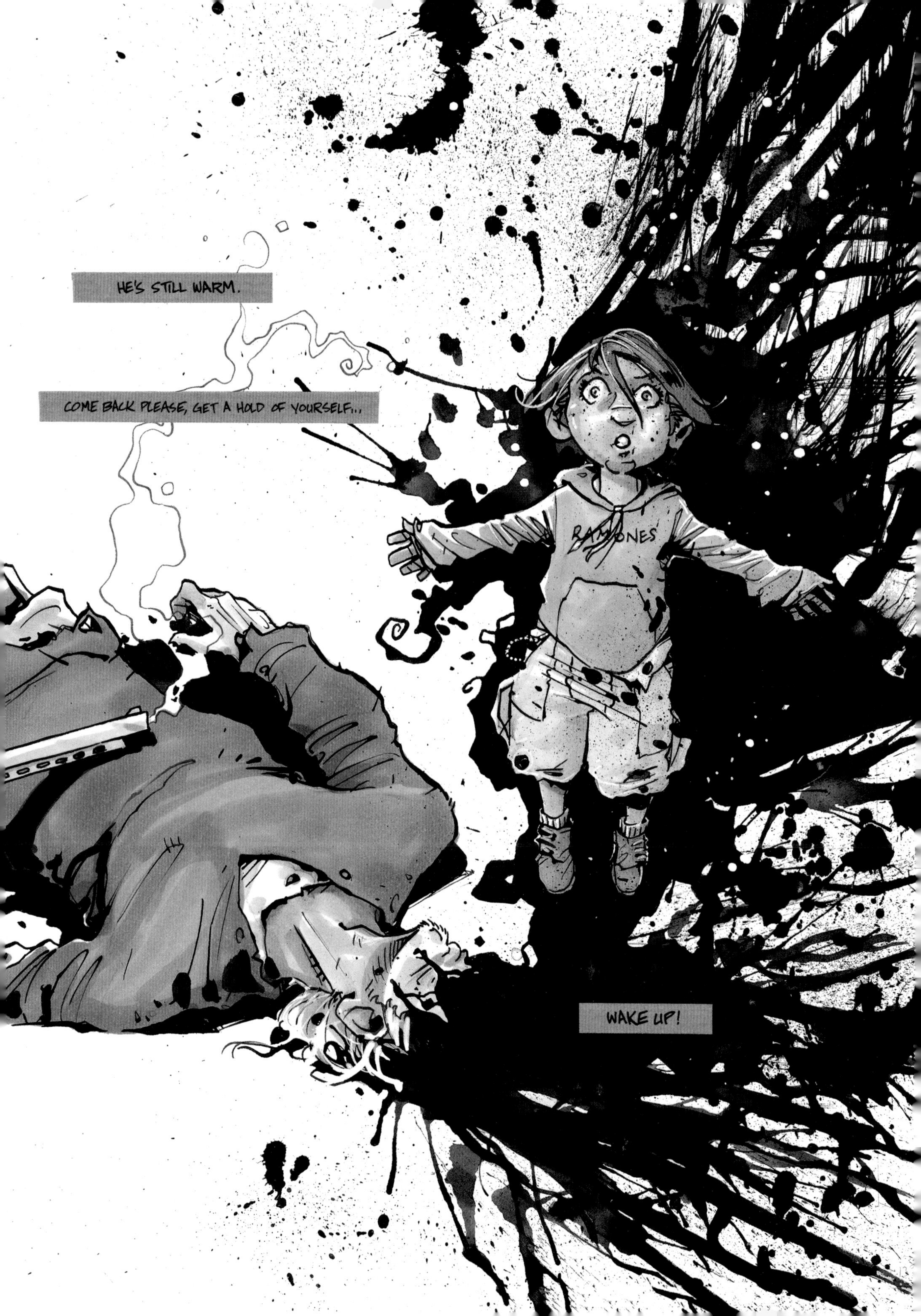
HE'S STILL WARM.
COME BACK PLEASE, GET A HOLD OF YOURSELF...
RAMONES
WAKE UP!

SHE KNEW THAT IT WAS GOING TO HAPPEN. SHE HADN'T HAD ANY DREAMS THE LAST TWO NIGHTS.

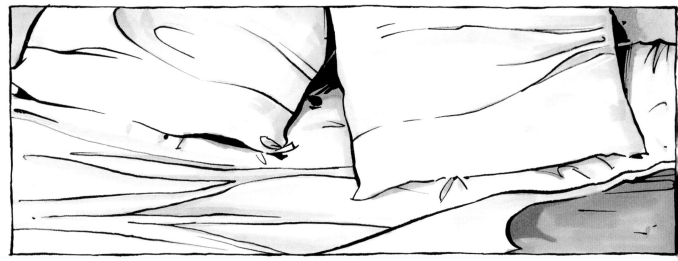

SHE DIDN'T SEE ANYTHING WHEN SHE LOOKED IN THE MIRROR.

144

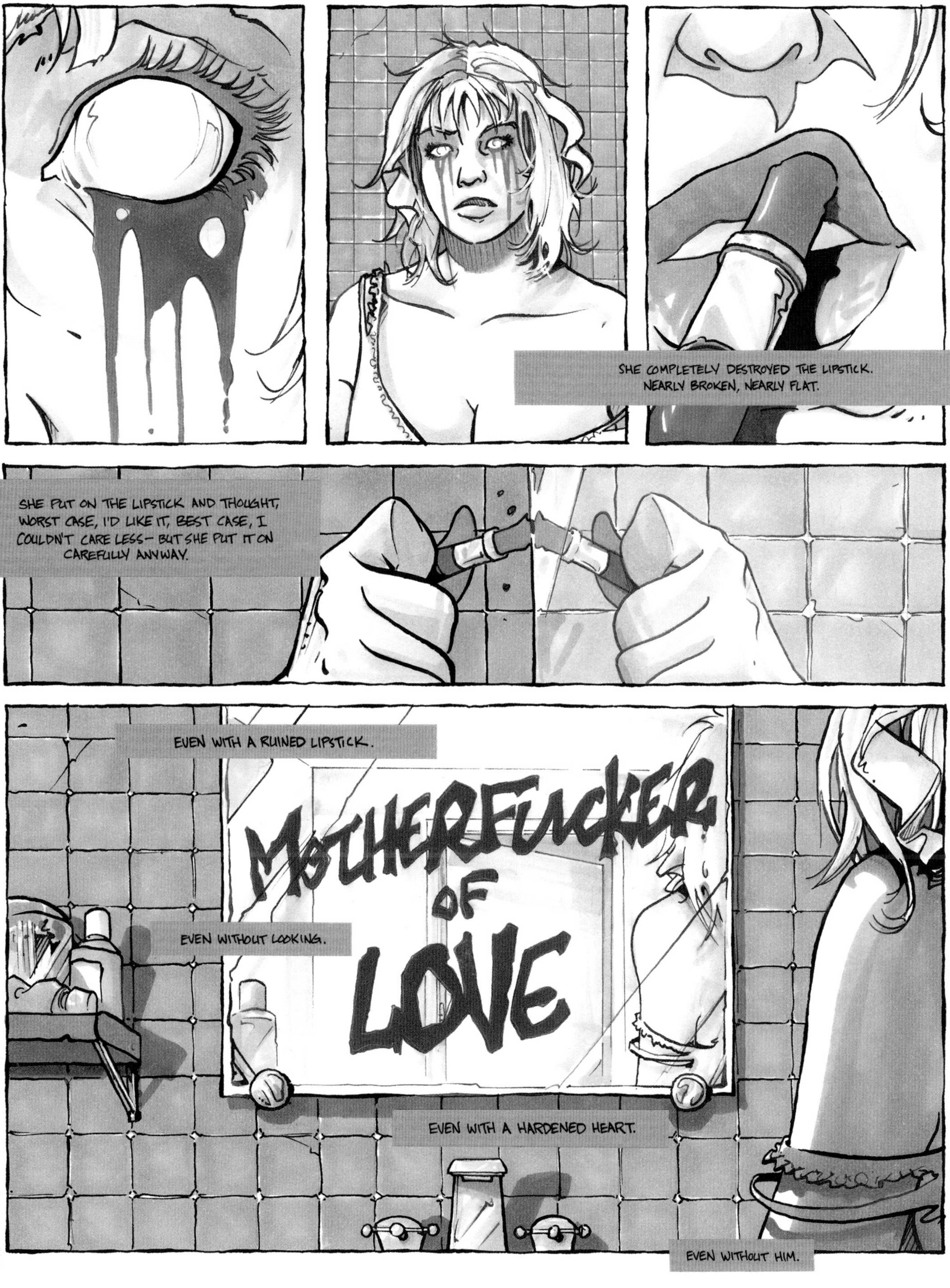
SHE COMPLETELY DESTROYED THE LIPSTICK. NEARLY BROKEN, NEARLY FLAT.
SHE PUT ON THE LIPSTICK AND THOUGHT, WORST CASE, I'D LIKE IT, BEST CASE, I COULDN'T CARE LESS— BUT SHE PUT IT ON CAREFULLY ANYWAY.
EVEN WITH A RUINED LIPSTICK.
MOTHERFUCKER OF LOVE
EVEN WITHOUT LOOKING.
EVEN WITH A HARDENED HEART.
EVEN WITHOUT HIM.

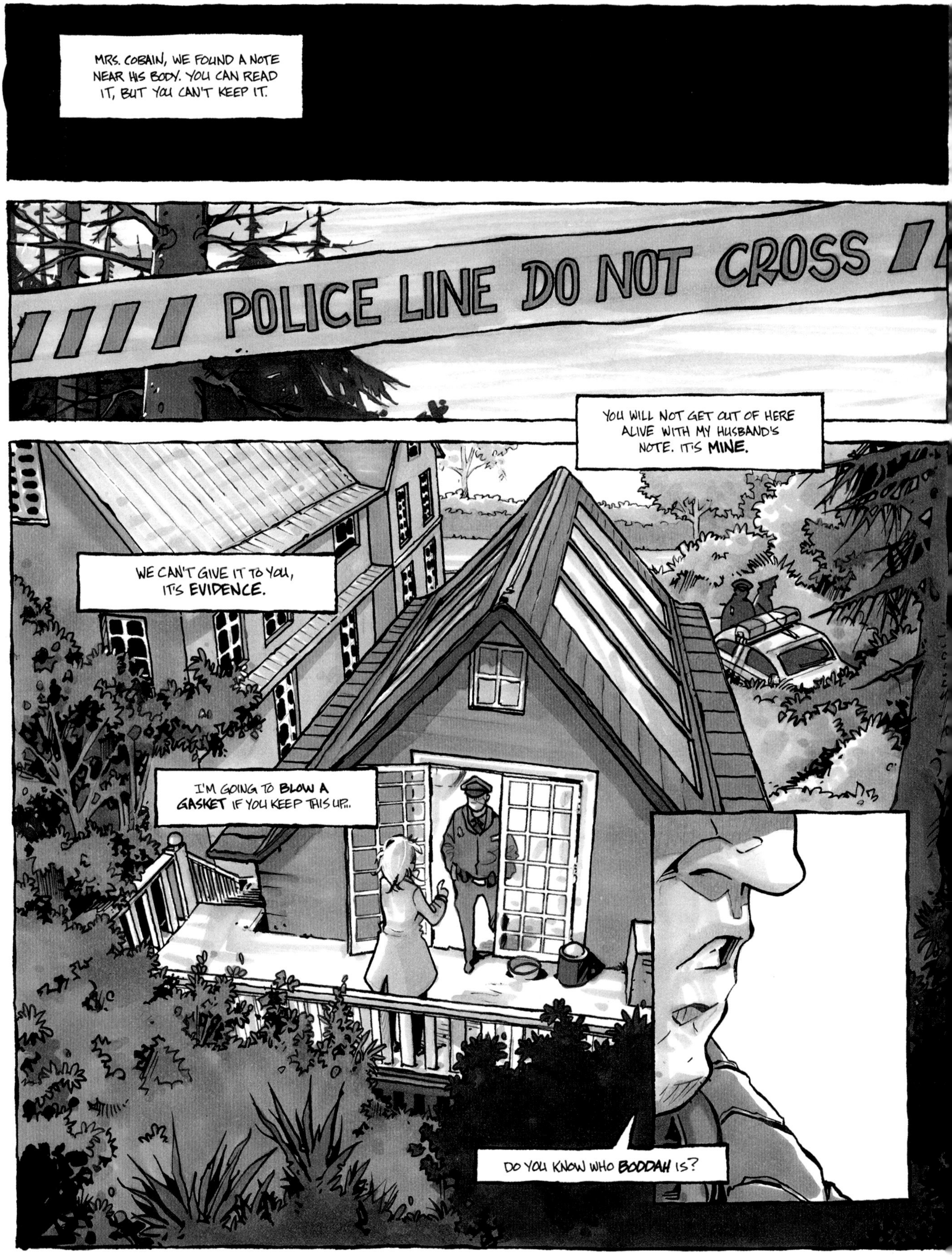
MRS. COBAIN, WE FOUND A NOTE NEAR HIS BODY. YOU CAN READ IT, BUT YOU CAN'T KEEP IT.
POLICE LINE DO NOT CROSS
YOU WILL NOT GET OUT OF HERE ALIVE WITH MY HUSBAND'S NOTE. IT'S MINE.
WE CAN'T GIVE IT TO YOU, IT'S EVIDENCE.
I'M GOING TO BLOW A GASKET IF YOU KEEP THIS UP...
DO YOU KNOW WHO BODDAH IS?

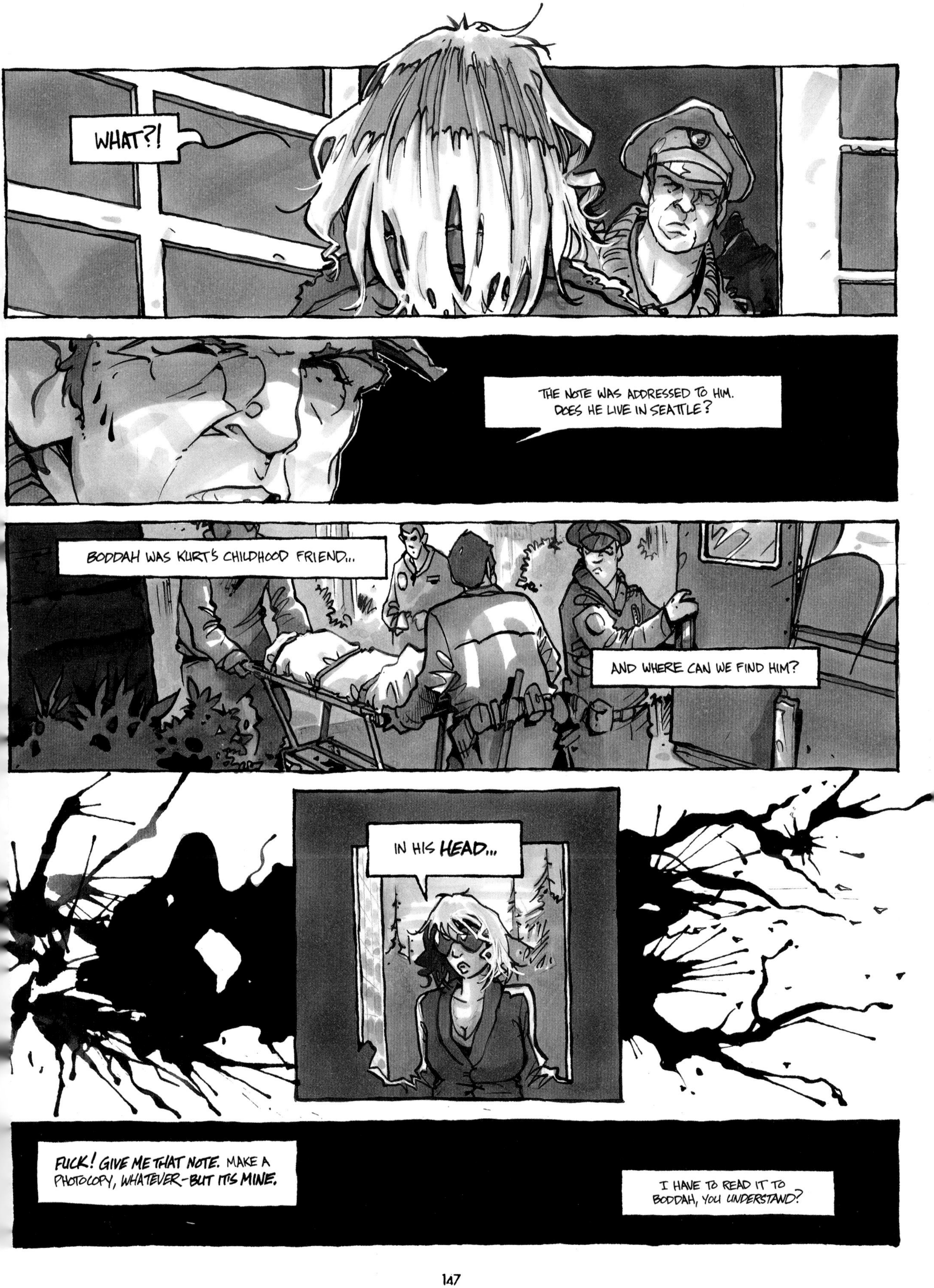
WHAT?!
THE NOTE WAS ADDRESSED TO HIM. DOES HE LIVE IN SEATTLE?
BODDAH WAS KURT'S CHILDHOOD FRIEND...
AND WHERE CAN WE FIND HIM?
IN HIS HEAD...
FUCK! GIVE ME THAT NOTE. MAKE A PHOTOCOPY, WHATEVER—BUT IT'S MINE.
I HAVE TO READ IT TO BODDAH, YOU UNDERSTAND?

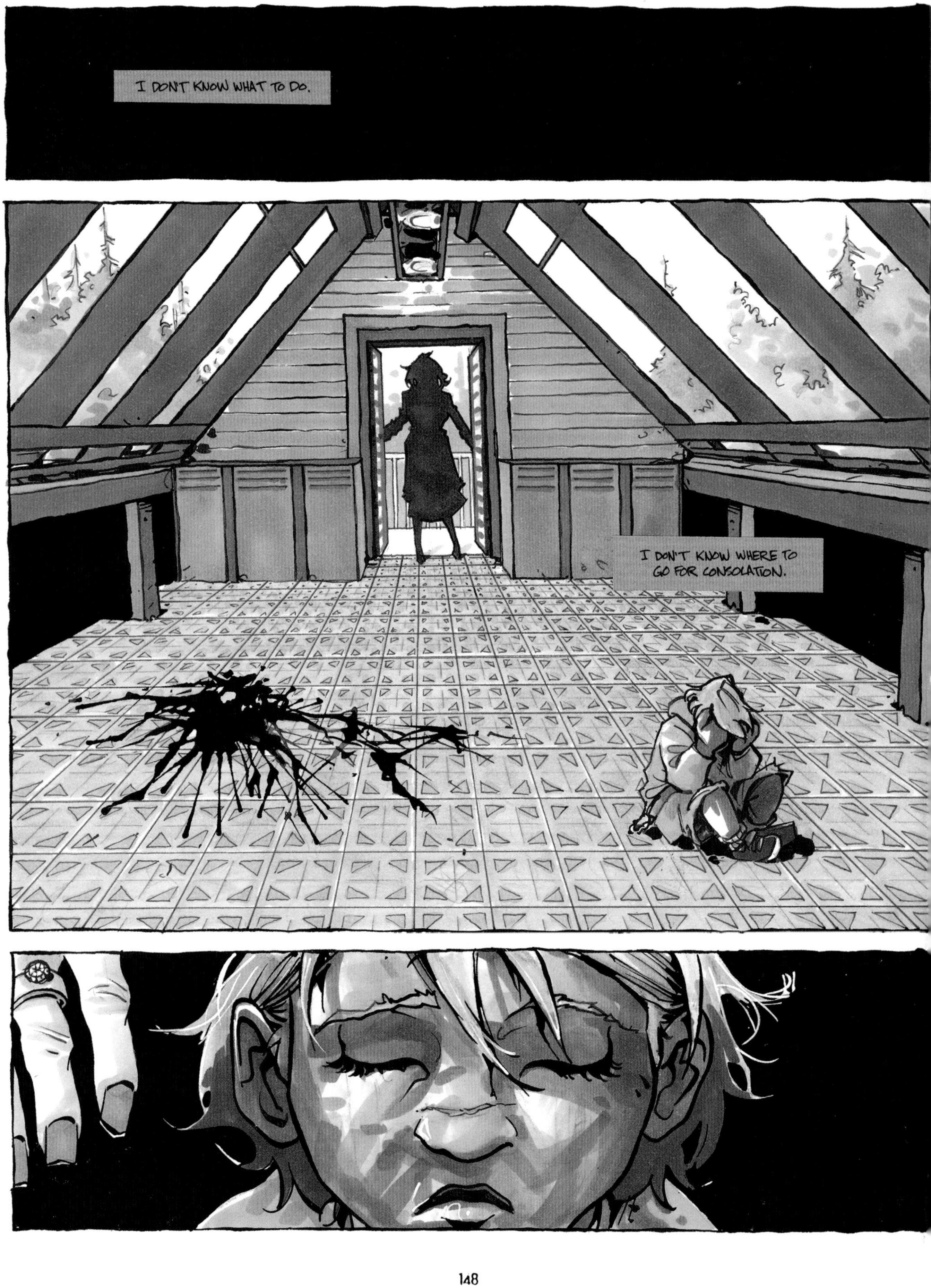
I DON'T KNOW WHAT TO DO.
I DON'T KNOW WHERE TO GO FOR CONSOLATION.

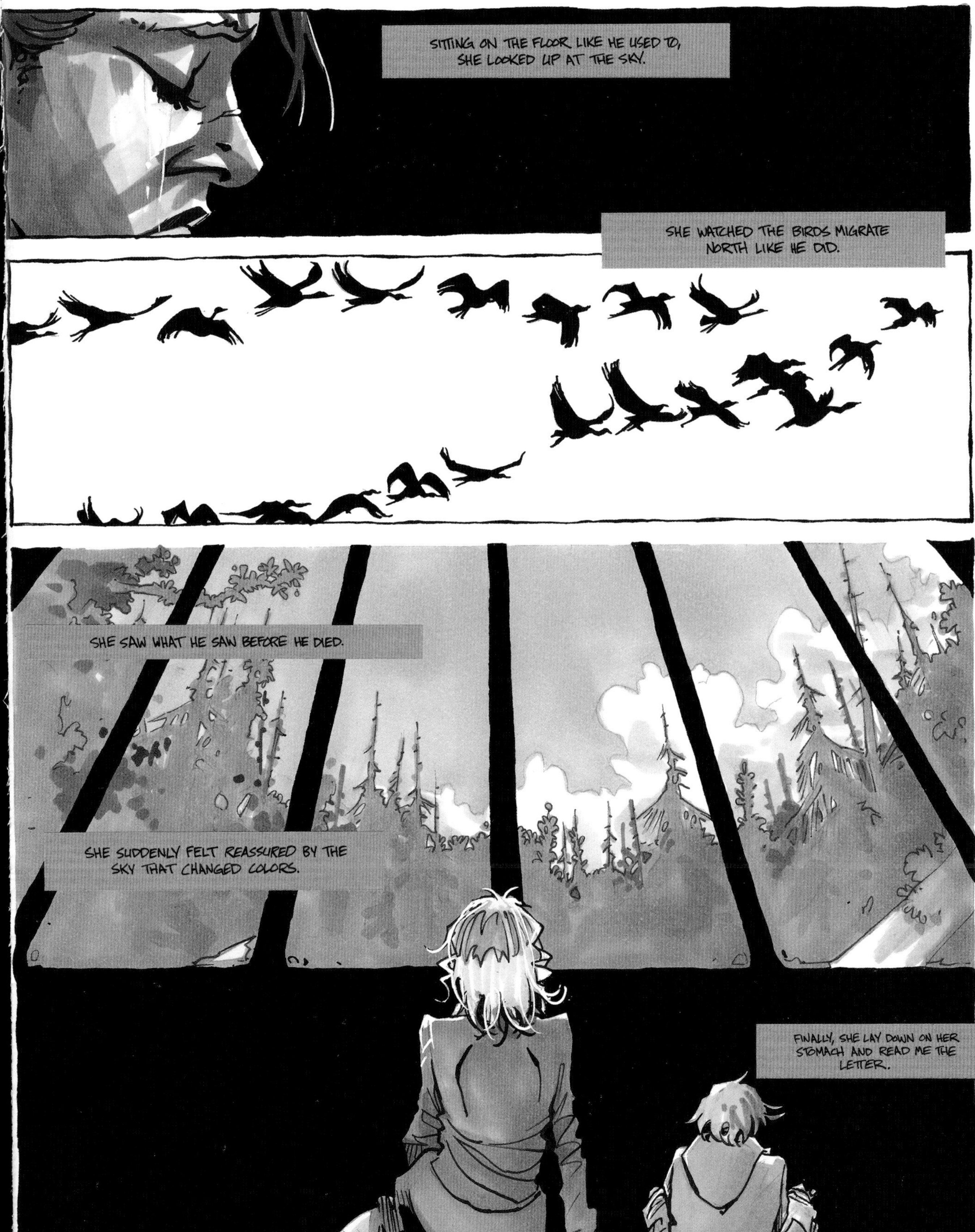
SITTING ON THE FLOOR LIKE HE USED TO, SHE LOOKED UP AT THE SKY.
SHE WATCHED THE BIRDS MIGRATE NORTH LIKE HE DID.
SHE SAW WHAT HE SAW BEFORE HE DIED.
SHE SUDDENLY FELT REASSURED BY THE SKY THAT CHANGED COLORS.
FINALLY, SHE LAY DOWN ON HER STOMACH AND READ ME THE LETTER.

TO BoddAH

Speaking from the tongue of an experienced simpleton who obviously would rather be emasculated, infantile complain-ee. This note should be pretty easy to understand.

ALL the warnings from the Punk Rock 101 courses over the years, since my first introduction to the, shall we say, ethics involved with independence and the embracement of your community has proven to be very true. I haven't felt the excitement of listening to as well as creating music Along with reading and writing for too many years now. I feel guilty beyond words about these things. For example when we're backstage and the lights go out and the manic roar of the crowd begins It doesn't affect me the way it did for Freddy Mercury, who seemed to love, relish in the love and adoration from the crowd which is something I totally admire and envy. The fact is, I can't fool you. Any one of you. It simply isn't fair to you or me. The worst crime I can think of would be to rip people off by faking it and pretending as if I'm having 100% fun. Sometimes I feel as if I should have a punch in time clock before I walk out on stage. I've tried everything within my power to appreciate it (and I do, GOD, believe me I do, but it's not enough). I appreciate the fact that I and we have affected and entertained a lot of people. I must be one of those narcissists who only appreciate things when they're gone. I'M too sensitive. I need to be slightly numb in order to regain the enthusiasm I once had as a child. On our last 3 tours, I've had a much better appreciation for all the people I've known personally, and as fans of music, but I still can't get over the frustration, the guilt and empathy I have for everyone.

There's good in all of us and I think I simply love people too much, so much that it makes me feel too fucking sad. The sad little, sensitive, unappreciative, Pisces, Jesus man! Why don't you just enjoy it? I don't know! I have a goddess of a wife who sweats ambition and empathy and a daughter who reminds me too much of what I used to be, full of love and joy, kissing every person she meets because everyone is good and will do her no harm. And that terrifies me to the point to where I can barely function.

I can't stand the thought of Frances becoming the miserable, self-destructive, death rocker that I've become. I have it good, very good, and I'm grateful, but since the age of seven, I've become hateful towards all humans in general. Only because it seems so easy for people to get along that have empathy. Only because I love and feel sorry for people too much I guess. Thank you all from the pit of my burning, nauseous stomach for your letters and concern during the past years. I'm too much of an erratic, moody baby! I don't have the passion anymore, and so remember, it's better to burn out than to fade away.

peace, love, Empathy. Kurt Cobain

Frances and Courtney, I'll be at your alter.
Please keep going Courtney.
for Frances
for her life which will be so much happier
without me. I love you I LOVE YOU!

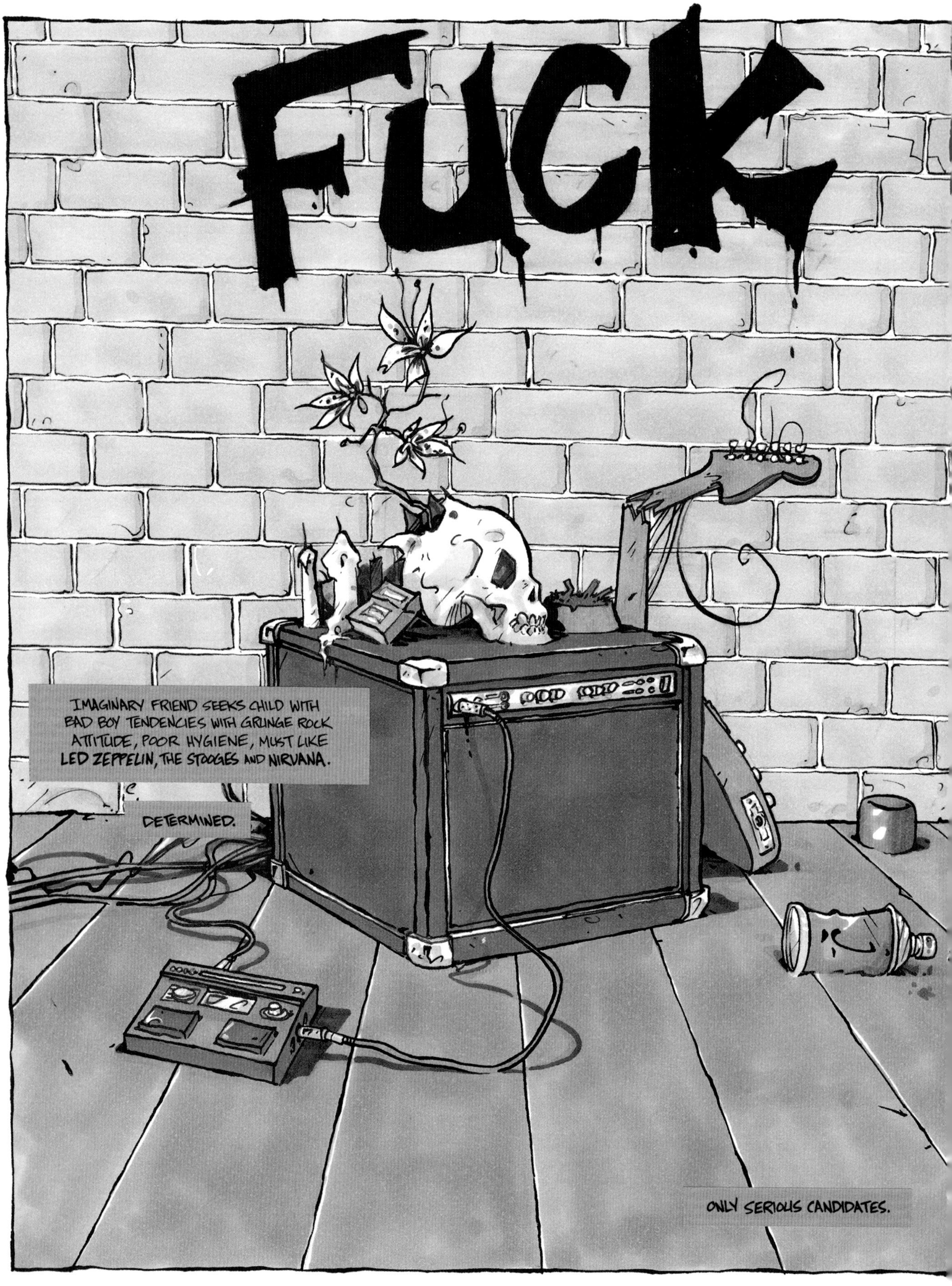
FUCK
IMAGINARY FRIEND SEEKS CHILD WITH BAD BOY TENDENCIES WITH GRUNGE ROCK ATTITUDE, POOR HYGIENE, MUST LIKE LED ZEPPELIN, THE STOOGES AND NIRVANA.
DETERMINED.
ONLY SERIOUS CANDIDATES.